1

Cyberbullying in the Global Playground

Cyberbullying in the Global Playground

Research from International Perspectives

Edited by
Qing Li, Donna Cross,
and Peter K. Smith

WILEY-BLACKWELL
A John Wiley & Sons, Ltd., Publication

This edition first published 2012

Blackwell Publishing was acquired by John Wiley & Sons in February 2007.
Blackwell's publishing program has been merged with Wiley's global Scientific,
Technical, and Medical business to form Wiley-Blackwell.

Registered Office
John Wiley & Sons Ltd, The Atrium, Southern Gate, Chichester, West Sussex,
PO19 8SQ, UK

Editorial Offices
350 Main Street, Malden, MA 02148-5020, USA
9600 Garsington Road, Oxford, OX4 2DQ, UK
The Atrium, Southern Gate, Chichester, West Sussex, PO19 8SQ, UK

For details of our global editorial offices, for customer services, and for information about how
to apply for permission to reuse the copyright material in this book please see our website at
www.wiley.com/wiley-blackwell.

Library of Congress Cataloging-in-Publication Data

Cyberbullying in the global playground: research from international perspectives / edited by Qing Li,
Donna Cross, and Peter K. Smith.
p. cm.
Includes bibliographical references and index.
ISBN 978-1-4443-3376-3 (hbk. : alk. paper)
1. Cyberbullying. 2. Bullying in schools. I. Li, Qing, 1964– II. Cross, Donna, PhD.
III. Smith, Peter K.
LB3013.3.C93 2012
371.5′8–dc23

2011032985

A catalogue record for this book is available from the British Library.

This book is published in the following electronic formats: ePDFs [ISBN 9781119954453];
Wiley Online Library [ISBN 9781119954484]; ePub [ISBN 9781119954460];
Mobi [ISBN 9781119954477]

Set in 10.5/13pt Minion by SPi Publisher Services, Pondicherry, India
Printed in Malaysia by Ho Printing (M) Sdn Bhd

1 2012

Contents

About the Editors

Qing Li is a Professor in the Department of Educational Technology and Literacy at Towson University, USA. She received her PhD in educational technology from the University of Toronto in 2001, and her MA in mathematics education and MSc in mathematics from the University of British Columbia, Canada. She is one of the first researchers to study and publish work related to cyberbullying. She has published over 50 papers in peer-reviewed academic journals and numerous articles in refereed conference proceedings. She was a visiting scholar at the Massachusetts Institute of Technology (MIT) in 2009 and a visiting professor at the University of Idaho in 2006.

Donna Cross is the Foundation Professor of Child and Adolescent Health in the School of Exercise, Biomedical and Health Sciences, Edith Cowan University, in Western Australia and Director of the University's Child Health Promotion Research Center. She received her doctorate at Columbia University, New York in 1993. She has conducted bullying and cyberbullying research in Australian schools since 1999 and leads the first empirical cyber bullying intervention trial in Australia, the Cyber Friendly Schools project. She has published 62 peer-review papers, three books, and five book chapters on children's health-related issues. She is a non-European member of the COST IS0801 "Action on Cyberbullying: Coping with negative and enhancing positive uses of new technologies in relationships in educational settings," and an invited member of the 2010 Arizona-based International Cyberbullying Thinktank.

Peter K. Smith is Emeritus Professor at the Unit for School and Family Studies at Goldsmiths, University of London; he is a Fellow of the British Psychological Society. He received his BSc at the University of Oxford and his PhD from the University of Sheffield. He is co-author of *Understanding Children's Development* (Blackwell, 1988, 1991, 1998, 2002, and Wiley-Blackwell, in press), and co-editor of *School Bullying: Insights and Perspectives* (Routledge, 1994), *Tackling Bullying in*

Your School: A Practical Handbook for Teachers (Routledge, 1994), *The Nature of School Bullying* (Routledge, 1999), *The Family System Test* (Routledge, 2001), and the *Blackwell Handbook of Childhood Social Development* (Blackwell, 2002; Wiley-Blackwell, 2nd ed., 2011), and editor of *Violence in Schools: The Response in Europe* (Routledge, 2002). He directed the DFE Sheffield Anti-Bullying project from 1991–1994, advised on the UK Department for Education (DfEE) pack *Don't Suffer in Silence* (1994, 2nd ed., 2000), and has coordinated a European Commission-funded project (1997–2001) on *The Nature and Prevention of Bullying* (www.gold.ac.uk/tmr) and another project (1999–2002) on *Violence in Schools* (www.gold.ac.uk/connect). He is currently Chair of COST IS0801 "Action on Cyberbullying: Coping with negative and enhancing positive uses of new technologies, in relationships in educational settings."

About the Contributors

Ana Maria Tomás de Almeida is an Associate Professor at the University of Minho and leads the Child Studies Research Center, Portugal.

Ikuko Aoyama is a post-doctoral researcher at Chiba University in Japan.

Sheri Bauman is Associate Professor and Director of the School Counselling Program at the University of Arizona, USA.

Antonella Brighi is a researcher and lecturer in Developmental Psychology at the University of Bologna, Italy.

Juan Calmaestra is a doctoral student at the University of Cordoba, Spain.

Pamela Calussi is a post-doctoral researcher at the University of Florence, Italy.

Isabel Correia is Associate Professor at the University of Lisbon Institute and leads the Research Center for Social Intervention, Portugal.

Donna Cross is Professor of Child and Adolsescent Mental Health at Edith Cowan University, Australia.

Julian Dooley is a post-doctoral research fellow at Edith Cowan University, Australia.

Melanie Epstein is a research fellow at Edith Cowan University, Australia.

Tak Fung is a senior mathematical and statistical consultant in Information Technologies at the University of Calgary, Canada.

D'Jamila Garcia is a doctoral student at the University of Lisbon, CIS-Centro de Investigaçãoe Intervenção Social/ISCTE-Instituto Universitário de Lisboa, Portugal.

Maria Luisa Genta is Professor in Developmental Psychology and Education at the University of Bologna, Italy.

Mark Grabe is a Professor of Psychology at the University of North Dakota, USA.

Petra Gradinger is a post-doctoral researcher at the University of Vienna, Austria.

Annalisa Guarini is a psychologist and researcher in developmental psychology at the University of Bologna, Italy.

Motohiro Hasegawa is an Associate Professor at Kinjo Gakuin University in Japan.

Lydia Hearn is senior post-doctoral fellow at Edith Cowan University, Australia.

Brett Holfeld is a doctoral student at the University of North Dakota, USA.

Keumjoo Kwak is Professor of Psychology at Seoul National University, Korea.

Qing Li is a Professor in the Department of Educational Technology and Literacy at Towson University, USA.

Sylvie Marinho is a doctoral student at the University of Minho, Portugal.

Giannino Melotti is researcher and lecturer in Social Psychology and in Conflicts in Social Groups and Mediation Processes at the University of Bologna, Italy.

Ersilia Menesini is Professor of Psychology at the University of Florence, Italy.

Helen Monks is a senior research fellow at Edith Cowan University, Australia.

Joaquín Mora-Merchán is Associate Professor at the University of Seville, Spain.

Annalaura Nocentini is a researcher at the Department of Psychology at the University of Florence, Italy.

Rosario Ortega is Professor and Head of the Department of Psychology, University of Cordoba, Spain.

Virpi Pöyhönen is a graduate student of psychology at the University of Turku, Finland.

Christina Salmivalli is Professor of Psychology at the University of Turku, Finland.

Therese Shaw is a biostatistician at Edith Cowan University, Australia.

Peter K. Smith is Emeritus Professor at the Unit for School and Family Studies, Goldsmiths, University of London, UK.

Christiane Spiel is Professor of Bildung, Psychology, and Evaluation, and department head at the University of Vienna, Austria.

Dagmar Strohmeier is Professor for Intercultural Competence at the Upper Austria University of Applied Sciences, Austria.

Fran Thompson is a researcher at Goldsmiths, University of London, UK.

Neil Tippett is a doctoral student at the University of Warwick, UK.

Shoka Utsumi is a doctoral course student in the Faculty of Humanities and Sciences, Ochanomizu University, Tokyo, Japan.

Preface

This book is the first thorough comparative account of the recent research into the emerging phenomenon of cyberbullying, across Europe, North America, Australia, and Asia. Attempting to enhance our understanding of cyberbullying, we include reports of projects from Australia, Austria, Canada, England, Finland, Italy, Japan, Portugal, South Korea, Spain, and the United States. Reflecting on recent studies, we have chosen the countries discussed in this book because quality active research in relation to cyberbullying is being carried out there. Although each project has its unique approaches, methods employed, and outcome identified, the common objective of this collection is to reduce or prevent cyberbullying by providing a comprehensive understanding of the issue.

Chapter 1 sets the scene by offering background information on technology and a discussion of the general features of cyberbullying. It also includes definitions of the key terms and basic research designs of current studies related to the topic. This opening chapter is followed by 12 chapters reporting first-hand accounts of recent studies by leading researchers in the area. Collectively, these studies provide an international perspective on the prevalence and nature of cyberbullying, its underlying mechanisms, group dynamics, and possible effect on the social, emotional, and psychological development of young people.

The three chapters in Part II, European Studies Within a DAPHNE Project, bring together contributions from four European countries (Italy, England, Spain, and Finland) that have participated in an EU-funded DAPHNE project. These chapters present some corresponding data and analyses, while also discussing specific aspects of each country. In the context of previous research and national policies in each country, Chapters 2 and 4 examine traditional bullying and cyberbullying, their interrelations, and the impact they have on the victims. Chapter 3 investigates the role of self-esteem and perceived loneliness in association with episodes of cyber-aggression acted or received, adapting Bandura's theory of moral disengagement in the new cyber-context.

Part III contrasts findings in two Commonwealth countries, Australia and Canada. Chapter 5 assesses the extent, mechanisms, and characteristics of cyberbullying, and its social, emotional, cognitive, and behavioral impacts on Australian youth who are bullied and who bully others. It also explores the degree to which youth have participated in, or been perpetrators of, cyberbullying and the reasons for their involvement, as well as the cyberbullying beliefs of children, their parents, and teachers. Chapter 6 examines cyberbullying through the lens of Canadian high school students' beliefs and their behaviors, focusing on social and affective perspectives to uncover important patterns related to cyberbullies, cybervictims, and bystanders.

Part IV contains two contributions from the USA. Chapter 7 discusses the frequency of cyberbullying, and analyzes the methodological procedures used in generating these data. Chapter 8 reports on two studies: one is a survey conducted in a rural, diverse intermediate school focusing on self-blaming attributions, moral disengagement, and prevalence. The second compares deaf and hearing-impaired students to a group of hearing students in a secondary charter school.

Part V contains two chapters exploring cyberbullying in the Pacific Rim. Chapter 9 discusses two recent empirical studies in Japan. One examines the relationship between parental monitoring, relational aggression, Internet use, and cyberbullying involvement among junior high school students; the other is a cross-cultural comparison between Japanese and US high school students, in terms of cyberbullying, parental monitoring, and help-seeking behaviors. Chapter 10 reviews recent research in South Korea, and describes findings from a recent survey, drawing particular attention to the phenomenon of online game bullying.

Part VI links three chapters which focus on psychological factors related to cyberbullying; notably moral disengagement, empathy, psychological health, and types of aggressiveness. Chapter 11 focuses on the sociocognitive measures of moral disengagement and empathy related to being a cyberbully, a cybervictim, or a bystander, and considers the possible effects of these roles on the social and emotional development of adolescents. Chapter 12 not only describes the degree of involvement in different typologies of cyberbullying in relation to gender and school types, but also analyzes the relationship between involvement in cyberbullying and concurrent health symptoms. Chapter 13 investigates prevalence rates of cyberbullying and cybervictimization and relates them to bullying and victimization in general. It also examines the aggressiveness of bullies versus cyberbullies and the adjustment of victims versus cybervictims.

Following these 12 empirical projects, our final chapter reflects on the existing literature on cyberbullying, including that reported in this book, and discusses its implications for intervention. By reviewing and commenting on practical guidelines for schools, governments, corporations, and society as a whole to reduce the effects of cyberbullying, our enhanced understanding helps us to design intervention, evaluation, and policy strategies for effective efforts to address cyberbullying to build and sustain healthy relationships among children and youth.

Qing Li, Donna Cross, and Peter K. Smith
March 2011

Part I
Introduction

1

Research Into Cyberbullying
Context

Qing Li, Peter K. Smith, and Donna Cross

Technology continues to develop rapidly and is changing our ways of functioning in society. New doors are opening, bringing opportunities but these also lead to questions about the ethical use of technology in schools. The Internet, mobile phones, and other communication technologies, while providing us with convenience, also potentially expose our students to dangerous interactions which put their safety and emotional wellbeing at risk. One negative use of technology is cyberbullying, a relatively new form of bullying, with some overlaps but also some distinct differences from traditional bullying.

School bullying has been recognized as a serious problem worldwide for some decades now. Many children are likely to experience aggression in their relationships with schoolmates (see Jimerson, Swearer, & Espelage, 2010). But with the advent of modern forms of communication, children are now able to harass their peers using electronic tools. This form of aggression involves the use of information and communication technology such as mobile phones, videoconferencing, emails, and web pages to post or send harassing or embarrassing messages to another person.

Research studies have shown that a substantial number of students are victims of cyberbullying, with various international studies demonstrating a significant level of cyberbullying in schools, which leads to the increased recognition that cyberbullying is becoming a serious problem (Willard, 2006; Li, 2006, 2007; Cross, 2008; Smith, 2011). One of the most devastating outcomes of cyberbullying victimization is suicide. It is reported that, in the US alone, at least three teenage children have committed suicide linked to cyberbullying (Hinduja & Patchin, 2009). Because cyberbullying can occur anywhere, anytime, it blurs the boundaries for adult supervision and responsibility, and introduces unprecedented legal and

Cyberbullying in the Global Playground: Research from International Perspectives, First Edition.
Edited by Qing Li, Donna Cross, and Peter K. Smith.

educational concerns for schools. The development of effective policies and practices to reduce cyberbullying requires a sound understanding of how it differs from face-to-face bullying, including the potential harm caused by cyberbullying; the barriers and misconceptions that have enabled cyberbullying to flourish; as well as ways this issue can be effectively addressed by schools, families, and students. Most importantly, since cyberbullying occurs in a network that connects the globe, geographical limits no longer exist. An international perspective, therefore, has never been so critical.

In this chapter we document the increase in use of the new communication technologies that make cyberbullying possible; give some definition of terms; summarize some distinctive features of cyberbullying, compared to traditional bullying; and mention some issues around research findings and research design.

Technology Use

The technological revolution, particularly in digital communicational tools such as the Internet, has brought significant changes to our lives and blurs real and virtual worlds and spaces. The drastic increase of handheld devices and mobile phones, quickly embraced by young people, enables today's youth to live in a highly mediated world and always stay connected.

Research conducted by the US government in 2002 indicated that at that time, about 90% of adolescents used computers (National Telecommunications and Information Administration, 2002). The Organization for Economic Cooperation and Development (OECD)'s 2006 study, analyzing the first international comparative data of 41 different countries in youth technology use based on PISA (Program for International Student Assessment) 2003, showed that almost all 15-year-old students have used computers and, in particular, over 90% of US or Canadian youth used computers almost every day for a wide range of purposes. In Canada, about 95% of the students had access to computers at home or at school (OECD, 2006).

In the US, the Pew Internet Project regularly conducts large-scale surveys that provide information on issues and trends related to online technology. Their 2006 survey (Madden, 2006) indicates that the proportion of active online users increased from 66% in 2005 to 73% (i.e. 147 million people) in 2006. Of these online users, about 42% (84 million) use broadband connections at home. A more recent Pew study (Lenhart, Arafeh, Smith, & Macgill, 2008) showed that 94% of American teenagers (12–17-year-olds) now use the Internet, while 89% of them have Internet access and 66% have broadband Internet access at home. In addition, 71% of teenagers owned a mobile phone and 58% had a social network site profile. Teens and young adults (aged 18–28) lead the way in using Internet services, and are more likely than older users to use instant messaging (IM), play digital games, create blogs or use a social network, download music, and search for information. The number of teenagers using the Internet has increased by 24% in the past four years, and 87% of those between the ages of 12 and 17 are connected.

Several large-scale studies (Rideout, Roberts, & Foehr, 2005; Lenhart et al., 2008; USC, 2008) indicate a steady increase in teen Internet use, from 73% in 2000, to 87% in 2004, and 95% in 2007; and a rapid increase in mobile phone ownership, from 45% in 2004 to 71% in 2007. Pew's 2007 survey (Lenhart et al., 2008) found that 63% of teens go online daily, 36% send text messages, and 35% talk on a mobile phone. The nature of social communication in cyberspace means the increased likelihood of being contacted by strangers. In fact, Lenhart and Madden (2007) discovered that about one in three online teens reported being contacted by complete strangers while close to one-fifth include people, whom they have never met face-to-face, as their "friends" on their social network profile.

Rideout, Foehr, and Roberts (2010; see www.kff.org) sampled a section of US 8–18-year-olds in 1999, 2004, and 2009. The average number of hours the teens spent in a typical day on a computer was 0.27 in 1999, 1.02 in 2004, and 1.29 in 2009. Time spent talking on mobile phones was 0.33 hours in 2009, and time spent texting was 1.33 hours (in 1999 there was no question about mobile phones at all, and in 2004 only one about talking on mobile *or* landline phones).

The Australian Bureau of Statistics conducted a survey of 15,233 randomly selected private dwelling households across Australia in 2008–2009 (Pink, 2009). The data found that 78% of households had computers and 72% had home Internet access. From 1998 to 2008, household computer access increased from 44% to 78%, and Internet access from 16% to 72%. In addition, about two-thirds (62%) of all households in Australia have broadband access, and 94% of Australian youth aged 15–17 use the Internet.

European countries share similar patterns. For example, a survey (Eurobarometer, 2008) was conducted in 29 European countries in 2008. About 12,800 randomly selected parents of 6–17-year-olds participated in the study, describing their children's Internet activities. The report suggests that more and more children are using the Internet and use it more frequently. In general, three-quarters of the parents indicated that their children aged between 6 to 17 go online, although the number of children using the Internet varied considerably across different European countries. The lowest proportion of children online was in Italy (45%) and the highest in Finland (94%), with in-between countries such as the UK (91%), Spain (70%), and Portugal (68%). Older children (15–17-year-olds), compared to younger ones (6–10-year-olds), were more likely to use the Internet on their own computer at home (47% versus 22%), at school (57% versus 49%), at friends' homes (32% versus 16%), or in Internet cafés (6% versus 1%).

Not only has the number of users increased, but the variety of technological tools that teens use to support their communication, research, and entertainment desires has also grown. For example, in the US, for online users aged between 18 and 35, about one in five have used Twitter or similar services (Lenhart & Madden, 2007). In a similar vein, cellular (mobile) phones have become more popular. In the mid-2005, the number of total cell phone carriers reached 2.4 billion. In the US alone, the number of text messages sent each month was 7.2 billion in 2005, but this number had jumped to 75 billion by June 2008 (CTIA, 2008). These numbers have continued to multiply steadily over recent years, and cell phones are increasingly commonly used by young people aged 10–19 (McKeown, 2008). European countries share a similar trend, with almost two-thirds of the parents of 6–17-year-olds reporting that their child had a mobile phone, an increase from 48% in 2005/6 (Eurobarometer, 2008).

These numbers paint a picture of how new technologies are used by youth, both in and out of schools, suggesting an augmentation of our traditional activities and behaviors. While providing invaluable tools to enhance student learning, these new technologies can also be used for deviant purposes such as cyberbullying (Patchin & Hinduja, 2006). For example, the anonymity, the lack of supervision in chatrooms, the possibility of allowing people to contact others anytime, anyplace, all contribute to increased opportunities for cyberbullying. This calls for further exploration of this relatively new phenomenon.

Cyberbullying: Some Definitions

Just like traditional bullying (Rigby, Smith, & Pepler, 2004), no universally agreed definition of cyberbullying is available. Although cyberbullying can be briefly defined as "sending or posting harmful or cruel text or images using the Internet or other digital communication devices" (Willard, 2006), a more detailed definition is:

> Cyberbullying involves the use of information and communication technologies such as email, cell phone and pager text messages, instant messaging, defamatory personal websites, and defamatory online personal polling websites, to support deliberate, repeated, and hostile behavior by an individual or group that is intended to harm others. (Belsey, 2004)

Another widely adapted definition is proposed by Smith and colleagues, who define cyberbullying as "an aggressive, intentional act carried out by a group or individual, using electronic forms of contact, repeatedly and over time against a victim who cannot easily defend him or herself" (Smith et al., 2008, p. 376).

It is generally agreed that cyberbullying can take various forms ranging from flaming, to harassment, to cyberstalking. Although several research studies have explored different forms of cyberbullying, the most comprehensive categorization to date is provided by Willard (2006), with the following formal definition for each form:

flaming—sending angry, rude, vulgar messages directed at a person or persons privately or to an online group;
harassment—repeatedly sending a person offensive messages;
cyberstalking—harassment that include threats of harm or is highly intimidating;
denigration (put-downs)—sending or posting harmful, untrue, or cruel statements about a person to other people;

masquerade—pretending to be someone else and sending or posting material that makes that person look bad or places that person in potential danger;
outing and trickery—sending or posting material about a person that contains sensitive, private, or embarrassing information, including forwarding private messages or images. Engaging in tricks to solicit embarrassing information that is then made public;
exclusion—actions that specifically and intentionally exclude a person from an online group. (Willard, 2006)

In general, the terms "cyberbullying" and "cyber-harassment" are used interchangeably. The fact that Willard's definition above includes cyber-harassment as one sub-category of cyberbullying suggests that cyberbullying is a term that has been used to include cyber-harassment in most research studies of young people, if not all.

Cyberbullying can occur in blogs (interactive web journals), websites, emails, listserves, chat, instant messaging, and text/digital image messaging via mobile devices. It can relate to racial, religious, and cultural biases.

Aggressiveness, intention, repetitiveness, and the *power imbalance* are commonly accepted as the core characteristics of cyberbullying (Dooley, Pyzalski, & Cross, 2009). As with face-to-face bullying, aggressiveness and intention are easily understandable. The issues of repetition and power imbalance applied in cyberbullying, however, are more intricate than first appears. For example, one can post a nasty message on the Internet which can last forever: would this be considered as a single aggressive act or a repeated act? Similarly, how can one determine power imbalance in cyberspace? Is it merely a measure of technology skills, or there are other factors to be considered? Dooley and colleagues (Dooley et al., 2009) have discussed such issues in more detail, yet a unanimously accepted conclusion is still lacking, and the distinction between cyberbullying and cyber-aggression can be argued to be less clear than that between traditional bullying and aggression (Smith, 2011).

Distinctive Features of Cyberbullying

Cyberbullying has some particular characteristics that distinguish it from most traditional bullying, despite some similarities between them. These can be important in considering the impact of cyberbullying, and in finding effective coping strategies (Smith, 2011). These include the following:

1. Cyberbullying depends on some degree of technological expertise: although it is easy enough to send emails and text messages, more sophisticated attacks such as masquerading (pretending to be someone else posting denigrating material on a website) require more skill.

2. It is primarily indirect rather than face-to-face. Thus there is some "invisibility" of those doing the bullying. Perpetrators of cyberbullying have more opportunity to remain anonymous, minimizing the risk they will be caught. A perpetrator may try to withhold identification in text or Internet postings, to maintain anonymity.
3. Relatedly, the perpetrator does not usually see the victim's reaction, at least in the short term. On the one hand, this delayed gratification can enhance moral disengagement from the victim's plight (Hymel, Rocke-Henderson, & Bonanno, 2005) and thus might make cyberbullying easier; without such direct feedback there may be fewer opportunities for empathy or remorse. On the other hand, many perpetrators enjoy the feedback of seeing the suffering of the victim, and would not get this satisfaction so readily through cyberbullying.
4. The variety of bystander roles in cyberbullying is more complex than in most traditional bullying. There can be three main bystander roles rather than one: the bystander is with the perpetrator when an act is sent or posted; the bystander is with the victim when it is received; or the bystander is with neither, but receives the message or visits the relevant Internet site.
5. One motive for bullying is thought to be the status gained by showing (abusive) power over others, in front of witnesses (Salmivalli, Lagerspetz, Bjorkqvist, Osterman, & Kaukiainen, 1996). The perpetrator will often lack this in cyberbullying, unless steps are taken to use more public cyber-places such as a chatroom or to tell others what has happened or publicly share the material.
6. The breadth of the potential audience is increased. Over time, cyberbullying can reach particularly large audiences in a peer group compared with the small groups that are the usual audience in traditional bullying. For example, when nasty comments are posted on a website, the audience who may see these comments is potentially very large.
7. It is difficult to escape from cyberbullying—there is "no place to hide." The victim may be sent messages to their mobile or computer, or access nasty website comments, wherever they are. Unlike traditional forms of bullying, where once the victim gets home he is away from the bullying until the next day, cyberbullying is harder to escape from; the victim may continue to receive text messages or emails, or view nasty postings on a website, wherever he is.
8. Cyberbullying is more likely to be experienced outside of school than in school (Smith et al., 2008), but it is a foreseeable risk to schooling, with consequences often washing back into the school and affecting student learning (Bhat, 2008).

These are important distinctions; but they should not be overstated, as some forms of traditional bullying (such as spreading rumors) are not face-to-face, for example. A case can be made that these are differences in degree rather than differences in kind (Pyzalski, 2011).

Basic Research Design

Although increasingly more scholars are starting to examine cyberbullying, the research, as a field, is still relatively new. This is reflected in various aspects, ranging from the number of studies conducted, to the limited existing guiding theories. Specifically, most, if not all, studies conducted to date employ qualitative research design, exploring the issues through online or face-to-face surveys, with many either using small sample sizes or convenience samples (Griezel, Craven, Yeung, & Finger, 2008). For example, a study by Raskauskas and Stoltz (2007) used a small sample size of 84 adolescents to explore the relationship between involvement in cyberbullying and traditional bullying. Patchin and Hinduja (2006) conducted an online survey of 384 respondents who were under 18 at the time they completed the questionnaire. This study, however, used convenience sampling, with 84.6% of female respondents.

Although several large-scale studies exist, many are not carefully designed using field-tested instruments. Even for the limited available quantitative research studies, our search of existing literature confirms the conclusion by other scholars (Griezel et al., 2008) and points to the need for the further development of research methodology in this field: there is a lack of measurement tools that are based on sound theoretical frameworks and empirically validated, and little psychometric evaluation of instrumentation is employed.

Cross-cultural psychological and sociological concerns

Previous research about traditional bullying has identified, with ample evidence, various psychological and sociological consequences for those victimized and the perpetrators. Such negative consequences range from deterioration in academic performance (Gini & Pozzoli, 2006), feelings of humiliation and anxiety (Olweus, 2003), to depression, low self-esteem (Salmon, James, Cassidy, & Javaloyes, 2000), and health problems (Rigby, 2003). Many scholars express serious concerns for similar negative impacts of cyberbullying, although only limited evidence is available to date.

Parallel to the negative effects of traditional bullying, many victims of cyberbullying, especially the younger ones (preadolescents) and those who are chronically victimized are emotionally distressed (Ybarra, Mitchell, & Finkelhor, 2006). Also, cybervictims report increased levels of anxiety (Nishina, Juvonen, & Witkow, 2005; Ybarra et al., 2006) and feelings of humiliation (Breguet, 2007). Other emotional/psychological consequences include frustration and anger (Beran & Li, 2005; Hinduja & Patchin, 2007; Ortega, Elipe, Mora-Merchan, Calmaestra, & Vega, 2009), low self-esteem and feelings of hopelessness (Strom & Strom, 2005; Vandebosch & van Cleemput, 2008, 2009). For example, a Canadian study conducted in 2005 involving a survey of 432 high-school students showed that over half of cyberbullying victims report feeling angry on several occasions and over a third experience sadness and hurtful feelings (Beran & Li, 2005). As well, a significant gender difference is identified: male cybervictims, compared to their female counterparts, are less likely to feel frustrated or angry (Hinduja & Patchin, 2007). Further, a few research studies (Ybarra & Mitchell, 2004; Ybarra et al., 2006) report that clinical features of depression are correlated to cybervictimization. Vandebosch and van Cleemput (2009) discovered that cybervictims are three times more likely to report depression than others.

Sociological concerns are another important consequence of cyberbullying. The victims of cyber-harassment report feelings of loneliness and insecurity (Breguet, 2007). Not only are they more likely to experience poor relationships with people other than their non-cyberbullied counterparts, but they also often have difficulty making emotional and social adjustments (Hinduja & Patchin, 2007).

In a nutshell, it is argued by many scholars (Hinduja & Patchin, 2007; Heirman & Walrave, 2008) that the consequences of cyberbullying go far beyond hurt feelings. Rather, its effects can be far-reaching and have the potential to permanently damage young people, both psychologically and sociologically. Nevertheless there is a continuing argument about the relative impacts of cyberbullying and traditional bullying, which we return to in Chapter 14. There is no doubt however that it is a serious problem, one that is worldwide, and one that continues to develop as cyber-technologies develop. The "global playground" is truly international and, like the traditional playground, can be a place of danger as well as fun and excitement.

References

Belsey, B. (2004). *Cyberbullying*. Retrieved July 15, 2004 from www.cyberbullying.ca

Beran, T., & Li, Q. (2005). Cyber-harassment: A new method for an old behavior. *Journal of Educational Computing Research, 32*, 265–277.

Breguet, T. (2007). *Frequently asked questions about cyberbullying*. New York: Rosen.

Cross, D. (2008, July). *Cyberbullying: International comparisons, implications and recommendations*. Paper presented at the 20th Biennial International Society for the Study of Behavioural Development Conference, Wurzburg, Germany.

CTIA. (2008). *Wireless quick facts*. Retrieved December 19, 2008 from CTIA: The Wireless Association website: www.ctia.org/consumer_info/service/index.cfm/AID/10323

Dooley, J., Pyzalski, J., & Cross, D. (2009). Cyberbullying versus face-to-face bullying. *Zeitschrift für Psychologie/Journal of Psychology, 217*, 182–187.

Eurobarometer. (2008). *Towards a safer use of the Internet for children in the EU—A parent's perspective*. Luxembourg: European Commission.

Gini, G., & Pozzoli, T. (2006). The role of masculinity in children's bullying. *Sex Roles, 54*, 585–588.

Griezel, L., Craven, R., Yeung, A., & Finger, L. (2008, December). *The development of a multidimensional measure of cyberbullying*. Paper presented at the Australian Association for Research in Education Conference, Brisbane.

Heirman, W., & Walrave, M. (2008). Assessing concerns and issues about the mediation of technology in cyberbullying. *Cyberpsychology: Journal of Psychosocial Research on Cyberspace, 2*, 1–18.

Hinduja, S., & Patchin, J. (2007). Offline consequences of online victimization: School violence and delinquency. *Journal of School Violence, 6*, 89–112.

Hinduja, S., & Patchin, J. W. (2009). *Bullying beyond the schoolyard: Preventing and responding to cyberbullying*. Thousand Oaks, CA: Corwin Press.

Hymel, S., Rocke-Henderson, N., & Bonanno, R. A. (2005). Moral disengagement: A framework for understanding bullying among adolescents. *Journal of Social Sciences, 8*, 1–11.

Lenhart, A., Arafeh, S., Smith, A., & Macgill, A. R. (2008). *Writing, technology and teens*. Washington, DC: Pew Internet & American Life Project.

Lenhart, A., & Madden, M. (2007). *Teens, privacy & online social networks: How teens manage their online identities and personal information in the age of MySpace*. Washington, DC: PEW Internet & American Life Project.

Li, Q. (2006). Cyberbullying in schools: A research of gender differences. *School Psychology International, 27*, 157–170.

Li, Q. (2007). New bottle but old wine: A research on cyberbullying in schools. *Computers and Human Behavior, 23*, 1777–1791.

Madden, M. (2006). *Internet penetration and impact*. Washington, DC: Pew Internet & American Life Project.

McKeown, D. (2008). *Cell phone use by children and youth* (staff report). Toronto: Medical Officer of Health.

National Telecommunications and Information Administration. (2002). *A nation online: How Americans are expanding their use of the Internet*. Retrieved July 17, 2011 from www.ntia.doc.gov/ntiahome/dn/anationonline2.pdf

Nishina, N., Juvonen, J., & Witkow, M. R. (2005). Sticks and stones may break my bones, but names will make me sick: The psychosocial, somatic, and scholastic consequences of peer harassment. *Journal of Clinical Child and Adolescent Psychology, 34*, 37–48.

OECD. (2006). *Are students ready for a technology-rich world? What PISA studies tell us*. Paris: Organization for Economic Cooperation and Development (OECD).

Olweus, D. (2003). A profile of bullying at school. *Educational Leadership, 60*, 12–19.

Ortega, R., Elipe, P., Mora-Merchan, J., Calmaestra, J., & Vega, E. (2009). The emotional impact on victims of traditional bullying and cyberbullying: A study of Spanish adolescents. *Zeitschrift für Psychologie/Journal of Psychology, 217*, 197–204.

Patchin, J. W., & Hinduja, S. (2006). Bullies move beyond the schoolyard: A preliminary look at cyberbullying. *Youth Violence and Juvinile Justice, 4*, 148–169.

Pink, B. (2009). *Household use of information technology: Australia 2008–09*. Sydney: Australian Bureau of Statistics.

Pyzalski, J. (2011). Electronic aggression among adolescents: An old house with a new facade (or even a number of houses). In C. Hällgren, E. Dunkels, & G-M. Frånberg (Eds.), *Youth culture and net culture: Online social practices* (pp. 278–295). Hershey, PA: IGI Global.

Raskauskas, J., & Stoltz, A. D. (2007). Involvement in traditional and electronic bullying among adolescents. *Developmental Psychology, 43*, 564–575.

Rideout, V. J., Foehr, U. G., & Roberts, D. F. (2010). *Generation M2. Media in the lives of 8–18-year-olds*. Washington, DC: Henry J. Kaiser Foundation. Available online from www.kff.org

Rideout, V., Roberts, D., & Foehr, U. (2005). *Generation M: Media in the lives of 8–18-year-olds.* Menlo Park, CA: Kaiser Family Foundation.

Rigby, K. (2003). Consequences of bullying in schools. *Canadian Journal of Psychiatry, 48,* 538–590.

Rigby, K., Smith, P. K., & Pepler, D. (2004). Working to prevent school bullying: Key issues. In P. K. Smith, D. Pepler & R. K. Rigby (Eds.), *Bullying in schools: How successful can interventions be?* (pp. 1–12). Cambridge: Cambridge University Press.

Salmivalli, C., Lagerspetz, K. M. J., Bjorkqvist, K., Osterman, K., & Kaukiainen, A. (1996). Bullying as a group process: Participant roles and their relations to social status within the group. *Aggressive Behavior, 22,* 1–15.

Salmon, G., James, A., Cassidy, E. L., & Javaloyes, M. A. (2000). Self reported anxiety, depression, and self-esteem in secondary school children. *British Medical Journal, 317,* 348–352.

Smith, P. K. (2011). Cyberbullying and cyber aggression. In S. R. Jimerson, A. B. Nickerson, M. J. Mayer, & M. J. Furlong (Eds.), *Handbook of school violence and school safety: International research and practice.* New York: Routledge.

Smith, P. K., Mahdavi, J., Carvalho, M., Fisher, S., Russell, S., & Tippett, N. (2008). Cyberbullying: Its nature and impact in secondary school pupils. *Journal of Child Psychology & Psychiatry, 49,* 376–385.

Strom, P. S., & Strom, R. D. (2005). When teens turn cyberbullies. *The Educational Digest, 71,* 35–41.

USC. (2008). *Finds shifting trends among adults about the benefits and consequences of children going online.* Los Angeles, CA: University of Southern California.

Vandebosch, H., & van Cleemput, K. (2008). Defining cyberbullying: A qualitative research into the perceptions of youngsters. *CyberPsychology & Behavior, 11,* 499–503.

Vandebosch, H., & van Cleemput, K. (2009). Cyberbullying among youngsters: prevalence and profile of bullies and victims. *New Media & Society, 11,* 1–23.

Willard, N. E. (2006). *Cyberbullying and cyberthreats.* Eugene, OR: Center for Safe and Responsible Internet Use.

Ybarra, M. L., & Mitchell, J. K. (2004). Online aggressor/targets, aggressors, and targets: A comparison of associated youth characteristics. *Journal of Child Psychology and Psychiatry, 45,* 1308–1316.

Ybarra, M. L., Mitchell, K. J., & Finkelhor, D. (2006). Examining characteristics and associated distress related to Internet harassment: Findings from the second youth Internet safety survey. *Pediatrics, 118,* e1169–e1177.

Part II

European Studies Within a DAPHNE Project

2

Comparative Aspects of Cyberbullying in Italy, England, and Spain

Findings From a DAPHNE Project

Maria Luisa Genta, Peter K. Smith, Rosario Ortega, Antonella Brighi, Annalisa Guarini, Fran Thompson, Neil Tippett, Joaquín Mora-Merchán, and Juan Calmaestra

The last 10 years have seen the increasing use of Information and Communication Technologies (ICT) among adolescents. Bullying too has been examined in relation to the growth in the use of ICT by adolescents and young people, opening up a line of research investigating "cyberbullying" behavior.

In the study of cyberbullying among preadolescents and adolescents it is important to consider the relationship between young people and ICT, highlighting the amount of use of different digital media and the preference and choices made by young people in their free time (relating to Internet, mobile phones, television, etc.).

The Accessibility of ICT

In Italy the first systematic national study on young people and ICT was conducted by Censis-Ucsi (2004) with a further study carried out in 2008 (Censis-Ucsi, 2008). Over the four years, there had been a substantial increase in the use of the Internet by young people aged 14–29: from 61% to 83% used the Internet at least once a week, and from 40% to 74% using it at least three times a week. The use of mobile phones increased from 95% to 97% in the same period. There was little gender difference in the use of the Internet: 75% of young males used the Internet at least three times a week and 72% of young females. Comparing two age levels

Cyberbullying in the Global Playground: Research from International Perspectives, First Edition.
Edited by Qing Li, Donna Cross, and Peter K. Smith.

(14–18 versus 19–24 years), younger participants were more frequent users of electronic technology, with the characteristic of *nomadism*: the ability to use every kind of electronic medium, skipping easily from one to another (preferring mobile phones, the Internet, and television to radio and newspapers).

In Spain, the National Statistical Institute (INE) carried out the first national survey about the use of and access to ICT in 2002. Here we focus our attention on the period 2004–2010, when a unified data collection system was used and the Spanish population experienced a significant growth in ICT use (INE, 2010). This increase has been in Internet access (from 33.6% in 2004 to 59.1% in 2008), and in access to mobile phones (from 82.4% in 2004 to 94.6% in 2010). If we focus on children from 10 to 15 years, almost all, 94.6%, had access to a computer in 2010 (INE, 2010).

In the UK, the Mobile Life Youth Report (2006) found that 51% of 10-year-olds and 91% of 12-year-olds had a mobile phone. The UK Children Go Online project (Livingstone & Bober, 2005) reported that 98% of 9–19-year-old British children have regular access to the Internet, with almost three-quarters having a computer connected to the Internet within their home. Around one fifth (22% of boys and 19% of girls) have Internet access in their bedrooms. Findings also showed that 41% of participants use the Internet daily, while a further 43% use it once a week or more often.

Censis-Ucsi (2008) also compared the habits of young people in the main countries in Europe; in all countries surveyed, they use a varied number of media, and the use of the Internet has increased enormously in young people of both genders. The study, however, stressed some differences among young Europeans. In particular, the researchers of the CENSIS study hypothesized two different styles of access to the digital media: an *Italian way*, in which the use of mobile phones is primarily compared to the use of the Internet; and a *Northern way* (the UK, Germany) in which the Internet is the central focus of a digital culture in young people. Spanish young people seem to use a different style again, using both mobile phones and the Internet less frequently.

A further aspect of the CENSIS study concerns the preferences of young European people in the use of digital media during their free time. The order of choices is different in Italy, the UK, and Spain. In Italy the first choice is mobile phones, followed by television and the Internet. In the UK, young people's first choice is time on the Internet, followed by mobile phones and television. In Spain the first choice is television, followed by the use of the Internet and then mobile phones. It may be that the prevalence of cyberbullying episodes among these (and other) different European countries is affected by differential "styles" in the use of new technologies.

Previous Research on Cyberbullying in Italy, England, and Spain

In Italy, research related to cyberbullying has been underway since 2008 (Pisano & Saturno, 2008; Guarini, Brighi, & Genta, 2009; Genta, Brighi, & Guarini, 2009a). Pisano and Saturno (2008) showed that 14% of middle-school students (aged 12–14) were cyberbullied, with no differences found between males and females.

Among high school students, the overall rate of victimization was similar, at 16%, but girls (23%) were much more likely to be victimized than boys (6%). Guarini and colleagues (2009) distinguished between mobile phone and Internet bullying, presenting data from the Italian sample collected during the DAPHNE project. For mobile phone bullying, 9.5% of middle and high school students (aged 12–17 years) were cyberbullied, 9.1% had cyberbullied others, and 23.2% reported having seen such aggression (bystanders). For Internet bullying, the figures were lower; with 6.8% reporting they were cyberbullied, 7.3% reporting they had cyberbullied others, and 17.2.% reporting they were bystanders.

Early studies on the prevalence of cyberbullying in England indicated a level of variability. Oliver and Candappa (2003) found that 4% of students aged 12–13 had suffered threats or insults via text messages on their mobile phones and 2% via emails. Rivers and Noret (2010), in a longitudinal study carried out from 2002–2005 with 11,227 students, found that 7% had received threatening or unpleasant messages on their mobile phones. This level increased over the years of the study, particularly for girls. Smith and colleagues (2008) found that 22% had experienced cyberbullying, but only 6.6% had suffered frequently during the last two months.

In Spain, the study by the Ombudsman (Defensor del Pueblo-UNICEF, 2007) carried out with a representative sample of Spanish young people, found that 5.5% of students were cyberbullied, while 4.8% admitted to being cyberbullies. Other studies in Spain, by Calmaestra, Ortega, and Mora-Merchán (2008), Mora-Merchán and Ortega (2007), and Ortega, Calmaestra, and Mora-Merchán (2008), conducted using questionnaires specifically designed to examine cyberbullying, have shown that more than 25% of secondary students are involved in cyberbullying occasionally (less than twice a week, 22.8%) or frequently (at least once per week, 3.8%).

Different Types of Cyberbullying

Several authors have distinguished between cyberbullying via mobile phones and cyberbullying using the Internet, since the two technologies can be used aggressively in different ways (Raskauskas & Stoltz, 2007; Dehue, Bolman, & Vollink, 2008; Ortega, Calmaestra, & Mora-Merchán, 2008; Slonje & Smith, 2008; Smith et al., 2008). It is possible to send videos, photos, or messages from mobile phones to people whose telephone numbers are known and, when aggressive messages are received via mobile phones, in many cases the victim knows the aggressor, who is often at the same school (Slonje & Smith, 2008; Smith et al., 2008). In contrast, on the Internet the people sending and receiving bullying messages could be anywhere around the globe and may be unknown to each other, thus exponentially amplifying the humiliation suffered by students who are cyberbullied (Kowalski & Limber, 2007; Wolak, Mitchell, & Finkelhor, 2007).

The effects of age and gender in cyberbullying are varied in different studies, but Ortega, Calmaestra, and Mora-Merchán (2008) suggest a differential effect of the age and gender variables depending on the type of technology used. For Internet bullying, younger students were more likely to be cyberbullied, and older students were more likely to cyberbully others; for mobile phone bullying, there were no age differences. Conversely, for Internet bullying there were no gender differences, but for mobile phone bullying, girls were more often cyberbullied than boys.

The Research Project

This project was approved and financed by the DAPHNE II Program, promoted by the European Union (EU). It was entitled "An investigation into forms of peer–peer bullying at school in preadolescent and adolescent groups: New instruments and preventing strategies." The project (see www.bullyingandcyber.net) was coordinated by Professor Genta (Department of Psychology, University of Bologna) and involved three other EU countries (Spain, University of Cordoba; Finland, University of Turku; the UK, Goldsmiths College, London); as well as Bosnia-Herzegovina (University of Tuzla) as an associate partner, and another Italian team (Promeco, Ferrara). (For a detailed description of the project see Genta, Brighi, & Guarini, 2009b.) This project aimed to develop a new questionnaire, studying aspects of cyberbullying in the countries concerned, and developing resources for teachers and educators. Here we report cross-sectional data from three countries (Italy, England, and Spain) in which the same questionnaire was used in a large-scale survey.

Aims and Research Questions

We first report data on the accessibility of ICT (mobile phone and Internet) for European adolescents, analyzing the differences between Italy, England (some data are for the UK generally), and Spain. Then we describe the diffusion of cyberbullying (by mobile phones or via the Internet) among secondary school students. We also consider age and gender variables, and the national differences, in the light of the diffusion of various forms of ICT.

A comparison between cyberbullying carried out via mobile phone and the Internet allows us to understand how European adolescents implement their acts of aggression, thus providing interesting insights for future intervention and prevention practice and policies.

Method

Participants

Cross-sectional data were gathered in early 2008. The study involved a total of 5862 students from secondary schools in Italy, England, and Spain. There were approximately equal numbers of boys and girls in each country, and the sample was

Table 2.1 Numbers of Young People in the Survey, by Country, Gender, and Age (Year Group).

	Italy	*UK*	*Spain*	*Total*
Total N	1964	2227	1671	5862
Boys	1024	1105	857	2986
Girls	921	1114	812	2847
Year 8	695	846	536	2077
Year 10	689	851	534	2074
Year 12	580	526	598	1704

approximately split equally between three age groups: Year 8 (around 12 years), Year 10 (around 14 years), and Year 12 (around 16 years); see breakdown in Table 2.1 (29 pupils did not indicate gender, 7 did not indicate year group). Pupils with disabilities represented around 3% (n = 171) of the total sample (data were missing for 77 students on this variable). Regarding parents' education levels, 14.5% (n = 794) of the fathers and 12.8% of the mothers (n = 718) did not study beyond primary school; 41.7% of the fathers (n = 2274) and 42.8% (n = 2397) of the mothers finished secondary school, and 43.8% (n = 2391) and 44.4% (n = 2492) had university degrees (data were missing for 403 pupils on fathers' education level and 255 pupils on mothers' education level).

In Italy young people from 39 secondary schools in Emilia Romagna (a region in the center of Italy; in particular in the areas of Bologna, Ferrara, and Forlì) were studied. The schools chosen included all possible type of school (lower secondary schools, upper secondary schools, lyceums, technical institutes, professional institutes) and they were located in areas with different socioeconomic statuses. In each school all classes of the corresponding age level were recruited. The main nationality was Italian (1705), with other European countries (117), African (36), Asian (61), South American (25), and North American (1); nationality information was missing for 19 students. These figures are representative of the nationalities present in central Italy.

In the UK young people from 14 different secondary schools in various parts of England were studied. The main ethnic breakdown was white (1555), Asian (437), black (116), and dual heritage (160); ethnicity information was missing for 30 pupils. This is a reasonably representative ethnic mix for pupils in England generally.

In Spain young people were surveyed from seven private and public secondary schools in the region of Cordova in the south of Spain. In each school all classes of the corresponding age level were recruited. It was not possible to ask about ethnicity in the Spanish sample, but the proportion of immigrant or minority families in the area is low (around 3%). Schools from areas with different socioeconomic levels were selected through random cluster sampling. These samples are representative of the province of Cordoba, a southern area in the Andalucía region.

Questionnaires

The questionnaire, which was based on previous questionnaires (Smith, Mahdavi, Carvalho, & Tippett, 2006; Ortega, Calmaestra, & Mora-Merchán, 2007), consisted of three separate sections with a total of eighty-two questions. The first section covered demographic aspects, including gender and ethnicity. The second section included items on loneliness and self-esteem (see Chapter 3). The third section included questions regarding bullying and cyberbullying. Brief definitions of bullying and of cyberbullying were given at the beginning of this section so that pupils had a clear understanding of the behaviors classified as bullying and cyberbullying and did not confuse them with other aggressive behaviors:

> Bullying is behavior carried out by an individual, or a group, which is repeated over time in order to hurt, threaten or frighten another individual with the intention to cause distress. It is different from other aggressive behavior because it involves an imbalance of power which leaves the victim defenseless.
>
> Cyberbullying is a new form of bullying which involves the use of mobile phones (texts, calls, video clips) or the Internet (e-mail, instant messaging, chatrooms, websites) or other forms of information and communication technology to deliberately harass, threaten, or intimidate someone.

Questions were then asked about four kinds of bullying, two traditional and two cyber, introduced and defined as follows:

> Traditional types of bullying (this doesn't include cyberbullying). Direct forms of bullying include hitting, tripping up, taking belongings, name-calling, and taunting (perhaps about race, gender, sexuality, or disability) to someone in person, face-to-face. Indirect forms of bullying include telling lies or spreading false rumors about someone behind their back, sending mean notes to try and make someone disliked, or excluding someone from a social group on purpose. Again, this doesn't include cyberbullying.
>
> Cyberbullying using a mobile phone includes sending or receiving upsetting phone calls, taking, sending, or receiving unpleasant photos and/or videos using mobile phones (such as being flamed, happy slapping etc.), or sending or receiving abusive text messages by mobile phone. Cyberbullying using the Internet includes malicious or threatening emails directly, or about someone to others, intimidation or abuse when participating in chatrooms, abusive instant messages (MSN, Yahoo, etc.), websites where secret or personal details are revealed in an abusive way or where nasty or unpleasant comments are being made (such as social networking websites (MySpace, Facebook, Bebo, Piczo, etc.); file-sharing websites (YouTube, flickr, etc.); blogs (blogger, blogspot, LiveJournal, etc.).

Data from the following questions were analyzed for this chapter. Two were on accessibility to technology, with yes/no response options:

1. Do you have a mobile phone?
2. Do you have any computers linked to the Internet in your home? And in your own room?

A further four questions were on experiences as a student who was bullied and/or bullied others; the response options for each were on a five-point scale (scored from one to five): "I haven't been bullied/I haven't bullied anyone;" "It has only happened once or twice;" "Two or three times a month;" "About once a week;" and "It happens several times a week."

1. Have you been bullied through mobile phone use in the last two months?
2. Have you bullied anyone else using your mobile phone in the last two months?
3. Have you been bullied on the Internet in the last two months?
4. Have you bullied anyone else using the Internet in the last two months?

Of the responses, "it has only happened once or twice" was defined as being "occasional;" while "two or three times a month" or more frequently was defined as being "severe."

Procedure

The questionnaires were filled out by students during school hours. The researchers first explained the definition of cyberbullying (following that in the questionnaire), and clarified that the questionnaire was voluntary and anonymous; all the information was treated confidentially and no one in the respondents' school would know what they had answered. Students could omit any questions they did not wish to answer. The researchers remained in the classroom while the questionnaires were filled in, to answer any queries and then collect the questionnaires. The pupils' parents and the school management board gave their consent, and the project was approved by the appropriate institutional ethics committees in each country.

Statistical analysis

Statistical analyses were run using SPSS 17 for Windows. The significance level was set at 5%. Chi square analyses were carried out in order to investigate the association between country and ICT accessibility. Four logistic analyses were run to investigate the predictive values of several factors (gender, age as year level, country, and ICT accessibility) on the frequency of cyberbullying through mobile phones and the Internet. Since students who were involved in severe cyberbullying were very rare (see descriptive analyses) we decided to compute the prevalence of occasional and severe cyberbullying in these analyses. Moreover, we must emphasize that in

Table 2.2 Percentages of Adolescents (Male and Female) Involved in Victimization/Bullying Via Mobile Phones and the Internet (Not Involved, Occasional, and Severe: Percentages and Sample Size), for the Total Sample.

	Gender	*Not involved*	*Occasional*	*Severe*	*Total*
Mobile victimization	Boy	95.0 (2786)	3.4 (99)	1.6 (47)	100.0 (2932)
	Girl	93.1 (2625)	5.2 (146)	1.7 (48)	100.0 (2819)
Internet victimization	Boy	94.4 (2783)	3.8 (111)	1.8 (54)	100.0 (2948)
	Girl	91.5 (2578)	6.5 (182)	2.1 (58)	100.0 (2818)
Mobile bullying	Boy	93.3 (2768)	4.0 (120)	2.6 (78)	100.0 (2966)
	Girl	96.0 (2723)	3.2 (92)	0.8 (22)	100.0 (2837)
Internet bullying	Boy	94.3 (2790)	3.9 (116)	1.8 (53)	100.0 (2959)
	Girl	96.4 (2724)	2.7 (77)	0.9 (25)	100.0 (2826)

cyberbullying, differently from traditional bullying, a one-off episode can be as upsetting as continuous acts of aggression. Before running logistic regression analyses, multicollinearity was tested.

Results

Accessibility to mobile phones and the Internet

Almost all the adolescents surveyed owned their own personal mobile phones (n = 5494, 94.6%). More Italian students had a personal mobile (n = 1859, 95.9%) than Spanish students (n = 1570, 94.1%) and English students (n = 2065, 93.8%), χ^2 (2) = 10.17, $p = 0.006$. While a large proportion of students had access to a computer connected to the Internet at home (n = 5114, 87.7%), more English students (n = 2106, 95.0%) than Italian (n = 1635, 83.5%) and Spanish students (n = 1373, 82.7%) had such access, χ^2 (2) = 180.30, $p < 0.001$. Nearly half of the students had a computer connected to the Internet in their own bedrooms (n = 2441, 41.8%). This applied more for Italian (n = 949, 48.5%) than Spanish (n = 641, 38.6%) and English students (n = 851, 38.4%), χ^2 (2) = 53.20, $p < 0.001$.

The prevalence of cyberbullying

The prevalence of cyberbullying via mobile phones and the Internet, taking into account the distinction between occasional and severe bullying, is shown in relation to gender in Table 2.2, in relation to age (year group) in Table 2.3 and in relation to country in Table 2.4. In total 5.9% of students were cyberbullied via mobile phones

Table 2.3 Percentages of Children in Each Year Group (Year 8, Year 10, and Year 12) Involved in Victimization/Bullying Via Mobile Phone and the Internet (Not Involved, Occasional, Severe: Percentages and Sample Size), for the Total Sample.

	Year	*Not involved*	*Occasional*	*Severe*	*Total*
Mobile victimization	Year 8	94.1 (1928)	4.2 (86)	1.7 (34)	100.0 (2048)
	Year 10	93.7 (1917)	4.4 (89)	1.9 (39)	100.0 (2045)
	Year 12	94.3 (1585)	4.3 (73)	1.3 (22)	100.0 (1680)
Internet victimization	Year 8	92.7 (1903)	5.1 (104)	2.2 (45)	100.0 (2052)
	Year 10	93.0 (1908)	5.1 (104)	1.9 (39)	100.0 (2051)
	Year 12	93.1 (1568)	5.2 (87)	1.7 (29)	100.0 (1684)
Mobile bullying	Year 8	95.6 (1971)	3.2 (65)	1.3 (26)	100.0 (2062)
	Year 10	93.5 (1930)	4.2 (86)	2.4 (49)	100.0 (2065)
	Year 12	94.7 (1608)	3.8 (65)	1.5 (25)	100.0 (1698)
Internet bullying	Year 8	96.9 (1993)	2.2 (46)	0.8 (17)	100.0 (2056)
	Year 10	94.8 (1955)	3.4 (70)	1.8 (38)	100.0 (2063)
	Year 12	93.9 (1586)	4.6 (78)	1.5 (25)	100.0 (1689)

Table 2.4 Percentages of Adolescents by Country (Italy, England, and Spain) Involved in Victimization/Bullying Via Mobile Phone and the Internet (Not Involved, Occasional, Severe: Percentages and Sample Size), for the Total Sample.

	Country	*Not involved*	*Occasional*	*Severe*	*Total*
Mobile victimization	Italy	90.5 (1738)	7.3 (140)	2.2 (42)	100.0 (1920)
	England	95.9 (2121)	2.1 (47)	2.0 (44)	100.0 (2212)
	Spain	95.7 (1574)	3.7 (61)	0.5 (9)	100.0 (1644)
Internet victimization	Italy	92.7 (1795)	5.4 (104)	1.9 (37)	100.0 (1936)
	England	93.4 (2061)	4.0 (88)	2.6 (57)	100.0 (2206)
	Spain	92.5 (1527)	6.2 (103)	1.3 (21)	100.0 (1651)
Mobile bullying	Italy	90.9 (1778)	6.4 (126)	2.7 (53)	100.0 (1957)
	England	97.5 (2158)	1.0 (22)	1.5 (33)	100.0 (2213)
	Spain	94.9 (1577)	4.2 (69)	0.9 (15)	100.0 (1661)
Internet bullying	Italy	93.2 (1814)	5.1 (100)	1.6 (32)	100.0 (1946)
	England	96.9 (2147)	1.5 (34)	1.5 (34)	100.0 (2215)
	Spain	95.4 (1578)	3.6 (60)	1.0 (16)	100.0 (1654)

(4.3% occasionally and 1.6% severely) and 7.1% through the Internet (5.1% occasionally, 2% severely); 5.4% of students cyberbullied others through mobile phones (3.7% occasionally and 1.7% severely) and 4.7% through the Internet (3.3% occasionally, 1.4% severely).

Table 2.5 Logistic Regression for Cybervictimization Via Mobile Phones (Not Involved Versus Students who Were Cyberbullied by Others).

Predictors	B	SE	*Wald*	Df	P	e^B
Gender	−0.611	0.221	7.637	1	0.006	0.543
Age						
12–8	−0.413	0.394	1.099	1	0.294	0.662
12–10	−0.028	0.185	0.023	1	0.879	0.972
Country						
Spain–Italy	0.846	0.146	33.517	1	0.000	2.330
Spain–England	−0.064	0.164	0.153	1	0.695	0.938
Own mobile	0.159	0.285	0.310	1	0.578	1.172

Note: e^B = exponentiated B. $\chi^2(7) = 72.45, p < 0.001$.

Students who were cyberbullied via mobile phones

The first logistic regression analysis was run on 5709 students and it investigated the effect of gender, age, country, and accessibility to personal mobile phones on the frequency of students who were cyberbullied via mobile phones (dependent variable: students not involved versus students who were cyberbullied by others). The model was significant, although it explained very little of the variance between students who were cyberbullied (Nagelkerke $R^2 = 0.085$). As shown in Table 2.5, gender and country were significant predictors of victimization. In particular, females were more likely to be a target of cyberbullying than males. Moreover, more students in Italy than in Spain declared themselves to be cyberbullied by others, while no differences were found between Spanish and English students.

Students who were cyberbullied via the Internet

The second logistic regression analysis was run with 5742 students testing the predictive values of gender, age, country, and accessibility to an Internet connection in their own rooms, on the prevalence of students who were cyberbullied via the Internet. As already found with students who were cyberbullied through mobile phones, the model, although significant, can explain only a small amount of the variance in the frequency of students who were cyberbullied by others via the Internet (Nagelkerke $R^2 = 0.043$). As shown in Table 2.6, the only significant predictor was accessibility to the Internet, with higher percentages of victimization among students who had an Internet connection in their own rooms.

Students who cyberbullied others via mobile phones

The third logistic regression analysis was conducted with 5759 students and it tested the effects of gender, age, country, and accessibility to own mobile phones on the frequency of students who cyberbullied others via mobile phones. The

Table 2.6 Logistic Regression on Cybervictimization Through the Internet (Not Involved Versus Students who Were Cyberbullied by Others).

Predictors	B	SE	*Wald*	Df	P	e^B
Gender	−0.218	0.194	1.263	1	0.261	0.804
Age						
12–8	0.634	0.364	3.030	1	0.082	1.886
12–10	0.210	0.172	1.480	1	0.224	1.233
Country						
Spain–Italy	−0.077	0.130	0.349	1	0.554	0.926
Spain–England	−0.186	0.129	2.091	1	0.148	0.830
Connection in own room	0.268	0.105	6.501	1	0.011	1.308

Note: e^B = exponentiated B. $\chi^2(7) = 30.48, p < 0.001$.

Table 2.7 Logistic Regression on Cyberbullying Via Mobile Phones (Not Involved Versus Students who Cyberbullied Others).

Predictors	B	SE	*Wald*	Df	P	e^B
Gender	0.566	0.226	6.289	1	0.012	1.762
Age						
12–8	−0.059	0.462	0.016	1	0.898	0.943
12–10	0.237	0.236	1.013	1	0.314	1.268
Country						
Spain–Italy	0.605	0.138	19.123	1	0.000	1.831
Spain–England	−0.773	0.180	18.547	1	0.000	0.462
Own mobile	0.020	0.287	0.005	1	0.945	1.020

Note: e^B = exponentiated B. $\chi^2(7) = 117.97, p < 0.001$.

model was significant, explaining 10% of variance of students who cyberbullied others through mobile phones (Nagelkerke $R^2 = 0.102$). Significant predictors were gender and country (see Table 2.7). In particular, more males than females cyberbullied others in Italy compared to Spain, and in Spain compared to England.

Students who cyberbullied others via the Internet

The last logistic regression analysis was conducted with 5763 students and it investigated the effect of gender, age, country, and accessibility to Internet connection in students' own rooms on the prevalence of students who cyberbullied others

Table 2.8 Logistic Regression on Cyberbullying Via the Internet (Not Involved Versus Students who Cyberbullied Others).

Predictors	B	SE	*Wald*	Df	P	e^B
Gender	0.579	0.213	7.399	1	0.007	1.783
Age						
12–8	−0.355	0.458	0.601	1	0.438	0.701
12–10	−0.217	0.245	0.786	1	0.375	0.805
Country						
Spain–Italy	0.376	0.151	6.220	1	0.013	1.457
Spain–England	−0.416	0.174	5.698	1	0.017	0.660
Connection in own room	0.449	0.128	12.379	1	0.000	1.567

Note: e^B = exponentiated B. $\chi^2(7) = 89.19$, $p < 0.001$.

via the Internet. The model was significant and it explained about 12% of variance of prevalence of students who cyberbullied others through the Internet (Nagelkerke $R^2 = 0.121$). As shown in Table 2.8, significant predictors of the model were gender, country, and accessibility to Internet. In summary, a higher percentage of students who cyberbullied others was male compared to female, and a higher percentage was found in Italy than in Spain, and in Spain than in England. Moreover, a higher percentage of students who had an Internet connection in their own rooms cyberbullied others than their peers who had no connection in their own room.

Discussion

This study has provided cross-national information on the phenomenon of cyberbullying in its two most frequent and recognized forms by students (via mobile phones and through the Internet). The findings indicate that there are different forms of cyberbullying, depending on whether it is conducted via mobile phones or through the Internet, in terms of the structural variables involved, including roles, levels of severity, gender, and country differences.

The percentages of cyberbullying arising from our data with respect to prevalence can be compared to previous and other contemporary studies, while bearing in mind differences in samples and methodology. In Italy, the prevalence of cyberbullying found in the present study is similar to recent data presented by Pisano and Saturno (2008).

In England, the figures are lower than those reported by Smith et al. (2008) (22% occasional, 6.6% frequent); however, this latter study had a relatively small sample size. It also appears slightly less than the figures of around 7% reported by Rivers and Noret (2010). The evidence for a decrease in cyberbullying is far from strong, given differences in samples and methodology, but if there was such a decrease, it could possibly be related to government action on bullying and cyberbullying (see below).

In Spain, there have been no national surveys carried out, except the last Ombudsman's report (Defensor del Pueblo-UNICEF, 2007) on school violence, which includes some information about cyberbullying. Hence the prevalence of cyberbullying throughout the country is unknown. Our results show higher levels of prevalence than the Ombudsman's report (2007: 5.5% occasional, 0.4% frequent) but lower than Orte (2006) and Sureda et al. (2009) (around 20% of students involved in occasional and frequent bullying). However, the data are similar to those collected by Ortega's research team (Calmaestra, Ortega, & Mora-Merchán, 2008; Ortega, Calmaestra, & Mora-Merchán, 2008).

Overall, the percentages from these European samples point mostly to occasional forms of mobile phone and Internet cyberbullying, and they are generally lower than those reported in North American studies (Beran & Li, 2005; Li, 2006; Patchin & Hinduja, 2006). Moreover, the percentages of reported victimization and cyberbullying are quite similar, indicating that, in general, both media are involved in the phenomenon.

The availability of mobile phones and the Internet among the sample was very high, especially concerning mobile phones, where almost all students had access to one, although with some country differences. More Italian adolescents owned a mobile phone than English and Spanish peers. Also, Internet availability at home was reported to be very high in the sample. Availability was highest among students in England in comparison to Italy and Spain. In Italy, Internet availability, although lower than in England, is also associated with an increased likelihood of adolescents using a computer in their own rooms. It was remarkable that our data suggest that adolescents who use a computer in their own room, that is, without adult supervision, are at higher risk of engaging in cyberbullying behavior and being cyberbullied by others. We think that a low level of awareness of cyberbullying among many adults leads to poor monitoring of their children's online behavior. Such awareness should be the outcome, among other things, of good policies to inform educators and adults in general, and through providing specific and useful tools to counteract cyberbullying.

Concerning gender differences in cyberbullying behavior, our results showed different effects of this variable in the cyberbullying roles, as already highlighted by Dehue, Bolman, and Vollink (2008). In particular, we found that females are more likely to be cyberbullied by others, while males are generally more likely to cyberbully others. The greater prevalence of cyberbullying in males has been observed in previous studies (Aricak et al., 2008; Slonje & Smith, 2008). Similar to studies conducted by Li (2007), this study suggests that females were more likely to be victimized than males. However, gender differences were not found in several international studies (Wolak, Mitchell, & Finkelhor, 2007; Smith et al., 2008), highlighting how the influence of gender on cyberbullying is still unclear.

In the present research, no significant relationships were found between age (assessed by year group) and cyberbullying behavior. The effect of age is still debated in the literature, since some authors observed a significant increase in the involvement of adolescents in the phenomenon of cyberbullying with an increase in age (Ybarra & Mitchell, 2004; Kowalski & Limber, 2007; Smith et al., 2008), while other studies have highlighted a decrease in the percentages of cyberbullying in the move from primary to middle school (Dehue, Bolman, & Vollink, 2008) and from middle to secondary school (Slonje & Smith, 2008).

Concerning differences among countries, Italian students were more involved in cyberbullying behavior than English and Spanish students when they were cyberbullied (via both mobile phones and the Internet) and were cyberbullying others (via mobile phones). Moreover, differences between Spain and England emerged among students who cyberbullied others (via both mobile phones and the Internet), with a more active involvement of Spanish adolescents. We hypothesized that these differences between countries can be explained by cultural factors and different national policies to prevent bullying and cyberbullying.

In Italy, the lack of a sustained national policy against bullying and cyberbullying is remarkable. In fact, the first national legislation to prevent bullying was published by the Ministry of Education in 2007. The aim of this document was to indicate some opportunities, resources, and tools for school in order to manage bullying, in collaboration with other institutions and educational settings. Several national actions were described: the creation of a network of permanent regional institutes to research, train, monitor, and inform, the creation of a national website (www.smontailbullo.it), the activation of a national bullying phone helpline, collaboration with the police to monitor aggression through the Internet and to inform students about the risks of the Internet and about the legal issues connected to cyberbullying. For a more detailed review of this, see Genta, Berdondini, Brighi, & Guarini (2009). In 2007 the Ministry of Education also published guidelines on the use of mobile phones and other electronic devices during teaching, imposing disciplinary sanctions on students who refused to comply with instructions, and highlighting the co-responsibility of parents and teachers. This document bans the use of mobile phones by teachers and pupils during school hours. However, such initiatives are localized and sporadic and not always evaluated.

In England, there are national policies in place to deal with cyberbullying (Safe to Learn: Cyberbullying, 2008). The guidance includes the definition and forms of cyberbullying, legal powers available to schools (Education and Inspections Act, 2006) and ways of preventing cyberbullying, including awareness-raising and promoting understanding through the curriculum. Schools are advised to promote e-safety and the responsible use of ICT, publish reporting methods, and have a clear range of sanctions for perpetrators and bystanders. A school's anti-bullying policy should include cyberbullying, and the guidance suggests that it is important for schools to refer to Acceptable Use Policies (AUPs) for Internet and mobile use. Technology-specific sanctions for pupils engaged in cyberbullying behavior could include limiting Internet access for a period of time or removing the right to use a mobile phone on the school site. See www.digizen.org/downloads/cyberbullying.pdf for more information.

In Spain there are no national initiatives concerning policies that specifically address cyberbullying. However, some regional administrations and non-governmental organizations (NGOs) have developed proposals to prevent cyberbullying, most of them using the structure of guidelines for the safe use of ICTs (related to Internet safety). There are also some prevention programs supported by regional administrations which include anti-bullying initiatives (for example, in Andalusia the "Schools: Spaces of Peace" program, and the PREVI plan in Valencia). INTECO (2008), a national platform promoted by the Ministry of Education, reports on the legal consequences of cyberbullying behaviors.

The strength of the study includes its cross-cultural design, using the same theoretical background and methodological approach. One possible limitation of this study could be the use of a questionnaire that did not allow a more systemic view of cyberbullying (that is, the parallel use of qualitative and quantitative methodologies).

In conclusion, when looking at the diffusion of this phenomenon and at the relevant variables which can influence it, the importance of prevention policies clearly emerges. First, on the basis of our main results we can point out the importance of addressing interventions to boys, girls, preadolescents, and adolescents since they are all involved in the cyberbullying phenomenon. Second, the interventions must be tailored according to the needs of each country, taking into consideration any differences in cultural and political orientation. Last, we stress the necessity of promoting prevention policies that take into consideration a more global approach; not only considering students and their relationships but also engaging parents, teachers, educators, school managers, and policy-makers in a common effort involving the whole community.

Acknowledgments

This research was supported by the DAPHNE Program II 2004-2008 (Proposal No. 06-1/0) "To prevent and combat violence against children, young people and to protect victims and groups at risk." We would like to thank Silvia Galli for her support in statistical analyses. We are also grateful to all the students, teachers, and parents who agreed to participate in the study.

References

Aricak, T., Siyahnan, S., Uzunhasanoglu, A., Saribeyoglu, S., Ciplak, S., & Yilmaz, N. (2008). Cyberbullying among Turkish adolescents. *CyberPsychology & Behavior, 11*, 253–261.

Beran, T., & Li, Q. (2005). Cyber-harassment: A study of a new method for an old behaviour. *Journal of Educational Computing Research, 32*, 265–277.

Calmaestra, J., Ortega, R., & Mora-Merchán, J. A. (2008). Las TIC y la convivencia. Un estudio sobre formas de acoso en el ciberespacio. *Investigación en la Escuela, 64*, 93–103.

Censis-Ucsi. (2004). *Terzo rapporto Censis-Ucsi sulla comunicazione. Testo completo.* Retrieved October 1, 2010 from www.censis.it/5?resource_23=4785&relational_resource_24=4785&relational_resource_396=4785&relational_resource_26=4785&relational_resource_78=4785&relational_resource_296=4785&relational_resource_342=4785&relational_resource_343=4785

Censis-Ucsi. (2008). *Settimo rapporto sulla comunicazione. Sintesi dei Risultati.* Retrieved October 1, 2010 from www.governo.it/GovernoInforma/Dossier/rapporto_censis/Sintesi_7_rapcom.pdf

Defensor Del Pueblo-UNICEF. (2007). *Violencia escolar: el maltrato entre iguales en la educación secundaría obligatoria. 1999–2006.* Madrid: Publicaciones de la Oficina del Defensor del Pueblo.

Dehue, F., Bolman, C., & Vollink, T. (2008). Cyberbullying: youngsters' experiences and parental perception. *CyberPsychology & Behavior, 11*, 217–223.

Genta, M. L., Berdondini, L., Brighi A., & Guarini, A. (2009). Il fenomeno del bullismo elettronico in adolescenza. *Rassegne di Psicologia, 26*, 141–161.

Genta, M. L., Brighi, A., & Guarini, A. (Eds.) (2009a). *Bullying and cyberbullying in adolescence.* Rome: Carocci.

Genta, M. L., Brighi, A., & Guarini, A. (2009b). European project on bullying and cyberbullying, granted by DAPHNE II Program. *Zeitschrift für Psychologie/Journal of Psychology, 217*, 233.

Guarini, A., Brighi, A., & Genta, M. L. (2009). Traditional bullying and cyberbullying in Italian secondary schools. In M. L. Genta, A. Brighi, & A. Guarini (Eds.), *Bullying and cyberbullying in adolescence* (pp. 77–95). Rome: Carocci.

INE. (2010). *Encuesta sobre equipamiento y uso de tecnologías de la información y comunicación en los hogares 2010.* Retrieved June 28, 2011 from www.ine.es/jaxi/menu.do?type=pcaxis&path=/t25/p450/a2010/&file=pcaxis

INTECO. (2008). *Protección del derecho al honor, a la intimidad y a la propia imagen en Internet.* Retrieved on June 28, 2011 from www.inteco.es/Seguridad/Observatorio/manuales_es/guiaManual_honor_internet

Kowalski, R. M., & Limber, S. P. (2007). Electronic bullying among middle school students. *Journal of Adolescent Health, 41*, 822–830.

Li, Q. (2006). Cyberbullying in schools: A research of gender differences. *School Psychology International, 27*, 157–170.

Li, Q. (2007). New bottle but old wine: a research of cyberbullying in schools. *Computers in Human Behavior, 23*, 1777–1791.

Livingstone, S., & Bober, M. (2005). *UK children go online: Final report of key project findings.* London: LSE Report.

Mobile Life Youth Report. (2006). *The impact of the mobile phone on the lives of young people.* Carphone Warehouse. Retrieved July 23, 2011 from www.yougov.co.uk/extranets/ygarchives/content/pdf/CPW060101004_2.pdf

Mora-Merchán, J. A., & Ortega, R. (2007). The new forms of school bullying and violence. In R. Ortega, J. A. Mora-Merchán, & T. Jäger (Eds.), *Acting against school bullying and violence. The role of media, local authorities and the Internet* (pp. 7–34). Landau: Verlag Empirische Pädagogik (www.bullying-in-school.info).

Oliver, C., & Candappa, M. (2003). *Tackling bullying: Listening to the views of children and young people.* Nottingham: Department for Education and Skills.

Orte, C. (2006). Nuevas perspectivas sobre la violencia y el bullying escolar. *Infancia y Juventud: Nuevas Condiciones, Nuevas Oportunidades, 3*, 27–41.

Ortega, R., Calmaestra, J., & Mora-Merchán, J. A. (2007). *Cuestionario cyberbullying*. Cordoba: Universidad de Córdoba.

Ortega, R., Calmaestra, J., & Mora-Merchán, J. A. (2008). Cyberbullying. *International Journal of Psychology and Psychological Therapy, 8*, 183–192.

Patchin, J., & Hinduja, S. (2006). Bullies move beyond the schoolyard: A preliminary look at cyberbullying. *Youth Violence and Juvenile Justice, 4*, 148–169.

Pisano, L., & Saturno, M. E. (2008). Le prepotenze non terminano mai: tipologie, proprietà e aspetti epidemiologici del cyberbullismo. *Psicologia Contemporanea, 210*, 40–45.

Raskauskas, J., & Stoltz, A. D. (2007). Involvement in traditional and electronic bullying among adolescents. *Developmental Psychology, 43*, 564–575.

Rivers, I., & Noret, N. (2010). 'I h8 u': Findings from a five-year study of text and email bullying. *British Educational Research Journal, 36*, 643–671.

Slonje, R., & Smith, P. K. (2008). Cyberbullying: Another main type of bullying? *Scandinavian Journal of Psychology, 49*, 147–154.

Smith, P. K., Mahdavi, J., Carvalho, M., Fisher, S., Russell, S., & Tippett, N. (2008). Cyberbullying: Its nature and impact in secondary school pupils. *Journal of Child Psychology and Psychiatry, 49*, 376–385.

Smith, P. K., Mahdavi, J., Carvalho, M., & Tippett, N. (2006). *An investigation into cyberbullying, its forms, awareness and impact, and the relationship between age and gender in cyberbullying*. Research brief no. RBX03-06: Anti-Bullying Alliance.

Sureda, J., Comas, R., Morey, M., Mut, B., Salva, F., & Oliver, M. (2009). *Les TIC i els joves a les Illes Balears: Equipament i usos de les tecnologies de la informació i la comunicació per part dels joves de les Illes Balears d'entre 15 i 16 anys*. Balearic Islands: Fundació IBIT (see www.ibit.org/dades/doc/2190_ca.pdf).

Wolak, J., Mitchell, K. J., & Finkelhor, D. (2007). Does online harassment constitute bullying? An exploration of online harassment by known peers and online-only contacts. *Journal of Adolescent Health, 41*, 851–858.

Ybarra, M. L., & Mitchell, K. J. (2004). Youth engaging in online harassment: associations with caregiver–child relationships, Internet use, and personal characteristics. *Journal of Adolescence, 27*, 319–336.

3

Self-Esteem and Loneliness in Relation to Cyberbullying in Three European Countries

Antonella Brighi, Giannino Melotti, Annalisa Guarini, Maria Luisa Genta, Rosario Ortega, Joaquín Mora-Merchán, Peter K. Smith, and Fran Thompson

The continuous expansion of electronic space gives adolescents the opportunity to free themselves from restrictions relating to their age and offers them easy access to a world which is beyond that of their families and schools. Recent European surveys show that the diffusion of the Internet is a worldwide phenomenon, compared to the Internet diffusion reported 10 years ago. Italy reports an Internet penetration of 51.7% and a 127.5% percentage increase compared to the former data collection; the UK reports an Internet diffusion of around 82.5% and a percentage increase of 234.0%; and in Spain the rate of increase is even higher, at 440.0%, reaching 62.6% of the population (source: www.internetworldstats.com/stats.htm).[1]

The possibility of establishing virtual social interactions has become increasingly important for 10–13-year-olds. In the first years of adolescence, numerous friendships are created and young people want to manifest their own identity in terms of their relations with others (Arcuri, 2008), and new technologies offer immense opportunities to do this.

Young people use these means as a form of expression to communicate information about themselves. Some scholars consider the Internet to be a means by which young people can explore and build their own identity (Calvert, 2002) and experiment with diverse roles in interactive games (Turkle, 1995; McDonald & Kim, 2001). They can explore various ways of presenting themselves (Harter, 1998), find useful information, receive, and send instant messages (IM), create personal web pages (Schmitt, Dayanim, & Matthias, 2008), or write blogs (Huffaker & Calvert, 2005). In a US study, Schmitt, Dayanim, and Matthias (2008) interviewed 500 preadolescents

Cyberbullying in the Global Playground: Research from International Perspectives, First Edition.
Edited by Qing Li, Donna Cross, and Peter K. Smith.

and adolescents aged 8 to 17 and found that 66% of those who had a personal home page or blog had been contacted by people they had never met before. This was true mainly for adolescents (71.4%), but less so for preadolescents (37.5%).

This function is in line with the process of psychosocial moratorium (Erikson, 1950; Marcia, 1980) in which the adolescent is given time and space to acquire a stable identity. In preadolescence such Internet applications constitute a way of exploring one's own identity and later, in adolescence, become a way of giving it form, allowing this identity to be explored, tested, and remodeled under the guarantee of anonymity.

Bullying in Traditional and Virtual Contexts

This present generation is the first generation of adolescents growing up in a society in which "being connected" represents a fact of life, an experience ingrained in day-to-day living (Raskaukas & Stoltz, 2007). The possibility of also always being "elsewhere," in reality and parallel universes, offers adolescents a new and stimulating context of interaction and, at the same time, it forces researchers to investigate the new scenarios of communication which may require a quite different paradigm from those that were used for face-to-face communication. Despite the enormous possibilities offered by ICT, the data concerning the diffusion of ICT allows us to also foresee a positive correlation between the diffusion of episodes of misuse and bullying. The distorted and improper use of ICT to intentionally attack defenseless people and cause damage to their reputation, facilitated by anonymity and by the potential planetary diffusion of insults, has been called *cyberbullying*. Cyberbullying describes an aggressive and intentional act conducted by an individual or a group of individuals using various forms of electronic contact, repeatedly over time against a victim (Smith et al., 2008).

With the advent of cyberbullying, persons who bully others do not act solely in the "real world," but can also target victims in the "virtual world" offered by the Internet. Adolescents in particular may be the target of aggression online as the virtual world is a major part of their socializing. The high frequency with which people meet, communicate and interact online has given the emergence of deviant behavior more importance—in the sense that it is different from "real life interactions" and true acts of delinquency and criminality in the "real" world. Chisholm (2006) calls this behavior "disinhibition" and it explains how people do not behave in the same way in cyberspace as in real life, especially when engaging in violent or fraudulent conduct. This disinhibition in communication and hence in the system of relationships with others when using the Internet or mobile phone communication can lead to hostile interactions (Willard, 2006).

The widespread use of virtual interactions which extend from purely work-related environments to all the areas of daily life, leads social psychologists to ask whether these interactions are regulated by the same social processes and mechanisms that take place in the "real" world. Is it useful to use the same explanations and theories with which we analyze the environment of everyday life for what takes place in a virtual world? Moreover, what are the consequences of cybervictimization in the "real lives" of victims?

As a social or psychological phenomenon, aggression accomplished through the new communication media is often more subtle and more encompassing than traditional face-to-face forms (Suler, 2004; Willard, 2006; Brighi, Guarini, & Genta, 2009). The features of the Internet that may facilitate aggression may be considered within a general framework suggested by the social learning theorist Bandura (1996), focusing on the causes of aggressive behavior. This perspective considers the role of interactive multiple factors: those creating the motivation to commit aggression, those reducing internal and external inhibitions that may prevent acting out the desire to aggress, and those providing the opportunity for the act to occur. Motivational, disinhibitory, and opportunity factors may create a blend in the virtual world with peculiar characteristics still not well understood, but clearly our understanding of bullying behavior must be considered from a different perspective. It is within this context that the presumed invisibility, the weakening of ethical qualms, the high degree of spontaneity and immediacy, the absence of spatio-temporal limits, and disinhibition become the means through which most adolescents begin to cyberbully.

A psychosocial approach may suggest further points to be considered, as studies on traditional bullying inspired by this approach reveal. Aggressive behavior is seen as the result of the interaction between individual dispositions and the context in which it takes place. The latter context is mainly characterized by its social dimension; that is, the presence of various social groups, the normative and evaluative system that regulates interactions among individuals and groups, and the historical/cultural system of reference. As Ojala and Nesdale (2004) note, most studies on (traditional) bullying are interested in an analysis of the psychosocial characteristics of students who bully or their victims and the consequences of such victimization (Olweus, 1994; Boulton & Smith, 1994; Bernstein & Watson, 1997; Craig, 1998; Hawker & Boulton, 2000; Rigby, 2001; Smith, Shu, & Madsen, 2001; Ortega & Del Rey, 2008), while some researchers have analyzed bullying as a group process (Salmivalli, Lagerspetz, Bjorkquist, Osterman, & Kaukianinen, 1996; Ortega & Mora-Merchán, 1996, 2008; Salmivalli, Huttunen, & Lagerspetz, 1997; Atlas & Pepler, 1998; Genta, 2002). Most cases of bullying do not only involve the bully and the victim but rather entire groups of people of the same age who take part, more or less actively, in the aggressive action while playing diverse roles (assistants or followers, supporters, defenders of the victim, bystanders, and those neutral to such scenes).

A key psychosocial concept that has been proposed to understand bullying as a phenomenon dependent upon group processes and dynamics is that of *social identity* defined as "that part of an individual's self-concept which derives from his knowledge of his membership in a social group (or groups) together with the value and emotional significance attached to that membership" (Tajfel, 1981, p. 255).

Social identity does not limit itself to being a category that individuals use to describe their own belonging to a group but, because particular emotive states and values are associated with it, it is prescriptive that a member of a group must have certain attitudes and modes of behavior if he is to remain such a member. This system establishes both the internal and external functioning of the group and prescribes what the attitudes, behavior modes, and rules of conduct are that every member must observe regarding people their own age, adults, other adolescent groups and, more generally, collectively. In a period of experimentation and "psychosocial moratorium" as adolescence (Erikson, 1950; Marcia, 1980), where the individual makes an effort to respond to the demand for differentiation from parental figures, the identification with peers is functional to the process of the adolescent's social identity construction. This is because she earns the status of "belonging" to a group in which she can make her own rules within the group which are shared by members her own age and she can behave towards adults, other groups, and society in accordance with the dictates of this group (Berti, 1993, 2005).

The concepts proposed by social identity theory, concerning group normative systems, values, and affiliative behaviors of group members, can be complemented by the "theory of deviance as management of reputation" put forward by Emler and Reicher (1995), established with the intention of explaining for the more general phenomenon of adolescent deviance. According to this view, adolescents behave in a transgressive way simply to communicate something about themselves to the public. Deviant actions (but also those that conform to social rules) correspond to a strategy that the individual adopts so as to build and maintain a certain reputation within the social context in which she interacts and that reflects her orientation towards formal authority. Infringing social rules becomes a way of managing her own reputation, a means of strengthening her own identity within a group that collectively endorses such norms of antisocial behavior.

According to this perspective, bullying should not be interpreted as simply an act of aggression by the bully, but also as an act of communication relative to the identity of both the bully and the victim. The bully, in this sense, without spectators and without followers would not be anyone and would not be recognized as having the identity of a bully. The Internet, as a means of communication, therefore becomes fundamental for "publicizing," divulging acts of bullying, and "creating" an audience which contributes to strengthening the bully's identity. The bully, in fact, feels proud and responsible for her own acts which she judges as demonstrations of her own strong self as aggressor.

The act of bullying, especially when it becomes "known to the public domain" (as in some cases of cyberbullying), contributes to a defining of the identity and social reputation of the victim. This is particularly true in those cases of electronic aggression where the person who perpetrates bullying uses the medium (that is, text messaging, social networks, blogs, YouTube) for committing acts of cyberbullying with the aim of smearing the victim's reputation. The unfortunate victim finds himself being an object of a negative identity and reputation that he did not choose but which undoubtedly impresses upon his social relations.

Melotti, Passini, and Biolcati (2009) stressed the particular characteristics of this form of cyberbullying as being more indirect forms of cyberbullying, where there exists a relationship of direct aggression from bully to victim and the new media are used as tools to reach the victim:

> We have defined such an approach as indirect cyberbullying to distinguish it from direct cyberbullying and to emphasize the media-oriented character in such an act. In this case, in fact, the new technological means are not used as a direct instrument of communication from bully to victim but as a means for divulging and creating a negative image of the victim with the aim of denigrating him and psychologically destroying him. (Melotti et al., 2009, p. 82)

In this indirect mode, the Internet, mobile phones, and/or videophones are used for obtaining rapid and effective defamation and the creation of a negative reputation for the victim in the eyes of the peer group, and also in the eyes of an even more vast group, the Internet. In this sense, Ortega, Elipe, Mora-Merchán, Calmaestra, and Vega (2009) have found the emotional profiles of victims of cyberbullying are very similar to victims of indirect bullying, yet different to those of victims of direct bullying. Victims (25% of the total sample) were distributed in three groups: 60% victims of only traditional bullying; 20% victims of only cyberbullying forms; 20% victims of both traditional and cyberbullying simultaneously. Analyses were carried out by types of bullying (traditional direct, traditional indirect, cyber mobile, cyber Internet). Multivictims (those who suffered more than one type at the same time) were not considered.

From the above considerations we may infer that the theme of social reputation (of bully and victim) is a central element in cyberbullying, and it can play a crucial role in determining the effects of cyber-aggression.

Loneliness and Self-Esteem in Victims

In traditional bullying, victims report psychosocial problems such as anxiety, depression, and withdrawal as well as lower self-esteem and feelings of loneliness (Hazler, 1996; Haynie et al., 2001; Graham, Bellmore, & Mize, 2006). Gofi, Parti, and Goldon (2002) reported that being bullied was associated with poor self-confidence, feelings of loneliness, and difficulty in making friends among boys, and being ignored by others and being excluded among girls. Nansel, Craig, Overpeck, Saluja, and Ruan (2004) found that victims of bullying have poorer emotional adjustment compared with bullies and uninvolved children.

Loneliness among children is not only related to overt (direct) victimization, but perhaps especially to relational (indirect) victimization (Crick & Grotpeter, 1996). Ireland and Qualter (2008) argue that this association can also be explained considering the nature of indirect aggression. Such aggression is largely based on the ability of a perpetrator to utilize the social group to ostracize and exclude: "It could be speculated that social loneliness would thus occur first with such aggression (i.e., as the group excludes/ostracizes and makes the victim feel unwelcome via their behavior), followed by emotional loneliness as the behavior continues and the need for a close, supportive attachment figure is increased" (Ireland & Qualter, 2008, p. 27).

The effects established for traditional bullying victimization may suggest similar developmental trajectories for cybervictims: school problems, substance use, suicidal ideation, eating disorders, depression, extreme violence toward themselves or other individuals, and generally a serious threat to their psychological and physical well-being (Hawker & Boulton, 2000; Card, 2007). But the nature of cyberbullying may greatly expand the reach of victims by students who bully and augment the intensity of interpersonal harm that occurs among this population. Little research has explored the effects of a desynchronized relationship between the person who perpetrates bullying and the victim, and the peculiar context where the person who perpetrates bullying does not receive any direct emotional feedback from the victim, as happens in the cyber context. The particular features of cyberbullying also raises new questions, if we take into consideration the role of variables related to the management of social reputation (Emler & Reicher, 1995).

Brighi, Genta, and Guarini (2008) compared victims of traditional bullying (direct and indirect) with victims of cyberbullying along the dimensions of self-esteem and loneliness in a sample of Italian students aged from 12 to 16. Cybervictims scored higher than traditional bullying victims on some self-esteem measures—Efficacy in Peer Relationships, and Global Self-Evaluation ("I like the kind of person I am")—and lower on Perceived Loneliness. A second comparison was done between those participants who reported being both traditional and cybervictims ("poly-victims"), and those not bullied in either way. Poly-victims scored lower in Body Self-esteem, Peer Relationships, Family, and Global Self-Evaluation, and had higher scores on Parent Low Support, Peer Low Support, and Affinity to Loneliness. The results suggest that, for victims, the social exclusion experienced in "real world" exchanges may be more psychologically demanding than those experienced in virtual contexts. The high-risk group however is the "poly-victims." Brighi et al. (2008) point out the need for further research to investigate separately the victimization phenomenon across different forms of bullying (direct, indirect, cyber via mobile, and cyber via the Internet) and to take into consideration the intensity of the aggression reported (occasional versus severe). Moreover, it is necessary to consider the possible outcomes on self-esteem and loneliness of different forms of bullying, taking account of whether there is an attack to self reputation. In some cyber-attacks the bullying action is not "confined" to the person who perpetrates bullying and the victim, but is intentionally extended to a worldwide arena (for example, when an embarrassing video is posted on YouTube).

Aims of This Study

The study reported here is part of an international project devised to investigate new forms of bullying across Europe, with the partnership of four countries (University of Bologna, Italy; Goldsmiths College, London, UK; University of Cordoba, Spain; and University of Turku, Finland) and one non-EU country (University of Tuzla, Bosnia). It was funded by the European Commission through the DAPHNE II Program. Here only the data, collected in early 2008, from the Italy, Spain, and UK samples will be reported.

The first aim was to analyze the effects of victimization (not involved, occasional victim, and severe victim)[2] in traditional bullying (direct and indirect) on self-esteem and loneliness. We hypothesized that victims of traditional bullying would feel lower self-esteem and report higher feelings of loneliness compared to peers not involved in bullying.

The second aim was to investigate the effects of victimization in cyberbullying (not involved, occasional victim, and severe victim) on self-esteem and loneliness. We hypothesized, as for traditional bullying, that victims would feel lower self-esteem and report higher feelings of loneliness compared to uninvolved peers.

The third aim was to analyze the effect of victimization in cyberbullying on self-esteem and loneliness dimensions as a function of the presence of attacks to the reputation of the victims. Following the hypothesis about the potential use of new technologies to carry out attacks on the reputation of the victim, we selected those students who had reported being victimized via videos on YouTube, blogs, and social networks (such as a message or a movie posted on YouTube with embarrassing content).We hypothesized that they would have the lowest scores for self-esteem and a worse attitude for loneliness compared to cybervictims where there was no attack to reputation, as well as to uninvolved participants.

The last aim was to compare self-esteem and loneliness among victims of traditional bullying, victims of cyberbullying, and poly-victims (victims of both traditional bullying and cyberbullying). We hypothesized that the combination of traditional and cyber-aggression suffered by such victims would result in lower scores along all the dimensions of self-esteem and higher perceptions of loneliness, especially in the relationships with parents and peers.

We were interested in investigating how the phenomenon of victimization can assume different characteristics as a function of the following variables: the intensity of the attack (not involved versus severe), the kind of context (traditional versus cyberbullying), if an attack to reputation is implied or not, and the combined effect of being victim in traditional and cyber context, so we will not discuss here in detail the results concerning the role of gender, age, and country. We are aware that these variables may have an effect, as reported in the literature, but here we choose not to report each interaction, since this would make the presentation of the results very complex.

Method

Participants

The study involved 5862 students from secondary schools in Italy (n=1964), the UK (n=2227), and Spain (n=1671); altogether 2986 boys (51.2%) and 2847 girls (48.8%). Three age ranges took part: 2077 students (35.5%) attended Year 8 (in the English education system: around 12 years), 2074 pupils (35.4%) attended Year 10 (around 14 years) and 1704 pupils (29.1%) attended Year 12 (around 16 years). Students with disabilities represented around 3% (n=171) of the sample; none of these students requested any support to complete the questionnaire. The adolescents indicated that 14.5% (n=794) of fathers and 12.8% of mothers (n=718) did not study beyond primary school; 41.7% of fathers (n=2274) and 42.8% of mothers (n=2397) finished secondary school; and 43.8% of fathers (n=2391) and 44.4% of mothers (n=2492) had one university degree or more.

Questionnaire

The questionnaire was administered to the students by a researcher and investigated forms of traditional and electronic bullying carried out by students. Brief definitions of bullying and cyberbullying were given before specific questions so that pupils had a clear understanding of the behaviors classified as bullying and cyberbullying and did not confuse them with other aggressive behaviors. Four questions (one for each type of bullying) measured whether a student was bullied and/or bullied others; the response options for each were on a five-point scale (scored 1 to 5): "I haven't been bullied/I haven't bullied anyone"; "it has only happened once or twice"; "two or three times a month"; "about once a week"; and "several times a week"(see also Chapter 2). A second section contained scales to measure self-esteem and loneliness. For the self-esteem measure the SEQ (Self-esteem questionnaire) from DuBois, Felner, Brand, Phillips, and Lease (1996) was used with 18 items obtained from the Italian version (Melotti & Passini, 2002). For loneliness, the LLCA (Louvain Loneliness Scale for Children and Adolescents) (Marcoen, Goossens, & Caes, 1987; Marcoen & Goossens, 1993) was adopted, using 12 items obtained from the Italian version (Melotti, Corsano, Majorano, & Scarpuzzi, 2006).

The SEQ stems from a multidimensional concept of self-esteem and has been used for preadolescents and adolescents. It measures six sub-scale dimensions: body self-esteem, school self-esteem, family self-esteem, sport self-esteem, peer self-esteem, and global self-esteem. This latter dimension is excluded from the factorial analysis and was treated as a dependent variable in a regression model with the other five dimensions as independent variables. In the reduced version adopted in this study, each dimension is measured by the mean obtained from three items rated on a four-point scale of agreement/disagreement (1=totally disagree, 2=disagree, 3=agree, and 4=totally agree).

The LLCA is constituted from four sub-scales:

1. *Loneliness in relationships with parents* (L-Parent): feelings of rejection, abandonment, and desertion occurring within the relationships with parents;
2. *Loneliness in relationships with peers* (L-Peer): feelings of rejection, abandonment, and desertion occurring within the relationships with peers;
3. *Aversion to loneliness* (A-Neg): a negative attitude to loneliness leading the person concerned to seek to avoid moments when feeling alone;
4. *Affinity for loneliness* (A-Pos): a positive attitude to loneliness connected to seeking times when able to remain alone.

In the reduced version used in this study, each dimension is measured using the mean obtained from three items rated over a four-point frequency scale (1 = never, 2 = seldom, 3 = sometimes, and 4 = often).

The multidimensional nature of this instrument differentiates the sense of social isolation experienced in a family context (sub-scale L-Parent) and within the peer group (L-Peer). The other two other sub-scales (A-Neg and A-Pos) investigate loneliness experienced negatively or positively, in the context of being alone generally; this could discriminate subjects who reported loneliness as a condition to be actively sought and desired from those who fear to be alone. In order to evaluate the validity and consistency of each instrument, both the SEQ and LLCA were piloted.

For the SEQ, we first checked that the items relating to global self-esteem had a satisfactory reliability; Cronbach's alpha was found to be 0.69. We ran an exploratory factor analysis (EFA) on the remaining items with the method of maximum likelihood with direct oblimin rotation, hypothesizing that it would yield five factors concerning self-esteem in the *body*, in *school*, in *family*, in *sports activities*, and in *peer relationships*. The results confirmed this; see Table 3.1.

In order to test the hierarchic model of self-esteem as proposed by DuBois et al. (1996), a linear regression analysis was conducted with global self-esteem as the dependent variable and with self-esteem in *body*, *school*, *family*, *sport*, and *peers* as predictors. The value of $R^2 = 0.50$ confirms the proposed model, and the use of the shortened version of our scale to measure self-esteem in a reliable way.

For the LLCA we ran an EFA with the method of maximum likelihood with direct oblimin rotation, hypothesizing that it would yield four factors, as reported by the original authors. The results shown in Table 3.2 confirm the hypothesis and suggest that the reduced version of LLCA adopted in our study is a valid instrument for measuring loneliness.

Results

Data were analyzed using SPSS for Windows, release version 17.0 (© SPSS, Inc., 2001, Chicago, IL; www.spss.com). A set of descriptive analyses and nonparametric analyses were used (Kruskall–Wallis), in order to deal with the non- normality of the distribution. Then we ran ANOVA analyses which confirmed the results obtained by nonparametric tests; for reasons of clarity we present here the ANOVA results, since the output is easier to interpret, dealing with mean value and not with ranks. In the composition of the victims' sample, we excluded those subjects who reported to be both victims and students who bully. Missing data were excluded from the analysis.

A general overview of mean values (range 1–4) along each dimension of the SEQ showed that the young people in our sample evaluate themselves as "positive" with regard to their body image ($M = 2.87$, $SD = 0.68$), their family relationships ($M = 3.35$, $SD = 0.60$), in sport activities ($M = 3.01$, $SD = 0.68$), in peer relationships ($M = 3.11$, $SD = 0.52$), and on global self-esteem ($M = 3.17$, $SD = 0.51$). By contrast, school

Table 3.1 SEQ Factor Analysis: Structure Matrix Using Method of Maximum Likelihood, With Direct Oblimin Rotation. Total Variance Explained: 60.0% (n=5579).

	Factor				
Item	*Body*	*School*	*Family*	*Sport*	*Peers*
7: I like my body just the way it is	**0.91**	0.28	0.28	0.46	0.39
3: I am happy with the way I look	**0.74**	0.26	0.26	0.41	0.41
11: I feel good about my height and weight	**0.69**	0.27	0.27	0.42	0.37
2: I am as good a student as I would like to be	0.27	**0.84**	0.28	0.17	0.20
16: I feel OK about how good a student I am	0.29	**0.82**	0.35	0.19	0.26
6: I am doing as well on school work as I would like to	0.28	**0.78**	0.32	0.18	0.27
18: I am happy with how much my family loves me	0.24	0.27	**0.81**	0.19	0.30
14: My family pays enough attention to me	0.27	0.31	**0.80**	0.20	0.31
10: I get along as well as I would like to with my family	0.31	0.35	**0.72**	0.22	0.32
9: I feel OK about how well I do when I participate in sports/physical activities	0.44	0.19	0.21	**0.85**	0.43
4: I am as good at sports/physical activities as I want to be	0.45	0.14	0.16	**0.81**	0.37
12: I am happy about how many different kinds of sports/physical activities I am good at	0.42	0.22	0.24	**0.75**	0.45
17: I feel good about how well I get along with other people my own age	0.34	0.22	0.38	0.35	**0.72**
5: I am as good as I want to be at making new friends	0.30	0.17	0.21	0.34	**0.65**
13: I am as well liked by other people my own age as I want to be	0.41	0.27	0.22	0.38	**0.61**

Note: **Items for global self-esteem are in bold font in all tables:** Item 1, "I am happy with the way I can do most things"; item 8, "I like being just the way I am"; item 15, "I am the kind of person I want to be." Alpha values: School: 0.86; peers: 0.69; family: 0.81; body: 0.82; sport: 0.84; global: 0.69.

self-esteem had the lowest mean score ($M=2.76$, $SD=0.66$), very close to the neutral point ($M=2.5$). Examining gender differences, males report higher scores of self-esteem across all the dimensions than girls; this is significant for all dimensions except school self-esteem. Self-esteem scores decrease significantly across all dimensions with decreasing age.

On the LLCA, the mean values of the four dimensions (range 1–4) show that our students seldom experience feelings of abandonment and loneliness from their parents ($M=1.41$, $SD=0.58$) or from their peers ($M=1.54$, $SD=0.64$). They seldom search actively for moments that they can be alone (A-Pos: $M=2.31$, $SD=0.70$), and seldom find it difficult to cope with loneliness (A-Neg: $M=2.46$, $SD=0.75$). Examining gender differences, males report significantly lower scores in the scales of

Table 3.2 LLCA Factor Analysis. Structure Matrix Method of Maximum Likelihood, With Direct Oblimin Rotation. Total Variance Explained: 53.1% (n = 5611).

	Factor			
Item	*L-peer*	*L-parent*	*A-neg*	*A-pos*
5: I feel left out by my friends	**0.83**	−0.21	0.23	0.33
3: I feel abandoned by my friends	**0.82**	−0.21	0.23	0.32
11: I feel sad because I have no friends	**0.59**	−0.15	0.18	0.23
7: My parents are ready to listen to me or to help me*	0.21	**−0.83**	0.06	0.17
9: My parents show real interest in me*	0.22	**−0.82**	0.07	0.17
1: My parents make time to pay attention to me*	0.18	**−0.72**	0.02	0.16
8: When I am lonely, I don't know what to do	0.26	−0.07	**0.72**	0.03
2: When I am lonely, I feel bored	0.19	−0.04	**0.72**	−0.06
10: Time drags when I'm on my own	0.16	−0.03	**0.65**	−0.09
4: I want to be alone	0.33	−0.16	−0.10	**0.72**
6: I like being on my own	0.23	−0.09	−0.03	**0.71**
12: At home I like to be alone, so that I can do things on my own	0.22	−0.17	−0.01	**0.51**

Note: *reverse coded. Alpha values: L-parent: 0.83; L-peer: 0.78; A-pos: 0.67; A-neg: 0.74.

L-Peers, A-Neg and A-Pos. Examining age differences, L-Parents and A-Pos increase with age, while A-Neg decreases; L-Peers shows a nonlinear trend, decreasing from Year 8 to Year 10 and then increasing again by Year 12.

Loneliness and Self-Esteem in Victims of Traditional Bullying

Several one-way ANOVAs were run in order to test the hypothesis that the victims of traditional bullying would feel lower self-esteem and higher feelings of loneliness compared to peers who are not involved in bullying. Tables 3.3 and 3.4 show results for the two distinct forms of traditional bullying, direct and indirect.

As predicted, an inverse trend is observed from the SEQ between the severity of bullying and the lowering of self-esteem. When the degree of victimization increases from "not involved" or "occasional" to "severe," there is a significant reduction in scores along all the self-esteem subscales, with one exception: in victims of direct bullying, school self-esteem did not follow this trend (Table 3.3). From the LLCA, as the degree of victimization increases, feelings of loneliness (from peers and parents) perceived by the victims increase as well, both for direct and indirect bullying.

An apparently puzzling result emerges: when the degree of victimization increased, the victims showed an increase in their aversion to loneliness (A-Neg), but also an increase for a positive evaluation of being alone (A-Pos). This indicates an ambivalent attitude toward loneliness, with feelings both of affinity and aversion. A reason for this could be that victims are often attacked by peers, and this leads to the isolation

Table 3.3 Effect of Victimization in Direct Traditional Bullying [Not Involved (n=4818), Occasional Victim (n=554), and Severe Victim (n=245)] on Self-Esteem and Loneliness Dimensions (Using One-Way ANOVAs).

	Victimization in direct bullying					
	Not involved	*Occasional victim*	*Severe victim*	*Df/sample size*	*F*	*p*
	Self-esteem (1=totally disagree to 4=totally agree)					
Body	2.90	2.71	2.68	2 (5527)	28.09	<0.001
School	2.77	2.72	2.79	2 (5561)	1.20	n.s.
Family	3.37	3.26	3.21	2 (5554)	17.19	<0.001
Sport	3.03	2.92	2.84	2 (5541)	13.37	<0.001
Peers	3.14	2.96	2.76	2 (5529)	87.10	<0.001
Global	3.19	3.05	3.00	2 (5549)	34.85	<0.001
	Loneliness dimensions (1=never to 4=often)					
L-parent	1.38	1.49	1.60	2 (5550)	26.41	<0.001
L-peer	1.47	1.82	2.22	2 (5526)	235.96	<0.001
A-neg	2.44	2.59	2.62	2 (5538)	16.80	<0.001
A-pos	2.28	2.39	2.55	2 (5548)	21.44	<0.001

Note: Df=degrees of freedom; the number in parentheses is the number of subjects in each sub-sample. The same applies to all subsequent tables in this chapter.

Table 3.4 Effect of Victimization in Indirect Traditional Bullying [Not Involved (n=4575), Occasional Victim (n=775), and Severe Victim (n=257)] on Self-Esteem and Loneliness Dimensions (Using One-Way ANOVAs).

	Victimization in indirect bullying					
	Not involved	*Occasional victim*	*Severe victim*	*Df/sample size*	*F*	*p*
	Self-esteem (1=totally disagree to 4=totally agree)					
Body	2.91	2.71	2.59	2 (5517)	52.27	<0.001
School	2.78	2.73	2.61	2 (5554)	10.42	<0.001
Family	3.38	3.27	3.12	2 (5547)	31.34	<0.001
Sport	3.03	2.91	2.77	2 (5531)	26.64	<0.001
Peers	3.14	3.01	2.75	2 (5519)	81.75	<0.001
Global	3.20	3.06	2.95	2 (5540)	51.49	<0.001
	Loneliness dimensions (1=never to 4=often)					
L-parent	1.37	1.45	1.60	2 (5542)	24.65	<0.001
L-peer	1.46	1.77	2.12	2 (5518)	204.41	<0.001
A-neg	2.44	2.53	2.60	2 (5530)	9.24	<0.001
A-pos	2.27	2.40	2.61	2 (5539)	36.56	<0.001

Table 3.5 Effect of Victimization in Cyberbullying [Not Involved (n=5117), Occasional Victim (n=435), and Severe Victim (n=125)] on Self-Esteem and Loneliness Dimensions (Using One-Way ANOVAs).

	Victimization in cyberbullying					
	Not involved	*Occasional victim*	*Severe victim*	*Df/sample size*	*F*	*p*
	Self-esteem (1=totally disagree to 4=totally agree)					
Body	2.90	2.69	2.58	2 (5590)	29.66	<0.001
School	2.78	2.60	2.53	2 (5626)	22.33	<0.001
Family	3.37	3.23	2.91	2 (5619)	45.74	<0.001
Sport	3.02	2.88	2.87	2 (5606)	11.11	<0.001
Peers	3.12	3.03	2.97	2 (5594)	10.75	<0.001
Global	3.19	3.04	2.95	2 (5607)	28.44	<0.001
	Loneliness dimensions (1=never to 4=often)					
L- Parent	1.38	1.47	1.92	2 (5613)	59.77	<0.001
L-Peer	1.51	1.66	1.93	2 (5588)	37.37	<0.001
A-Neg	2.45	2.53	2.60	2 (5599)	4.46	0.012
A-Pos	2.29	2.45	2.48	2 (5607)	14.94	<0.001

of victims, who suffer accordingly. This could explain the aversion to loneliness (A-Neg). At the same time, when attacks are more intense, victims may tend to avoid social interactions, preferring to remain alone than with peers who are potential offenders, justifying the higher scores in the affinity for loneliness (A-Pos) reported by victims of "severe" bullying. So, while social withdrawal is an outcome for a victim, it is also a defensive strategy chosen intentionally to avoid further aggression. Further support for this idea comes from paired *t*-tests between affinity (A-Pos) and aversion (A-Neg) to loneliness which found no significant statistical differences in victims of severe direct bullying ($t_{245}=1.17$, n.s.) and victims of indirect bullying ($t_{257}=0.85$, n.s.).

Self-esteem and loneliness in victims of cyberbullying

Several one-way ANOVAs were used to test the hypothesis that cybervictims could feel lower self-esteem and higher feelings of loneliness than traditional bullying victims. The results, shown in Table 3.5, reveal that when the degree of cyber-victimization increases, self-esteem decreases, while feelings of loneliness from parents and peers increase.

As for traditional victims, the results show a parallel increase for both affinity (A-Pos) and aversion (A-Neg) to loneliness (paired *t*-test for A-Pos and A-Neg: Severe victims $\bar{x}_{aversion}=2.60$, $\bar{x}_{affinity}=2.48$, $t=1.49$, $df=125$, $p=0.14$) differently from

Table 3.6 Effect of Victimization in Cyberbullying [Not Involved (n=5378), Victim Without Attacks to Reputation (n=270), Occasional Victim With Attacks to Reputation (n=79), and Severe Victim With Attacks to Reputation (n=33)] on Self-Esteem and Loneliness Dimensions (Using One-Way ANOVAs).

	Victimization in cyberbullying						
	Not involved	*Victims without attacks to reputation*	*Victims with occasional attacks to reputation*	*Victims with severe attacks to reputation*	*Df/sample size*	*F*	*p*
			Self-esteem (1=totally disagree to 4=totally agree)				
Body	2.89	2.69	2.52	2.27	3 (5668)	23.06	<0.001
School	2.77	2.59	2.46	2.45	3 (5705)	214.24	<0.001
Family	3.37	3.18	3.15	2.67	3 (5699)	25.57	<0.001
Sport	3.02	2.88	2.63	2.77	3 (5686)	13.14	<0.001
Peers	3.12	3.03	2.92	2.72	3 (5671)	11.35	<0.001
Global	3.18	3.03	2.94	2.77	3 (5687)	20.43	<0.001
			Loneliness dimensions (1=never to 4=often)				
L- parent	1.39	1.58	1.49	2.09	3 (5694)	27.42	<0.001
L-Ppeer	1.52	1.68	1.69	2.28	3 (5668)	22.90	<0.001
A-neg	2.45	2.54	2.55	2.78	3 (5680)	3.72	0.011
A-pos	2.29	2.40	2.59	2.70	3 (5688)	9.65	<0.001

what was reported by not involved students (paired *t*-test for A-Pos and A-Neg: not involved $\bar{x}_{aversion}=2.45$, $\bar{x}_{affinity}=2.29$, $t=11.00$, $df=5117$, $p < 0.001$).

Cybervictims: Loneliness and self-esteem in a sub-sample of subjects who received attacks to reputation

Sub-samples of victims were selected through analysis of the responses to items concerning the kind of cybervictimization experienced. We selected those students who had reported being victimized via modalities such as denigration diffused by video on YouTube, blogs, and social networks.

Several one-way ANOVAs were run comparing students who were not involved, cybervictims who received no attacks to their reputation, cybervictims who received occasional attacks to their reputation and victims who reported severe attacks to their reputation. The results, shown in Table 3.6, show that self-esteem scores decrease as a function of the received attacks to reputation, with pupils who reported receiving severe attacks to reputation showing the lowest scores. LLCA scores show that severe victims report significantly higher scores than those in the other subgroups, denoting the worst experience with solitude and, indirectly, a higher risk condition.

Table 3.7 Effect of Severe* Victimization [Victim of Traditional Bullying (n=362), Victim of Cyberbullying (n=81), and Victim of Both Traditional and Cyberbullying (n=60)] on Self-Esteem and Loneliness Dimensions (Using One-Way ANOVAs).

	Only traditional	*Only cyber*	*Traditional and cyber*	*Df/sample size*	*F*	*p*
			Self-esteem (1=totally disagree to 4=totally agree)			
Body	2.64	2.74	2.42	2 (490)	2.76	0.06
School	2.68	2.56	2.57	2 (496)	1.55	n.s.
Family	3.23	3.03	2.83	2 (490)	9.75	0.000
Sport	2.82	3.05	2.64	2 (492)	4.91	0.008
Peers	2.78	3.13	2.79	2 (491)	10.05	0.000
Global	2.98	3.08	2.82	2 (493)	2.35	0.04
			Loneliness dimensions (1=never to 4=often)			
L- parent	1.52	1.75	2.03	2 (498)	14.87	0.000
L-peer	2.08	1.79	2.13	2 (489)	4.49	0.01
A-neg	2.60	2.57	2.51	2 (496)	0.28	n.s.
A-pos	2.54	2.31	2.74	2 (495)	5.55	0.004

Note: This table only presents a comparison between severe victims of traditional bullying, cyberbullying, and victims of both traditional and cyberbullying. We excluded from the analysis victims who also reported being bullies.

Here too, when cybervictimization increases and includes damage to reputation, the scores for affinity to loneliness (A-Pos) and aversion to loneliness (A-Neg) get closer and become higher, so that the difference is no longer significant. Moreover in the case of occasional victims (t_{79}=0.19, $p > 0.05$) and severe victims (t_{33}=0.34, $p > 0.05$) with attacks to reputation, the score of loneliness affinity (A-Pos) are actually higher than those for loneliness aversion (L-Neg), although the difference is non-significant.

Comparison among victims of traditional bullying, victims of cyberbullying, and poly-victims (both traditional and cyberbullying)

The last aim was to investigate the perception of self-esteem and loneliness among victims of traditional bullying, victims of cyberbullying, and poly-victims (victims of both traditional and cyberbullying). The victim group was divided into three subgroups: "only traditional bullying victims," "only cyberbullying victims," and "victims of both traditional and cyberbullying." Then these subgroups were compared through one-way ANOVAs on LLCA and SEQ subscales.

The results reported in Table 3.7 confirm, in part, the hypothesis: the poly-victim group reported significantly lower scores along almost all the dimensions of SEQ, but not in school self-esteem (the difference between the three groups here was not statistically significant, although the trend was similar to that found for the other dimensions).

Moreover, poly-victims had higher LLCA scores in all dimensions, although the three groups did not differ significantly in the aversion scale (A-Neg).

Discussion

These findings, based on an extensive sample of nearly 6000 students aged 12–16 years, confirm some of our hypotheses, and some previous findings related to traditional bullying and self-esteem, but also yield some new findings related to cyberbullying, and to the dimensions of loneliness not previously investigated in relation to victimization. Our first aim was to analyze the effects of victimization in direct and indirect traditional bullying on self-esteem and loneliness. We hypothesized that victims of traditional bullying would feel lower self-esteem and report higher feelings of loneliness than their peers who were not involved in bullying. This was generally confirmed (see Tables 3.3 and 3.4). A number of previous studies have shown that victimization is significantly associated with poor self-concept (Slee & Rigby, 1993; Boulton & Smith, 1994; Neary & Joseph, 1994; Callaghan & Joseph, 1995; Grills & Ollendick, 2002). A meta-analysis conducted by Hawker and Boulton (2000) found that victimization was moderately associated with lower social and global self-esteem. Our data show a relationship between frequency of victimization and a decrease in self-esteem, and this was true both for direct and indirect bullying; it was also true for all the dimensions of self-esteem measured here, with one exception. For direct bullying there was no significant relationship between victimization and school self-esteem; victims do not feel bad in their role as a student or in their schoolwork, which may be considered independently of their social self-esteem. Interestingly, there was such a relationship for indirect bullying, a finding that deserves further investigation. In general, the scores for self-esteem were lower for victims of (severe) indirect bullying, compared to victims of severe direct bullying. In interpreting these results, we should also consider the gender of the victims involved in the two kinds of bullying, since the literature reports some evidence of girls being more affected by indirect bullying and boys more by direct bullying (Genta, Brighi, & Guarini, 2009). Given that it has been reported that adolescent girls typically begin to experience a decrease in self-esteem, whereas the self-esteem of boys typically increases or stays the same (Rosenberg, 1985; McLeod & Owens, 2004), the differences in the two samples could be due to the larger number of girls affected by indirect victimization. It could be also that the pervasiveness of indirect bullying, which necessarily involves the victim's social network (schoolmates, friends, etc.) may affect self-esteem in a more substantial way than direct bullying.

Our data do not allow us to make a causal link between low self-esteem and victimization, but a number of previous studies on traditional bullying provide some evidence for such a link (Kochenderfer & Ladd, 1996; Troop-Gordon & Ladd,

2005; Arsenault et al., 2006) or for victimization and low self-esteem being related in a bi-directional way (Egan & Perry, 1998; Kochenderfer-Ladd & Wardrop, 2001), consistent with transactional models of development (Sameroff, 1987). Salmivalli and Isaacs (2005), in a longitudinal study of 11–13-year-old Finnish pupils over one year, found that negative self-perception did predict peer-nominated victim status, and victim status in turn predicted more negative perceptions of peers (how peers thought about them), although not more negative self-perceptions.

Also as expected, we found that severity of victimization was associated with higher feelings of loneliness, both for loneliness with peers and loneliness with parents. This was true both for direct and indirect victimization, but direct victimization has a greater relationship with loneliness with peers, compared to severe indirect victimization. It is also worth noting that indirect victimization has a more negative relationship with family self-esteem than direct victimization (see Tables 3.3 and 3.4). Again, if such a link is replicated, any causal direction is open to question; it may be that pupils with poor family relationships are more likely to get involved with or be vulnerable to indirect (often relational) bullying, or it may be that indirect victimization has some impact on family relationships (more than direct bullying).

For both direct and indirect victimization, frequency is associated with both positive and negative feelings about loneliness, indicating a more ambivalent attitude. Victims, very often, receive attacks from peers that result in the isolation of the victim, who suffers in this situation. This could explain the aversion to loneliness (A-Neg). At the same time, when attacks are more intense, victims may have the tendency to avoid social interactions, preferring to remain alone than with peers who are potential offenders, justifying the higher scores in the affinity for loneliness (A-Pos) reported by severe victims. So, victims withdraw socially, perhaps as a defensive strategy to avoid further aggressive behavior.

Our second aim was to investigate the effects of victimization in cyberbullying on self-esteem and loneliness. We hypothesized, as for traditional bullying, that victims would feel lower self-esteem and report higher feelings of loneliness than not involved peers. This was confirmed as a negative relationship between frequency of cybervictimization and all the measures of self-esteem and loneliness (see Table 3.5). Comparing Table 3.5 with Tables 3.3 and 3.4, it can be seen that the relationships for self-esteem are similar, but for cybervictimization the relationship tends to be stronger (compared to traditional bullying) for family self-esteem, but not so strong for peer self-esteem (which is lower in the two forms of traditional bullying when compared to cyberbullying). This trend is consistent with findings for loneliness, where the negative relationship is greater for loneliness with parents in cybervictimization, but greater for loneliness with peers in traditional victimization. Again this finding deserves replication and further investigation, but may give interesting indications of differing motives for, or impacts of, traditional and cybervictimization, as well as a possible differential role of parental support across the context where bullying takes place. It is possible that feelings of efficacy in family relationships could reflect different levels of reciprocal involvement among family members, which could also imply lower parental monitoring of adolescents' activity on the Internet and longer periods of time spent online by adolescents, thus increasing the possibility of receiving online attacks.

Some research confirms this assumption, since it has demonstrated an association between positive parenting styles and a "healthy" use of the Internet in adolescence while, by contrast, lack of emotional involvement, lack of parental monitoring, and an authoritative or neglectful parenting style are connected with online harassment. Li Lei and Wu (2007) investigated how the use of the Internet is associated with individual differences in father–adolescent attachment in China. Pathological use of the Internet was positively associated with alienation, and negatively with trust and communication. Adolescents who experience alienation from their fathers can lack social abilities and appropriate strategies of coping in a real-world context. As a consequence they may consolidate relationships online, spending a lot of time on the Internet, which renders them more vulnerable to negative experiences. This may also be the case for cybervictims, who can be more exposed to virtual interaction, increasing their risk of being exposed to cyberbullying and reducing, at the same time, their already poor ability to interact in a real-world context. Smith et al. (2008) found in an English sample that being a cybervictim (but not a cyberbully) correlated with high Internet use.

Our third aim was to analyze the effect of victimization in cyberbullying on self-esteem and loneliness as a function of attacks to the reputation of the victims. We hypothesized that students who reported being victimized via modalities such as denigration diffused by video on social networking sites would have the lowest scores for self-esteem and a poorer attitude to loneliness compared to cybervictims where there was no attack to reputation, as well as to not involved participants. This was confirmed, as shown in Table 3.6. There is in most cases a strong relationship, and the self-esteem scores for severe victims with attacks to reputation are particularly low. Comparing Table 3.6 with Tables 3.3, 3.4, and 3.5, it can be seen that these victims have noticeably lower self-esteem than severe victims of direct, indirect, or general cyberbullying, for all dimensions. Also, severe cybervictims with attacks to their reputation have markedly higher loneliness scores with both parents and peers, and highly ambivalent attitudes to loneliness.

Social networking sites potentially provide a large audience of peers who may see denigrating and abusive material about a victim. This can have very damaging effects for the victim. Although we cannot be certain of cause and effect, it is a plausible hypothesis that such acts do cause suffering, as exemplified by low self-esteem and loneliness (it may also be plausible that a lonely child is more likely to have denigrating material posted about him on social networking sites). Smith et al. (2008) and Slonje and Smith (2008) found that so-called "happy slapping" (circulating of nasty or malicious videoclips on mobile phones) was perceived by young people (in England and in Sweden) as having a very strong negative impact on the victim, and this was often ascribed to the potentially large audience and the consequent damage to reputation of the victim.

Cyberbullying using social networking sites may be on the increase, as the popularity of such sites has increased rapidly in recent years (Nielsen Online, 2010). The negative impact of this may be amplified by the potentially larger audience seeing such negative material. These results suggest that the management of reputation during adolescence may be a crucial task for adolescents, as suggested by Emler and Reicher (1995), and ICT contexts may denote a new scenario where young people have to deal with new challenges to their own reputation.

Our fourth aim was to compare self-esteem and loneliness among victims of traditional bullying, victims of cyberbullying, and poly-victims (victims of both traditional bullying and cyberbullying). We hypothesized that poly-victims would have lower scores along all the dimensions of self-esteem, and higher perceptions of loneliness than victims of only traditional (summing over direct and indirect), or only cyberbullying. This was broadly confirmed, as shown in Table 3.7. Poly-victims' scores were lower on all dimensions except for school self-esteem. A similar finding was reported by Ybarra and Mitchell (2004). It is possible that, since the items linked to school self-esteem evaluate the level of satisfaction reached in academic tasks, the victims in this sample could have been identified from some peers as the outstanding students in the group, and become a target of attacks. Concerning aversion to loneliness (A-Neg), our data show there are no differences among the three groups of victims, but there are differences between nonvictims and victims. This suggests that, regardless of the different kinds of bullying (traditional, cyber, or both), the attack can produce a real sense of isolation in the victim which is perceived as a strong fear of being rejected by her peers. Peers act as a "mirror for the self" (Mead, 1934), contributing to the widening of personal experiences of the adolescent, and are with her from childhood to adult life. For this reason, being excluded by their peers can be very traumatic for adolescents.

Our findings provide some new insights into the likely impacts of cybervictimization, and suggestions for further research. An important limitation of our study is reliance on self-reports for all measures, with the possibility of shared method variance. Also, we lack longitudinal data, and thus cannot make inferences about the causal direction of effects. However, the sample is large, allowing satisfactory power even for smaller subgroup analyses (our smallest subgroup, cybervictims with severe attacks to their reputation, still had 33 pupils). An important suggestion for further research is to examine what appears to be a greater link with relationships to parents in cybervictimization, but with relationships to peers in traditional victimization. The likely severe effects of cyber-attacks on reputation are also an important finding.

It is important to highlight that these results, even if stimulating, need further investigations, since our study did not account for clustering of students by school, age, and gender. Another variable to be taken into consideration in further analysis is cultural differences between countries, which may affect students' perceptions of bullying.

Our findings suggest some hints for intervention. First, too often teachers, researchers, educators, and psychologists tend to adopt intervention strategies based mainly on a descriptive level of analysis and assuming the continuity of roles (bully, victim, bully-victim, bystander) over time and across different contexts without trying to understand the complex plot of different factors which define each context (and each person) as unique. We suggest, instead, adopting a systemic perspective that could interpret the victimization phenomenon as a developmental outcome, the aetiology of which should be rooted in a complex interplay of individual and contextual variables along the development continuum (Bronfenbrenner, 1979, 1992). In this sense, we think it would be helpful to integrate into theoretical approaches suggestions arising from studies inspired by "developmental psychopathology" (Sroufe & Rutter, 1984; Cicchetti, 1989; Rutter, 1990; Rolf, Masten, Cicchetti, Neuchterlein, & Weintraub, 1990; Sroufe, 1990; Cicchetti & Aber, 1998), a discipline which integrates contributions from different areas of psychology (developmental, clinical, and social psychology) as well as psychiatry, sociology, and epidemiology. Its contextualist and interactionist approach suggests a focus on risk and protective factors which underlie positive and negative adjustments along the individual developmental trajectories, investigating both "normal" and atypical development. This theoretical approach, applied to bullying phenomena, could highlight the risk processes underlying not only the bullying behaviors and the risk conditions experienced by the victims, but also the experiences of those not involved in the bullying. This would allow the researchers to design interventions that can account for the complexity and the specificity of each context in which bullying takes place. According to this perspective, intervention programs should help the whole class to reflect upon the identity dimensions implied in bullying behavior, or to help the group to weaken the positive representation associated with bullying.

Second, those responsible for managing new media should be sensitive to the potential risks of some messages, and should work to limit their function as amplifiers of the social reputation of those persons who perpetrate bullying, for example, giving less coverage to news that shows adolescents acting aggressively. The media often report realistic factual acts of bullying which are rare events in real life, or they allow the diffusion of humiliating content without any kind of filter. Some editors and website managers do spontaneously adopt "self-censorship" in this respect, but we think that Europe should push for more prescriptive rules.

Also, privacy and anonymity, which are a feature of many exchanges on the Internet, should be discussed further. There is a debate among Internet users concerning issues of regulation and anonymity, with the risk that any form of "control" may lead to limitations in the freedom of the Internet. It is not our aim to point to solutions to this problem, but our contribution, as researchers, is to underline that some groups of people, such as isolated adolescents, may experience real threats in virtual worlds that may increase their psychological vulnerability, feeding a vicious circle with an unpredictable outcome.

Acknowledgments

This research was funded by a grant from the EU DAPHNE II Program to the Department of Psychology at the University of Bologna and coordinated by Professor M. L. Genta. We are grateful to the many people who helped to collect data for each country; for Italy we would like to thank Drs. E. Buccoliero, S. Nicoletti, F. Gallingani, S. Passini, and L. Berdondini; and for England, Mr. Neil Tippett. Grateful thanks are also due to the Regional Observatory of Regione Emilia Romagna, and to all the teachers and students who took part in the research.

Notes

1 Accessed June 2011. For a more detailed description of adolescents' use of ICT across Europe, see Chapter 2 in this book.
2 The intensity of victimization was coded as "occasional" if it had happened once or twice in the last two months and "severe" if it occurred more than two/three times a month.

References

Arcuri, L. (2008). *Crescere con la tv e Internet* [*Growing up with TV and the Internet*]. Bologna: Il Mulino.

Arsenault, L., Walsh, E., Trzesniewski, K., Newcombe, R., Caspi, A., & Moffitt, E. (2006). Bullying victimization uniquely contributes to adjustment problems in young children: A nationally representative cohort study. *Pediatrics, 118*, 130–138.

Atlas, R. S., & Pepler, D. J. (1998). Observations of bullying in the classroom. *Journal of Educational Research, 92*, 86–99.

Bandura, A. (1996). Moral disengagement in the perpetrations of inhumanities. *Journal of Personality and Social Psychology, 71*, 364–374.

Bernstein, J. Y., & Watson, M. W. (1997). Children who are targets of bullying. *Journal of Interpersonal Violence, 12*, 483–498.

Berti, C. (1993). La devianza adolescenziale [Adolescent deviance]. In A. Palmonari (Ed.), *Psicologia dell'adolescenza* [*Psychology of Adolescence*] (pp. 327–373). Bologna: Il Mulino.

Berti, C. (2005). *Antisocialità, devianza e rischio nell'adolescenza* [*Antisocial behavior, deviance and risk in adolescence*]. In G. Speltini (Ed.), *Minori, disagio e aiuto psicosociale* [*Children, maladjustment and psychosocial support*] (pp. 155–199). Bologna: Il Mulino.

Boulton, M. J., & Smith, P. K. (1994). Bully-victim problems in middle-school children: Stability, self-perceived competence, peer perceptions and peer acceptance. *British Journal of Developmental Psychology, 12*, 315–329.

Brighi, A., Genta, M. L., & Guarini, A. (2008). *Cyberbullying among Italian students: an explorative study of bullying through new technologies and its psychological impact*. Paper presented to the 4th World Conference on Violence at School and Public Policies, Lisbon, July 23–26.

Brighi, A., Guarini, A., & Genta M. L. (2009). Bullying in the digital age. In M. L. Genta, A. Brighi, & A. Guarini (Eds.), *Cyberbullying*. Rome: Carocci.

Bronfenbrenner, U. (1979). *The ecology of human development: Experiments by nature and design*. Cambridge, MA: Harvard University Press.

Bronfenbrenner, U. (1992). Ecological system theory. In R. Vasta (Ed.), *Six theories of child development* (pp. 187–250). London: Jessica Kingsley.

Callaghan, S., & Joseph, S. (1995). Self-concept and victimization among schoolchildren. *Personality and Individual Differences, 18*, 161–163.

Calvert, S. L. (2002). Identity construction on the internet. In S. L. Calvert, A. B. Jordan & R. R. Cocking (Eds.), *Children in the digital age: Influences of electronic media on development* (pp. 57–70). Westport, CT: Praeger.

Card, N. A. (2007). Correlates of school victimization: Implications for prevention and intervention. In J. E. Zins, M. J. Elias, & C. A. Maher (Eds.), *Bullying, victimization, and peer harassment* (pp. 339–366). New York & London: Haworth Press.

Chisholm, J. L. (2006). Cyberspace violence against girls and adolescent females. *Annals of the New York Academy of Sciences, 1087*, 74–89.

Cicchetti, D. (1989). How research on child maltreatment has informed the study of child development: Perspective from developmental psychopathology. In D. Cicchetti & J. Carlson (Eds.), *Child maltreatment: Theory and research on the causes and consequences of child abuse and neglect* (pp. 377–431). Cambridge: Cambridge University Press.

Cicchetti, D., & Aber, J. L. (1998). Contextualism and developmental psychopathology. *Development and Psychopathology, 10*, 137–141.

Craig, W. M. (1998). The relationship among bullying, victimization, depression, anxiety, and aggression in elementary school children. *Personality and Individual Differences, 24*, 123–130.

Crick, N. R., & Grotpeter, J. K. (1996). Children's treatment by peers: Victims of relational and overt aggression. *Development and Psychopathology, 8*, 367–380.

DuBois, D. L., Felner, N., Brand, S., Phillips, R. S. C., & Lease, A. M. (1996). Early adolescent self-esteem: A developmental–ecological framework and assessment strategy. *Journal of Research on Adolescence, 6*, 543–579.

Emler, N., & Reicher, S. (1995). *Adolescence and delinquency: the collective management of reputation*. Oxford: Blackwell.

Erikson, E. H. (1950). *Childhood and society*. New York: Norton.

Genta, M. L. (2002). *Il bullismo: Bambini aggressivi a scuola* [*Bullying: aggressive children at school*]. Rome: Carocci.

Genta, M. L., Brighi, A., & Guarini, A. (Eds.) (2009). *Cyberbullying*. Rome: Carocci.

Graham, S., Bellmore, A. D., & Mize, J. (2006). Peer victimization, aggression, and their co-occurrence in middle school: Pathways to adjustment problems. *Journal of Abnormal Child Psychology, 34*, 349–364.

Grills, A. E. & Ollendick, T. H. (2002). Peer victimization, global self-worth, and anxiety in middle school children. *Journal of Clinical Child and Adolescent Psychology, 31*, 59–68.

Harter, S. (1998). The development of self-representations. In W. Damon & N. Eisenberg (Eds.), *Handbook of child psychology vol. 3: Social, emotional, and personality development* (5th ed., pp. 553–617). New York: Wiley.

Hawker, D. S. J., & Boulton, M. J. (2000). Twenty years' research on peer victimization and psychosocial maladjustment: A meta-analytic review of cross sectional studies. *Journal of Child Psychology and Psychiatry, 41*, 441–445.

Haynie, D., Nansel, T., Eitel, P., Crump, A., Saylor, K., Yu, K., & Simons-Morton, B. (2001). Bullies, victims, and bully-victims: Distinct groups of at-risk youth. *Journal of Early Adolescence, 21*, 29–49.

Hazler, R. J. (1996). *Breaking the cycle of violence: Interventions for bullying and victimization*. Athens, OH: Ohio University.

Huffaker, D., & Calvert S. (2005). Gender, identity, and language use in teenage blogs. *Journal of Computer-Mediated Communication,* 10, Article 1. Retrieved 28 June, 2011 from http://jcmc.indiana.edu/vol10/issue2/huffaker.html

Ireland, J. L., & Qualter, P. (2008). Bullying and social and emotional loneliness in a sample of adult male prisoners. *International Journal of Law and Psychiatry, 31*, 19–29.

Kochenderfer, B. J., & Ladd, G. W. (1996). Peer victimization: Cause or consequence of school maladjustment? *Child Development, 67*, 1305–1317.

Kochenderfer-Ladd, B., & Wardrop, J. L. (2001). Chronicity and instability of children's peer victimization experiences as predictors of loneliness and social satisfaction trajectories. *Child Development, 72*, 134–151.

Li Lei, Y. & Wu, M. A. (2007). Adolescents' paternal attachment and Internet use. *Cyberpsychology & Behavior, 10*, 633–639.

Marcia, J. E. (1980). Identity in adolescence. In J. Adelson (Ed.), *Handbook of adolescent psychology* (pp. 159–187). New York: Wiley.

Marcoen, A., & Goossens, L. (1993). Loneliness, attitude towards aloneness, and solitude: Age differences and developmental significance during adolescence. In S. Jackson & H. Rodriguez-Tomé (Eds.), *Adolescence and its social worlds* (pp. 197–228). Hove: Lawrence Erlbaum.

Marcoen, A., Goossens, L., & Caes, P. (1987). Loneliness in pre- through late adolescence: exploring the contributions of a multidimensional approach. *Journal of Youth and Adolescence, 16*, 561–576.

McDonald, D. G., & Kim, H. (2001). When I die, I feel small: Electronic game characters and the social self. *Journal of Broadcasting and Electronic Media, 45*, 241–258.

McLeod, J. D., & Owens, T. J. (2004). Psychological well-being in the early life course: Variations by socioeconomic status, gender, and race/ethnicity. *Social Psychology Quarterly, 67*, 257–278.

Mead, G. H. (1934). *Mind, self and society*. Chicago, IL: University of Chicago Press.

Melotti, G., Corsano, P., Majorano, M., & Scarpuzzi, P. (2006). An Italian application of the Louvain Loneliness Scale for Children and Adolescents (LLCA). *TPM-Testing, Psychometrics, Methodology in Applied Psychology, 13*, 237–255.

Melotti, G., & Passini, S. (2002). L'applicazione ad un gruppo di adolescenti italiani del Self Esteem Questionnaire (SEQ) [The application of the Self Esteem Questionnaire to a sample of Italian adolescents]. *Bollettino di Psicologia Applicata, 238*, 59–70.

Melotti, G., Passini, S., & Biolcati, R. (2009). Una lettura psicosociale del bullismo nel web [A psychosocial reading of cyberbullying]. In M. L. Genta, A. Brighi, & A. Guarini (Eds.), *Il bullismo elettronico* [*Cyberbullying*] (pp. 78–103). Rome: Carocci.

Nansel, T. R., Craig, W., Overpeck, M. D., Saluja, G., & Ruan, W. J. (2004). Cross-national consistency in the relationship between bullying behaviors and psychosocial adjustment. *Archives of Pediatrics and Adolescent Medicine, 158*, 730–736.

Neary, A., & Joseph, S. (1994). Peer victimization and its relationship to self-concept and depression among school girls. *Personality and Individual Differences, 16*, 183–186.

Nielsen Online. (2010). *UK web use up 65% since 2007—Social networking more than doubles*. Retrieved June 28, 2011 from http://blog.nielsen.com/nielsenwire/global/u-k-web-use-up-65-since-2007-social-networking-more-than-doubles/

Ojala, K., & Nesdale, D. (2004). Bullying and social identity: The effects of group norms and distinctiveness threat on attitudes towards bullying. *British Journal of Developmental Psychology, 22*, 19–23.

Olweus, D. (1994). Bullying at school: Long-term outcomes for the victims and an effective school-based intervention program. In L. R. Huesmann (Ed.), *Aggressive behavior: Current perspectives* (pp. 97–130). New York: Plenum Press.

Ortega, R., & Del Rey, R. (2008). La víctima de maltrato y acoso entre compañeros [The victim of school bullying]. In M. Herrera (Ed.), *Hostigamiento y hábitat social: una perspectiva victimológica [Harrasment and social habitat: A victimological perspective]* (pp. 209–234). Granada: Comares.

Ortega, R., Elipe, P., Mora-Merchán, J. A., Calmaestra, J., & Vega, E. (2009). The emotional impact on victims of traditional bullying and cyberbullying. A study of Spanish adolescents. *Zeitschrift für Psychologie/Journal of Psychology, 217*, 197–204.

Ortega, R., & Mora-Merchán, J. A. (1996). El aula como escenario de la vida afectiva y moral [The classroom as setting of affective and moral life]. *Cultura y Educación, 3*, 5–18.

Ortega, R., & Mora-Merchán, J. A. (2008). Las redes de iguales y el fenómeno del acoso escolar: explorando el esquema dominio-sumisión [Peer networks and the bullying phenomenon: Exploring the control–submission schema]. *Infancia y Aprendizaje, 31*, 511–528.

Rigby, K. (2001). Health consequences of bullying and its prevention in schools. In J. Juvonen & S. Graham (Eds.), *Peer harassment in school: The plight of the vulnerable and victimized* (pp. 310–331). New York: Guilford.

Rolf, J., Masten, A., Cicchetti, D., Neuchterlein, K. M., & Weintraub, J. (Eds.) (1990). *Risk and protective factors in the development of psychopathology*. Cambridge: Cambridge University Press.

Rosenberg, M. (1985). Self-concept and psychological well-being in adolescence. In R. L. Leahy (Ed.), *The development of the self* (pp. 205–246). New York: Academic Press.

Rutter, M. (1990). Psychosocial resilience and protective mechanisms. In J. Rolf, A. Masten, D. Cicchetti, K. M. Neuchterlein, & J. Weintraub (Eds.), *Risk and protective factors in the development of psychopathology* (pp. 181–214). Cambridge: Cambridge University Press.

Salmivalli, C., Huttunen, A., & Lagerspetz, K. (1997). Peer networks and bullying in schools. *Scandinavian Journal of Psychology, 38*, 305–312.

Salmivalli, C., & Isaacs, J. (2005). Prospective relations among victimization, rejection, friendliness, and children's self- and peer-perceptions. *Child Development, 76*, 1161–1171.

Salmivalli, C., Lagerspetz, K., Bjorkqvist, K., Österman, K., & Kaukiainen, A. (1996). Bullying as a group process: Participant roles and their relations to social status within the group. *Aggressive Behaviour, 22*, 1–15.

Sameroff, A. J. (1987). The social context of development. In N. Eisenberg (Ed.), *Contemporary topics in developmental psychology* (pp. 273–291). New York: Wiley.

Schmitt, K. L., Dayanim, S., & Matthias, S. (2008). Personal homepage construction as expression of social development. *Developmental Psychology, 44*, 496–506.

Slee, P. T., & Rigby, K. (1993). The relationship of Eysenck's personality factors and self-esteem to bully-victim behaviour in Australian schoolboys. *Personality and Individual Differences, 14*, 371–373.

Slonje, R. & Smith, P. K. (2008). Cyberbullying: Another main type of bullying? *Scandinavian Journal of Psychology, 49*, 147–154.

Smith, P. K., Mahdavi, J., Carvalho, M., Fisher, S., Russell, S., & Tippett, N. (2008). Cyberbullying: its nature and impact in secondary school pupils. *Journal of Child Psychology and Psychiatry, 49*, 378–385.

Smith, P. K., Shu, S., & Madsen, K. (2001). Characteristics of victims of school bullying: Developmental changes in coping strategies and skills. In J. Juvonen & S. Graham (Eds.), *Peer harassment in school: The plight of the vulnerable and victimized* (pp. 332–351). New York: Guilford.

Sroufe, L. A. (1990). Considering normal and abnormal together: The essence of developmental psychopathology. *Development and Psychopathology, 2*, 335–347.

Sroufe, L. A., & Rutter, M. (1984). The domain of developmental psychopathology. *Child Development, 55*, 17–29.

Suler, J. (2004). The psychology of cyberspace. *CyberPsychology and Behavior, 7*, 321–326.

Tajfel, H. (1981). *Human groups and social categories. Studies in social psychology*. Cambridge: Cambridge University Press.

Troop-Gordon, W., & Ladd, G. (2005). Trajectories of peer victimization and perceptions of the self and schoolmates: Precursors to internalizing and externalizing problems. *Child Development, 76*, 1072–1091.

Turkle, S. (1995). *Life on the screen: Identity in the age of the Internet*. New York: Simon & Schuster.

Willard, N. E. (2006). *Cyberbullying and cyberthreats*. Eugene, OR: Center for Safe and Responsible Internet Use.

Ybarra, M., & Mitchell, K. (2004). Online aggressor/targets, aggressors, and targets: A comparison of associated youth characteristics. *Journal of Child Psychology and Psychiatry, 45*, 1308–1316.

4

Cyberbullying in Finland

Christina Salmivalli and Virpi Pöyhönen

Although cyberbullying has raised considerable public concern in Finland, empirical studies on the phenomenon are scarce, and are almost exclusively based on web-based surveys with possibly highly selected samples. Thus, even basic information about cyberbullying, including prevalence rates and sex differences, is still limited. The studies presented in this chapter are the first ones investigating cyberbullying and cybervictimization in a large, representative sample of Finnish students.

After reviewing background facts about Internet and mobile phone use among Finnish youth, findings from existing surveys on cyberbullying in our country, and concerns related to these phenomena, we will present results from a large-scale study conducted in the context of the DAPHNE project, "An investigation into forms of peer–peer bullying at school in preadolescent and adolescent groups: New instruments and preventing strategies (2006–2009)." The study concerned the prevalence, sex, and age differences in cyberbullying and cybervictimization, the most typical devices utilized (the Internet versus mobile phones), and the associations between traditional and cyberbullying/victimization. Finally, we will discuss the effects of a new Finnish anti-bullying program, KiVa, on students' likelihood of being bullied via the Internet or mobile phones (Salmivalli, Kärnä, & Poskiparta, 2011).

Finnish Children and Electronic Communication Tools: Lots of Use and Few Limits

Finnish children and adolescents are frequent users of the Internet and mobile phones. According to a recent Eurobarometer survey by the European Commission (Flash Eurobarometer, 2008), 94% of Finnish children aged between 6 and 17 use

Cyberbullying in the Global Playground: Research from International Perspectives, First Edition.
Edited by Qing Li, Donna Cross, and Peter K. Smith.

the Internet and 87% own a mobile phone. These numbers are higher than in any other country in the European Union. According to Finnish children themselves, their parents set relatively few limits to their Internet usage. In Microsoft's European Online Safety Survey conducted in early 2009 and including ten countries across Europe (http://www.microsoft.com/presspass/emea/presscentre/pressreleases/OnlinebullyingPR_100209.mspx), only 8% of Finnish adolescents said that they had been given limits to their Internet use. By comparison, 28% of Norwegian and 21% of Spanish adolescents reported that they had parental limits set on their Internet use. As many as 44% of Finnish youth reported that they had *no limits at all* for their Internet usage, and 41% said that limits were set *sometimes*. In a Finnish survey, only half of 10–12-year-old children and fewer than 12% of 14–15-year-old adolescents reported that their parents know what they do on the Internet (that is, who they meet, which sites they visit; Tossavainen, 2008). Overall, it seems that parental supervision of Internet use is relatively loose among Finnish youth.

The most common forms of internet usage among 10–18-year-old Finnish youth include visiting social networking sites such as MySpace (in Finland, Irc-gallery) and playing games (Tossavainen, 2008). Time spent on the Internet increases with age (Tossavainen, 2008; Save the Children Finland, 2008) and boys use the Internet more than girls. During adolescence, the social communication function of the Internet becomes more important, whereas using the Internet for playing games becomes less popular (Save the Children Finland, 2008).

Cyberbullying in Finland

In Finland, much public attention has focused on peer-to-peer bullying in schools since the early 1990s. Within the last ten years, this focus has widened to include electronic or cyberbullying. In the Finnish language, there are separate words for bullying on the Internet (*nettikiusaaminen*) and bullying via mobile phones (*kännykkäkiusaaminen*), but no single construct to refer to both types collectively. In public discussion, the most frequently mentioned forms of cyberbullying include sending insulting or threatening messages by mobile phone or email, and posting embarrassing or demeaning photos or videos on websites. Phenomena such as "happy slapping" seem to be less known and are very rarely mentioned in Finnish discussions concerning cyberbullying.

Despite a lot of media interest and public concern, there has been little research on these new forms of bullying. Some non-governmental organizations have done surveys on cyberbullying utilizing online questionnaires. In a recent survey by the Mannerheim League for Child Welfare (www.mll.fi) it was found that 9% of adolescents reported having been bullied in the Internet at least *sometimes*. In Microsoft's European Online Safety Survey conducted in early 2009, (www.microsoft.com/presspass/emea/presscentre/pressreleases/OnlinebullyingPR_100209.mspx), 21% of Finnish adolescents reported having been bullied on the Internet sometimes, whereas 4% had been targeted repeatedly. In another survey by

Save the Children Finland (2008), 11–20% of girls and 9–17% of boys said they had experienced Internet bullying by their peers. The frequencies showed a decreasing trend among both boys and girls, being highest among children below 11 years and lowest among 16–17-year-olds. Among girls, however, Internet harassment increased with age, with 26% of 16–17-year-olds having experienced some. In 1995, Save the Children Finland reported that 25% of 7–15-year-olds had been targets of mobile phone bullying. This prevalence was highest among the youngest children, aged 7–9.

These surveys provide some important initial information about the experiences youth have with cyberbullying. There are two problems, however. First, the samples might be highly selected as they often consist of children who just happened to find the questionnaires on the Internet and respond to them (thus excluding children and young people who spend little or no time in cyberspace, or who are not motivated to respond to questions concerning cyberbullying). Second, the definition of cyberbullying is often not optimal, as many surveys ignore the repeated nature of attacks which is included in standard definitions of bullying (Olweus, 1978, 1995; Salmivalli & Peets, 2009). Thus, the high incidences reported in some studies might be partly due to different definitions of cyberbullying, as compared with traditional bullying. For instance, surveys on cyberbullying might just ask whether a child has *ever* been targeted (e.g., received a nasty message), without specifying any time frame (during lifetime, versus during the past couple of months), or taking into account whether the incidence only took place once or happened repeatedly. International studies examining traditional and cyberbullying using identical questions (Smith et al., 2008) suggest that traditional bullying is clearly more prevalent. Similar comparisons are lacking in Finland, and overall, valid information on the prevalence, risk factors, and correlates of cyberbullying and cybervictimization is still scarce.

Finnish schools are expected to prevent and tackle bullying taking place among children. The Finnish Basic Education Act (since 1999) states that every student has the right to a safe school environment. Education providers have the responsibility of making sure that students do not experience acts of violence or bullying while at school. The legislation concerns all educational levels. It was further amended in 2003, stating that "the education provider shall draw up a plan, in connection with curriculum design, for safeguarding pupils against violence, bullying, and harassment, execute the plan and supervise adherence to it and its implementation." Many teachers and other school personnel wonder, however, whether it is their responsibility to tackle cyberbullying, which usually does not occur during school hours and not necessarily even between children from the same school. It can be assumed, however, that in many cases children bullied at school are also targets of cyberbullying (see Raskauskas & Stolz, 2007; Smith et al., 2008; Katzer, Fetchenhauer, & Belschak, 2009), and thus attacked by the very same perpetrators who are harassing them at school. It is unclear, however, whether general anti-bullying programs implemented in schools can also reduce cyberbullying, along with more traditional forms. One might even argue that as a result of an anti-bullying program, bullying might get more hidden and move from the schoolyard to the "virtual playground."

The DAPHNE Project on Cyberbullying and Victimization

In the context of the DAPHNE project (2006–2009), we investigated the prevalence of cyberbullying and cybervictimization among Finnish children and youth, sex and age differences in these phenomena, the most typical devices utilized (the Internet versus mobile phones), and the associations between traditional and cyberbullying/victimization.

As the data came from a large research project (the KiVa project; see Salmivalli, Kärnä, & Poskiparta, 2010a, 2010b, and www.kivakoulu.fi) and were collected in schools during regular school hours, supervised by well-instructed teachers, the findings can be considered more generalizable than the results of previous online surveys. Furthermore, we chose to use criteria for cyberbullying and victimization that were identical to those used in the context of traditional bullying and victimization, producing comparable prevalence estimates.

Methods

Participants and procedure

The data utilized in the DAPHNE project on cyberbullying and cybervictimization were the pre-test data collected in third to fifth grades and seventh to eighth grades in the context of evaluation of the KiVa anti-bullying program. The target sample consisted of 21,364 children and adolescents in comprehensive education. From among these students, 83% had active consent from their parents to participate and were present at the time of the data collection (i.e., provided self-report data). This resulted in a sample of 17,627 students (50% boys). As students in Finland typically start comprehensive education at the age of seven (with some starting, with special permission, at the age of 6), the age range of students was from 8 to 15, and they were from 156 different schools representing all five provinces of mainland Finland.

All data were concurrent (only pre-test, or time 1 data) but collected in two phases, in May 2007 (grades 3, 4, and 5) and May 2008 (grades 7 and 8). Students filled out Internet-based questionnaires in the schools' computer labs during regular school hours. The process was administered by the teachers, who were supplied with detailed instructions about two weeks prior to data collection. Detailed description of the procedures for obtaining consent and instructing teachers and students can be found elsewhere (Kärnä et al., 2011).

Instruments

All participants responded via an Internet-based questionnaire using their personal passwords. As the passwords were created by the research team, in the University of Turku, the sex and grade level of each student was known (although students also reported them at the beginning of the questionnaire). In the following, we describe the questions utilized in the present study, that is, self-report measures to assess the frequency of different forms of bullying and victimization.

The questionnaire first introduced the standard definition of bullying (Olweus's Bully/Victim questionnaire; Olweus, 1996), which emphasizes the repetitive nature of bullying and the power imbalance between the bully and the victim. Several examples covering different forms of bullying were given. Moreover, an explanation of what is *not* bullying (teasing in a friendly and playful way; fighting between children of equal strength) was also provided. To help students keep the definition in their mind during responding, a shortened version of it always appeared on the upper part of the computer screen when students responded to any bullying-related question.

After the definition, the students were presented with a global victimization item, asking about the frequency with which they had been bullied in general (without specifying the form) during the past few months. After that, they were presented with nine items representing different forms of victimization including verbal, physical, social exclusion, spreading lies and nasty rumors, taking or damaging property, racist, sexual, threatening/forcing to do things, and cybervictimization. For each form, the students were asked how frequently, during the past few months, they had been bullied in this specific way. The questions regarding victimization were followed by corresponding questions (global + nine specific forms) about bullying others. All answers were given on a five-point scale (0=not at all, 1=only once or twice, 2=two or three times a month, 3=every week, 4=several times a week). All questions about bullying and victimization in their different forms are presented in the Appendix to this chapter.

The students who reported bullying others or being bullied via the Internet or mobile phones were further asked whether they had bullied/been bullied via the Internet, mobile phone, or via both the Internet and mobile phones.

Analyses

To identify "cyberbullies" and "cybervictims," we followed the suggestion by Solberg and Olweus (2003) to use the cut-off criterion of the student reporting bullying others or being bullied by others *at least 2–3 times a month* during the past couple of months.

We analyzed the frequency distributions of students fulfilling the above criteria across sex and grade levels. Furthermore, we tested whether the distribution of students reporting that they bullied others or were bullied by others by means of a mobile phone, the Internet, or both, differed across grade levels. Finally, at a descriptive level, we also explored the extent to which students who repeatedly bullied others or were bullied by electronic means were also perpetrators or targets of other forms of bullying.

Results

Prevalence of cyberbullying and cybervictimization

In presenting the results, as above, we used Solberg and Olweus's (2003) definition of cyberbullies" or "cybervictims" students who reported bullying others or being bullied by others at least two to three times per month or more often during the past couple of months.

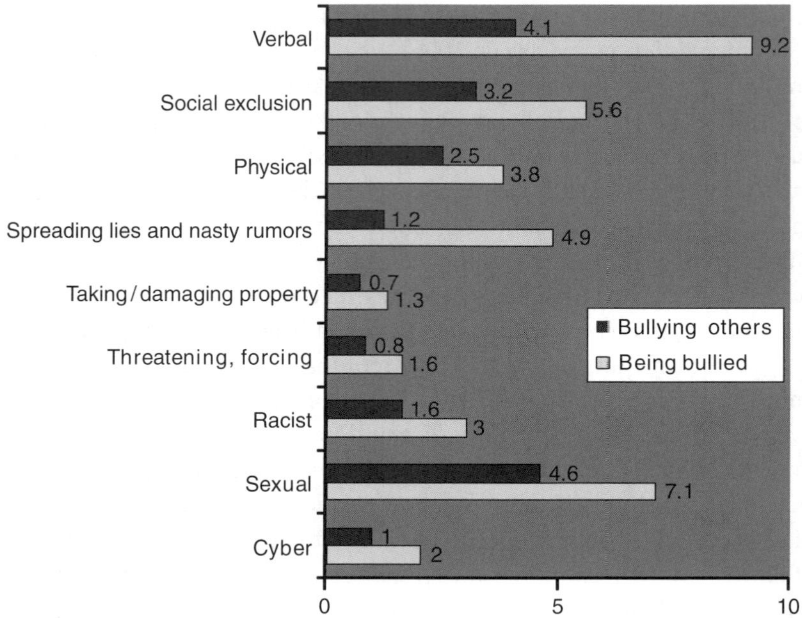

Figure 4.1 Frequencies of Students Reporting That They Have Bullied Others or Been Bullied by Others at Least 2–3 Times per Month or More Often During the Past Few Months. N = 17,598–17,627 Students From Grades 3–5 and 7–8. Created by Christina Salmivalli and Virpi Pöyhönen.

The frequencies of students reporting bullying others or being bullied by others at least two to three times per month or more often in different ways across the whole sample are presented in Figure 4.1. The most common forms of bullying as well as being bullied were sexual (the high prevalence mostly due to these forms being common among secondary school students), verbal, social exclusion, and physical bullying. Social manipulation by lies and nasty rumors was relatively commonly reported by the targets, but rarely admitted by the bullies. Together with material bullying (taking or damaging property) and threatening and forcing, cyberbullying was one of the very rarely reported forms of bullying/being bullied. Only 1% (177 out of 17,627 children responding to this question) said they had been cyberbullying others on a regular basis, whereas 2% (348 out of 17,274 students) reported having been cyberbullied repeatedly.

Sex and grade differences in cyberbullying and cybervictimization

Although the overall frequency of cyberbullies and cybervictims are small, they might still vary by sex and grade level. It is conceivable, for instance, that with increasing use of the Internet, the prevalence of cyberbullying will also increase. We therefore examined the frequencies of cyberbullies and victims in each grade level, separately among boys and girls. The prevalence rates are presented in Table 4.1.

With respect to sex differences, there were significantly more boys than girls who admitted to cyberbullying (χ^2 (1) = 82.85, $p < 0.001$). The overall increase

Table 4.1 Percentages of Students Reporting Cyberbullying Others/Being Cyberbullied Themselves (2–3 Times per Month or More Often) Among Girls and Boys in Different Years at School.

	Cyberbullying others			*Being cyberbullied*		
	Boys	*Girls*	*Total*	*Boys*	*Girls*	*Total*
Grade						
Primary school						
3	0.9%	0.3%	0.6%	2.9%	1.9%	2.4%
4	0.7%	0.2%	0.4%	1.4%	2.7%	2.0%
5	0.5%	0.5%	0.5%	2.2%	2.5%	2.4%
Secondary school						
7	2.0%	0.4%	1.1%	2.1%	1.7%	1.9%
8	2.9%	0.4%	1.6%	2.4%	1.0%	1.7%
Total (primary and secondary)	1.7%	0.3%	1.0%	2.2%	1.8%	2.0%

in cyberbullying from primary to secondary school years (see the third column in Table 4.1) was due to a strong increase among boys, who were over-represented in the upper grades (χ^2 (4)=50.89, $p<0.001$) whereas females who cyberbullied others were evenly distributed across grade levels. It should be noted, however, that even among secondary school boys the reported frequencies were still relatively small, representing 2% and 3% of the boys in the seventh and eighth grades, respectively.

When it comes to being a victim of cyberbullying, boys were targeted somewhat more often but the overall sex difference did not quite reach the level of significance. Girl victims tended to be in the lower rather than in the upper grades (χ^2 (4)=19.04, $p<0.001$), whereas boys who reported being cyberbullied were evenly distributed across grade levels. As a consequence, there were more male than female cybervictims at the secondary school level.

Internet versus mobile phone cyberbullying

The students who had bullied others or been bullied by others repeatedly (again, at least two to three times a month) via electronic devices were asked whether that had happened via mobile phone, the Internet, or both. The distributions of responses, separately for each grade level, are presented in Table 4.2. It should be remembered that the proportions are calculated from very small subsamples (from among the 1% and 2% of the total sample, that is, 177 and 348 students identified as cyberbullies and cybervictims, respectively) as most children did not report any involvement either in cyberbullying or in being a victim.

The devices used in cyberbullying changed as a function of age (χ^2 (8)=32.90, $p<0.001$), and the same was true of the experience of being bullied (χ^2 (8)=36.58, $p<0.001$). Whereas bullying others via mobile phone was more common than bullying via the Internet in the third and fourth grades, the opposite was true from fifth grade onwards. In seventh grade and (especially) eighth, students bullying

Table 4.2 The Proportions of Cyberbullies/Victims Who Themselves Utilize, or Are Targeted by, Mobile Phone Only, the Internet Only, and by Both Mobile Phone and Internet.

	Bullying others			*Being bullied*		
	Mobile phone only	*Internet only*	*Both*	*Mobile phone only*	*Internet only*	*Both*
Grade						
Primary school						
3	**53.8%**	30.8%	15.4%	**58.2%**	14.5%	27.3%
4	**66.7%**	22.2%	11.1%	41.7%	31.3%	27.1%
5	15.4%	46.2%	5.4%	29.5%	42.6%	27.9%
Secondary school						
7	19.0%	25.9%	55.2%	23.73%	36.1%	40.2%
8	23.5%	44.9%	**56.5%**	17.2%	35.6%	**47.1%**

Note: The cells in which there are significantly more cases than would be expected by chance (adjusted residuals > 2) are marked in bold.

others via electronic means were most likely to utilize *both* mobile phone and the Internet. Self-reports of being bullied showed a similar pattern, as students being bullied by mobile phone only were over-represented in third grade and those bullied by both mobile phone and the Internet were most likely to be eighth-graders. The patterns remained similar even when we looked at the children who had bullied others or been bullied by others *at least once* during the past couple of months.

Associations with other forms of bullying and victimization

Cyberbullying was related to each of the other eight forms of bullying included in our questionnaire (Spearman's rank order correlations ranged from 0.18 to 0.32). Accordingly, cybervictimization correlated positively with all other forms of victimization, with correlations of similar magnitude (Spearman's rank order correlations 0.19–0.30). Cybervictimization correlated most strongly ($r=0.30$) with "lies and nasty rumors being spread about oneself," whereas the lowest correlation was observed between cybervictimization and physical victimization.

To further explore the extent to which cyberbullying and victimization overlapped with the other forms, we created nine dichotomous variables indicating whether a child bullied others repeatedly (two to three times a month or more often) in each of the nine ways, and corresponding nine variables which indicated whether the child had been repeatedly bullied in each of these ways or not. Cross-tabulations of the nine dichotomous bullying variables on one hand, and of the nine victimization variables on the other, showed that (a) cyberbullies often bullied others in other ways too, and (b) cybervictims were often victimized in many other ways too.

As many as 90% of cyberbullies and 85% of cybervictims reported at least one other way in which they bullied others or were bullied by others on a regular basis. On average, cybervictims reported 3.4 other ways by which they were repeatedly victimized, and cyberbullies reported 4.6 other forms in which they bullied others repeatedly. Finally, only 0.2% of the whole sample (51 students) were regular cybervictims, but were *not* repeatedly tormented in any other way and only 0.1% (18 students) were regular cyberbullies who did *not* engage repeatedly in any other form of bullying. Together, these findings suggest that cyberbullying and cybervictimization are *almost always accompanied by other, more traditional, forms of bullying and victimization.*

Can Cyberbullying Be Reduced via a School-Based Anti-Bullying Program?

The KiVa anti-bullying program, currently being disseminated for national use in Finnish comprehensive schools (Salmivalli et al., 2010a, 2010b) includes both universal and specific actions to prevent the occurrence of bullying as well as to intervene in individual bullying cases. The program has a multifaceted theoretical background (e.g., Salmivalli et al., 2010a). It is based on research on participant roles in bullying that started over a decade ago (Salmivalli, Lagerspetz, Björkqvist, Österman, & Kaukiainen, 1996) as well as on recent studies into the social standing of aggressive children in general (e.g., Rodkin, Farmer, Pearl, & Van Acker, 2006; Cillessen & Mayeux, 2004) and bullies in particular (Juvonen, Graham, & Schuster, 2003). More specifically, the program is predicated on the idea that bystanders often contribute to the emergence and maintenance of bullying by assisting and reinforcing the bully, which in turn provides bullies with the status and power they seek (Salmivalli & Peets, 2009; Sijtsema, Veenstra, Lindenberg, & Salmivalli, 2009). It is thus assumed that a positive change in the behaviors of classmates can reduce the social rewards gained by bullies and consequently their motivation to bully.

The *universal actions* include a series of student lessons (primary school) and themes (secondary school) delivered by teachers in classrooms. The lessons and themes aim to make bystanders aware of the role they play in the bullying process, to make them show the bully they are against bullying, and to provide them with safe strategies to support the victim, instead of encouraging the bully. They involve discussion, group work, role-play exercises, and short films about bullying. A unique feature of the universal actions is an anti-bullying computer game (primary school) and a virtual learning environment called KiVa Street (secondary school), the contents of which are closely tied to the topics handled during the student lessons and themes.

As well as universal actions, the specific actions represent an equally important element of the KiVa program. They involve a systematic procedure for handling any acute bullying cases that come to the attention of school staff.

KiVa is a generic anti-bullying program in the sense that it is not designed to tackle either cyberbullying or any other specific form of bullying specifically. However, it devotes some time to cyberbullying, as the topic is handled in the student lessons and themes during a school year. Cyberbullying is also brought up in some of the video materials and in the computer game/virtual learning environment involved in the KiVa program. Thus, students should be aware of the fact that cyberbullying is part of bullying among peers and it has similar negative consequences for the victims as more traditional bullying.

The first evaluation of program effects in fourth to sixth grades (Kärnä et al., 2011) showed remarkable reductions in both bullying others and being bullied, assessed via global items not specifying the form(s) of negative acts delivered or received. The reductions in bullying and being bullied were confirmed by peer reports. More importantly for the present chapter, in a further study (Salmivalli et al., 2011) we examined changes in different *specific forms of being bullied* during the first nine months of implementation of the KiVa program (in comparison to changes taking place in control schools which did not implement KiVa) in fourth to sixth grades. Similar evaluations are not yet available for the other grades.

Although we assumed that the KiVa program reduces multiple forms of being bullied, including cyberbullying, it might have had quite different consequences as well. It has been suggested that intervention programs might only be able to reduce visible, direct forms of bullying, and may even increase indirect and/or cyberbullying (e.g., Woods & Wolke, 2003). The reasoning is that as a consequence of the intervention, bullying moves from the schoolyard into cyberspace, where it is less likely to be punished.

Our findings (Salmivalli et al., 2011) indicated, however, that the frequency of victims bullied via the Internet and/or mobile phone (again, using the criterion of being targeted *2-3 times a month or more often*) decreased by 36% in the intervention schools, whereas it increased by 14% in the control schools. This means a reduction of 50% in KiVa schools in comparison to control schools. The odds of being a victim of cyberbullying, calculated while correcting the standard errors for clustering at the school level with the average cluster size (for the formulas, see Ttofi, Farrington, & Baldry, 2008), was 1.81 (80% CI=1.11–2.93). This means that after the first nine months of implementing the KiVa program, the likelihood of being a target of cyberbullies was 1.81 times higher for a control school student than it was for a student in an intervention school (for comparison, the average OR across all nine forms of being bullied assessed in the study was 1.58, meaning that cybervictimization was affected relatively greatly compared with the other forms assessed).

By using an even stricter criterion to define a cybervictim, that of being treated negatively *every week* or *several times a week,* the odds ratio was found to be as high as 2.57, indicating that the likelihood of a child being cyberbullied that often was 2.6 times higher for a control school student than for a student in a school implementing KiVa.

These remarkable reductions in the frequencies of cybervictimizatiojn indicate that a generic program such as KiVa can be very effective in reducing cyberbullying as well as other forms of peer-to-peer bullying. It should be mentioned that other types of "hidden" bullying such as social manipulation were significantly reduced by KiVa as well. Thus, an anti-bullying program does not only result in decreases in visible bullying but also forms of bullying that are not directly observable by adults in the school context.

Conclusion

When identified by using the same frequency criterion (two to three times per month or more often) than is usual when assessing traditional bullying and victimization (see Solberg & Olweus, 2003), cyberbullying and cybervictimization were found to be relatively rare among Finnish children and youth. For instance, whereas 9.2% of students in our sample reported being repeatedly verbally bullied (the most common form of victimization), only 2% reported that the same had happened via the Internet or by mobile phone. Bullying others by electronic means was uncommon as well: While 4.1% of students admitted that they had repeatedly bullied others by verbal means, only 1% reported bullying others repeatedly on the Internet or by mobile phone. Taking into account that Internet use is common and poorly supervised by parents in Finland, and the vast majority of children and youth have their own mobile phones, it seems that Finnish youth can use these devices in responsible ways.

Some previous surveys have suggested that as many as 20–30% of Finnish youth are cyberbullied. The considerable difference with the present findings probably partly stems from the selected samples, but especially from using a different criterion for identifying the victimized youth (e.g., many previous studies have asked whether a child or an adolescent has *ever experienced* cyberbullying or victimization). Also in our representative sample, 91.4% of all students reported they had *never* been cyberbullied, meaning that almost 10% had at least some experience of being targeted, such as receiving one or two nasty emails. We strongly suggest that such incidents should not be taken to represent cyberbullying, but researchers should apply the same criteria to define cybervictims as they do when studying bullying in general. Otherwise we might get a highly distorted view of the prevalence of cyberbullying and cybervictimization, compared to the other forms.

We argue that one reason why cyberbullying is not more widespread stems from the function of bullying for the perpetrator(s). It has been suggested (e.g., Pellegrini, 2002; Salmivalli & Peets, 2009) that one motive underlying bullying is gaining and maintaining group status. If the bully wants to demonstrate his power and status to peers, public attack with several witnesses is likely to best serve this goal. In cyberbullying, the humiliation can be widespread but it is not public in the same way as an attack taking place in the playground. In cyberspace, the bully can neither see the reactions of others (at least immediately), nor the reactions of the victim. He cannot be seen "in action" by others either. As this element of *public, successful abuse of power over another person* is missing in many forms of cyberbullying (such as sending insulting or threatening messages, posting embarrassing photos on a public website), cyberbullying might never become as common as other forms of harassment among school-aged children.

Our data suggest, however, that cyberbullying tended to become more common among boys (but not girls) when entering secondary school. Whereas mobile phones were the most common device used for cyberbullying in the lower grades, this had already begun to change around fifth grade (when Finnish students are aged about 11–12). With increasing age, the Internet became the more common tool for bullying. This is in line with findings showing how time spent on the Internet increases as a function of age (Tossavainen, 2008). It should be noted, however, that in secondary school it was relatively common to bully others/be bullied by the means of *both* mobile phones and the Internet.

Similarly to previous studies carried out in other countries (Katzer et al., 2009) we found that cyberbullying and cybervictimization are not distinct from more traditional forms. Children and youth who bully their peers online tend to torment them in multiple ways. Similarly, being cyberbullied is related to being bullied in other ways as well. It is very rare that a child only bullies others on the Internet or by mobile phone, or is only bullied by such means.

Our finding concerning the intervention effects showed that reducing cyberbullying does not necessarily require programs specially tailored to target these specific forms of bullying, but a general anti-bullying program, such as KiVa as discussed in this chapter, can have significant effects on cyberbullying as well. This result might reflect the fact that both cyberbullying and cybervictimization appear along with more traditional forms of bullying (see also Raskauskas & Stolz, 2007; Smith et al., 2008; Katzer et al., 2009). When a child is no longer targeted, this is reflected in the reduction of multiple forms of harassment, including online/mobile phone attacks. Furthermore, the awareness and skills that students acquire when participating in an anti-bullying intervention such as KiVa may positively influence their behavior outside school as well. Based on our results, it seems clear that a general anti-bullying program does not result in bullying becoming more hidden or secretive (for example, moving from a school setting to cyberspace) but, rather, the positive effects of intervention can be seen in both traditional bullying and cyberbullying.

Implications for Research and Practice

Future research on cyberbullying should investigate in more detail the multiple forms it can take. In our study, we only asked about bullying "via the Internet or by mobile phone," thus leaving open the different modes of attack, such as insults delivered by instant messaging or in chatrooms, spreading video clips, and so on (see Smith et al., 2008). Second, the motives behind cyberbullying (as well as bullying in general) should be addressed in more depth. Finally, research on the harmful effects of cybervictimization should take into account the fact that this form of victimization is usually accompanied by multiple other forms of harassment. In other words, it is necessary to control for the shared variance with other forms in order to find out whether cybervictimization has *unique* or *additional* harmful effects on the individuals targeted.

Our study has practical implications as well. Although teachers might feel that preventing and reducing cyberbullying is beyond their responsibility (and capability), our findings suggest that cyberbullying can be reduced by a well-planned, general anti-bullying intervention implemented at school, such as KiVa in Finland. It is impossible to say whether student lessons focusing especially on cyberbullying, or the more general program components, were most influential, however. As a general recommendation, it could be concluded that it is important to address several forms of harassment (including cyberbullying) in anti-bullying programs, rather than develop specific, separate programs to tackle the various forms.

Acknowledgments

The studies presented in this chapter were supported by the European DAPHNE project, "An investigation into forms of peer–peer bullying at school in preadolescent and adolescent groups: New instruments and preventing strategies (2006–2009)" and by the Academy of Finland (grant no. 121091 to the first author).

Appendix: The definition and questions concerning bullying others and being bullied in the KiVa study, based on the OBV questionnaire; Olweus (1996)

It is *bullying* when another student makes a child feel bad *on purpose and repeatedly*. The child being bullied finds it *difficult to defend himself/herself*.

A student is being bullied when one or more other students

- say mean or hurtful things, make fun of him, or call him mean and hurtful names;
- completely ignore him, exclude him from their group of friends, or leave him out of things on purpose;
- hit, kick, shove or order him about or lock him inside a room;
- try to make other students dislike him by spreading lies about him or by sending mean notes;
- do other hurtful things like those above.

Also, it is bullying when a student is teased repeatedly in a mean and hurtful way.

Friendly and playful teasing *is not bullying. Neither is it bullying* when two more or less equally strong students argue or fight.

Please keep this explanation of bullying in mind when you answer the following questions.

When you answer the following questions about bullying, do not concentrate on how things are right now. Instead, think about **the time after winter break** *[as the questionnaires were filled out in May, this meant a 2–3 -month period before answering]*.

[SHORT DEFINITION]

It is *bullying* when another student makes a child feel bad *on purpose and repeatedly*.

[GLOBAL QUESTION]
How many times have you bullied others/been bullied at school during the past couple of months?

a) I have not bullied/ been bullied
b) Once or twice
c) Two or three times a month
d) About once a week
e) Several times a week

[SPECIFIC QUESTIONS—DIFFERENT FORMS OF BULLYING / BEING BULLIED]
Have you bullied others/been bullied by others at school during the past couple of months in this way?

[The short definition and this question were presented before each item. Each question was presented on separate page, so that they were seen one by one on the computer screen.]

(verbal)
I called someone names, made fun of her or teased her in a hurtful way.
I was called mean names, was made fun of or teased in a hurtful way.

(social exclusion)
I ignored someone completely or excluded her from things or from my group of friends.
Other students ignored me completely or excluded me from things or from their group of friends.

(physical)
I hit, kicked, or shoved someone.
I was hit, kicked, or shoved.

(social manipulation)
I tried to make others dislike someone by spreading lies about him.
Other students tried to make others dislike me by spreading lies about me.

(taking/damaging property)
I took money or other things from someone or damaged someone's belongings.
Somebody took money or other things from me or damaged my belongings.

(threatening, forcing)
I threatened someone or forced someone to do things she did not want to do.
I was threatened or forced to do things I did not want to do.

(racist)
I made nasty remarks about someone's ethnicity or skin color.
I was bullied by making nasty remarks or gestures about my ethnicity or skin color. Such a name can be, for example, *nigger*.

(sexual)
I bullied someone by sexual name calling, gestures, or actions.
I was bullied by sexual name calling, gestures, or actions.

(cyber)
I bullied someone by cell phone or through the Internet. I sent mean or hurtful messages, calls, or pictures [Please also report any other ways of bullying by means of a cell phone or a computer.]
I was bullied by cell phone or through the Internet: I received mean or hurtful messages, calls, or pictures. [Please also report any other ways of bullying by means of a cell phone or a computer.]

References

Cillessen, A. H. N., & Mayeux, L. (2004). From censure to reinforcement: Developmental changes in the association between aggression and social status. *Child Development, 75*, 147–163.

Flash Eurobarometer. (2008). Towards a safer use of the Internet for children in the EU—A parent's perspective. Survey requested by the Directorate General Information Society and Media, and coordinated by Directorate General Communication, European Commission.

Juvonen, J., Graham, S., & Schuster, M. (2003). Bullying among young adolescents: The strong, the weak, and the troubled. *Pediatrics, 112*, 1231–1237.

Kärnä, A., Voeten, M., Little, T., Poskiparta, E., Kaljonen, A., & Salmivalli, C. (2011). A large-scale evaluation of the KiVa anti-bullying program: Grades 4–6. *Child Development, 82*, 311–330.

Katzer, C., Fetchenhauer, D., & Belschak, F. (2009). Cyberbullying. Who are the victims? A comparison of victimization in Internet chatrooms and victimization in school. *Journal of Media Psychology, 21*, 25–36.

Olweus, D. (1978). *Aggression in schools: Bullies and whipping boys*. Washington, DC: Hemisphere.

Olweus, D. (1995). Bullying or peer abuse at school: facts and interventions. *Current Directions in Psychological Science, 4*, 196–200.

Olweus, D. (1996). *The revised Olweus bully/victim questionnaire*. Bergen, Norway: Research Center for Health Promotion (HEMIL Center), University of Bergen.

Pellegrini, A. (2002). Bullying, victimization, and sexual harassment during the transition to middle school. *Educational Psychologist, 37*, 151–163.

Raskauskas, J., & Stolz, A. D. (2007). Involvement in traditional and electronic bullying among adolescents. *Developmental Psychology, 43*, 564–575.

Rodkin, P., Farmer, T., Pearl, R., & Van Acker, R. (2006). They're cool: Social status and peer group supports for aggressive boys and girls. *Social Development, 15*, 175–204.

Salmivalli, C., Kärnä, A., & Poskiparta, E. (2010a). From peer putdowns to peer support: A theoretical model and how it translated into a national anti-bullying program. In S. Jimerson, S. Swearer, & D. Espelage (Eds.), *Handbook of bullying in schools: An international perspective* (pp. 441–454). New York: Routledge.

Salmivalli, C., Kärnä, A., & Poskiparta, E. (2010b). Development, evaluation, and diffusion of a national anti-bullying program (KiVa). In B. Doll, W. Pfohl, & J. Yoon (Eds.), *Handbook of youth prevention acience* (pp. 238–252). New York: Routledge.

Salmivalli, C., Kärnä, A., & Poskiparta, E. (2011). Counteracting bullying in Finland: The KiVa Program and its effects on different forms of being bullied. *International Journal of Behavioral Development, 35*, 405–411.

Salmivalli, C., Lagerspetz, K., Björkqvist, K., Österman, K., & Kaukiainen, A. (1996). Bullying as a group process: Participant roles and their relations to social status within the group. *Aggressive Behavior, 22*, 1–15.

Salmivalli, C., & Peets, K. (2009). Bullies, victims, and bully–victim relationships. In K. Rubin, W. Bukowski, & B. Laursen (Eds.), *Handbook of peer interactions, relationships, and groups* (pp. 322–340). New York: Guilford Press.

Save the Children Finland. (2008). *Lapsen ääni -kysely. Raportti lasten netin käytöstä*. Helsinki: Pelastakaa lapset ry.

Sijtsema, J., Veenstra, R., Lindenberg, S., & Salmivalli, C. (2009). An empirical test of bullies' status goals: Assessing direct goals, aggression, and prestige. *Aggressive Behavior, 35*, 57–67.

Smith, P. K., Mahdavi, J., Carvalho, M., Fisher, S., Russell, S., & Tippett, N. (2008). Cyberbullying: its nature and impact in secondary school pupils. *Journal of Child Psychology and Psychiatry, 49*, 376–385.

Solberg, M. E., & Olweus, D. (2003). Prevalence estimation of school bullying with the Olweus Bully/Victim questionnaire. *Aggressive Behavior, 29*, 239–268.

Tossavainen, T. (2008). Internet lasten ja nuorten elämässä—selvitys pääkaupunkiseudun 10–18 -vuotiaiden lasten ja nuorten elämästä Internetissä. Helsinki: Toinen elämä – hanke.

Ttofi, M., Farrington, D. P., & Baldry, A. C. (2008). *Effectiveness of programmes to reduce school bullying: A systematic review*. Report prepared for the Swedish National Council for Crime Prevention. Västerås, Sweden: Edita Norstedts.

Woods, S., & Wolke, D. (2003). Does the content of anti-bullying policies inform us about the prevalence of direct and relational bullying behavior in primary schools? *Educational Psychology, 23*, 381–401.

Part III

Studies in Commonwealth Countries

5

Cyberbullying in Australia

Is School Context Related to Cyberbullying Behavior?

Donna Cross, Therese Shaw, Melanie Epstein, Helen Monks, Julian Dooley, and Lydia Hearn

Information and Communication Technology (ICT) permeates all aspects of society in Australia. Since the introduction of the Internet into Australia some 20 years ago the majority of Australian households (72% in 2008–2009) have access to the Internet (Australian Bureau of Statistics, 2009). By mid-2009 over 24 million active mobile phone services were used in Australia, amounting to more than one phone per person (Australian Communications and Media Authority, 2010). Increasingly, young people are entering the mobile phone market with 76% of 12–14-year-olds having their own phone (Australian Bureau of Statistics, 2010). Despite the infiltration of mobile phones into the youth market, the majority of phone contact (60%) made is among family members rather than peers (Australian Bureau of Statistics, 2009).

Recent Australian estimates suggest that Internet use (that is, hours per day) among young people increases significantly with age (Australian Communications and Media Authority, 2009). Eight- to eleven-year-olds in Australia reported using the Internet for an average of 30 minutes per day, which steadily increased to two hours and 24 minutes per day among 15–17-year-olds. Likewise, the reason for using the Internet varied with age with younger children (5–11-year-olds) using it to play online games and for educational activities, whereas older children (12–14-year-olds) were more likely to interact with other people online as well as search for music, send and receive emails, and search for information for school homework and projects. These types of peer-to-peer related activities can result in specific types of safety risks and, consistently, the most likely risk for young people comes from their peers in the form of bullying (that is, cyberbullying; Dooley, Cross, Hearn, & Treyvaud, 2009).

Cyberbullying was first mentioned in the Australian press in August 2003 following an informal survey of student cyberbullying behaviors in 40 schools in

Cyberbullying in the Global Playground: Research from International Perspectives, First Edition.
Edited by Qing Li, Donna Cross, and Peter K. Smith.

New South Wales. The first Australian peer-reviewed research publications addressing cyberbullying followed in 2004 (Fleming & Rickwood, 2004) and 2005 (Campbell, 2005). Despite growing public concern about cyberbullying in Australia and young people's increasing access to technology, very little was known by adults about this online behavior (Campbell, 2005).

Data collected prior to the study reported in this chapter (2005 and 2006) found that 8–10% of young people aged 12–14 years reported being cyberbullied and 6% reported cyberbullying others every few weeks or more often in the previous term at school. In these studies cyberbullying was described as sending nasty or threatening messages via a mobile phone or the Internet (for example, through MSN Messenger or email), where private emails, messages, pictures, or videos are sent to others to hurt someone, or where an identity or password is "stolen" to send hurtful messages online to others (Waters, Epstein, Cross, & Shaw, 2007).

Although there are obvious differences between cyber- and face-to-face bullying (for example, repetition effect, anonymity effect; see Dooley, Pyzalski, & Cross, 2009), there are also many important similarities. The vast majority of young people who reported being cyberbullied online also reported being bullied offline, and similarly the majority of young people who reported bullying others online also reported bullying others offline (Cross et al., 2009). These findings highlight the behavioral basis of cyberbullying and face-to-face bullying and provide strong evidence that these two forms of bullying are more similar than not.

School-Level Initiatives to Reduce All Forms of Bullying in Australia

The Australian Commonwealth government has implemented numerous ecological initiatives that acknowledge the strong influence of schools' structural, functional, and physical environment and interpersonal relationships on the academic and health outcomes of students. Australian-based research conducted by Waters, Cross, and Runions (2009) suggests the structure of a school including its size, sector, and organization (such as leadership and policies) and functionality (for example, pastoral care practices and teaching practices) help to create a positive school ecology which appears to directly influence adolescent behavior.

The most recent and widespread of these ecological initiatives in Australia is the National Safe Schools Framework (NSSF) which aimed to embed whole school policies and practices to enhance and maintain student safety and wellbeing (Ministerial Council on Education, Employment Training and Youth Affairs, 2003). Through the NSSF, schools throughout Australia are encouraged to provide policy and practices that positively influence the school context to reduce all forms of bullying behavior. The NSSF was developed to address Australia's concerns regarding both the extent and serious effects of youth violence, harassment, child abuse, and bullying among Australian students (Commonwealth Government of Australia, 1994; Rigby & Slee, 1999).

It aimed to promote the importance of a shared vision of physical and emotional safety and wellbeing for all students in Australian schools (Ministerial Council on Education, Employment Training and Youth Affairs, 2003).

In 2007, in response to young people's increasing access to ICT and general concern that cyberbullying and other forms of covert bullying (that is, bullying behaviors that are not easily seen) may become more prevalent among school-age students in Australia, the government commissioned several studies to better understand how to address young people's covert and especially cyberbullying behavior (Bhat, 2008; Hanewald, 2008). One of these studies was the Australian Covert Bullying Prevalence Study (ACBPS) (Cross et al., 2009), and the other, "Behind the Scenes: Insights into the Human Dimension of Covert Bullying," was a smaller-scale qualitative study (Spears, Slee, Owens, Johnson, & Campbell, 2008).

The ACBPS, conducted by the authors, aimed to redress the lack of current and reliable evidence about the school context, nature, and prevalence of cyber and other covert bullying behaviors among fourth to ninth-grade students in Australia, and to use these data as a benchmark to identify further feasible, promising, and sustainable policy and practice options for Australian schools. The ACBPS comprised five qualitative and quantitative phases of data collection as described in Figure 5.1.

The largest of the ACBPS data collection phases was Phase 4, a nationally representative quantitative study. This chapter describes the prevalence of cyber-bullying as reported by this representative sample of 9–14-year-old primary and secondary Australian students in 2007 and 2008. We also examine the association between these students' reported cyberbullying experiences and their aggregated school-level (versus individual level) perceptions of: (a) staff and students' attitudes to cyberbullying; (b) staff management of bullying; (c) academic achievement; (d) engagement in problem behaviors; (e) school rules related to mobile phone and Internet use; (f) loneliness at school; and (g) connectedness to school. Specifically, this chapter describes the prevalence of cyberbullying in Australia and school-level contextual factors associated with student reported rates of cyberbullying victimization and perpetration.

Method

The ACBPS involved a cross-sectional quantitative survey of 7418 Australian school students aged 8 to 14 years from 106 schools. Schools across all education sectors and States and Territories of Australia were recruited into the study.

Sampling schools

This study aimed to recruit and sample a total of 100 schools (50 primary and 50 secondary schools) across the eight Australian states and territories. The target population for the survey was all students enrolled in grades 4 to 9 (aged 9–14 years)

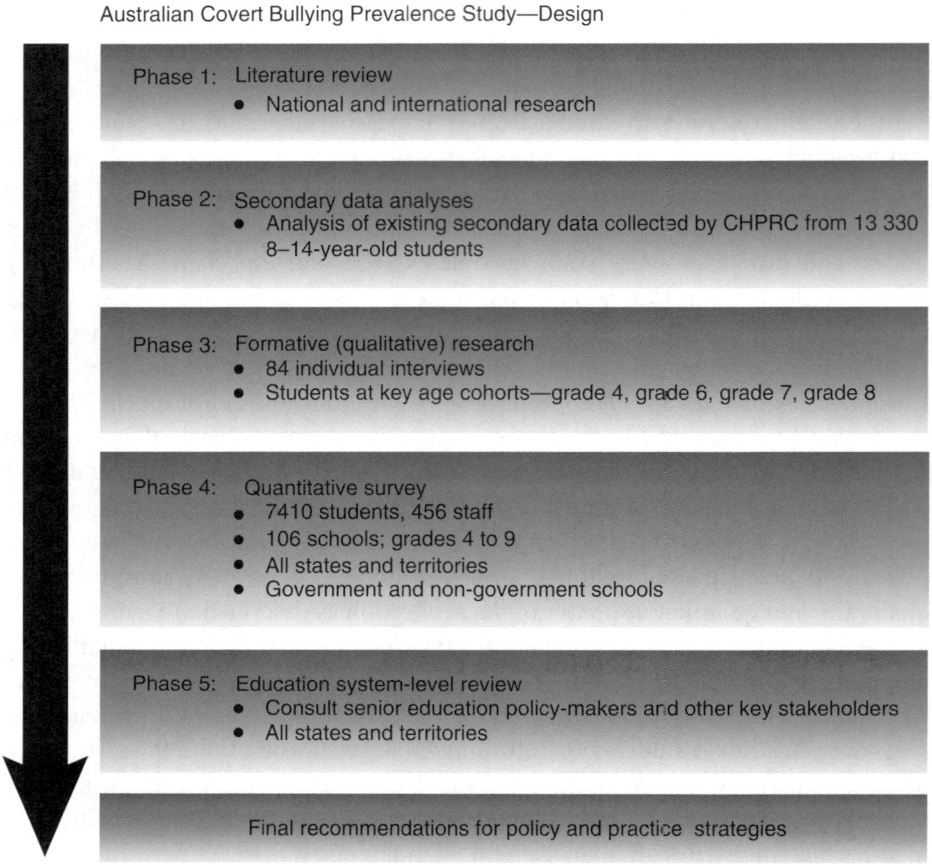

Figure 5.1 Australian Covert Bullying Prevalence Study—Design. Created by Donna Cross, Therese Shaw, Melanie Epstein, Helen Monks, Julian Dooley, & Lydia Hearn.

across all the education sectors in Australia. There are two main education sectors in Australia, government and non-government schools. Government schools are non-denominational, and the majority of students in Australia attend these public schools. Non-government schools, which are attended by approximately 30% of students in Australia, include Catholic schools, or independent schools, some of which may have a religious affiliation and some of which are non-denominational.

The target population included all primary and secondary schools in Australia. The transition from primary to secondary school occurs at slightly different times in the different states and territories of Australia, with secondary schools in some Australian states/territories beginning with grade 7 students, whereas in other states/territories students transition to secondary school in grade 8. Thus, the sub-sample of grade 7 students in this study includes students in their final year of primary school and others in their first year of secondary school, depending on when the transition to secondary school occurred in each state/territory.

Schools were sampled using a stratified sampling technique. Sufficient students were sampled within each stratum to enable adequate precision of prevalence estimates—this equated to approximately 100 primary and 100 secondary students per stratum. All schools that met the inclusion criteria were stratified by state and then by location (metropolitan or non-metropolitan). Some of the strata were further divided by sector (i.e., government or non-government) or, where school numbers permitted, by government or Catholic or other independent schools. A total of 25 strata were formed and the study aimed to recruit two primary and two secondary schools, randomly drawn from each stratum. Schools were therefore not sampled proportionately but instead to ensure that sufficient students were recruited in each stratum to generate prevalence estimates (i.e., by state, sector, and location).

Sampling classes and students

Schools were selected at the first stage of the sampling and classes within the schools at the second stage. Samples were drawn separately for primary schools (grades 4 to 6/7; ages 9 to 11/12) and secondary schools (grades 7/8 to 9; ages 12/13 to 14). Each school was asked to randomly select the required number of classes of students. Schools were asked to choose from heterogeneous classes (i.e., those not streamed by academic ability). Two to three classes of students were selected randomly per grade level per school to obtain 17–25 completed questionnaires per grade level per school.

Parental/caregiver consent was necessary for any student to participate in the project. Ethics approval was obtained by the relevant authority in each state/territory before the project commenced (this process took approximately three months).

Response rates

In total 106 schools (55 primary and 51 secondary) participated in the study. This represents 46% of the 229 schools approached, of whom 124 agreed to participate in the study (54%). Eighteen schools (15%) did not return surveys due to time constraints and flood damage to survey forms. An overall parental/caregiver consent rate of 62% was achieved. Approximately 4% of parents approached returned consent forms indicating they *did not* wish their child to participate. In total, of the 8782 students whose parents provided consent, useable surveys (i.e., surveys which were completed appropriately) were obtained from 85% (n = 7418). The frequency and percentage of respondents by grade level, gender, and location are shown in Table 5.1.

Table 5.1 Student Respondents by Key Demographics.

	Frequency	*Percentage*
Grade level		
Grade 4	1412	19
Grade 5	1291	17
Grade 6	1279	17
Grade 7—Primary	686	9
Grade 7—Secondary	628	9
Grade 8	1094	15
Grade 9	1028	14
Gender		
Male	3521	48
Female	3874	52
Area		
Metropolitan	4760	64
Non-metropolitan	2658	36
Total	7418	

Instruments and measures

The student survey instrument developed for this study was used for primary and secondary students, to ensure comparability of data across school grade levels.

Global measures of bullying (any form)

Student reports of how often they were bullied and/or bullied others were measured using two items adapted from the Olweus Bully/Victim Questionnaire (Olweus, 1996) and the Rigby and Slee Peer Relations Questionnaire (Rigby, 1998). These adapted global bullying items were previously tested for reliability with Australian students ($n \approx 140$) and found to have moderate levels of reliability (being bullied $\kappa_w = 0.54$ and bullying others $\kappa_w = 0.45$). Consistent with previous research, response choices referred to a specific time period (i.e., during the last 10-week term at school) and referred to the repeated nature of bullying behavior (Solberg & Olweus, 2003).

To obtain prevalence estimates students were categorized, based on their responses to the two global questions, as having been bullied or having bullied others (in any way, including cyberbullying) if they indicated they were bullied by another student or group of students or had bullied another student(s) every few weeks or more often in the last 10-week term at school. The requirement that the behavior was experienced or perpetrated "every few weeks or more often" when defining groups that are bullied or bully others was made to incorporate the repeated nature of bullying behavior.

Measures of cyberbullying behaviors

The items used to measure specific cyberbullying behaviors were generated using focused semi-formal (qualitative) interviews with 84 students aged 10 to 14 years, who represented but were not part of the study cohort. Students recommended using a list of cyberbullying behaviors that they described. Scales were developed listing these common cyberbullying behaviors experienced (see below) and perpetrated by these young people. Internal consistency reliability for these data was good for the victimization items (Cronbach's alpha = 0.86; item-to-total correlation coefficients ranged from 0.51 to 0.67) and perpetration items (Cronbach's alpha = 0.88; item-to-total correlations ranged from 0.60 to 0.70).
The cybervictimization items were:

- being sent threatening emails
- being sent nasty messages on the Internet (e.g., through MSN Messenger)
- being sent nasty text messages or receiving prank calls on their mobile phone
- someone pretending to be the student (using their screen name or password) to hurt him
- someone sending a student's private emails, messages, pictures, or videos to others
- mean or nasty comments or pictures about the student being sent or posted to websites (e.g., MySpace, Facebook)
- mean or nasty messages or pictures about the student being sent to other students' mobile phones
- being deliberately ignored or left out of things over the Internet.

Perpetration of cyberbullying behaviors was measured with the same items reworded accordingly.

The four cyberbullying scales were used to categorize the respondents according to their exposure to and engagement in cyberbullying behaviors: (a) "exposure to cyberbullying behaviors" was defined as having experienced any one of eight listed forms of cyberbullying behaviors once or more often in the last term, and (b) "being cyberbullied" was defined as repeatedly being cyberbullied every few weeks or more often in the preceding term. Students were defined as (c) "having perpetrated cyberbullying behaviors" and (d) "having cyberbullied others" in a similar way. Once again students needed to be exposed to/perpetrate this behavior repeatedly to be categorized as being cyberbullied/having cyberbullied others.

Measures of school context

Several variables, aggregated to the school level, were used to measure the association between cyberbullying outcomes and school context. These contextual variables included staff attitudes to/management of bullying; students' support for students who are bullied; student perception of their academic achievement; student engagement in problem behaviors; school rules related to mobile phone and Internet use; loneliness at school; and connectedness to school.

Staff attitudes to/management of bullying was used to determine whether students perceive their school promotes a culture that discourages bullying behavior. Students were asked to indicate their perception on a ten-item scale, their level of agreement on a Likert scale, ranging from strongly disagree (1) to strongly agree (5), and a mean score was calculated at the school level. The ten items were as follows: Most staff are friendly to each other; most staff try to stop bullying; most staff are available to talk to about bullying; most staff take bullying seriously; reports of bullying are dealt with immediately; help is provided to students who are bullied; help is provided to students who bully others; the way students are expected to behave is fair; the way most staff deal with bullying is fair; and we have a policy about how the school will respond to bullying. Internal consistency was α = 0.85, with item-to-total correlations ranging from 0.43 to 0.67.

Students' support for students who are bullied was calculated at the school level as the mean of student responses to two items ("Most students in my grade level stick up for someone who is being bullied" and "Most students in my grade level report bullying") on a Likert scale ranging from strongly agree to strongly disagree. As there were only two items in this scale, reliability statistics were not calculated.

Student perception of their academic achievement was calculated at the school level as the percentage of students who reported perceiving that they achieved worse results than others in their grade level in their last school report. This variable was measured using one item with four response options. Students were asked to indicate whether they performed better than, about the same as, or not as well as most other students in their grade level or whether they didn't know.

Student engagement in problem behaviors was measured using a 12-item scale adapted from a questionnaire developed by Resnicow, Ross-Gaddy, and Vaughan (1995). Students were asked how many times in the past month they had engaged in 12 problem behaviors such as stealing from a shop, getting into an argument with their friends or parents, destroying property, drinking alcohol, or smoking. The response choices were: "never," "once," "twice," "three times," or "more than three times." Internal consistency reliability for these items was 0.84, with item-to-total correlations between 0.44 and 0.61. A school-level problem behavior engagement score was calculated as the mean of the twelve items.

School rules related to mobile phone and Internet use measures asked students if they have rules about when and for how long they can use the Internet and/or mobile phone at school, using one of three response options; "yes," "no," or "I don't have access to this." Two scores were calculated: The percentage of students at the school level who identify there are rules at their school about their mobile phone use and the percentage of students at the school level who identify there are rules about their Internet use.

The *loneliness at school* nine-item scale was adapted from the Loneliness and Social Dissatisfaction Questionnaire developed by Cassidy and Asher (1992). This scale asked students to indicate their level of agreement to a list of seven statements, including: "I have nobody to talk to in my classes," "It's hard for me to make friends at school," "I feel left out of things at school," and "I'm lonely at school." The internal consistency of the scale was good (Cronbach's alpha = 0.84, item-to-total correlations ranged from 0.49 to 0.74). A mean of students' scores was calculated and ranged from 1 (strongly disagree) to 5 (strongly agree), across nine items.

A *connectedness to school* score was adapted from the National Longitudinal Study of Adolescent Health (Resnick et al., 1997; McNeely, Nonnemaker, & Blum, 2002). This scale asks students how they feel about their school and provides four response options: "I feel close to people at this school," "I feel like I am part of this school," "I am happy to be at this school," and "I am treated fairly by teachers at this school." A fifth item was added to this scale, adapted from the Peer Relations Questionnaire (Rigby, 1998), which measured how often students feel safe at school ("always," "usually," "sometimes," "never," or "unsure"). The internal consistency for the scale was good (Cronbach's alpha = 0.80, item-to-total correlations ranged from 0.49 to 0.69). The school level score was calculated as the mean of the five items.

Other school-level variables included in these analyses were the location of the school (metropolitan versus non-metropolitan), the total number of students enrolled at each school, grade level, and each school's Socio-Economic Status (SES) which was calculated using the Socio-Economic Indexes for Areas (SEIFA) combined index of social advantage/disadvantage (Australian Bureau of Statistics, 2001). Where required, analyses controlled for school sector (government versus non-government), Australian state/territory, and student gender.

Data collection methods

Surveys were administered during school time in the months of October and November, 2007 by the teachers of the fourth to ninth grade classes. Teachers were given a standardized survey administration protocol and briefed by a staff member in their school previously trained by the research team. The self-administered questionnaire was read aloud by the classroom teacher to the grade 4 to 6 students only (grade 7 to 9 students read their own questionnaires, but teaching staff were available to clarify any instructions).

Respondents' anonymity was maintained through the use of identification numbers and teachers were asked not to answer any questions students may have relating to the questionnaire content while administering the questionnaire, or look at students' responses. Student surveys were collected by the classroom teacher and mailed to the research team.

Data analysis

Prevalence of cyberbullying

Prevalence figures were obtained (using the survey estimate commands in the software program Stata 10 after weighting the survey data to account for the sampling methods and allow for inferences to be drawn regarding the Australian population.

The key demographic variables considered were each student's sex, whether they lived in metropolitan or non-metropolitan areas, and their grade level at school. As noted earlier, since the transition from primary to secondary school differs between states/territories in Australia a distinction was made between grade 7 students in primary and those in secondary schools. Associations between these demographic variables and bullying behaviors were tested in multivariable logistic regression models with random intercepts fitted in Stata 10.

School-level contextual factors associated with cyberbullying

Analyses were conducted separately for primary and secondary schools to assess school-level contextual factors associated with cyberbullying. To reduce the impact of skew in the data, the cyberbullying mean scores were analyzed using three categories ("not involved," "1–2 times last term," "every few weeks or more often last term"). Contextual effects were assessed using the mean centering and modeling approach described in Raudenbush and Bryk (2002). This approach tests for differences between students with the same characteristics, in schools that differ with regard to the contextual variable being assessed. Thus the tests were not assessing individual differences between students on the contextual factor, but differences between schools with different levels of the contextual factor. For example, when assessing the role of school connectedness, the test determined whether there are differences in the cyberbullying scores of two students who have the same connectedness to school but are in schools where the average connectedness of the student body in the schools is different. Random coefficient linear models were fitted in Stata 10 to account for school-level clustering.

Results

Prevalence of bullying

Overall, 27% of students reported being bullied (any form including cyber), and 9% reported they bullied others (any form including cyber) in the previous 10-week school term (see Figures 5.2 and 5.3).

Prevalence of cyberbullying

Six percent of students reported they were cyberbullied (repeatedly exposed—every few weeks or more often) (Table 5.2), whereas about a quarter (23%) reported being

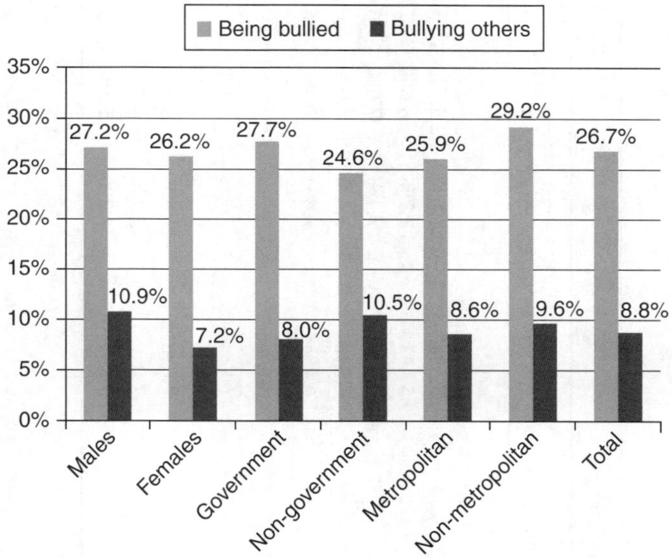

Figure 5.2 Prevalence of Being Bullied and Bullying Others by Key Demographics. "Bullying" is defined as occurring every few weeks or more often. Created by Donna Cross, Therese Shaw, Melanie Epstein, Helen Monks, Julian Dooley, & Lydia Hearn.

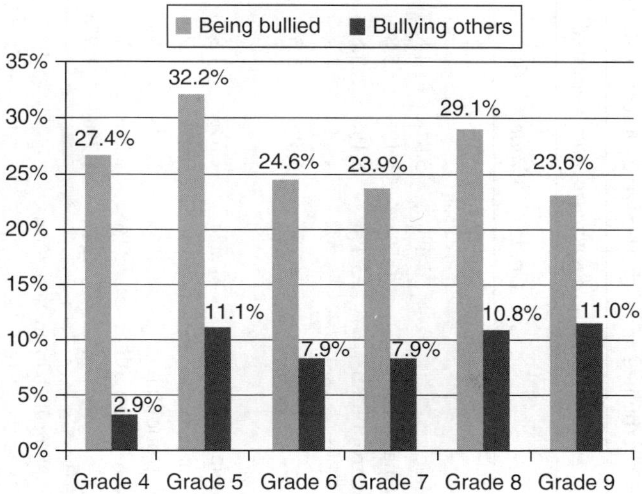

Figure 5.3 Prevalence of Being Bullied and Bullying Others by Grade Level. "Bullying" is defined as occurring every few weeks or more often. Created by Donna Cross, Therese Shaw, Melanie Epstein, Helen Monks, Julian Dooley, & Lydia Hearn.

exposed to cyberbullying behaviors once or more often in the prior term (Table 5.3). Similar differences were observed for cyberbullying others: 3% reported they cyberbullied others (repeatedly perpetrated—every few weeks or more often) and 18% reported they engaged in cyberbullying behaviors at least once in the previous term (Tables 5.3 and 5.4).

Table 5.2 Prevalence of Being Cyberbullied and Cyberbullying Others by Key Demographics.

		Prevalence rates: Repeated[a] *cyberbullying behaviors*							
		Grade 4	*Grade 5*	*Grade 6*	*Grade 7—Primary*	*Grade 7—Secondary*	*Grade 8*	*Grade 9*	*Total*
Being cyberbullied									
By gender	Male	1.4%	5.8%	4.8%	4.2%	8.3%	5.0%	5.7%	5.0%
	Female	6.5%	5.1%	5.8%	7.1%	5.4%	8.7%	8.6%	7.0%
By area	Metropolitan	3.4%	6.1%	4.8%	6.4%	6.4%	7.4%	7.0%	6.0%
	Non-metropolitan	6.8%	3.4%	6.8%	3.2%	6.5%	7.4%	8.9%	6.7%
Total being cyberbullied		**4.1%**	**5.5%**	**5.3%**	**5.7%**	**6.4%**	**7.4%**	**7.5%**	**6.2%**
Cyberbullying others									
By gender	Male	.3%	2.5%	1.9%	2.4%	7.0%	4.0%	6.1%	3.4%
	Female	.1%	.9%	1.7%	.8%	2.1%	4.3%	4.9%	2.7%
By area	Metropolitan	.1%	1.7%	1.9%	1.8%	2.6%	3.9%	5.6%	2.8%
	Non-metropolitan	.5%	1.7%	1.7%	1.1%	7.0%	5.1%	4.6%	3.6%
Total cyberbullying others		**.2%**	**1.7%**	**1.9%**	**1.6%**	**3.8%**	**4.2%**	**5.3%**	**3.0%**

Note: [a]*Repeated*—every few weeks or more often in previous term.

Table 5.3 Prevalence of Exposure to or Perpetration of Cyberbullying Behaviors by Key Demographics.

		Prevalence rates: Any[a] *exposure to/perpetration of cyberbullying behaviors*							
		Grade 4	*Grade 5*	*Grade 6*	*Grade 7—Primary*	*Grade 7—Secondary*	*Grade 8*	*Grade 9*	*Australia*
Exposure									
By gender	Male	16.5%	16.8%	16.4%	12.7%	16.5%	16.2%	15.7%	16.1%
	Female	27.5%	25.5%	25.9%	28.3%	27.9%	31.2%	29.4%	28.3%
By area	Metropolitan	22.0%	20.7%	19.8%	23.2%	26.2%	24.4%	23.8%	22.8%
	Non-metropolitan	23.5%	22.6%	23.5%	12.9%	17.7%	29.4%	24.9%	23.7%
Total bullied		**22.3%**	**21.2%**	**20.7%**	**20.7%**	**24.0%**	**25.8%**	**24.1%**	**23.0%**
Perpetration									
By gender	Male	13.4%	8.8%	14.2%	12.3%	17.0%	18.2%	18.2%	14.7%
	Female	9.9%	13.0%	17.9%	17.1%	25.3%	29.5%	23.7%	21.1%
By area	Metropolitan	11.5%	10.4%	15.9%	16.0%	22.3%	26.8%	22.3%	18.6%
	Non-metropolitan	12.1%	13.0%	15.6%	10.8%	23.7%	21.2%	19.3%	17.6%
Total bullying others		**11.6%**	**11.0%**	**15.9%**	**14.8%**	**22.7%**	**25.3%**	**21.5%**	**18.3%**

Note: [a]*Any*—one or more times in previous term.

Table 5.4 Prevalence of *Repeated* and *Any* Cyberbullying Behaviors.

Being cyberbullied	Repeated[a]	Any[b]
Sent threatening emails	1.7%	4.9%
Sent nasty messages on the Internet (MSN)	3.0%	10.0%
Sent nasty text messages or prank calls to my mobile phone	1.9%	6.6%
Used my screen name or passwords, pretending to be me to hurt someone else	1.6%	6.4%
Sent my private emails, messages, pictures, or videos to others	0.7%	2.8%
Posted mean or nasty comments or pictures on websites about me	1.4%	5.8%
Sent mean or nasty messages or pictures about me to others' mobile phones	0.6%	2.8%
Deliberately ignored or left out of things over the Internet	2.4%	10.6%
Cyberbullying others		
Sent nasty or threatening emails	0.6%	2.5%
Sent nasty messages on the Internet (e.g., MSN)	1.5%	7.0%
Sent nasty text messages or prank calls to another student's mobile phone	1.2%	7.1%
Used another student's screen name or passwords, pretended to be them	0.8%	4.7%
Sent another student's private emails, messages, pictures, or videos to others	0.8%	2.2%
Posted mean or nasty comments or pictures on websites	0.7%	3.7%
Sent mean or nasty messages or pictures about another student to others' mobile phones	0.8%	2.2%
Deliberately ignored or left another student out of things over the Internet to hurt them	1.3%	6.2%

Note: [a]*Repeated*—every few weeks or more often in previous term. [b]*Any*—one or more times in previous term.

Being cyberbullied

As illustrated by the percentages in Table 5.3 and tested in multivariable logistic regression models, girls were more likely to be cyberbullied than boys (odds ratio = 1.5, 95% confidence interval (CI) range = 1.2–1.8) and were also more likely to report exposure to cyberbullying behaviors that occurred at least once in the previous term at school (Table 5.4; odds ratio = 1.7, 95% CI range = 1.5–1.9). The prevalence of being cyberbullied was slightly higher (although not statistically significant, $p = 0.074$) in secondary compared to primary school years (Table 5.2), and students in metropolitan and non-metropolitan areas did not differ with regard to their odds of being cyberbullied ($p = 0.347$). Likewise, the likelihood of any exposure is similar across grade levels ($p = 0.164$).

Cyberbullying others

In contrast to being cyberbullied, girls were less likely than boys to report cyberbullying others (odds ratio = 0.6, 95% CI range = 0.4–0.7). Older students were more likely to cyberbully others ($p < 0.001$), with all grade levels except grade 8 reporting significantly lower levels of cyberbullying than grade 9 students. Similarly, perpetration of one or more cyberbullying behaviors among older students is more common than among younger students ($p < 0.001$), with students in grades 4 to 6 less likely than those in grade 9 to report perpetrating cyberbullying behaviors at least once in the last term. The likelihood is similar for students in grades 7, 8, and 9. When comparing students in metropolitan and non-metropolitan areas, as for cybervictimization, there were no significant differences for cyberbullying others ($p = 0.578$) or exposing others to such behaviors at least once ($p = 0.863$).

When considering the different types of cyberbullying behaviors perpetrated using different media, the prevalence of *any* exposure/perpetration (i.e., once or more often in the previous term) for different cyberbullying behaviors was 1% to 9% higher than the prevalence of *repeated* exposure/perpetration (i.e., every few weeks or more often in the previous term) (Table 5.4). The most commonly reported cyberbullying behaviors experienced by students as a victim or a perpetrator were the same. As reported by students who were victimized, these behaviors included being sent nasty messages on the Internet (3% "repeated" and 10% "any") or on a mobile phone (2% "repeated" and 7% "any"), and being deliberately ignored or left out of things over the Internet (2% "repeated" and 11% "any"). The most commonly reported behaviors perpetrated were sending nasty messages on the Internet (2% "repeated" and 7% "any") or to someone's mobile phone (1% "repeated" and 7% "any") and deliberately ignoring or leaving someone out of things over the Internet to hurt them (1% "repeated" and 6% "any").

The relationship between all forms of bullying and cyberbullying

While the results for victimization and perpetration are presented separately above, it is of interest to assess the extent of the overlap between being cyberbullied and cyberbullying others and, additionally, the extent to which students involved in cyberbullying behaviors were also involved in other bullying.

Overall, most students (92%) reported not being cyberbullied or cyberbullying others. Five percent reported being cyberbullied but not cyberbullying others, 2% reported cyberbullying others but not being cyberbullied themselves, and 1% reported they were both cyberbullied and cyberbullied others.

A high reported overlap of cyberbullying and offline bullying behaviors were found in this study. Of those students who were cyberbullied, most (87%) reported also being bullied offline, with only 13% being cyberbullied only. Likewise of those

Table 5.5 School Contextual Factors for Cyberbullying Behaviors.

Variable	*Coefficient (SE)*	*Test of significance*
Primary schools—Likelihood of experiencing cyberbullying behaviors[a]		
Engagement in problem behaviors	0.21 (0.063)	z = 3.33, $p = 0.001$
Primary schools—Likelihood of perpetrating cyberbullying behaviors[b]		
Engagement in problem behaviors	0.20 (0.052)	z = 3.90, $p < 0.001$
School rules about Internet use	−0.11 (0.055)	z = −1.96, $p = 0.049$
School rules about mobile phone use	−0.25 (0.057)	z = −4.36, $p < 0.001$
Grade level		
Grade 5	0.03 (0.014)	z = 2.08, $p = 0.038$
Grade 6	0.08 (0.014)	z = 6.08, $p < 0.001$
Grade 7	0.10 (0.018)	z = 5.63, $p < 0.001$
Secondary schools—Likelihood of experiencing cyberbullying behaviors[c]		
Connectedness to school	0.10 (0.046)	z = 2.10, $p = 0.036$
Lower academic achievement	−0.62 (0.213)	z = −2.92, $p = 0.004$

Note: [a,c]Controlling for Australian state and student gender. [b]Controlling for Australian state.

who reported they cyberbullied others, about a quarter (23%) only cyberbullied others, whereas 77% bullied other students offline as well.

School-level contextual factors associated with cyberbullying

Contextual school effects were tested separately for primary and secondary schools. As shown in Table 5.5, students in primary schools with higher levels of self-reported engagement in problem behaviors were *more* likely to experience cyberbullying behaviors (z = 3.33, $p = 0.001$) and to perpetrate such behaviors (z = 3.90, $p < 0.001$). Further, students in primary schools with higher percentages of students who identify the school has rules related to the use of the Internet (z = −1.96, $p = 0.049$) and mobile phones (z = −4.36, $p < 0.001$) were *less* likely to report engagement in cyberbullying behaviors. Students in higher primary grades reported higher levels of perpetration of cyberbullying than those in lower grades.

The contextual factors associated with cyberbullying in secondary schools were different to those found in primary schools. Students in secondary schools with higher overall levels of school connectedness among students were *more* likely to experience cyberbullying behaviors (z = 2.10, $p = 0.036$). However, students in secondary schools with higher percentages of students reporting they do worse on average academically than their peers, were *less* likely to be exposed to cyberbullying (z = −2.92, $p = 0.004$). None of the other contextual variables tested (engagement in problem behaviors, grade level, school rules about mobile and Internet use) was significantly associated with secondary students' scores for perpetration of cyberbullying.

Discussion

Cyberbullying behaviors in Australia

The vast majority of Australian students aged 10 to 14 years report they are not cyberbullied and do not cyberbully others. Only 6% indicate they were cyberbullied every few weeks or more often during the last term (10 weeks) at school. Although the prevalence estimates of cyberbullying in countries other than Australia varied widely, largely due to different definitions of cyberbullying and the duration over which this behavior was measured (Smith & Slonje, 2010), the Australian findings for cyberbullying are similar to the reported prevalence of cyberbullying over comparable time periods and among similar age groups of students in other countries. For example, Smith and colleagues (2008) found 5% of UK students aged 11–16 years were cyberbullied in the last week or month; Ybarra, Diener-West, and Leaf (2007) found 8% of 10–15-year-old students in the US were harassed on the Internet monthly or more often; and Kapatzia and Sygkollitou (2007) found 6% of 14–19-year-old students in Greece reported being cyberbullied two or three times a month or more often.

While difficult to compare directly, 3% of Australian students report they cyberbullied others every few weeks or more often last term at school, and Smith et al. (2008) and Kapatzia and Sygkollitou (2007) found 7% cyberbullied others in the last week or month. As young people's access to ICT becomes more universal and mobile, these online bullying behaviors may well increase to levels akin to offline bullying. It is possible that since the ACBPS data collection (2007) this may already be the case.

Analogous to data reported in this chapter where 87% of Australian students who report they were cyberbullied also report they were face-to-face bullied, Smith and colleagues (2008) found 82% of 11–16-year-olds and Raskauskas and Stolz (2007) found 85% of 13–18-year-olds who were cyberbullied were also face-to-face bullied.

In terms of perpetration, the rates of students who reported they cyberbullied others and also face-to-face bullied others in Australia (77%) and those of Smith et al. (2008) in the UK (75%) and Raskauskas and Stolz (2007) in the US (94%) were also very similar. This high level of behavior transfer strongly suggests that ICT provides another means to experience/deliver "virtually" the same types of bullying behavior. Thus, if schools and families have effective strategies in place to prevent and manage young people's face-to-face bullying, these may also be effective to reduce the likelihood of cyberbullying behaviors.

Some research suggests students who are bullied by others in the schoolyard and other "real" environments often feel more comfortable communicating online, and are significantly more likely (51%) to engage in cyberbullying as a means of retaliating against serious conventional bullying (Ybarra, 2004), while other research found contrary evidence (Vandebosch & van Cleemput, 2009). In this Australian study, only 1% of the students bullied in any way reported bullying others online but not offline, therefore there is no evidence in these data that this form of retaliation is occurring in Australia at this time.

School-level contextual factors associated with cyberbullying behaviors

Lee (1999) suggests school-level (socio-ecological) factors that encourage positive relationships between and support for others, along with other structural and functional features such as size, leadership, policies, pastoral care practices, and teaching practices, are key to shaping the academic, health, and social outcomes of students. This study involving over 100 Australian schools provides a unique opportunity to investigate the extent to which school-level contextual factors are associated with cyberbullying behaviors.

Most research to date has examined individual and classroom-level factors associated with cyberbullying behavior (e.g., peer support, loneliness, safety at school, school connectedness). Identifying significant school-level socio-ecological factors that moderate the effects of individual differences on cyberbullying behaviors will help to enhance whole-school interventions to reduce cyberbullying. In this study only five of the eight school-level contextual variables tested were associated with cyberbullying behaviors; three in primary schools and two in secondary schools.

School rules about mobile phone and Internet use

Farrington and Ttofi (2009) found that among the most important program elements associated with a reduction in bullying others were classroom rules against bullying and effective classroom management techniques to identify and respond to instances of bullying. Given most cyberbullying typically occurs outside of school hours, it is important to know whether school rules about mobile phone and Internet use are associated with fewer cyberbullying behaviors. Interestingly, in this study school rules about mobile phone use and Internet use were associated with a lower likelihood of exposure to cyberbullying, but only in primary schools, not secondary schools. This relationship may be because the majority of primary school students have more limited access to a mobile phone and the Internet and/or are more willing to comply with school rules than secondary students. It may also be that in schools with raised student awareness of school rules, there is also raised awareness regarding cyber issues and thus less cyberbullying.

Students' active involvement in decision making about school rules in primary and especially secondary schools may result in them developing a better understanding of the purpose of these rules, and ultimately view these rules more as behavioral expectations with rights and responsibilities than draconian measures designed to take the fun out of spending time online.

Internet filters to enforce school rules are another necessary but potentially insufficient measure to keep young people safer online. Internet filters appear to be more effective for primary school students than secondary students, who may use proxy servers to bypass filters used in schools and on home computers (Agatston & Limber, 2007). Hence, understanding and ownership of rules by young people and close positive support and monitoring of these rules rather than relying on only filters may enhance the effectiveness of school rules to reduce cyberbullying. Last, it may also be helpful to policy makers, practitioners, and parents to know if school Internet and mobile phone rules need to comprise a balance of social rules and usage rules such as restrictions on time and places the technology is allowed, to reduce the occurrence of cyberbullying.

Problem behaviors

According to Problem Behavior Theory, one reason why young people's "problem" behaviors tend to cluster is that society views each of them as unacceptable, deviant, or rebellious (Resnicow, Ross-Gaddy, & Vaughan, 1995). Accordingly, it may be that adolescents who engage in bullying behaviors, due to societal norms, feel they have crossed the boundary of acceptable conduct, and become part of a "deviant" subculture, where these behaviors are more prevalent and acceptable. In this study students' involvement with cyberbullying was more likely in primary schools if the schools had higher overall levels of reported problem behaviors. These findings are similar to research conducted in US schools, suggesting that many common problem behaviors such as engaging in smoking, drinking alcohol and substance abuse (Kaltiala-Heino, Rimpela, Rantanen, & Rimpela, 2000; Nansel, Overpeck, Pilla, & Ruan, 2001; Strabstein & Piazza, 2008), as well as intentionally hurting animals or other people and weapon-carrying (Strabstein & Piazza, 2008), are associated with the perpetration of face-to-face bullying and cyberbullying (Hinduja & Patchin, 2007; Sourander et al., 2010).

Problem Behavior Theory suggests that if students felt less disapproval or marginalization for their poor behavior, they may be more likely to remain within common societal bounds. In other words, it may be beneficial for schools to emphasize that cyberbullying is a teenage behavior with potential negative health effects and other consequences that need to be addressed rather than a discipline problem only. This approach is used somewhat effectively to reduce both the onset and regular use of cigarettes (Hamilton, Cross, Resnicow, & Hall, 2005).

Connectedness to school is described by Resnick et al. (1997, p. 823) as an "adolescent's experience of caring at school and sense of closeness to school personnel and environment." It has been associated with numerous positive student outcomes including decreased risk of violence and depressive symptoms, enhanced emotional well-being, fewer substance use problems, and reduced suicide ideation (McBride, Midford, & James, 1995; Resnick et al., 1997; Catalano, Haggerty, Oesterle, Fleming, & Hawkins, 2004; McNeely & Falci, 2004; Patton et al., 2006). The findings in this study suggest that the likelihood of being exposed to cyberbullying was higher in secondary schools if school-level connectedness was *higher*. This finding is counter to connectedness research conducted at an individual level. Williams and Guerra (2007) found students who reported greater connectedness to school and a positive school climate had a reduced likelihood of bullying and cyberbullying others. It appears in this study that connectedness as measured was not a protective factor for secondary school students' cyberbullying behaviors.

Also counter to expectations, students were *less* likely to report being cyberbullied if *higher* percentages of students at the school level see themselves as achieving below average compared to schools where fewer students report this. Some other cross-sectional studies indicate that being bullied (Eisenberg, Neumark-Sztainer, & Perry, 2003; Glew, Fan, Katon, Rivara, & Kernic, 2005), bullying others (Nansel et al., 2001), concurrently being bullied and bullying others (Nansel et al., 2001; Glew et al., 2005), and being cyberbullied (Erdur-Baker & Kavsut, 2007) are all associated with impaired academic achievement. One study suggests that students with poor academic performance report the highest frequency of being bullied (Eisenberg et al., 2003), possibly due to factors such as absenteeism or poor concentration. Nonetheless, the school-level assessment of academic achievement examined in this study provided the opposite result. This finding may, however, be confounded by students' social-economic status (SES), such that students attending schools reporting lower than average mean achievement may (a) reside in lower SES areas and have poorer access to technology in their schools and homes, which may help to explain the lower rates of cyberbullying; or (b) may be attending more academically competitive schools with higher academic standards (possibly with less cyberbullying) which may have affected the students' assessment of their own achievement relative to other students.

It will be important to determine longitudinally if increased technology knowledge, media literacy, and access to ICT at a school level, such as the roll-out of school laptop programs (in a structural context), consequently increases the likelihood of cyberbullying or if it provides a platform for teaching and learning to encourage positive uses of technology.

Limitations

The findings in this study are tempered by three major limitations related to the design, instrumentation, and data collection procedures. First, the cross-sectional nature of the data precludes conclusions being drawn about the causal nature of the relationships identified. Second, the data were collected using self-completion questionnaires. Thus, reports of cyberbullying behaviors may be under- or over-estimates of these outcomes depending on the nature of the behavior concerned and the age and literacy skills of the students involved. Third, the questionnaires were administered by school staff. While the staff were sent a strict protocol for questionnaire administration, the mode of administration may have impacted on students' responses.

Conclusions

The findings from this research may be relevant to policy makers who have (for the most part) directed school-level changes via building programs, appointment of school leaders and staff, provision of policies, and other system-level directives. Further evidence is needed to see to what extent these system-delivered school-level changes can influence the likelihood of student cyberbullying. Moreover, the effectiveness of these system-level changes to address cyberbullying are limited by the speed of technological change and the corresponding shifts in the culture and activity of young people and a general lack of knowledge and understanding of how adolescents use digital technology to communicate and form social networks (Tapscott, 1998).

Disentangling, through longitudinal research, the school-level effects observed in this cross-sectional study will help to determine if these effects operate similarly to the classroom-level effects on face-to-face bullying as identified by Kärnä, Voeten, Poskiparta, and Salmivalli (2010). This raises the question of what, if anything, about the school context enables or inhibits cyberbullying behavior. This question is especially relevant given that most cyberbullying happens outside school hours. Classroom-level differences are largely explained by Salmivalli (2010) as related to class norms. In order to intervene more effectively at the school level it will be necessary to determine which factors, including norms, may help to explain some of the school-level differences observed in cyberbullying behavior.

References

Agatston, P. W., & Limber, S. (2007). Students' perspectives on cyberbullying. *Journal of Adolescent Health, 41*, S59–S60.

Australian Bureau of Statistics. (2001). Socio-economic indexes for areas, Australia. Canberra: Australian Bureau of Statistics.

Australian Bureau of Statistics. (2009). Household use of information technology 2008–09. Canberra: Australian Bureau of Statistics.

Australian Bureau of Statistics. (2010). Square eyes and couch potatoes: children's participation in screen-based activities. *Perspectives on Sport, June 2010*. Canberra: Australian Bureau of Statistics.

Australian Communications and Media Authority. (2009). ACMA Communications Report 2007–08. Melbourne: Australian Communications and Media Authority.

Australian Communications and Media Authority. (2010). ACMA Communications Report 2008–09. Melbourne: Australian Communications and Media Authority.

Bhat, C. S. (2008). Cyberbullying: Overview and strategies for school counsellors, guidance officers, and all school personnel. *Australian Journal of Guidance and Counselling, 18*, 53–66.

Campbell, M. A. (2005). Cyberbullying: An old problem in a new guise? *Australian Journal of Guidance and Counselling, 15*, 68–76.

Cassidy, J., & Asher, S. R. (1992). Loneliness and peer relations in young children. *Child Development, 63*, 350–365.

Catalano, R. F., Haggerty, K. P., Oesterle, S., Fleming, C. B., & Hawkins, J. D. (2004). The importance of bonding to school for healthy development: Findins from the Social Development Research Group. *Journal of School Health, 74*, 252–261.

Commonwealth Government of Australia. (1994). *Sticks and stones: A report of violence in schools.* Canberra: Australian Publishing Service.

Cross, D., Shaw, T., Hearn, L., Epstein, M., Monks, H., Lester, L., & Thomas, L. (2009). *Australian Covert Bullying Prevalence Study (ACBPS).* Retrieved June 4, 2009 from www.deewr.gov.au/Schooling/NationalSafeSchools/Pages/research.aspx

Dooley, J. J., Cross, D., Hearn, L., & Treyvaud, R. (2009). A review of the Australian and international cyber-safety literature. A report prepared for the Department of Broadband, Communications and the Digital Economy. Perth: Edith Cowan University.

Dooley, J., Pyzalski, J., & Cross, D. (2009). Cyberbullying versus face-to-face bullying: a theoretical and conceptual review. *Zeitschrift für Psychologie/Journal of Psychology, 217*, 182–188.

Eisenberg, M. E., Neumark-Sztainer, D., & Perry, C. L. (2003). Peer harassment, school connectedness, and academic achievement. *Journal of School Health, 73*, 311.

Erdur-Baker, O., & Kavsut, F. (2007). Cyberbullying: A new face of peer bullying. *Eğitim Araştrmaları—Eurasian Journal of Educational Research, 7*, 31–42.

Farrington, D. P., & Ttofi, M. M. (2009). School-based programs to reduce bullying and victimization. *Campbell Systematic Reviews.* Oslo: The Campbell Collaboration.

Fleming, M. J., & Rickwood, D. J. (2004). Teens in cyberspace: Do they encounter friend or foe? *Youth Studies Australia, 23*, 46–52.

Glew, G., Fan, M., Katon, W., Rivara, F., & Kernic, M. (2005). Bullying, psychosocial adjustment and academic performance in elementary school. *Archives of Pediatric and Adolescent Medicine, 159*, 1026–1031.

Hamilton, G., Cross, D., Resnicow, K., & Hall, M. (2005). A school-based harm minimization smoking intervention trial: Outcome results. *Addiction, 100*, 689–700.

Hanewald, R. (2008). Confronting the pedagogical challenge of cyber safety. *Australian Journal of Teacher Education, 33*, 1–16.

Hinduja, S., & Patchin, J. W. (2007). Offline consequences of online victimization: School violence and delinquency. *Journal of School Violence, 6*, 89–112.

Kaltiala-Heino, R., Rimpela, M., Rantanen, P., & Rimpela, A. (2000). Bullying at school—an indicator of adolescents at risk for mental disorders. *Journal of Adolescence, 23*, 661–674.

Kapatzia, A., & Sygkollitou, E. (2007). *Cyberbullying in middle and high schools: prevalence, gender and age differences.* University of Thessaloniki, Greece.

Kärnä, A., Voeten, M. J. M., Poskiparta, E., & Salmivalli, C. (2010). Vulnerable children in variable classroom contexts: Bystanders' behaviors moderate the effects of risk factors on victimization. *Merrill-Palmer Quarterly, 56*, 261–282.

Lee, V. E. (1999). School size and the organization of secondary schools. In M. T. Hallinan (Ed.), *Handbook of the sociology of education* (pp. 327–344). New York: Kluwer Academic/Plenum.

McBride, N., Midford, R., & James, R. (1995). Structural and management changes that encourage schools to adopt comprehensive health promotion programs. *Health Promotion Journal of Australia, 5*, 17–23.

McNeely, C., & Falci, C. (2004). School connectedness and the transition into and out of health-risk behavior among adolescents: A comparison of social belonging and teacher support. *Journal of School Health, 74*, 284–292.

McNeely, C. A., Nonnemaker, J. M., & Blum, R. W. (2002). Promoting student connectedness to school: Evidence from the National Longitudinal Study of Adolescent Health. *Journal of School Health, 72*, 138–146.

Ministerial Council on Education, Employment Training and Youth Affairs. (2003). *National Safe Schools Framework*. Retrieved July 15, 2011 from www.mceecdya.edu.au/verve/_resources/natsafeschools_file.pdf

Nansel, T., Overpeck, M., Pilla, R., & Ruan, J. (2001). Bullying behaviors among US youth: Prevalence and association with psychosocial adjustment. *Journal of the American Medical Association, 285*, 2094.

Olweus, D. (1996). The Revised Olweus Bully/Victim Questionnaire. Bergen, Norway: Research Center for Health Promotion, University of Bergen.

Patton, G. C., Bond, L., Carlin, J. B., Thomas, L., Butler, H., Glover, S., Catalano, R., & Bowes, G. (2006). Promoting social inclusion in schools: A group randomized trial of effects on student health risk behavior and well-being. *American Journal of Public Health 96*, 1582–1587.

Raskauskas, J., & Stoltz, A. D. (2007). Involvement in traditional and electronic bullying among adolescents. *Developmental Psychology, 43*, 564–575.

Raudenbush, S. W., & Bryk, A. S. (2002). *Hierarchical linear models: Applications and data analysis methods* (2nd ed.). Newbury Park, CA: Sage.

Resnick, M. D., Bearman, P. S., Blum, R. W., Bauman, K. E., Harris, K. M., Jones, J., Tabor, J., Beuhring, T., Sieving, R. E., & Shew, M. (1997). Protecting adolescents from harm: Findings from the National Longitudinal Study on Adolescent Health. *Journal of the American Medical Association, 278*, 823–832.

Resnicow, K., Ross-Gaddy, D., & Vaughan, R. D. (1995). Structure of the problem and positive behaviors in African-American youths. *Journal of Consulting and Clinical Psychology, 63*, 594–603.

Rigby, K. (1998). *The Peer Relations Questionnaire*. Point Lonsdale, VIC: The Professional Reading Guide for Educational Administrators.

Rigby, K., & Slee, P. (1999). Suicidal ideation among adolescent schoolchildren, involvement in bully–victim problems, and perceived social support. *Suicide and Life Threatening Behavior, 29*, 119–130.

Salmivalli, C. (2010). Bullying and the peer group: A review. *Aggression and Violent Behavior, 15*, 112–120.

Smith, P. K., Mahdavi, J., Carvalho, M., Fisher, S., Russell, S., & Tippett, N. (2008). Cyberbullying: Its nature and impact in secondary school pupils. *Journal of Child Psychology and Psychiatry, 49*, 376–385.

Smith, P. K., & Slonje, R. (2010). Cyberbullying: The nature and extent of a new kind of bullying, in and out of school. In S. Jimerson, S. Swearer & D. Espelage (Eds.), *Handbook of bullying in schools: An international perspective* (pp. 249–262). New York & London: Routledge.

Solberg, M., & Olweus, D. (2003). Prevalence estimation of school bullying with the Olweus bully/victim questionnaire. *Aggressive Behavior, 29*, 239–268.

Sourander, A., Klomek, A. B., Ikonen, M., Lindroos, J., Luntamo, T., Koskelainen, M., Ristkari, T., & Helenius, H. (2010). Psychosocial risk factors associated with cyberbullying among adolescents. *Archives of General Psychiatry, 67*, 720–728.

Spears, B., Slee, P., Owens, L., Johnson, B., & Campbell, A. (2008). *Behind the scenes: Insights into the human dimension of covert bullying*. Retrieved August 3, 2009 from www.deewr.gov.au/schooling/nationalsafeschools/pages/research.aspx

Strabstein, J., & Piazza, T. (2008). Public health, safety and educational risks associated with bullying behaviors in American adolescents. *International Journal of Adolescent Medicine and Health, 20*, 223–233.

Tapscott, D. (1998). *Growing up digital: The rise of the net generation*. New York: McGraw-Hill.

Vandebosch, H., & van Cleemput, K. (2009). Cyberbullying among youngsters: Profiles of bullies and victims. *New Media and Society, 11*, 1349–1371.

Waters, S., Cross, D., & Runions, K. (2009). Social and ecological structures supporting adolescent connectedness to school: A theoretical model. *Journal of School Health*. 79, 516–524.

Waters, S., Epstein, M., Cross, D., & Shaw., T. (2007). *Final report: A randomised control trial to reduce bullying and other aggressive behaviors in secondary schools*. Child Health Promotion Research Centre, Perth.

Williams, K. R., & Guerra, N. G. (2007). Prevalence and predictors of Internet bullying. *Journal of Adolescent Health, 41*, S14–S21.

Ybarra, M. (2004). Linkages between depressive symptomology and internet harassment among young regular Internet users. *CyberPsychology and Behavior, 7*, 247–257.

Ybarra, M. L., Diener-West, M., & Leaf, P. J. (2007). Examining the overlap in Internet harassment and school bullying: Implications for school intervention. *Journal of Adolescent Health, 41*, S42–S50.

6

Predicting Student Behaviors
Cyberbullies, Cybervictims, and Bystanders

Qing Li and Tak Fung

Living in a highly mediated world, cyberbullying is almost a logical outcome of the technological revolution of the last decade and has increasingly gained the attention of educators and journalists (e.g., NBC4.com, 2006; Spero News, 2006) as well as the research community (Patchin & Hinduja, 2006; Li, 2007b; Sijtsema, Veenstra, Lindenberg, & Salmivalli, 2009). Although the number of youth experiencing online harassment varied widely by data collection methods reported in the existing literature, many current studies (Ybarra & Mitchell, 2004; Li, 2006; Beran & Li, 2007) demonstrate that approximately 20–25% of young people have experienced harassment online, bullied others via electronic means, or performed both classes of behaviors, with a few such as i-Safe Survey (i-SAFE America, 2005) reporting a much higher rate of cybervictimization whereby 57% of fourth to eighth grade students were cyberbullied.

Previous research on traditional bullying indicated that gender, different dimensions of student school life, and students' attitudes and beliefs all contribute to the prevalence and significance of adolescents' bullying behaviors (Pellegrini & Bartini, 2000; Ma, 2001). Considering the close ties between traditional bullying and cyberbullying identified in previous research (Beran & Li, 2007; Li, 2007a; Smith et al., 2008), we suspect that gender, school life, student beliefs, and other related factors may play a major role in cyberbullying. Understanding the relationships between cyberbullying and these various factors may, therefore, help to address the problem of cyberbullying.

The History of Cyberbullying in Canada

Beran and Li's (2005) study was one of the earliest Canadian studies to specifically examine the issue of cyberbullying. They reported a paper-and-pencil survey of 432 students from grades seven to nine in Canadian schools. More than two-thirds of

Cyberbullying in the Global Playground: Research from International Perspectives, First Edition.
Edited by Qing Li, Donna Cross, and Peter K. Smith.

students (69%) had heard of incidents of cyber-harassment, about one quarter (21%) had been cyber-harassed several times, and a few students (3%) admitted engaging in this form of harassment. In addition, more than half of the victims (57%) stated that they felt angry on several occasions, and about one third (36%) reported feeling sad and hurt. Cyberbullying also impacted student behaviors, with over half (56%) experiencing poor concentration and 21% reporting lower marks.

A survey study (Li, 2007b) of 177 grade seven students in a Canadian city explored the nature and extent of adolescents' cyberbullying experience, their perception of the school climate, and the relationship between traditional bullying and cyberbullying. Over a quarter of the students were cybervictims and almost 15% were cyberbullies. About a third (32%) of the cybervictims had been harassed by school mates, but over 40% had no idea who the predators were. As well, a bully–cyberbully–victim cycle was identified: bullies in the physical world, compared to non-bullies, were more likely to be cyberbullies. In a similar vein, victims of face-to-face bullying were likely to be cybervictims. Finally, cyberbullies were more likely to be cybervictims than those who were not involved in cyberbullying.

Shariff and Hoff (Shariff, 2004; Shariff & Hoff, 2007) explored cyberbullying from legal and policy perspectives. Based on cases presented in the literature, these authors argued that we should (a) shun criminalizing children and adolescents; (b) understand the legal obligations of adults, particularly educators, to protect children from psychological harm; and (c) sustain safe school environments by clearly defining educators' legal obligations. Similarly, Brown, Jackson, and Cassidy's study (2006) discussed policy development to address cyberbullying by taking a policy analytical approach. By reviewing the existing literature related to cyberbullying, they recommended that (a) school policies should include both school and home use of technology; (b) school division policies should be connected to local school policies, which would therefore establish standards for response; (c) policy development should always give students an opportunity to share their ideas and thoughts; and (d) there is a strong need for critical evaluation of the effectiveness of policies.

Legislation, psychological, and sociological concerns

In Canada, the handbook about criminal harassment published by the Department of Justice (Department of Justice Canada, 2004) recognizes how serious cyber-harassment can be. Of course, there are different ways to describe cyber-stalking and online harassment and not all such conduct falls within Canada's definition of the Criminal Code. Depending on the level of severity and the activities involved, however, cyber-stalking and online harassment can be considered criminal harassment. Other charges such as "unauthorized use of a computer" (Sections 342.1), possession of device to obtain computer service (Section 342.2), and mischief in relation to data (Subsection 430(1.1)) can also be laid.

Although some parties (e.g., the Canadian Teachers Federation) urge amending the Criminal Code to specifically address cyberbullying, Shariff and Hoff (2007) are opposed to this idea for two main reasons. First, the Criminal Code already contains all the resources, including provisions for crimes of harassment and uttering threats, needed to prosecute bullying in its many varieties, including cyberbullying. Under existing legislation, teachers, parents, and others who work with children can and are even legally obliged to press charges against cyberbullies. Second, developing new legislation for cyberbullying will add opportunities to abuse freedom of speech.

Freedom of expression is a right of all Canadians, including children, and such rights are subject "only to such reasonable limits prescribed by law as can be demonstrably justified in a free and democratic society" (Section 2(b) of the Charter). School policies need to honor such individual rights, unless policy makers can justify an action to protect the greater good as a pressing and substantial objective. Whether occurring on or off school property, the critical issue of cyberbullying is the effect of such incidents. Schools have a responsibility to address cyberbullying if it is accessed/displayed at school, or if it results in substantial disruption to or poisons the learning environment for any student (Shariff & Hoff, 2007).

Research

Aims

A review of existing literature related to both traditional bullying and cyberbullying suggests that various factors contribute to cyberbullying. In this chapter, we explore the extent to which the following factors contribute to student behavior related to cyberbullying. These factors were selected because they have been previously reported as being predictors in the literature or have been found to be useful in our experience.

Beliefs: Research in traditional bullying has suggested the significance of students' beliefs in relation to their behavior, including their involvement in cyberbullying and subsequent actions. For example, students who hold aggressive attitudes are more likely to be persistent bullies (i.e., those who were identified as bullies for two or more years) (Carlson & Cornell, 2008), while victims with aggressive attitudes are more likely to engage in high-risk behaviors such as using alcohol, carrying weapons, and engaging in physical fights at school (Brockenbrough, Cornell, & Loper, 2002).

Gender: As reported in previous research and many news stories, gender plays a significant role in school violence and bullying. Moving to cyberspace, differences have also been identified across gender in the actual *experience* of being cyberbullied (Burgess-Proctor, Patchin, & Hinduja, 2009). Girls, compared to their male counterparts, are more likely to be involved in cyberbullying activities both as victims and perpetrators (Campbell, 2005; Keith & Martin, 2005; Smith et al., 2008; Hinduja & Patchin, 2009). One important factor to consider is that using aversive tactics with peers is an important social behavior for male students (Pellegrini & Bartini, 2000). In addition, it has been suggested that females might prefer to use electronic communication media such as chatrooms and email to bully others (Nelson, 2003;

Thorp, 2004). In keeping with the extant work on bullying (Boulton & Smith, 1994; Pellegrini, Bartini, & Brooks, 1999), it is posited that gender should predict cyberbullying and cybervictimization.

Access to technology: Since cyberbullying occurs in cyberspace, it is reasonable to assume that student access to information technology, such as the Internet at home or cell phones in school, should predict cyberbullying and cybervictimization.

Physical strength: Physical weakness or strength has proved to be a strong factor contributing to traditional bullying (Olweus, 1993; Guerin & Hennessy, 2002). Olweus's studies (1978, 1993) suggested that victims, in general, have less-than-average physical strength while bullies tend to be physically stronger than victims. For male students, physical strength is related to high popularity, and high popularity reduces their risk of being victimized. Although cyberbullying does not involve physical activity, the close tie between traditional bullying and cyberbullying (Beran & Li, 2005; Li, 2007a) leads us to hypothesize that physical strength predicates cyberbullying.

Social networks and extracurricular activities: Previous research showed that victims of bullying usually lacked the social networks that could keep them from being victimized (Shaffer, 2000). Peers as silent acceptors contributed greatly to the establishment and maintenance of bullying systems (Jeffrey, Miller, & Linn, 2001). In a similar vein, the level and frequency of student engagement in extracurricular activities may correlate with their popularity. As well, students' extracurricular activity is linked to both positive and deviant behaviors, including bullying-related behaviors (Peguero, 2008). Peguero's study indicated that students who were involved in three or more classroom-related extracurricular activities or intramural sports tended to be bullied, while interscholastic athletes were less likely to be victims of bullying.

Academic work: Previous research on bullying and victimization found that academic performance and academic pressure connect to bullying in schools (Ma, 2001; Brockenbrough, Cornell, & Loper, 2002; Guerin & Hennessy, 2002). Students experiencing lower academic pressure are more likely to bully than students in schools with high academic pressure. Victims, on the other hand, tend to have lower academic grades than the other groups (Schwartz, Farver, Chang, & Lee-Shin, 2002). Regardless of the type of bullying, victims suffer various negative consequences. Some important and well documented consequences include students having difficulty concentrating on schoolwork, decreased academic achievement levels, lower interest in school, and increased absences (National Association of State Boards of Education, 2003). This link between academic work and bullying suggests possible connections between academic achievement and cyberbullying. Consequently, it is hypothesized that academic achievement is connected to cyberbullying and cybervictimization.

Specifically, the first goal of this study is to determine the extent to which seven factors, namely *home access to the Internet*, *cell phone use at school*, *gender*, *beliefs*, *academic performance*, *physical strength*, and *extracurricular activities*, predict cyberbullying in secondary schools. We hypothesize that aggressive behaviors should be predicated by student beliefs about cyberspace. Further, it is posited that access to the Internet at home or via cell phones in schools, gender, physical strengths, and popularity should result in different cyberbullying behaviors. Also, lower academic performance should relate to more frequent cyberbullying or cybervictimization.

The second objective of this study is to examine the extent to which the above seven factors predict student actions after cybervictimization. These actions range from taking revenge through traditional bullying or cyberbullying others, to informing others, or directly confronting the predators, or passively accepting what happens.

As speculated in previous research, cyberbullying could result in some destructive consequences such as prompting victims to take revenge:

> [A]s a result of not receiving consequences for engaging in cyber-harassment, students may then continue the harassment when in close contact with a student at school. In addition, cyber-harassment may alter bullying at school. For example, if "electronic bullies" remain undetected, their bullying behaviors at school may become more severe and directly, rather than indirectly, exerted against a victim. (Beran & Li, 2005, p. 271)

Therefore, we posit that students who hold positive beliefs about cyberspace should take appropriate actions (i.e., inform others, confront cyberbullies, escape) after being cybervictimized. Those who hold negative beliefs should take deviant actions such as choosing to take revenge in the cyber or real world, or both.

The third objective of the study is to explore the extent to which the seven factors contribute to students' responses when witnessing cyberbullying incidents. These responses include both positive and negative ones, ranging from cheering the cyberbully on to trying to help or befriend the cybervictim.

Methods

Sample

Although a random selection of individual students was preferred, to ensure complete anonymity and protect students from any negative consequences, a random selection of classes rather than individual students was used. That is, 12 classes of grade 7–12 students (11–18-year-olds), enrolled in three suburban and rural schools (with a balanced male–female ratio) in Western Canada, were randomly selected from 96 classes. Originally, researchers (the first author and a graduate research assistant) accompanied by the technology coordinators of each school, with the help of teachers, distributed the survey to 293 students. Data were collected in 2008. Among these students, only 254 (135 males and 112 females; 7 did not enter gender) returned their completed survey, which formed the sample of this study. Over 90% of these students used the Internet at home and close to half used cell phones at school.

Measures

Because cyberbullying is a relatively new phenomenon, limited research is available in this field. Consequently, few measures have been developed to assess cyberbullying and related issues. This survey was built on the survey instrument created by Willard (2004) and the first author's previous research in this area. In addition, the existing literature on bullying and cyberbullying guided the development of this instrument.

For example, since student-perceived school/home climates contributed to cyberbullying, we asked students to comment on behaviors of school adults and family members related to cyberbullying. They were also asked to share their thoughts and experience as bystanders to explore another important group in the mix: the witnessing peers.

The Cyberbullying Student Survey consisted of four parts. The first part collected students' demographic data. The second and third parts examined students' behaviors and beliefs related to cyberbullying, as either participants or bystanders. The cyberbullying section dealt with students' experiences and scored in a dichotomous fashion. The witness section examined students' behaviors and opinions related to bystanders. The fourth part of the survey included students' opinions about online behaviors in general, as well as their social and physical life. Responses for each item in this section ranged from "strongly agree" (1 point) to "strongly disagree" (5 points) on a five-point Likert-type scale.

Procedure and analysis

An ethics review was sought from the Research Ethics Board (REB). After receiving the ethics approval, the survey was administered to students during a regular class period. Following the REB recommendation, we did not use consent forms but rather accepted unfilled questionnaires as an indication of unwillingness to participate to ensure complete anonymity. Students were informed that the purpose of the research was to study their experiences of and beliefs about cyberbullying. Letters and surveys were sent to the students' home. In the parent letter, it was stated that if parents allowed a student to participate, the student would put the completed questionnaire in the envelope provided (without names) and return it. If parents were not interested, students would simply return the envelopes with the blank questionnaires.

We employed quantitative analysis of student survey using SPSS™ for Windows. Eight questions were asked regarding student beliefs about the cyber-world in relation to cyberbullying. We first conducted an exploratory factor analysis in order to extract factors representing key elements of student beliefs (independent variable). We used 0.40 as a cut-off score to identify items with high loadings for inclusion with each factor (Conway & Huffcutt, 2003). Cronbach's alpha measures how well a set of items measures a single construct. We hence used Cronbach's alpha to test the internal consistency of the items within each construct, considering a reliability coefficient of 0.70 or higher as acceptable (Nunnally, 1978).

Factor analysis was first performed on eight questions asking students' opinions about cyberspace to extract the constructs related to student beliefs. The negatively worded items (i.e., "things that happen online should stay online," "I have the right to say anything I want online, even if what I say hurts someone or violates someone's privacy") were re-coded before they were entered in factor analysis. One item (i.e., "I know of someone who has been really hurt by cyberbullying") was discarded because it showed a very low factor loading (<0.40). From the remaining seven items, one factor, named as *belief*, was extracted and the minimum factor loading was 0.575. Belief was created by the sum of the seven items. It has a mean of 22.90, standard deviation of 5.90, with minimum of 7.00 and maximum of 35.00. Cronbach's alpha was 0.84.

Students' actions after being cyberbullied were categorized into positive or negative actions: there were four positive actions, namely *confront* ("tell the cyberbully to stop"), *avoid* ("get away from the cyberbully"), *inform adults* ("tell an adult"), *inform peer* ("tell a friend"), as well as three negative action variables, namely *no action* ("do nothing"), *cyberbully* ("cyberbully other people"), and *bully* ("bully other kids").

Student responses when they observed cyberbullying incidents were also grouped into positive and negative responses: five positive responses, namely *leave* ("leave the online environment"), *indirectly object* ("object to others, but not directly to the cyberbully"), *directly object* ("object to the cyberbully"), *help* ("try to help or befriend the victim"), *report* ("report the cyberbullying to someone who can help the victim"), as well as three negative response variables, namely *join in* ("join in"), *cheer on* ("cheer the cyberbully on"), and *watch* ("watch or look, but do not participate").

Next, stepwise regression was employed to examine the extent to which various factors contributed to cyberbullying. The selected potential predictors were: beliefs, gender, Internet use at home, cell phone use at school, school grade, extracurricular activities, and physical strength.

Finally, forward stepwise logistic regressions were performed to examine the extent to which the above seven factors predicted their actions after they were cybervictimized as well as their responses when witnessing cyberbullying incidents.

Results

Cyberbullying

Stepwise regression was used to predict frequencies of cyberbullying, and potential predictors were belief, gender, academic performance, extracurricular activities, Internet use at home, cell phone use and physical strength. Based on results from stepwise regression analysis, only belief (reg. coef = −0.07, t = −6.42, $p < 0.001$), Internet use at home (reg. coef = 0.70, t = 2.81, $p = 0.006$) and cell phone use (reg. coef. = 0.30, t = 2.14, $p = 0.03$) were significant predictors of cyberbullying (see Table 6.1 for details).

Table 6.1 Predicting Cyberbullying (N = 136).

Predictor	*Regression coefficient*	*t-ratio*	*P*
Belief	−0.07	−6.42	<0.001*
Internet at home	0.70	2.81	0.006*
Cell phone	0.30	2.14	0.034*

Note: *Significant at 0.05 level, R-squared = 0.29.

The signs of the significant predictors are what we expected; that is, students who held more positive beliefs about cyberspace less often cyberbullied others. Those who had access to the Internet at home and/or cell phones in schools cyberbullied others more often.

Actions after being cybervictimized

We hypothesized that the seven factors would affect student behaviors after they were cybervictimized. Forward stepwise logistic regressions were therefore performed to determine whether the seven potential predictors significantly predict different student actions (whether positive or negative action) after they were cyberbullied.

The variable *belief* was a significant predictor for all the subsequent actions of students when cybervictimized. For all the positive actions—confront, avoid, inform adult, and inform peers—the regression coefficients associated with belief are positive, which indicate that an increase in positive belief means a higher chance of taking positive action. Along with belief (+ve coef.), gender (−ve coef.), extracurricular activities (+ve coef.), and physical strength (+ve coef.) are significant predictors of "inform peers."

Belief is a significant predictor of all negative actions—for "no action," "cyberbully," and "bully," the regression coefficients are all negative, which indicate that decreases in belief leads to a higher chance of negative actions. Along with belief (−ve coef.), extracurricular activities (−ve coef.) is also a significant predictor of "bully" and it indicates that with a decrease in belief and extracurricular activities comes an increase in the chance of "bully." See Table 6.2 for details.

Witness responses

We also hypothesized that the seven factors predicted student responses when witnessing cyberbullying incidents. Forward stepwise logistic regressions were again conducted to determine whether the seven potential predictors significantly predict different student responses (whether positive or negative responses) when they observed cyberbullying incidents.

Table 6.2 Determinants of Actions (Dependent Variables, N = 122).

Dependent variable	*Predictors*	*B*	*S. E.*	*Wald's* χ^2	*Df*	*P*	*Exp (β) (OR)*
No action	*Belief*	−0.08	0.03	6.17	1	0.01*	0.92
Confront	*Belief*	0.11	0.04	6.83	1	0.01*	1.12
Avoid	*Belief*	0.14	0.04	13.66	1	<0.001*	1.15
Cyberbully	*Belief*	−0.84	0.33	6.29	1	0.01*	0.43
Bully	*Belief*	−0.52	0.21	6.32	1	0.01*	0.59
	Extracurricular activity	−1.70	0.85	3.96	1	0.047*	0.18
Inform adults	*Belief*	0.22	0.06	12.07	1	0.001*	1.24
Inform peers	*Belief*	0.14	0.06	5.41	1	0.02*	1.15
	Gender	−1.53	0.61	6.42	1	0.01*	0.22
	Extracurricular activity	0.60	0.22	7.29	1	0.01*	1.81
	Physical strength	0.77	0.30	6.71	1	0.01*	2.16

Note: *Significant at 0.05 level.

Table 6.3 Determinants of Witness Responses (N = 125).

Dependent variable	*Predictors*	*B*	*S. E.*	*Wald's* χ^2	*Df*	*P*	*Exp (β) (OR)*
Cheer on	*Belief*	−0.25	0.07	14.47	1	<0.001*	0.78
Leave	*Belief*	0.12	0.05	5.09	1	0.024*	1.13
Help	*Belief*	0.08	0.04	4.98	1	0.026*	1.09
Report	*Belief*	0.29	0.09	9.50	1	0.002*	1.33

Note: *Significant at 0.05 level.

Out of the seven potential predictors, only belief was a significant factor for four responses: cheer on, leave, help, and report. For the positive responses, that is, leave, help and report, the regression coefficients associated with belief were all positive which means that if belief increases then there is a higher chance of the positive responses. Belief (–ve coef.) was also a significant predictor of a negative response (cheer on). Students with more negative beliefs about cyberspace were more likely to cheer on the cyberbully when they saw cyberbullying. See Table 6.3 for details.

Discussion

This study advances our understanding of this issue by examining how various factors contribute to students' behavior, whether as a cyberbully, a cybervictim, or a bystander. The most important result of this exploration is that belief is a significant predictor and, in most cases the strongest or the only predictor, for almost all student actions we examined. This finding is consistent with previous research on traditional bullying that victim and perpetrator opinions and beliefs are often at issue (Hoover & Olsen, 2001) as in any interpersonal dynamics.

Predicting cyberbullying

The model predicting cyberbullying indicates that belief is the most significant predictor in the variables examined, followed by Internet access at home and cell phone use at school respectively. The more positive a student's beliefs about cyberspace, the less likely this student would cyberbully others. As well, students with no home Internet access or without a cell phone at school are less likely to cyberbully others. This makes sense because with less access to the tools, fewer opportunities exist for students to harass others using the tools. It is consistent with previous results that cyberbullies use the Internet more frequently and for longer than others (Ybarra, Alexander, & Mitchell, 2005). This fact, however, should not be taken as an argument against the use of technology in schools or at home. As demonstrated in previous work (Jenkins, Clinton, Purushotma, Robison, & Weigel, 2006), today technology is ubiquitous and students need to access it to acquire the skills needed for the twenty-first century. Rather, this model demonstrates the vital role student beliefs play in cyberbullying, and therefore underscores the need to create environments that support improved students' beliefs about cyberspace while providing technology-rich opportunities.

Predicting actions after being cyberbullied

The model predicting cybervictims' subsequent actions shows that belief again accounts significantly for their behavior after being cyberbullied. The more positive the belief a student holds about cyberspace or their responsibility for cyberbullying, the less likely they are to be passive victims or adopt deviant behaviors such as harassing others, in the cyber or real worlds. In a similar vein, such students are more likely to act appropriately by informing others, directly confronting the cyberbully, or getting away from the cyberbully.

In addition, the frequency of student engagement in extracurricular activities such as band and sport teams predicts their behaviors after cybervictimization. The more often the students engage in extracurricular activities, the higher the odds that they would inform friends about the cyberbullying incidents, and the less likely they would fight back by bullying other students. One possible explanation is that the more often students are involved in extracurricular work, the more friends they may have and the more opportunities for them to interact with friends. Hence, it is more likely they would discuss their life (including any cyberbullying) with friends. Consequently, with more friends and a busier life, these students may have a better chance of being distracted and recovering from cybervictimization, so they do not take revenge by harassing other students.

Further, our model demonstrates that physical strength predicts whether or not cybervictims tell friends about the cyberbullying incidents. Physically strong cybervictims, compared to their weaker counterparts, are more likely to tell friends about such incidents. Previous research (Olweus, 1993) on traditional bullying indicates that for boys, physical strength is related to popularity. Therefore, a logical explanation for this phenomenon is that physically strong students tend to have more friends, and therefore are more likely to discuss their cyberbullying experiences with friends.

Predicting responses of bystanders

Our logistic regression analysis has resulted in a model predicting bystanders' actions when witnessing cyberbullying. The model indicated that belief is the only predictor, out of the seven potential predictors, that contributes to bystander responses when witnessing cyberbullying. The more negative a belief the student holds, the more likely he is to participate in cyberbullying by cheering on the cyberbully. On the other hand, a student with a positive belief about cyberspace tends to leave the online environment, or solve the problem by helping or befriending the victim or reporting the incident to responsible people. Contrary to what we originally expected, gender, access to technology, school marks, involvement in extracurricular activities, and the physical strength of students are not predictors for bystander responses. This suggests that regardless of who the students are (male or female, strong or weak) and what they do (e.g., play in a sports team or not), their belief about the online world is the most fundamental and vital factor contributing to their actions when witnessing cyberbullying.

Conclusions and Implications

The most significant finding of this chapter is that students' beliefs about cyberspace and their understanding of responsibilities in relation to cyberbullying strongly impact their behavior, either as cyberbullies, cybervictims, or bystanders. This may be best explained by Bandura's moral disengagement model (Bandura, 1999) which claims that one's conduct, particularly in the early development stages, is largely regulated by

> external dictates and social sanctions … people adopt moral standards that serve as guides and as major bases for self-sanctions regarding moral conduct … They do things that give them satisfaction and build their sense of self-worth. They refrain from behaving in ways that violate their moral standards because such conduct will bring self-condemnation. (Bandura, 1999, p. 196)

Bandura (1999) argues that unless the morality is justified, people do not usually engage in harmful behavior. Students socialize in a world where the real and cyber-worlds are intertwined and entail different moral standards. Although netiquette has evolved for many websites and cyber-communities, the moral standards of cyberspace have not yet been completely developed. As well, no widely accepted guidelines exist for appropriate or inappropriate behavior in the online world. The use of technology may result in the "disengagement of personal control" (Bandura, 1999, p. 196), permitting justified acts that would be considered unjust in different circumstances. In other words, cyberbullies may attribute their behavior to the availability of electronic technology and the actions allowed by it. For example, it is probable that students regard cyberbullying as moral if they believe the online world should be a place to say whatever they want. Therefore their acts of cyberbullying or cheering on a cyberbully are justified. In the same breath, students holding more positive views about cyberspace would not only refrain from cyberbullying, because they know it is wrong, but would also act morally by supporting cybervictims.

Another result warranting discussion is the frequency of students' involvement in extracurricular activities, which predicts their actions in relation to cyberbullying, including informing friends and taking retribution by bullying other students. Perhaps taking part in frequent extracurricular activities allows students to create a strong and supportive social network. At the same time, their busy schedules distract them from cybervictimization. This leads to their sharing any negative incidents with friends rather than taking vengeance by bullying someone else.

Implications

The implications of the information obtained from this study go beyond adding to the Canadian research literature related to cyberbullying. This information contributes to the development of sustainable, shared knowledge about cyberbullying in general. The results show that students' attitudes and belief about cyberspace and cyberbullying are the most influential factors affecting their online and offline behaviors, whether as a cyber-predator, cybervictim or bystander. This result has vital implications in addressing cyberbullying. As discussed above, we first need to establish solid and comprehensive moral standards and social codes for online behavior. Next, education should be an essential component of any anti-bully/cyberbully intervention program to teach students and enhance their understanding of such moral standards and social codes. Finally, school policies should be modified to match such moral standards and social codes for cyber-conduct.

The fact that students' commitment to frequent extracurricular activity reduces their opportunity to retaliate by bullying others means that schools should consider establishing diversified and engaging extracurricular programs to attract more students. It is also desirable that schools establish relevant policies to encourage and promote extracurricular involvement. These policies will not only remedy cyberbullying and bullying, but also create a caring learning environment and social climate for students. This in turn, may reduce institutional violence and increase academic achievement.

One important point to be stressed is that schools should play a leading role in combating cyberbullying, yet restricting Internet use, email, or any other technological tools cannot stop bullies from finding ways around the schools' suspension of privileges (Heirman & Walrave, 2008). As suggested in previous research, young people are subject to ongoing social pressure to be online because it is an important construct of their social identity (Cavert, 2002) and limiting their access to cyberspace may result in other serious problems such as social isolation (Heirman & Walrave, 2008; Kowalski, Limber, & Agatston, 2008). Establishing effective anti-bullying programs as well as creating a culture of caring and kindness in schools has never been more important. Awareness is the first step and it is an absolute must. As indicated in student narratives in our survey, many students do not even know that cyberbullying is a form of bullying. If they do not even know they are being victimized, how can we help them? Similarly, cyberbullies sometimes do not understand that what they are doing is considered a form of bullying. Most students do not want a reputation as a bully, so once this becomes clear to them, some will stop. Most importantly, anti-bullying/cyberbullying programs should be systematic and joint effects by society rather than being a one-off or single-school project.

Addressing cyberbullying should be a collective effort on the part of schools, families, students, and society. Because cyberbullying can happen outside school boundaries, schools may direct such issues back to parents, saying that they have no legal jurisdiction. However, cyberbullying can be rooted in school or vice versa even if incidents appear to be initiated off school property. This requires schools to consider the development of comprehensive programs to fight cyberbullying, including detailed and unified policies as well as effective programs to educate students.

Recommendations for Future Research

Regarding implications for prevention, limited research has focused on cyberbullying and intervention strategies have not yet been evaluated. When determining the effect of cyberbullying, further research is recommended to examine whether this experience preceded socio-emotional behaviors to determine causality. Students' reports on the impact of cyberbullying are useful in understanding the child's perspective, while parents and teachers can provide information from different viewpoints. Additional reporting sources can be included in future research to compare children's and adults' perspectives.

Existing literature related to cyberbullying, including this study, relies mainly on student self-reported cyberbullying. It has been widely acknowledged in research related to bullying (Espelage & Holt, 2002; Cornell & Brockenbrough, 2004) that important differences occur between self-reported and peer-nominated bullies and victims. Considering the close ties between cyberbullying and traditional bullying

(Li, 2007a), further research is recommended to investigate cyberbullying through the lens of peer-nominated cyberbullying and its relationship with self-reported cyberbullying.

Other areas for further study include using school measures such as attendance records to understand children's experiences of bullying and cyberbullying. Also, direct and indirect bullying should be compared separately from cyberbullying. Our exploration of cyberbullying also indicates the need for qualitative methods to determine the nature and possible causes of this new phenomenon. The sample in this study was limited to secondary school students in Canadian schools who were willing to participate, and no grade differences were found in reports of cyberbullying. We suggest expanding the age range of the study in future studies, and including gender differences.

Given that students' behavior is largely affected by the significant people in their life, it is recommended that researchers examine cyberbullying by studying all the key players including the students, their teachers, and parents simultaneously. Such work will shed light on how the components—that is, home, school, and cyberspace—interact and how an individual's belief and behavior influence and are influenced by such interactions. The results will offer a comprehensive understanding of cyberbullying and consequently enable us to develop and evaluate strategies to mitigate cyberbullying.

References

Bandura, A. (1999). Moral disengagement in the perpetration of inhumanities. *Personality and Social Psychology Review, Special Issue on Evil and Violence, 3*, 193–209.

Beran, T., & Li, Q. (2005). Cyber-harassment: A new method for an old behavior. *Journal of Educational Computing Research, 32*, 265–277.

Beran, T., & Li, Q. (2007). The relationship between cyberbullying and school bullying. *Journal of Student Wellbeing, 1*, 15–33.

Boulton, M., & Smith, P. K. (1994). Bully/victim problems in middle school children: Stability, self-perceived competence, peer perceptions, and peer acceptance. *British Journal of Developmental Psychology, 12*, 315–329.

Brockenbrough, K., Cornell, D., & Loper, A. (2002). Aggressive victims of violence at school. *Education and Treatment of Children, 20*, 273–287.

Brown, K., Jackson, M., & Cassidy, W. (2006). Cyberbullying: Developing policy to direct responses that are equitable and effective in addressing this special form of bullying. *Canadian Journal of Educational Administration and Policy, 57*, 1–35.

Burgess-Proctor, A., Patchin, J., & Hinduja, S. (2009). Cyberbullying and online harassment: Reconceptualizing the victimization of adolescent girls. In V. Garcia & J. Clifford (Eds.), *Female crime victims: Reality reconsidered* (pp. 162–176). Upper Saddle River, NJ: Prentice Hall.

Campbell, M. A. (2005). Cyberbullying: An old problem in a new guise? *Australian Journal of Guidance and Counselling, 15*, 68–76.

Carlson, W., & Cornell, D. (2008). Differences between persistent and desistent middle school bullies. *School Psychology International, 29*, 442–451.

Cavert, S. (2002). Identity construction on the Internet. In S. Cavert, A. Jordan, & R. Cocking (Eds.), *Children in the digital age: Influences of electronic media on development* (pp. 57–70). Westport, CT: Praeger.

Conway, J. M., & Huffcutt, A. I. (2003). A review and evaluation of exploratory factor analysis practices in organizational research. *Organizational Research Methods, 6*, 147–168.

Cornell, D., & Brockenbrough, K. (2004). Identification of bullies and victims: A comparison of methods. *Journal of School Violence, 3*, 63–87.

Department of Justice Canada. (2004). *A handbook for police and crown prosecutors on criminal harassment.* Ottawa, ON: Authority of the Minister of Justice and Attorney General of Canada, Government of Canada.

Espelage, D., & Holt, M. (2002). Bullying and victimization during early adolescence: Peer influences and psychosocial correlates. In R. A. Geffner, M. Loring, & C. Young (Eds.), *Bullying behavior: Current issues, research, and interventions* (pp. 123–142). New York: Haworth Press.

Guerin, S., & Hennessy, E. (2002). *Aggression and bullying.* Oxford: Blackwell.

Heirman, W., & Walrave, M. (2008). Assessing concerns and issues about the mediation of technology in cyberbullying. *Cyberpsychology: Journal of Psychosocial Research on Cyberspace, 2*, 1–18.

Hinduja, S., & Patchin, J. W. (2009). *Bullying beyond the schoolyard: Preventing and responding to cyberbullying.* Thousand Oaks, CA: Corwin Press.

Hoover, J., & Olsen, G. (2001). *Teasing and harassment: The frames and scripts approach for teachers and parents.* Bloomington, IN: National Educational Service.

i-SAFE America. (2005). *National i-SAFE survey finds over half of students are being harassed online.* Carisbad, CA: i-Safe Inc.

Jeffrey, L., Miller, P., & Linn, M. (2001). Middle school bullying as a context for the development of passive observers to the victimization of others. In R. A. Geffner, M. Loring, & C. Young (Eds.), *Bullying Behavior: Current issues, research and interventions* (pp. 143–156). Binghamton, NY: Haworth Press.

Jenkins, H., Clinton, K., Purushotma, R., Robison, A., & Weigel, M. (2006). *Confronting the challenges of participatory culture: Media education for the 21st century* (Occasional paper). Washington, DC: The John D. and Catherine MacArthur Foundation.

Keith, S., & Martin, M. E. (2005). Cyberbullying: Creating a culture of respect in a cyber world. *Reclaiming Children and Youth, 13*, 224–228.

Kowalski, R., Limber, S., & Agatston, P. (2008). *Cyberbullying: Bullying in the digital age.* Malden, MA: Blackwell.

Li, Q. (2006). Cyberbullying in schools: A research of gender differences. *School Psychology International, 27*, 157–170.

Li, Q. (2007a). Bullying in the new playground: A research into cyberbullying and cyber victimization. *Australasian Journal of Educational Technology, 23*, 435–454.

Li, Q. (2007b). New bottle but old wine: A research on cyberbullying in schools. *Computers and Human Behavior, 23*, 1777–1791.

Ma, X. (2001). Bullying and being bullied: To what extent are bullies also victims? *American Educational Research Journal, 38*, 351–370.

National Association of State Boards of Education. (2003). Bullying in schools. *Policy Update, 11*, 1–2.

NBC4.com. (2006). *Youth falling victim to cyberbullying.* Retrieved December 1, 2007 from www.nbc4.com/news/9696618/detail.html

Nelson, M. (2003). *School bullies going high tech*. Retrieved July 14, 2004 from www.canoe.ca/NewsStand/LondonFreePress/News/2003/09/02/174030.html

Nunnally, J. C. (1978). *Psychometric theory*. New York: McGraw-Hill.

Olweus, D. (1978). *Aggression in the schools: Bullies and whipping boys*. New York: Wiley.

Olweus, D. (1993). *Bullying at school: What we know and what we can do*. Cambridge, MA: Blackwell.

Patchin, J. W., & Hinduja, S. (2006). Bullies move beyond the schoolyard: A preliminary look at cyberbullying. *Youth Violence and Juvinile Justice, 4*, 148–169.

Peguero, A. (2008). Bullying victimization and extracurricular activity. *Journal of School Violence, 7*, 71–85.

Pellegrini, A., & Bartini, M. (2000). A longitudinal study of bullying, victimization, and peer affiliation during the transition from primary school to middle school. *American Educational Research Journal, 37*, 699–725.

Pellegrini, A., Bartini, M., & Brooks, F. (1999). School bullies, victims, and aggressive victims: Factors relating to group affiliation and victimization in early adolescence. *Journal of Educational Psychology, 91*, 216–224.

Schwartz, D., Farver, J. M., Chang, L., & Lee-Shin, Y. (2002). Victimization in South Korean children's peer groups. *Journal of Abnormal Child Psychology, 30*, 113–125.

Shaffer, D. R. (2000). *Social and personality development* (4th ed.). Belmont, CA: Wadsworth.

Shariff, S. (2004). Keeping schools out of court: Legally defensible models of leadership to reduce cyberbullying. *Educational Forum, Delta Kappa Pi, 68*, 222–233.

Shariff, S., & Hoff, D. (2007). Cyberbullying: Clarifying legal boundaries for school supervision in cyberspace. *International Journal of Cyber Criminology, 1*, 76–118.

Sijtsema, J. J., Veenstra, R., Lindenberg, S., & Salmivalli, C. (2009). Empirical test of bullies' status goals: Assessing direct goals, aggression, and prestige. *Aggressive Behavior, 35*, 57–67.

Smith, P. K., Mahdavi, J., Carvalho, M., Fisher, S., Russell, S., & Tippett, N. (2008). Cyberbullying: its nature and impact in secondary school pupils. *Journal of Child Psychology & Psychiatry, 49*, 376–385.

Spero News. (2006, June 23). *1 in 3 teens are victims of cyberbullying*. Retrieved 22 July, 2011 from www.speroforum.com/site/article.asp?id=4994

Thorp, D. (2004). *Cyberbullies on the prowl in schoolyard*. Retrieved July 15, 2004 from http://australianit.news.com.au/articles/0,7204,9980900^15322^^nbv^15306,00.html

Willard, N. (2004). *An educator's guide to cyberbullying and cyberthreats*. Retrieved July 22, 2011 from http://csriu.org/cyberbully/docs/cbcteducator.pdf

Ybarra, M., Alexander, C., & Mitchell, K. J. (2005). Depressive symptomatology, youth Internet use, and online interactions: A national survey *Journal of Adolescent Health, 36*, 9–18.

Ybarra, M. L., & Mitchell, J. K. (2004). Online aggressor/targets, aggressors, and targets: A comparison of associated youth characteristics. *Journal of Child Psychology and Psychiatry, 45*, 1308–1316.

Part IV
Studies in the USA

7

An Examination of the History, Prevalence, Characteristics, and Reporting of Cyberbullying in the United States

Brett Holfeld and Mark Grabe

It has been estimated that at least 80% of adolescents in the US have a personal digital device allowing either Internet or cell phone access to online information and communication services (David-Ferdon & Hertz, 2007). These devices and related services collectively implicated here in the problem of cyberbullying seem associated with several characteristics that share a similar interesting property. A given characteristic often seems responsible for both positive and negative consequences. For example, parents may value cell phones because these devices offer a way to contact their children whenever necessary and whereever their children might be. This "anytime, anywhere" access is both convenient and reassuring to parents. However, the same characteristics of anytime, anywhere access also make it difficult for a victim to escape the taunts or threats of a cyberbully. Educators and researchers interested in increasing the participation of students in discussion have noted the benefits of isolation afforded by online discussion in encouraging contributions from those who are shy or slower to respond, severely limiting their involvement in face-to-face classroom discussion (Althaus, 1997). This same isolation allows cyberbullies the anonymity and escape from social cues that may encourage harassment and insensitivity.

Even access to the Internet has mixed consequences. Access offers the educational community inexpensive information resources, and communication and generative services. However, the same services used to communicate with an out-of-school expert or to author a content-related website can be used to bombard someone with spiteful messages or reveal embarrassing images. The point is that it is typically impractical to turn a service on or off or to limit the way in which it may be applied. We must rely on the decision-making of the participants and work to understand and modify the motives of those who turn the characteristics of the technologies to a destructive end.

Cyberbullying in the Global Playground: Research from International Perspectives, First Edition.
Edited by Qing Li, Donna Cross, and Peter K. Smith.

The History of Cyberbullying

In discussing the history of cyberbullying, Shariff (2008, p. 29) considers the original use of the term. The claim is made that the term originated either with Canadian Bill Belsey or US lawyer Nancy Willard (2003). Whatever the date at which the term was first used to describe the behavior, online harassment, and the careful study of such behavior, date back at least to the 1980s. In an age when being online may have meant communicating with others using a local area network, newsgroups, or accessing local Bulletin Board Systems (BBSs) with a telephone modem, there was concern over "flame wars," insensitivity and other forms of inappropriate interaction, theoretical models emphasizing anonymity and lack of visual cues, and research that, because it was usually conducted in more controlled environments, was more methodologically sophisticated than the typical survey study of cyberbullying conducted today (for example, Kiesler, Zubrow, & Moses, 1985; Postmes, Spears, & Lea, 1998). With this in mind, we will proceed with a brief review of the cyberbullying research conducted in the US.

We focus our attention mostly on articles appearing in peer-reviewed publications, focused on children and adolescents, and self-defined as focused on cyberbullying or cross-referenced by articles focused on cyberbullying. Our intentions are to describe the state of research on this topic conducted in the US, summarize prevalence data and correlates of bullying and victimization (both to establish what has been observed and to offer information for comparison with what is being established elsewhere), and to provide a general background to lead into a description of our own research.

Characteristics of the Research

It might be argued that the study of problematic, field-based human behaviors follows a predictable sequence; description, explanatory model-building attempting to demonstrate relationships among variables hypothesized as causes and consequences, and, when feasible, attempted interventions based on the manipulation of variables in the explanatory model. Because cyberbullying is commonly compared to bullying, it is noteworthy that while the study of bullying has reached the point at which meta-analyses of intervention success are possible (for example, Mishna, 2009; Ryan & Smith, 2009), the focus of research in the US on cyberbullying still seems to be on description and model building.

Prevalence

The most fundamental descriptive variables are the products of attempts to establish the commonality of cyberbullying and victimization. What proportion of pre-teens and adolescents are involved as perpetrators, victims, or both? Secondary to such basic information might be the breakdown of such typical levels of involvement by some secondary category (such as age or gender).

A common reaction of many researchers on reviewing the existing literature is just how variable reported levels of involvement actually are. For example, Juvonen and Gross (2008) summarize the existing findings on victimization by noting that the reported range of being cyberbullied at least once during the past year ranges across studies from 1% to 49%. In reporting data from their own research, these same researchers then state that 72% of Internet users report at least one incident during the previous year. Data such as these are confusing to those attempting to gain perspective on the problem, and some attempt must be made to account for what must be unlabeled sources of variability. Attempts to make comparisons of prevalance rates from published research based on categories of some type proposed post hoc are going to be extremely difficult to interpret and potentially misinformed.

One of the first questions to ask in bringing a perspective to this literature might be, how many of the existing studies were designed to be representative of the population of a specified age group within the US? These studies might be differentiated from studies tapping a population defined in some other way and not attempting to offer descriptive data representative of the nation. For example, the Pew Internet and American Life project involved a representative telephone survey of 12–17-year-olds (Lenhart, 2007). The Youth Internet Safety Surveys (YISS I and II) involved nationally representative telephone surveys of 10–17-year-olds (Ybarra & Mitchell, 2004a, 2004b; Wolak, Mitchell, & Finkelhor, 2007; Ybarra, Mitchell, Wolak, & Finkelhor, 2006). The Growing Up With Media survey involved a nationally representative telephone survey of 10–15-year-olds (Ybarra, Diener-West, & Leaf, 2007). These studies typically employ some minimal expectation for use of the Internet as an additional requirement.

Even within this set of studies, the range in rate of being cyberbullied is from 7% (Ybarra & Mitchell, 2004b) to 35% (Ybarra et al., 2007). The range in rate of engagement in cyberbullying is from 12% (Ybarra & Mitchell, 2004a) to 28% (Ybarra, Mitchell, Finkelhor, & Wolak, 2007).

Despite the similarities in these studies—national representative samples, phone interviews involving a small number of questions, similar and simple criteria based on whether or not the participant has had given experiences—the ranges reported are still substantial. Some differences in methodology are involved, but it is difficult to differentiate variables that may be responsible for the study to study variability when multiple variables are combined in various combinations. Lenhart (2007) identifies four categories of experience and asks, "Have you, personally, *ever* experienced any of the following things online?" Most of the other studies define the time period of interest as the *past year* (emphasis added). The survey questions also vary. For example, one of two items used to define a respondent as a cyberbully in the Youth Internet Safety Studies was "made a rude or nasty comment" (see, for example, Ybarra & Mitchell, 2004b). Twenty-eight percent of those surveyed indicated they had made such a comment. Such a statement might be interpreted as covering a fairly wide range of behaviors and some respondents may be referencing behaviors others might consider to be rather innocuous.

Contrast such a general statement with more specific statements used in other research. For example, the data reported by Lenhart (2007) asked whether someone had forwarded your private email or text message to someone else without permission or posted an embarrassing picture of you without permission. These descriptions likely lead to more similar interpretations on the part of respondents, but the sum of experience with a small number of specific behaviors may ignore other behaviors that reflect cyberbullying. It would seem that with a small number of questions, the severity of the behaviors described and the behaviors selected to represent the potentially vague concept of cyberbullying could generate significant differences in reported rates of cyberbullying and victimization. What is troublesome is that the variability locked in the details of specific studies is not communicated when cyberbullying is presented in textbooks or other secondary sources. Very different impressions are conveyed depending on the studies related to document the severity of the problem.

Bullying and Cyberbullying: Other Issues in Understanding the Prevalence of the Problem

The title of this book proposes a connection between bullying and cyberbullying, implying that, because of advances in technology and the availability of these advances to young people, bullying behavior is now evident in a new realm. Two questions related to this position will be considered here. The first concerns whether cyberbullying should be considered a category of bullying. This was discussed in Chapter 1. The second question ignores the definitional issue and considers the relationship or overlap between variables representing the prevalence of cyberbullying or online victimization and variables representing other forms of bullying and victimization.

Are bullying and cyberbullying interrelated?

A common assumption proposes that cyberbullying represents a progression or continuation made possible by new means of communication and sharing of information. Those prone to bullying now have new ways and more opportunities to attack their victims. Contrast this perspective with another that proposes the tools of cyberbullying change the balance of power present in face-to-face bullying in a way that allows some of those bullied to retaliate. In this case, the victim of face-to-face bullying becomes the perpetrator of online or cell phone attacks and does so targeting those who were the face-to-face aggressors (Ybarra & Mitchell, 2004a). Of course, being a victim within a given domain (face-to-face, online), does not preclude an individual from being aggressive toward others within that same domain.

Potentially, many relationships among forms of aggression, victimization, and method of interaction are possible. Several studies in the US have investigated the overlap between bullying and cyberbullying (Ybarra & Mitchell, 2004a; Raskauskas & Stoltz, 2007; Ybarra et al., 2007; Hinduja & Patchin, 2008). Basic descriptive data are offered for both online and face-to-face behavior and probabilities are tested to determine if involvement as a perpetrator or victim significantly influences the probability of also being a victim or perpetrator in the same or another domain.

In one of the original studies evaluating the overlap between bullying and cyberbullying in the US, Ybarra and Mitchell (2004a) determined that 19% of the adolescents surveyed had some involvement in cyberbullying or victimization; 12% as cyberbullies, 4% as victims, and 3% as both cyberbullies and victims. These categories were then used to determine the overlap with bullying. Fifty-six percent of these falling into the combination of cyberbully and victim category were also the targets of bullying. This was also true for 50% of cyberbullies and 44% of victims of cyberbullying, but only 29% of those with no involvement in either cyberbullying or victimization. The researchers concluded that these data indicate evidence both for overlap and exclusivity in these forms of aggression. A more recent study by Raskauskas and Stoltz (2007) examined the relationship between bullying and cyberbullying behavior and found a significant overlap between the two types of bullying. This led the researchers to hypothesize that being a victim of traditional bullying would predict victimization in cyberbullying.

Conversely, Hinduja and Patchin (2008) report their data on the interrelationship of face-to-face and online aggression in a slightly different way. They summarize their data by contending that real-life bullies are 2.5 times more likely to be involved in cyberbullying than those who do not bully. Victims of bullying were also determined to be 2.5 times more likely to be victims of cyberbullying that those who had not been bullied. The extent of overlap was extensive enough to encourage these researchers to propose that characteristics unique to categories of adolescents appear to make them likely to be general victims or perpetrators.

There appear to be important nuances in the relationship between face-to-face and online aggression. Ybarra, Diener-West, and Leaf (2007) indicate that 35% of their sample reported being cyberbullied, but that 64% of those cyberbullied had not been bullied. The frequency of being cyberbullied appeared to be a factor in the likelihood of being bullied. Among the 8% who reported being cyberbullied monthly, 50% reported being physically attacked at school while approximately 10% of those who were not cyberbullied reported being physically attacked. In a cross-sectional study, Williams and Guerra (2007) contrasted the rates of physical, verbal, and Internet bullying from elementary to high school. The overall rate of cyberbullying was 14%. Cyberbullying was significantly related to both verbal and physical bullying, with the strongest relationship found for verbal bullying. These forms of aggression followed different developmental trajectories. Physical and online bullying peaked in middle school and then declined. Verbal aggression increased into middle school and then remained high. Gender differences were noted for physical bullying only. Measures of moral beliefs, acceptance by peers, and interpretation of school climate were predictive of all forms of bullying, with the greatest similarity shown for cyberbullying and verbal bullying. These researchers conclude that cyberbullying is based in similar characteristics and as a practical matter should be part of educational and intervention programs already focused on bullying in schools.

The studies reported are typical of an approach that relies on survey data evaluating aggression and victimization with a small number of questions and a statistical approach attempting to answer questions about the commonality of bullying and cyberbullying based on self assignment to multiple categories of aggression and victimization. Varjas, Henrich, and Meyers (2009) take a different approach, relying on a more detailed survey including items concerning physical, verbal, relational bullying and victimization, cyberbullying and victimization, and a search for commonality involving confirmatory factor analysis. Higher order factors for aggression and victimization were evident. An intriguing result demonstrated that factors for physical, verbal, and relational bullying and victimization loaded more heavily on the corresponding higher order factors for aggression and victimization than did the factors for cyberbullying and cybervictimization.

Finally, retaliation represents a unique hypothesized explanation for the relationship between face-to-face and online experiences. Juvonen and Gross (2008) specifically addressed retaliation in a study focused on the behavior of victims. Seventy-seven percent of their sample claimed they had experienced at least one incident of bullying in the past year while 72% had been cyberbullied at least once, with a high overlap between the two forms of victimization. While 48% contended they retaliated, only 12% of those who responded to those who bullied them claimed they retaliated online. Most (60%) claimed they retaliated at school and 28% responded both at school and online.

Prevalence of cyberbullying and tools used

The online environment offers many options for communication and information sharing. Cell phone users typically also have several tools at their disposal. Several researchers have attempted to identify which tools seem most likely to be applied in cyberbullying and how these tools are used in aggressive acts. The information garnered from these studies offers several practical benefits. In some cases, the identification of frequent perpetration strategies can be used to inform the development of curricula to be used in educational programs designed to combat cyberbullying. Educational institutions and parents also frequently employ filtering software to prevent access to websites and online services potentially posing threats to young Internet users. As noted previously, the challenge in setting filters is making decisions that are not overly restrictive and limit access to beneficial services. The findings from these surveys should identify services that are most frequently problematic.

Both cyberbullies and their victims spend more time online than others from their cohort (Wolak et al., 2007; Hinduja & Patchin, 2008). Cyberbullies in the US do tend to use some tools more frequently than others. It appears that computer-based instant messaging (Kowalski & Limber, 2007; Wolak et al., 2007; Hinduja & Patchin, 2008; Juvonen & Gross, 2008) and chat (Kowalski & Limber, 2007; Wolak et al., 2007; Hinduja & Patchin, 2008) are the most frequent means of cyberbullying when comparisons are made among multiple tools. Wolak et al. (2007) observed that instant messaging was the most significant predictor when victims knew the perpetrator and chat was the most significant predictor when victims did not know the perpetrator. Perhaps most notable in these studies was that cell phone text messaging was not among the most significant predictors even though it was included in several of the lists researchers presented to victims.

An important issue associated with the tools through which adolescents experience bullying is whether victims of cyberbullying understand the opportunities built into these tools to resist aggression and whether adolescents take advantage of the protection these tools offer. The data seem to offer mixed reviews on these topics. Wolak et al. (2007) examine the reaction of victims to aggressors they both knew and did not know, and found that victims of aggression resulting from "online only" contacts were terminated in 75% of instances by taking "simple actions" (such as left site, blocked, ignored). These same techniques were applied in 41% of situations in which the victims knew the aggressors. A teacher or parent was contacted in 11% of cases involving known aggressors and no teacher or parent was contacted in situations involving online only aggressors. Data from Juvonen and Gross (2008) offer more specific detail on how victims respond to aggression by way of instant messaging. When asked about actions they had taken, 75% indicated they had blocked a screen name, 45% had restricted their buddy list, 44% had changed their own screen name, and 34% had sent an aggressor a warning message. What these data cannot indicate is some insight into specific situations and whether or not the victims in those situations felt no need to respond, were unaware of how they might respond, or were intimidated.

Emotional and Behavioral Consequences of Cyberbullying

Such outcomes are very difficult to determine, but researchers have made efforts to relate experiences of victimization to what might be described as negative characteristics and behaviors. The challenge here is separating cause from consequence. The power differential that is suggested to be inherent in bullying implies that characteristics that suggest weakness or uniqueness may mark certain adolescents as targets. So, for example, it is difficult to determine if low self-esteem invites cyberbullying, is a consequence of cyberbullying, or if both possibilities apply. However, Kowalski, Limber, and Agatston (2008) conclude that students with lower levels of self-esteem and higher levels of social anxiety were more vulnerable to being cyberbullied.

Very few studies have addressed how cyberbullying is negatively correlated with psychological/emotional issues. However, it is believed that victims of cyberbullying experience serious psychological and emotional harm and on some occasions even commit suicide (Patchin & Hinduja, 2006). According to Reid, Monsen, and Rivers

(2004), verbal and psychological bullying may have more long-term effects than physical bullying. Additionally, individuals who have been harassed online compared with those who have not been victimized online are more likely to experience depressive symptoms, interpersonal victimization, social skill deficits, and to harass others online (Ybarra, 2004).

Reporting cyberbullying

Much research and time has been devoted to encouraging students to come forward if they or someone they know have been bullied or harassed in any way. Consistently, we find this does not happen as much as we would like. According to Ybarra et al. (2006), 33% of victims of cyberbullying do not tell anyone about the incident. But why is this? Why do some students fail to tell anyone when they have been victimized? According to Juvonen and Gross (2008), students fail to report cyberbullying because they think they can deal with it on their own. Conversely, Agatston, Kowalski, & Limber (2007) believe students do not report cyberbullying at school because they feel school district personnel are not effective in dealing with the problem. These hypotheses will be examined in this chapter.

Additionally, it has long been assumed that when youth tell parents/teachers about a bullying incident, the behavior will stop. But what actually happens when youth report bullying? Does the behavior stop or continue? The current research attempts to answer these questions.

Summary of Trends in Cyberbullying

We regard cyberbullying research in the US as demonstrating characteristics typical of a new area of study. These studies focus on descriptive data and the investigation of hypothesized variable to variable relationships. Even basic descriptive data vary over a tremendous range, possibly as a consequence of unknown differences in populations studied or simple differences in the way problem behaviors are defined. Studies using nationally representative samples indicate that between 7% and 35% of youth have been cyberbullied and between 12% and 28% have cyberbullied others.

Investigating the relationship between bullying and cyberbullying has been motivated by theoretical and practical concerns. Victimization and perpetration in face-to-face and virtual settings demonstrate considerable overlap. Those involved in bullying are more than twice as likely to also cyberbully and those bullied are more than twice as likely to also be the victims of cyberbullying. Still, age- and gender-based differences in the relationships among forms of face-to-face and virtual aggression and victimization and the significant number of individuals victimized in only one environment indicate the need to understand what unique factors may be important in each setting. The significant overlap in these two areas of aggression suggests that both might be addressed in the same school intervention program.

The Present Study

The present study investigates the nature and extent of adolescents' experiences of cyberbullying. This study replicates earlier descriptive research on the prevalence of cyberbullying and related variables thought to influence the likelihood of being cyberbullied, such as gender. A number of hypotheses will be examined, many of which were discussed earlier in this chapter. Hypothesis one states that students with greater access to technology (Internet and cell phone) will be more vulnerable to being cyberbullied. The second hypothesis proposes that students with lower levels of self-esteem and higher levels of social anxiety will be more susceptible to being cyberbullied. The final hypothesis will examine the degree of overlap between traditional bullying and cyberbullying behavior. It is predicted that victims of traditional bullying will be more likely to also be victims of cyberbullying.

The second part of the study collects data on student reactions to cyberbullying attacks and the perception of reactions when reporting experiences to adults. For example, students who did not report the incident were asked to provide reasons for their behavior. Conversely, when students did report the incident, they were asked who they told and the resulting consequences. These are perhaps the most relevant questions for educators, yet the questions are seldom asked. Therefore, these data should be useful to school personnel, parents/guardians, and researchers.

Method

Participants

Participants included 383 students (190 males and 193 females) from four middle schools in a Northern American city. The average age of students was 13.5 years ($SD = 0.54$). Only eighth graders (with passive parental consent) in class on the day of survey administration were eligible to participate. The demographics of the participants are provided in Table 7.1.

Measures and procedure

A thorough search of the literature was unable to reveal a self-report survey that contained all the items of interest in the current study. Therefore, an anonymous paper and pencil survey, "A Look at Offline and Online Behaviors," was developed

Table 7.1 Participant Demographics (Percentages).

	Ethnicity					*Technology*		
Gender	*Caucasian*	*Aboriginal/ Native*	*Hispanic*	*Asian*	*Black*	*Own cell phone*	*Internet at home*	*Internet in bedroom*
Male	81	4	3	3	6	64	95	22
Female	80	7	3	5	1	73	95	27

for the purposes of this study (see Appendix A to this chapter). Two intact scales, Rosenberg's (1965) Self-Esteem Scale and Leary's (1983) Interaction Anxiousness Scale were used to supplement the questions created by the researchers.

Two specific measures were defined in this study; bullying and cyberbullying. The first measure, bullying, was adopted from Nansel et al. (2001) and defined as, "a repeated, aggressive, intentional behavior towards one person from another person or group of people causing the victim to feel hurt; physically, mentally or emotionally." Several questions examined students' bullying behaviors; victimization, perpetration, as well as witnessing bullying behaviors.

The second measure assessed cyberbullying behavior. Cyberbullying was defined as "the intentional and repeated harm of others through the use of computers, cell phones and other electronic devices." A number of questions examined students' cyberbullying behavior; victimization, perpetration, as well as witnessing cyberbullying behavior. These questions assessed cyberbullying behavior over one's lifetime, the last year, the last 30 days, and a few specific items focused on students' most recent experience.

A subset of questions investigated issues associated with the reporting of cyberbullying. Specific questions asked students who were victimized, who did you tell? What happened when you told someone? And did the behavior stop? An additional question offered students the option of reporting the reason(s) they chose not to report the incident.

Additionally, two intact scales were used to compliment the survey items described above: Rosenberg's (1965) Self-Esteem Scale and Leary's (1983) Interaction Anxiousness Scale. The Self-Esteem scale was a ten-item measure of how individuals felt about themselves. Higher scores on this scale reflected higher levels of self-esteem with scores ranging from 10 to 50. The Interaction Anxiousness Scale was a 15-item measure that reflected an individual's level of social anxiety. Higher scores indicated higher levels of social anxiety and ranged from 15 to 75.

Passive parental consent was obtained for all of the students who participated in the research. Additionally, students were asked to read and sign a consent form before filling out a questionnaire that took approximately 25 minutes to complete. Students were also told that they could withdraw from the research at any time.

Analysis

Frequency and descriptive statistics were used to explore the nature and extent of cyberbullying behavior. Chi-square analyses were used to examine associations between variables of interest while correlations were used to test the strength of various relationships.

Results

Prevalence

Across the sample ($N = 383$), 17% of respondents reported being cyberbullied at least once in their lifetime, while 16% reported incidence in the last year. Of those students who were cyberbullied in the last year, 62% were cyberbullied at least "once or twice" in the last 30 days. A chi-square analysis found a significant association between gender and cyberbully victimization, $\chi^2(1, N = 383) = 23.24, p < 0.05$ with females being bullied more frequently than would be expected by chance.

Conversely, only 11% of students reported cyberbullying others at least once in their lifetime and 9% in the last year. Of these students, 64% reported cyberbullying others at least "once or twice" in the last 30 days. A significant association was found between gender and cyberbullying using a chi-square analysis, $\chi^2(1, N = 383) = 4.01, p < 0.05$ as more females were cyberbullied than would be expected by chance.

Lastly, 39% of students reported witnessing cyberbullying. Again, a chi-square analysis revealed gender differences in witnessing cyberbullying, with more females being witness to cyberbullying than would be expected by chance, $\chi^2(1, N = 377) = 16.47, p < 0.05$.

Internet and cell phone correlates

Were students who used the Internet more frequently also more likely to be involved in cyberbullying? The answer is yes. A significant, but weak, relationship was found among cyberbullying victimization in the last year and frequency of Internet use; $r(382) = 0.10$, $p < 0.05$. Additionally, a significant relationship was found between cyberbully perpetration in the last year and frequency of Internet use; $r(382) = 0.15$, $p < 0.01$.

Would cell phone ownership leave adolescents more vulnerable to being cyberbullied? The answer is no. The relationship between cyberbully victimization in the last year and cell phone ownership was not significant; $r(382) = -0.08$, $p = 0.11$. However, a significant, but weak, relationship was found between cyberbully perpetration in the last year and cell phone ownership; $r(382) = 0.10, p < 0.05$.

In summary, partial support was found for the hypothesis that students who use the Internet more frequently are more likely to be involved in cyberbullying. However, cell phone ownership did not appear to play a role in the likelihood of being cyberbullied. Thus, it is unclear what specific role technology plays in the vulnerability of student involvement in cyberbullying behavior.

Method used to cyberbully

Victims of cyberbullying reported being bullied most often through cell phones (77%), instant messaging (75%), social networking sites (46%), email (28%), and chatrooms (7%). It is important to note that these categories were not mutually exclusive.

Do victims know the cyberbully?

Students reported being cyberbullied most often by classmates (56%) followed by ex-friends (52%), friends (44%), ex-boyfriends/girlfriends (36%), strangers (27%), many people (11%), and don't know (8%). Once again, these categories were not mutually exclusive.

One of the common assumptions associated with cyberbullying involves its anonymity. However, this study found little support for this. Only 8% of students who were cyberbullied did not know the identity of the cyberbully. This finding contradicts a previous report by Kowalski and Limber (2007) who reported that 48% of victims did not know the identity of the cyberbully.

Response to cyberbullying

The most common response used by 56% of the victims of cyberbullying was to block the cyberbully. This response was followed by getting revenge (25%), doing nothing (23%), leaving the site (17%), turning off their computer/cell phone (9%), and changing their screen name/email address (5%).

Psychological impact/distress

Victim level of distress was examined in relation to impact on school work, social relationships, and perceived safety at school. Nearly three in ten victims (28%) reported their school work was negatively impacted and 53% reported that the bullying was harmful to their social relationships. Additionally, 45% of students who were cyberbullied felt safe at school only "sometimes." These findings suggest that many students were significantly negatively impacted by their cyberbullying experience.

Additional analyses examined associations between self-esteem and social anxiety with cybervictimization. A significant association was found between students who had been cyberbullied in the past year and self-esteem, $r(367) = 0.19, p < 0.01$. This suggests students with lower levels of self-esteem were more likely to be cyberbullied. Conversely, the relationship between cybervictimization and social anxiety failed to yield a significant association. Thus, only partial support was found for the hypothesis posed by Agatston et al. (2007) who concluded that students with lower levels of self-esteem and higher levels of social anxiety were more vulnerable to being cyberbullied.

The relationship between traditional bullying and cyberbullying

A total of four chi-square analyses were conducted to examine the relationship between traditional bullying and cyberbullying. Significant relationships were found in each relationship and the results are presented in Table 7.2.

The first chi-square analysis examined the hypothesis of Raskauskas and Stoltz (2007) that victims of traditional bullying would be more likely to be cyberbullied. Our data found support for this hypothesis as a significant relationship was observed (see Table 7.2); 97% of students who were traditionally bullied were also cyberbullied.

A second chi-square analysis compared the relative frequency of victims of traditional bullying and those who cyberbullied others. Eighty-one percent of students who had cyberbullied others in the past year had also been bullied via traditional means. A significant association was found suggesting students who cyberbullied others were more likely to be traditionally bullied than would be expected by chance.

Table 7.2 Contingency Table Comparing Traditional Bullying and Cyberbullying Behavior ($N = 383$).

Traditional bullying	*Cyberbullying*	χ	df	p
Victim	Victim	33.77	1	<0.05
Victim	Bully	5.20	1	<0.05
Bully	Victim	31.61	1	<0.05
Bully	Bully	43.06	1	<0.05

Additional analyses examined associations between traditional bullying behavior with both victims of cyberbullying and cyberbullies. Significant relationships were found in both relationships (see Table 7.2). This suggests students who traditionally bullied others were more likely to be victims of cyberbullying as well as to cyberbully others.

Reporting

A central focus of this study concerned whether cyberbullying incidents were reported. Reporting was analyzed from the perspectives of the victim and witnesses of cyberbullying.

With traditional bullying, victims or witnesses have been encouraged to come forward with their knowledge of the event. Research has consistently shown many incidents go unreported. Presently, much of the research on cyberbullying has followed a similar pattern whereby many students do not report what they observe or experience. This study found 29% of students who were cyberbullied in the past year did not report the incident. This is consistent with previous research (Ybarra et al., 2006).

Open-ended questions examined the reasoning students used to explain their reporting behavior. The primary reasons students chose not to report were, "they didn't feel it was a big deal" and "they felt they could handle it on their own." These statements comprised 57% of the responses. These reasons were followed by students thinking "it would make it worse" or because they were "scared to tell." 29% of students reported these comments. Lastly, 14% of students either did not know why or just did not want to report the incident. These data are consistent with the hypothesis by Juvonen and Gross (2008) who concluded students fail to report cyberbullying because they think they can deal with it on their own.

Interestingly, what has been absent in the literature is an examination of the perceived outcome when students report cyberbullying experiences. Students are encouraged to come forward with information about cyberbullying but, when they do, what happens? Does the cyberbullying behavior stop? Both open- and close-ended questions were used to answer these questions.

In the current study, 71% of students reported the incident to someone after they were cyberbullied. Of these students, friend(s) were told 60% of the time followed

Table 7.3 An Examination of the Outcome When Students Reported Cyberbullying (CB).

Role in CB	*Told adults*	*Told peers*	*Chance of CB stopping (%)*
Victim	Yes	No	47
Victim	No	Yes	54
Victim	Yes	Yes	34
Witness	Yes	No	52
Witness	No	Yes	42
Witness	Yes	Yes	30

by parent(s) 46% of the time. The remaining 27% of students told teacher(s), sibling(s), or others. Perhaps most interestingly, teachers were told less than 6% of the time. The implications of the low rate of informing teachers are discussed later.

Chi-square analyses compared the relative frequency of outcome category by the group adolescents informed of their experience. The relationship between outcome and who was told was examined from the perspective of the victim as well as witness to cyberbullying. Due to small cell sizes for some categories, three categories were created for the variable "who was told:" adults (parents and/or teachers), peers (friends and/or siblings and/or cousins), and adults/peers (both adults and peers). The variable "outcome" was coded dichotomously as either the behavior stopped or it did not stop.

A chi-square analysis failed to demonstrate a significant association between the category of individuals informed and future experiences, $\chi^2(2, N = 52) = 2.70$, $p = 0.259$. Who victims of cyberbullying told did not appear to affect whether the experience of being cyberbullied continued (see Table 7.3). A similar outcome was demonstrated when witnesses reported cyberbullying. A chi-square analysis failed to find significant association between the category of individuals informed and future experiences, $\chi^2(2, N = 88) = 2.34$, $p = 0.311$. Who witnesses of cyberbullying told did not affect whether the experience of being cyberbullied continued (see Table 7.3). Perhaps of greatest interest from Table 7.3, it appears that when being bullied was reported to both adults and peers, the chances of the behavior stopping were actually at the lowest level of 30%. Perhaps victims seek assistance as widely as possible when bullying is more severe.

Discussion

The data suggest cyberbullying is an issue of concern among middle school students in the US. Nearly 17% of students in the sample reported being cyberbullied at least once in the past year. Of these students, 62% reported being bullied multiple times in the last 30 days. Fewer youth (11%) reported cyberbullying others and, of these students, 64% had cyberbullied others at least "once or twice" in the last 30 days. Lastly, four of every ten students had witnessed someone being cyberbullied in their life.

While it is difficult to compare prevalence rates of cyberbullying among the different published studies, students in this study are reporting cyberbully victimization at a lower rate than is the case in other studies (Juvonen & Gross, 2008). This difference may be due to the sample that was used in this study. The schools that participated were from a smaller city setting. Speculation might be that bigger city/urban youth are exposed to and have greater access to technology, which leads to greater risk of being cyberbullied. However, future research is needed to further explore the relationship between small/large city settings with cyberbullying behavior.

The data suggest that increased access to technology make adolescents more vulnerable to being cyberbullied. More than 90% of students in the sample had Internet access at home and more than 80% reported owning a cell phone. Of these students, females had significantly more access to the Internet in their bedroom than males and were more likely to own a cell phone. Interestingly, female students were also over-represented among all aspects of cyberbullying; victim, perpetrator, and witness. Thus, it would appear there is at least an indirect link between access to technology and cyberbullying.

Victims of cyberbullying reported being bullied most often through cell phones and by someone they knew. Only 8% of victims did not know the identity of the cyberbully. This provides little support for the assumption that cyberbullying is a particularly anonymous activity. More than half of the students responded by blocking the bully while a large number of students responded by getting revenge. It is unclear if students chose to get revenge by cyberbullying others. It will be important for future research to assess how many students only cyberbully others to avenge being cyberbullied themselves.

It appears some students were negatively impacted by the experience, as more than one in four students stated the bullying affected their school work and more than half of students' social relationships were affected. Interestingly, nearly 50% of students who were cyberbullied felt safe at school only "sometimes." Thus, it appears there are a large number of students who are truly distressed by the incident while a smaller number remain unaffected. It will be important to consider if students who are virtually unaffected by the incident should be counted as victims of cyberbullying or not.

Our data suggest students with lower levels of self-esteem were more vulnerable to being cyberbullied, thus providing partial support for our hypothesis. Schools may be prudent to provide workshops or activities geared towards building students' levels of self-esteem as it can provide them with a "buffer" against negative experiences such as cyberbullying.

Interestingly, the data identifies a considerable overlap between bullying (victim and bully) and cyberbullying (victim and bully) behavior. This suggests that cyberbullying may be an extension of traditional bullying and not two distinct types of behavior. However, future research is needed to identify if a causal relationship exists between the two types of bullying.

A focal point of this study concerned the reporting aspects of cyberbullying. Almost 30% of students who were cyberbullied did not tell anyone about the incident. Students' primary reasoning for this behavior were consistent with the hypothesis by Juvonen and Gross (2008) who concluded students fail to report their experiences to school officials because they think they can deal with it on their own. Other explanations were offered, such as students thinking that telling someone would make it worse or that they were afraid to tell. Collectively, many students are still opting not to report the incident to anyone for a variety of reasons. It is important we continue to look for ways to increase reporting among students.

When students did report incidence of cyberbullying, friends and parents were told most frequently. Perhaps most importantly, very few teachers were told. It is unclear if these students did not report to teachers because they felt teachers would not be able to help them or because they feared getting in trouble at school. Future research is needed to examine why students rarely tell teachers about cyberbullying as well as to identify teachers' knowledge of cyberbullying. Without this knowledge, many teachers are not equipped to effectively help youth who come forward with information about cyberbullying.

A unique aspect of this study addressed the relationship of who was told relative to the impact on future cyberbullying experiences. This relationship had not been examined previously in cyberbullying research. No significant associations were found between who was told relative to whether cyberbullying was reported by victims or witnesses to future experiences. In other words, the specific audience with which students shared negative experiences was not associated with the likelihood that the negative experience would stop. In fact, when both adults and peers were told, the chance of the cyberbullying behavior stopping was just 33% compared to almost 50% when only adults or peers were told. The results were similar when a witness reported the incident. Future research is needed to address what actually happens when adults and/or peers are told about an incident. What do these individuals do with this information? It is clear these individuals are not very successful in helping students deal with the problem, as the behavior often persists. As such, students may conclude it does not help to tell someone. Both adults and peers need to be taught better strategies to help youth who have been cyberbullied. Better outcomes in these situations will encourage more students to come forward with the critical information needed to address the problem of cyberbullying.

Implications

Our review of the published research in combination with our own experiences collecting data has encouraged reflection on what topics we and others might address next and how these issues might be addressed.

Some attempt should be made to standardize what is described as cyberbullying. Agreeing on standard definitions and perhaps instruments would be productive. Consider, for example, the efforts made by Konishi and colleagues (2009) to administer a common instrument used in the assessment of bullying in multiple countries. Perhaps the place to begin is to look at the ways in which the term is used in the research.

A practical definition of cyberbullying might combine variables determining the perception of personal distress and a period of time during which the victim was subjected to harassment. For example, feeling distressed for a month or more as the result of two or more identifiable damaging interactions might constitute cyberbullying.

It seems that the experience of being cyberbullied unfolds as a sequence of events and reactions and the individual differences in such sequences can vary considerably. For example, our interest was in the sequence—cyberbullying attack, perception of distress, decision regarding communication of distress with another, reaction of the other, and perception of change in likelihood of continued attacks. It is difficult to track this sequence through all possible options using traditional statistical procedures. It might make more sense to first attempt to understand likely sequences using qualitative methods. We attempted to include open-ended items in our survey but found participant response was unpredictable. The focus group approach already used by some (Agatston et al., 2007) would be an ideal approach.

Additionally, there are several implications for schools and policy makers. First, our data indicates that students rarely report cyberbullying to teachers. It is difficult to ascertain why this is. If schools are encouraging students to come forward with this information, it appears this message is being largely ignored. Perhaps different methods and strategies should be employed to encourage reporting, such as having drop boxes around school that would ensure anonymity.

Second, the data tells us that students confide in friends and parents/guardians most frequently. As such, greater efforts should be made to educate these individuals about the dangers of cyberbullying. This may include teaching youth recognition and awareness of placing yourself in vulnerable and susceptible positions; teaching peers to be more proactive in identifying when help is needed and what to do; and encouraging parents to be more aware of their children's computer habits and behaviors.

Third, since students frequently tell parents/guardians, better efforts should be made to teach these individuals about cyberbullying and its consequences. Since parents/guardians often see this as a problem associated with the school, an opportunity for discussion of the issue with school personnel might be welcomed by parents/guardians. It would be productive for schools to involve parents/guardians in these discussions because it will take a joint effort to deal with the problem of cyberbullying. For example, schools might schedule an open meeting or discussion with parents/guardians or develop a workshop to educate parents about cyberbullying.

Appendix: A look at offline and online behaviors

PART ONE: About yourself (please circle or fill your answer in the blank provided)

1. Sex: Maleapp Female
2. Year of birth: _____
3. Grade: _____

4. How do you describe yourself: a) Asian b) Hispanic c) Black d) White e) Aboriginal/Native f) Other
5. English is my second language? a) Yes b) No
6. My school grades are usually: a) As b) Bs c) Cs d) Ds e) Fs

PART TWO: Internet use (please circle or fill your answer in the blank provided)

7. How old were you when you first used the Internet? _____
8. Do you have Internet access at home? a) Yes b) No
9. Do you have a computer in your bedroom with Internet access? a) Yes b) No
10. Are there certain sites that you know of that you are **not allowed** to go to **at school**?
    a) Yes b) No
11. If **yes,** what are these sites? ________________________________
12. Are there certain sites that you know of that you are **not allowed** to go to **at home**?
    a) Yes b) No
13. If **yes,** what are these sites? ________________________________
14. Approximately how long are you on the Internet in a given week **at school**?
    a) 0–3 hours b) 4–7 hours c) 8–11 hours d) more than 11 hours
15. Approximately how long are you on the Internet in a given week **at home**?
    a) 0–3 hours b) 4–7 hours c) 8–11 hours d) more than 11 hours
16. Please estimate how much time you engage in each activity listed in a given week:

    (**Please write your response in hours**)
    a) Email _____ b) Social networking sites _____ c) Chatrooms _____
    d) Online games _____ e) Instant messaging _____
    f) School work _____

PART THREE: Cell phone use (please circle or fill your answer in the blank provided)

17. Do you own a cell phone? a) Yes b) No
18. If **yes**, how old were you when you first got a cell phone? _____
19. Do you use your cell phone ***during the school day***? a) Yes b) No
20. Do you think having a ban of cell phones ***during the school day*** would prevent kids being made fun of through text messaging, videos, or pictures?
    a) Yes b) No

21. Have you ever received repeated texts from a friend or stranger that made you sad, frustrated, or angry? a) Yes b) No

PART FOUR: Bullying

Definition of bullying: Bullying is a repeated, aggressive, intentional behavior towards one person from another person or group of people causing the victim to feel hurt, physically, mentally, or emotionally.

Please circle or fill in your response in the space provided.

22. In my lifetime, I have ***been bullied*** at school at least once. a) Yes b) No
23. If you have ***been bullied*** at school, how did you feel about it? ____________
____
____
24. Did you tell anyone about the incident(s)? a) Yes b) No c) I haven't been bullied
25. If ***yes***, who did you tell?
a) Parent(s) b) Teacher c) Friend(s) d) Sibling e) Other, please specify: _____
26. If ***no***, why did you not tell anyone? ____________________
____
____
27. In my lifetime, I have ***bullied others*** at school at least once. a) Yes b) No
28. If you have ***bullied others*** at school, why did you do it? ______________
____
____
29. Did you tell anyone about the incident(s)? a) Yes b) No c) I have not bullied others
30. Have you been a ***witness*** to someone else ***being bullied***? a) Yes b) No
31. If you have witnessed someone ***being bullied***, what did you do?
a) Nothing b) Tried to stop it c) Joined in with the bullying
d) I have not seen anyone being bullied e) Other, please specify: ________
____
32. If you have **witnessed bullying** and told someone about the incident, did it help to reduce the bullying behavior?
a) Yes b) No c) I have not witnessed bullying
33. Do you know if there is an ***anti-bullying prevention program*** in your ***school***?
a) Yes b) No

34. If there is, do you think it has helped to ***reduce bullying behavior***?
    a) Yes b) No

PART FIVE: Cyberbullying

Definition of cyberbullying: Cyberbullying is the intentional and repeated harm of others through the use of computers, cell phones, and other electronic devices. Some examples include:

- **Taking a picture of someone against their will and posting it online without the person's permission**
- **Hacking into a someone's email or MySpace account and sending messages to their friends**
- **Being humiliated and embarrassed in a chatroom**
- **Sending personal messages about a friend to everyone in your class**
- **Creating a website about a classmate to make fun of them.**

Please circle the response that fits you best.

35. In the last year, I have ***been cyberbullied.*** a) Yes b) No
36. In the last 30 days, I have ***been cyberbullied***:
    a) Never b) Once or twice c) A few times d) Many times e) Every day
37. I have ***been cyberbullied*** via (**please circle ALL that apply**):
    a) I have not been cyberbullied
    b) Instant messaging
    c) Chatrooms
    d) Cell phones
    e) Social networking sites (such as MySpace and Facebook)
    f) Email
    g) Other, please specify: _____
38. I have ***been cyberbullied*** by (**please circle ALL that apply**):
    a) No one has cyberbullied me
    b) Classmates
    c) Friend (s)
    d) Ex-friend
    e) Ex-boyfriend or girlfriend
    f) Stranger
    g) Many people
    h) I don't know
    i) Other, please specify: ____________

If you have experienced being cyberbullied, please tell me about your most recent experience (this refers to questions 39–46):

39. How did you respond to ***your cyberbullying*** experience?
    a) No one has cyberbullied me

b) Turned off my computer/cell phone
c) Left the site
d) Did nothing
e) Changed screen name or email address
f) Blocked the person
g) Called the police
h) Other, please specify: _____

40. Did I tell anyone when I ***was cyberbullied***?
a) Yes b) No c) I have not been cyberbullied

41. If you did **tell someone**, who did you tell?
a) Parent(s) b) Teacher c) Friend(s) d) Sibling e) Other, please specify: _____

42. If you did tell someone when you were ***being cyberbullied***, what happened? Did the behavior stop?
____
____
____
____

43. If you **did not tell anyone**, why did you choose not to?
____
____
____

44. Did it affect your school work? a) Yes b) No c) I have not been cyberbullied

45. Did it affect your social relationships? a) Yes b) No c) I have not been cyberbullied

46. How did you feel about getting ***cyberbullied***?
____
____

47. In the last year, I have ***cyberbullied others.*** a) Yes b) No

48. In the last 30 days, I have ***cyberbullied others***:
a) Never b) Once or twice c) A few times d) Many times e) Every day

49. I ***cyberbullied others*** via (**please circle ALL that apply**):
a) I have not cyberbullied others
b) Instant messaging
c) Chatrooms
d) Cell phones
e) Social networking sites (such as MySpace and Facebook)
f) Email
g) Other, please specify: ______________________________

If you have cyberbullied others, please tell me about your most recent experience (this refers to questions 50–54):

50. Why did you decide to ***cyberbully*** someone?
    a) I have not cyberbullied anyone
    b) For fun
    c) Because I don't like them
    d) Because others were doing it
    e) To demonstrate power
    f) For revenge
    g) Other, please specify:____________________________________

51. Did you know the person ***you were cyberbullying***?
    a) Yes b) No c) I have not cyberbullied anyone

52. How did you know the person ***you were cyberbullying***?
    a) I have not cyberbullied anyone
    b) Friend
    c) Ex-boyfriend or ex-girlfriend
    d) Ex-friend
    e) Someone from school
    f) Someone I met online
    g) Stranger
    h) Other, please specify: ____________________________________

53. What did you ***use to cyberbully*** the individual?
    a) Instant messaging
    b) Chatrooms
    c) Cell phone
    d) Social networking sites (such as MySpace or Facebook)
    e) Email
    f) Other, please specify: ____________________________________

54. If you used a computer ***to cyberbully***, whose computer did you use?
    a) I did not use a computer to cyberbully
    b) Home computer(s)
    c) School computer(s)
    d) Computer at a friend's house

55. Do you know someone who has ***been cyberbullied***? a) Yes b) No

56. If you knew someone was ***being cyberbullied,*** have you told:
    a) Parent(s)
    b) Teacher(s)
    c) Adult
    d) Friend(s)
    e) Sibling
    f) No one

57. If you have told when you knew someone was ***being cyberbullied***, what happened? Did the behavior stop? ______________________________
____
____
____

58. When **adults in school** know about ***cyberbullying***, do they try to stop it?
a) Yes b) No

59. I know personal safety strategies in cyberspace. a) Yes b) No

60. What safety strategies do you know about?
____
____
____

61. I learned these strategies from:
a) Taught myself
b) Teacher(s)
c) Parent(s)
d) Friend(s)
e) Other, please specify: ______________________________

62. Do you feel safe **at school**? a) Yes b) No c) Sometimes

How do you think about yourself? (Please circle only ONE response).

63. I feel that I am a person of worth, at least on an equal plane with others.
Strongly agree Agree Disagree Strongly disagree

64. I feel that I have a number of good qualities.
Strongly agree Agree Disagree Strongly disagree

65. I am inclined to feel that I am a failure.
Strongly agree Agree Disagree Strongly disagree

66. I am able to do things as well as most other people.
Strongly agree Agree Disagree Strongly disagree

67. I feel that I do not have much to be proud of.
Strongly agree Agree Disagree Strongly disagree

68. I take a positive attitude toward myself.
Strongly agree Agree Disagree Strongly disagree

69. On the whole, I am satisfied with myself.
Strongly agree Agree Disagree Strongly disagree

70. I wish I could have more respect for myself.
Strongly agree Agree Disagree Strongly disagree

71. I certainly feel useless at times.
Strongly agree Agree Disagree Strongly disagree

72. At times, I think I am no good at all.
Strongly agree Agree Disagree Strongly disagree

Please rate how you feel in different social situations (please only choose one number for each blank).

Indicate how characteristic each of the following statements is of you, according to the following scale:

1 = NOT AT ALL characteristic of me
2 = SLIGHTLY characteristic of me
3 = MODERATELY characteristic of me
4 = VERY characteristic of me
5 = EXTREMELY characteristic of me

73. _____ I often feel nervous, even in casual get-togethers.
74. _____ I usually feel comfortable when I'm in a group of people I don't know.
75. _____ I am usually at ease when speaking to a member of the opposite sex.
76. _____ I get nervous when I must talk to a teacher or boss.
77. _____ Parties often make me feel anxious and uncomfortable.
78. _____ I am probably less shy in social interactions than most people.
79. _____ I sometimes feel tense when talking to people of my own sex if I don't know them very well.
80. _____ I would be nervous if I was being interviewed for a job.
81. _____ I wish I had more confidence in social situations.
82. _____ I seldom feel anxious in social situations.
83. _____ In general, I am a shy person.
84. _____ I often feel nervous when talking to an attractive member of the opposite sex.
85. _____ I often feel nervous when calling someone I don't know very well on the telephone.
86. _____ I get nervous when I speak to someone in a position of authority.
87. _____ I usually feel relaxed around other people, even people who are quite different to me.

References

Agatston, P. W., Kowalski, R., & Limber, S. (2007). Students' perspectives on cyberbullying. *Journal of Adolescent Health, 41*, S59–S60.

Althaus, S. (1997). Computer-mediated communication in the university classroom: An experiment with online discussions. *Communication Education, 46*, 158–174.

David-Ferdon, C., & Hertz, M. H. (2007). Electronic media, violence, and adolescents: An emerging public health problem. *Journal of Adolescent Health, 41*, S1–S5.

Hinduja, S., & Patchin, J. W. (2008). Cyberbullying: An exploratory analysis of factors related to offending and victimization. *Deviant Behavior, 29*, 129–156.

Juvonen, J., & Gross, E. F. (2008). Extending the school grounds? Bullying experiences in cyberspace. *Journal of School Health, 78*, 496–505.

Kiesler, S., Zubrow, D., & Moses, A. M. (1985). Affect in computer mediated communication: An experiment in synchronous terminal-to-terminal discussion. *Human–Computer Interaction, 1*, 77–104.

Konishi, C., Hymel, S., Zumbo, B. D., Li, Z., Taki, M., Slee, P., Pepler, D., Sim, H., Craig, W., Swearer, S., & Kwak, K. (2009). Investigating the comparability of a self-report measure of childhood bullying across countries. *Canadian Journal of School Psychology, 24*, 892–893.

Kowalski, R. M., & Limber, S. P. (2007). Electronic bullying among middle school students. *Journal of Adolescent Health, 41*, S22–S30.

Kowalski, R. M., Limber, S. P., & Agatston, P. W. (2008). *Cyberbullying*. Malden, MA: Blackwell.

Leary, M. (1983). Social anxiousness: The construct and its measurement. *Journal of Personality Assessment, 47*(1), 66–75.

Lenhart. A. (2007). *Cyberbullying*. Pew Internet and American Life Project. Retrieved July 28, 2011 from http://www.pewinternet.org/Reports/2007/Cyberbullying.aspx

Mishna, F. (2009). An overview of the evidence on bullying prevention and intervention programs. *Brief Treatment and Crisis Intervention, 8*, 327–341.

Nansel, T. R., Overpeck, M., Pilla, R. S., Ruan, W. J., Simons-Morton, B., & Scheidt, P. (2001). Bullying behaviors among US youth: Prevalence and association with psychosocial adjustment. *Journal of the American Medical Association, 285*, 2094–2100.

Patchin, J. W., & Hinduja, S. (2006). Bullies move beyond the schoolyard: A preliminary look at cyberbullying. *Youth Violence and Juvenile Justice, 4*, 148–169.

Postmes, T., Spears, R., & Lea, M. (1998). Breaching or building social boundaries? Side-effects of computer mediated communication. *Communication Research, 25*, 689–715.

Raskauskas, J., & Stoltz, A. D. (2007). Involvement in traditional and electronic bullying among adolescents. *Developmental Psychology, 43*, 564–575.

Reid, P., Monsen, J., & Rivers, I. (2004). Psychology's contribution to understanding and managing bullying within schools. *Educational Psychology in Practice, 20*, 241–258.

Rosenberg, M. (1965). *Society and the adolescent self-image*. Princeton, NJ: Princeton University Press.

Ryan, W. & Smith, J. D. (2009). Antibullying programs in schools: How effective are evaluation practices? *Prevention Science*, 10, 248–259.

Shariff, S. (2008). *Cyberbullying: Issues and solutions for the school, the classroom and the home*. Abingdon, Oxon: Routledge.

Varjas, K., Henrich, C. C., & Meyers, J. (2009). Urban middle school students' perceptions of bullying, cyberbullying, and school safety. *Journal of School Violence, 8*, 159–176.

Willard, N. (2003). Off-campus, harmful online student speech. *Journal of School Violence, 2*, 65–93.

Williams, K. R., & Guerra, N. G. (2007). Prevalence and predictors of internet bullying. *Journal of Adolescent Health, 41*, S14–S21.

Wolak, J., Mitchell, K. J., & Finkelhor, D. (2007). Does online harassment constitute bullying? An exploration of online harassment by known peers and online-only contacts. *Journal of Adolescent Health, 41*, S51–S58.

Ybarra, M. L. (2004). Linkages between depressive symptomatology and Internet harassment among young regular Internet users. *Cyberpsychological Behavior, 7*, 247–257.

Ybarra, M. L., Diener-West, M., & Leaf, P. J. (2007). Examining the overlap in Internet harassment and school bullying: Implications for school intervention. *Journal of Adolescent Health, 41*, S42–S50.

Ybarra, M. L., & Mitchell, K. J. (2004a). Online aggressor/targets, aggressors, and targets: A comparison of associated youth characteristics. *Journal of Child Psychology and Psychiatry, 45*, 1308–1316.

Ybarra, M. L., & Mitchell, K. J. (2004b). Youth engaging in online harassment: Associations with caregiver–child relationships, Internet use, and personal characteristics. *Journal of Adolescence, 27*, 319–336.

Ybarra, M. L., Mitchell, K. J., Finkelhor, D., & Wolak, J. (2007). Internet prevention messages: Targeting the right online behaviors. *Archives of Pediatric Adolescent Medicine, 161*, 138–145.

Ybarra, M. L., Mitchell, K. J., Wolak, J., & Finklehor, D. (2006). Examining characteristics and associated distress related to Internet harassment: Findings from the second youth Internet safety survey. *Pediatrics, 118*, 1169–1177.

8

Cyberbullying in the United States

Sheri Bauman

The many advantages of communications technology (such as the Internet and cellular phones) are widely appreciated by US consumers. Education has also embraced technology, with virtually every school in the US having Internet access. These technological advances have impacted many sectors of society: print newspapers compete with online news sources, online merchants gain business that once was the exclusive domain of brick and mortar establishments, banking and other financial transactions are conducted online, and both business and personal communications now routinely occur technologically via instant messaging, text messaging, email, social networking, and cellular phone. Many homes no longer have telephone land lines, and use cellular phones exclusively (Alexander, 2008). Although some negative aspects of these practices (spam, phishing, etc.) are common knowledge, there is general agreement that technological innovations have been positive contributions to society, and there is no doubt that these are now seen as essential cultural tools rather than passing trends.

Cyberbullying has recently received considerable attention in the popular media in the US, with several sensational cases being widely covered. There appears to be heightened public concern about the dangers inherent in the use of technology, but there is no large-scale or national effort being made to understand and reduce the harm from cyberbullying. Such efforts are left to private organizations, states, school districts, or individual schools, and there are no evidence-based programs or practices that these entities can access. Further, despite increased public awareness of the potential negative consequences of cyberbullying, the educational establishment in the US is currently rather singularly focused on increasing academic achievement,

Cyberbullying in the Global Playground: Research from International Perspectives, First Edition.
Edited by Qing Li, Donna Cross, and Peter K. Smith.

due in large part to the national legislation that mandates such improvement. This climate relegates time and resources available to combat social issues that interfere with learning to a lower priority.

In recent years, scholars have also focused attention on this problem. In my work, I am interested in whether cyberbullying is confined to mainstream settings (such as urban and suburban areas where middle or higher income people reside) or whether it is a cultural phenomenon that reaches less advantaged groups, such as low-income, rural, and students with disabilities. As a prelude to the discussion of my research, I will begin with a description of the context in the US within which cyberbullying occurs.

The Context of Cyberbullying in the US

Use of technology

Access to Internet and cellular phones is common in the US. Although there is some variation by source of information, the lowest rate of Internet usage quoted is 73% of the population as of June 30, 2008 (www.internetworldstats.com). That site notes that Internet access was 44% in 2000, and increase has been steady each year since. Another site indicates that the US is second of 190 countries in the database for Internet access and first of 31 countries in broadband access (www.nationmaster.com/country/us-united-states/int-internet), but 16th in per capita broadband access. That is, there are more broadband lines in the US than anywhere else, but when the size of the population is taken into account, individual access to broadband ranks lower. The US is one of nine countries to have Internet access in 100% of schools (www.nationmaster.com/country/us-united-states/int-internet). In addition to Internet access in homes and schools, libraries and community centers typically have Internet access available at no cost to visitors.

From June 2000, when wireless phone penetration in the US was 34%, the rate of cellular phone penetration increased to 84% as of June 2008. There are almost 16% of US households that have only wireless service, with land lines being seen as obsolete and an unnecessary expense by many.

A national survey of teens with cell phones, conducted in July 2008 (Harris Interactive, 2008) revealed that 46% make and receive calls, 39% send or receive text messages, 19% use the camera, and 17% send or receive picture messages. Having the "latest and greatest" cell phone was important to 28% of respondents, with the importance decreasing with respondent age. Improved quality of life due to cell phones was endorsed by 57% of respondents; 52% felt that communicating with friends had become a "richer" experience since having a cell phone. Participants in the survey reported that the top two advantages of having a cell phone are the ability to stay in touch and to feel safe. Interestingly, cell phones were ranked number 2 (after clothing) in determinants of social status. A slight age-related preference for texting over talking was noted, with younger users doing more texting than talking, and older users describing the reverse pattern. Overall, females showed a stronger preference for texting. Participants in the survey most liked their phones' ability to multitask, with their speed being second. Surprisingly, 28% of respondents use their cell phones to access the Internet, with email and social networking sites being most frequently accessed from cell phones.

Legislation

There have been a number of high-profile cases of cyberbullying reported by the media. Those cases are the ones that led to suicides or other extreme consequences (Surdin, 2009). Arguably the most interesting is the case of Megan Meier, because it was ultimately heard in the courts. Megan Meier was a 13-year-old girl whose parents allowed her to create a MySpace profile (note that the rules for subscribers require a minimum age of 14). Megan had been bullied in school since elementary school. She began a MySpace friendship with a boy named Josh Evans who appeared to find her attractive and interesting. According to interviews with her mother, Megan was "ecstatic" about the attention and the flirting messages. After the two had exchanged messages for about six weeks, Megan began receiving cruel messages from Josh, including one that said in part, "The world would be better off without you." Megan, distraught, went to her room and hung herself, and despite the efforts of her parents to revive her, she died. As a result of their efforts to gather information about the boy, Megan's parents learned that Josh Evans did not exist in real life; rather, he was "created" by a neighbor, Lori Drew, age 49, ostensibly to find out what Megan would say about her own daughter, who had been a friend of Megan's. The parents took Ms. Drew to court, and on November 5, 2008, Ms. Drew was acquitted of the more serious felony conspiracy charge but was convicted of three misdemeanor charges of "unauthorized access" to the website, based on her falsified identity as Josh Evans. The convictions were eventually overturned by the judge.

The law that was used to prosecute this case is the 1986 federal Computer Fraud and Abuse Act, designed to prosecute hackers. Because Ms. Drew violated the terms of service agreement of MySpace.com (which requires users to be "truthful and accurate" in their postings) she was charged with a crime. Some legal experts wonder whether social networking sites can realistically enforce their terms of service and police their sites. MySpace and other social networking sites have mechanisms for reporting inappropriate behavior, and will cancel profiles of those who misuse the site when their infractions are reported. However, opening a new account with new information is easy to do to circumvent such barring. Perhaps more importantly, there are many reasons why individuals may need anonymity on the Internet (even police pose as others to catch predators, for example). It is debatable whether infractions of "terms of service" rules should result in legal action. The supporters of criminalizing such infractions say it would enable victims to have legal recourse when they are bullied online. Opponents argue that such problems should be resolved outside an already overloaded legal system.

Since the ruling in this case, the state of Missouri (the home of the Meiers) has amended an existing state law against harassment to include electronic bullying and stalking, and some cases have been prosecuted under the new law (see http://abcnews.go.com/TheLaw/story?id=6520260&page=1 for more information) including one case involving repeated taunting text messages. The sticking point for those who opposed such legislation is the First Amendment of the US Constitution, which provides protection for "free speech." The argument that alleged offenders are merely exercising their right to free speech is one that will surely be made in court.

In response to this incident and others with tragic consequences, Representative Linda Sanchez of California, along with 17 co-sponsors, introduced the Megan Meier Cyberbullying Prevention Act to the House of Representatives on April 2, 2009. This bill proposes to amend the federal criminal code "to impose criminal penalties [fine or imprisonment for up to two years or both] on anyone who transmits in interstate or foreign commerce a communication intended to coerce, intimidate, harass, or cause substantial emotional distress to another person, using electronic means to support severe, repeated, and hostile behavior" (www.opencongress.org/bill/111-h1996/text). The bill was referred to the subcommittee on crime, terrorism, and homeland security on April 26, 2009, and at the time of writing this chapter, had not yet come to the floor for a vote. A previous version of that bill (HB1628) was introduced in Spring 2008 and did not come to a vote, but Ms. Sanchez said in a radio interview on April 5, 2009 that she is confident that the bill will come to a vote in the current session of the legislature. Predictably, the bill has both supporters and detractors, and the ultimate outcome of the legislation is uncertain.

Several other states have passed legislation that typically amends existing laws by inserting terminology to include technological bullying. As of January 1, 2009, at least 19 states had passed laws intended to stop cyberbullying (Surdin, 2009). Most of these laws (in states including Minnesota, Oregon, and Washington) direct school districts to develop policies and procedures for handling cyberbullying. Some, such as the 2007 Arkansas law (and Florida, Oklahoma, and Idaho), direct districts to amend existing policies to include electronic bullying, but the Arkansas law also requires schools to include language to punish cyberbullying that originates off-campus when it results in a "substantial disruption" of the learning environment (Beckstrom, 2008, p. 291). Delaware has similar provisions for school action when there is a "school nexus," while Florida and New Jersey use the "substantial disruption" language. Maryland's new law (effective from July 1, 2009) allows school action when the cyberbullying creates a "hostile educational environment." Other state laws restrict schools to responding to incidents that involve the use of school technology, or at school or school-sponsored activities (such as Nebraska and Oregon). The 2007 Iowa law is silent on the issue of off-campus incidents, and the South Carolina statute is vague. Vermont's law is unique in that it allows for school action against off-campus cyberbullying and makes both bullying and cyberbullying criminal offenses which could bring a fine of up to $500. Idaho's law also makes cyberbullying a (misdemeanor) criminal act. California's law, which took effect on January 1, 2009, permits suspension or expulsion of students who cyberbully others.

These laws are all fairly recent, and have not been contested in court. There are many who are concerned that the language of the laws is unclear. For example, what constitutes "severe" behavior or "substantial emotional distress"? How is "substantial disruption" to be determined? In addition to these concerns about how these laws can be applied and enforced, there are others who oppose these laws because they infringe on the first amendment right to free speech. It is certain that some of these questions will be addressed in court.

Research on Cyberbullying in the US

Holfed and Grabe (see Chapter 7) review the research to date on cyberbullying in the US. The concept of the "digital divide" suggests that the advantages and use of technology are not accessible to everyone in society, and that those who are economically or socially outside the mainstream are excluded from the technological culture. My own research in this field has investigated cyberbullying in settings that are among those who might be less technologically equipped and adept than students in more affluent or mainstream schools: a rural school in a low-income area, and a school for the Deaf and Hard of Hearing (HOH). In both settings, I was interested in whether cyberbullying (and technology) extended to these non-mainstream settings, or whether this phenomenon is limited to more affluent and mainstream populations. I also wanted to discover what patterns and relationships could be detected that might increase our overall understanding of cyberbullying. These two studies, conducted in 2008 (see also Bauman, 2010, and Bauman & Pero, 2011), and a summary of the findings, are described next.

Study 1: Rural Intermediate School

In this quantitative study (Bauman, 2010), I used a survey developed for this purpose to investigate aspects of cyberbullying in a rural, low-income school. Because this study was exploratory in nature, conducted when few published studies were available, no specific hypotheses were proposed.

The study was conducted in a poor (average income was 78% of state average), rural (population density of 20 persons per square mile) community in southeastern Arizona. In 2007, 65% of rural households with comparable incomes had home computer access to the Internet (National Telecommunications and Information Administration, 2008), with some differences by race: 41% of Hispanic rural households had access compared to 61% of white non-Hispanic rural households.

Method

Participants

Participants were 221 students enrolled in an intermediate school (grades 5–8), of whom 118 (54%) were female. Most schools in the US are configured as elementary

Table 8.1 Subscales: Student Survey.

Scale	*# Items*	*Response options*	α	M	SD	n
Cyberbullying	9	never, once or twice, often, very often	0.89	1.4	0.58	207
Cybervictimization	12	never, once or twice, often, very often	0.85	1.17	0.33	202
Parental control of technology	4	never, once or twice, often, very often	0.97			
Parental use of technology	11	never, once or twice, often, very often	0.97	1.58	0.54	196
Parent–child techno-communication	3	never, once or twice, often, very often	0.91	1.79	0.72	204
Child use of technology	11	never, once or twice, often, very often	0.98	1.71	0.65	181
Risky online behavior	4	never, once or twice, often, very often	0.66	1.42	0.58	207
Self-blaming attributions (scenario)	10	definitely, probably, not sure, probably not, definitely not	0.91	2.68	1.09	207
*Distress (scenario)	6	definitely, probably, not sure, probably not, definitely not	0.82	3.09	1.01	207
*Acting out (scenario)	6	definitely, probably, not sure, probably not, definitely not	0.82	3.40	1.01	194
* Avoidance (scenario)	6	definitely, probably, not sure, probably not, definitely not	0.78	2.75	0.98	207
* Help-seeking from authority	3	definitely, probably, not sure, probably not, definitely not	0.71	2.73	1.15	206
Moral disengagement	8	strongly agree, agree, not sure, disagree, strongly disagree	0.86	2.54	0.94	207
Perceived school efforts to curb cyberbullying	4	strongly agree, agree, not sure, disagree, strongly disagree	0.78	2.60	0.95	214
Perceived level of cyberbullying in school	3	strongly agree, agree, not sure, disagree, strongly disagree	0.85	2.20	1.06	212
Perceived level of cyberbullying among friends	3	strongly agree, agree, not sure, disagree, strongly disagree	0.92	2.12	1.17	216
Cyberbullying interferes with school—self	4	never, once or twice, often, very often	0.70	1.12	0.29	217
Cyberbullying interferes with school—friends	5	never, once or twice, often, very often)	0.86	1.23	0.44	215

Note: Scales with * were derived by Principal Components Analysis (PCA). All others were rationally derived.

(grades K–5) and middle school (grades 6–8), but this school district uses a primary (K–4) and Intermediate (5–8) configuration. Students in the intermediate school are aged approximately 10–14. Grade levels of participants were as follows: 56 (25%) were in fifth grade, 61 (28%) in sixth, 76 (34%) in seventh, and 28 (13%) in eighth. Data on the school website indicate that 54% of students are Latino, 38% are Caucasian, 6% are Native American, and 3% are African-American. In the school, 86% of students qualify for free or reduced-price lunches, an indicator of low socioeconomic status.

Measure

I developed the student survey, *Student Use of Technology,* used here after a thorough search of the literature. Cyberbullying and cybervictimization are assessed by multiple items using behavioral descriptors rather than the term "cyberbullying," which may be socially undesirable. In addition to items inquiring about frequency of various experiences and behaviors related to technology, the survey included items about self-blaming attributions, levels of moral disengagement related to cyberbullying, and anticipated cognitive, emotional, and behavioral responses to a cyberbullying scenario. The attribution items were based on previous research on conventional bullying (Graham, personal communication, August 22, 2007) and the moral disengagement items were based on Bandura's work (Bandura, Barbaranelli, Caprara, & Pastoretti, 1996). Willard (2006) was the source of some of the items developed for the scales. Most scales used four-point Likert scale items (for example, never, sometimes, often, all the time or strongly agree, agree, disagree, strongly disagree).

The scales were rationally derived by grouping items with similar content. Each set of items was then subjected to Principal Components Analysis (PCA). If that analysis revealed a single factor solution, no further analysis was conducted on that scale, and the internal consistency reliability coefficient (Cronbach's alpha) was calculated. When the PCA indicated the presence of more than one factor, standard practice was employed to identify components. See Table 8.1 for a list of the scales, with alpha coefficients.

Cyberbullying and cybervictimization scale scores were obtained by summing the items describing behaviors consistent with those descriptors and dividing by the number of items, so that there was a mean score for each participant. *Z*-scores were then calculated for each score. Scores of participants whose *z*-score was +1.0 or greater were classified as cyberbullies (and the rest as not) and those whose victimization score was +1.0 or greater were classified as cybervictims. The complete survey (with additional items added for Study 2 below) is included in the Appendix to this chapter. Note that analyses reported here include the most useful findings; some variables were not used.

Procedure and analysis

The anonymous survey, *Student Use of Technology*, was administered by classroom teachers at the school as part of an effort to inform the staff about cyberbullying in their setting. Participation was voluntary for teachers and students. Completed

Table 8.2 Time Spent on the Internet and Cell Phones.

Internet: school days (n = 177)	*Internet: weekends (n = 166)*	*Cell phones (n = 142)*
0 hours: 28%	0 hours: 36%	0 hours: 36%
1 hour: 44%	1 hour: 24%	1 hour: 31%
2 hours: 11%	2 hours: 15%	2 hours: 15%
3 hours: 9%	3 hours: 10%	3 hours: 8%
4 hours: 3%	4 hours: 4%	4 hours: 6%

Note: Percentages are of those responding to the item.

Table 8.3 Descriptive Data About Technological Activities (Range = 1–4).

	M	SD
Parental monitoring of Internet activity	1.96	.82
Playing online games	2.43	1.1
Looking up information	2.16	1.1
Sending text messages	2.04	1.2
Visiting social networking sites	1.88	1.2
People at my school cyberbully by computer	2.06	1.27
People at my school cyberbully by cell phone	2.16	1.15

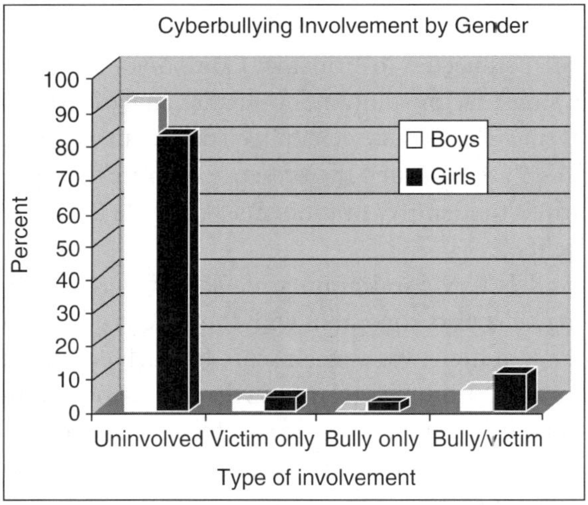

Figure 8.1 Cyberbullying Involvement by Gender in a Rural Low-Income School. Created by Sheri Bauman.

surveys were later provided to the researcher for analysis after the university's Institutional Review Board had approved the use of the archival data. All necessary school district approvals were also obtained. SPSS 16.0 was used to conduct all analyses.

Results

Descriptive data. Sixty percent of participants indicated they had Internet access at home. Of those, 78% reported that the computer was located in a public area of the home, while 22% said the computer was in their bedroom. Slightly less than half (48%) of participants reported having a personal cell phone.

In the total sample, 3% ($n = 6$) of students with complete data were classified as cyberbullies only, 4% ($n = 8$) as cybervictims only; and 5 % ($n = 10$) as cyberbully-victim, with a total of 12% ($n = 24$) involved in some way. Participants were asked what they would do if they were cyberbullied: 32% would bully back, 24% would ignore it, 12% would tell an adult at school, and 9% would tell a parent. Of those who had been cyberbullied, 50% did not know the identity of the perpetrator, while 23% said it was someone in one of their classes, 20% identified someone in their school they did not know, and 10% reported that the cyberbully was a close friend.

Table 8.2 presents the data on frequency of use of the Internet and cell phones, and Table 8.3 describes the technological activities reported by the participants.

Grade and gender differences

In order to determine whether access or use of technology varied by grade or gender, chi-square analyses were conducted. Proportionally fewer fifth graders reported having a cell phone than the other grades (χ^2 (3, $N = 217$) = 10.27, $p < 0.02$); sixth and eighth graders were 2.5 times as likely to have a cell phone as fifth graders; seventh graders were three times as likely to have one.

Chi-square tests found no difference in the proportions of girls and boys who had access to the Internet at home or had cell phones. For time spent on the Internet and cell phone, no difference was detected for using the Internet on schooldays, but girls spent slightly more time on the Internet on weekends ($U = 2721$, $z = -2.02$, $p < 0.04$, $r = 0.16$, a small effect) and on cell phones ($U = 1973.50$, $z = -2.15$, $p = 0.03$, $r = 0.18$, a small effect) than boys.

Because cell sizes were small, I compared the uninvolved and students involved in cyberbullying (as bullies, victims, or both) by gender. Females were disproportionately represented in the involved group (which included 8% of boys and 18% of girls), with $\chi^2(1, N = 197) = 4.48$, $p < 0.03$, $\varphi = 0.15$. Girls were almost three times (2.75) more likely than boys to be involved in cyberbullying in one of the three roles. Although cell sizes were too small to conduct an analysis by each role, Figure 8.1 shows a pattern of greater involvement in all roles by females.

To examine possible gender differences in cyber-activities, Mann–Whitney tests for independent groups were conducted on each of the 11 items describing the student's use of technology. A Bonferroni adjustment to alpha (0.05/11 = 0.005) found no significant difference by gender. No differences on the cybervictim scale was found by grade, but the mean scores on cyberbully scale did have a significant difference by grade ($\chi^2(3, N = 200) = 12.05, p < 0.007$) and showed a pattern increasing scores by grade. The post-hoc Mann–Whitney U-tests revealed that there was a significant difference in reporting cyberbullying behavior between grades five and six ($p < 0.04$), five and seven ($p < 0.001$), and five and eight ($p < 0.004$), with the fifth graders having significantly lower cyberbullying scores than each of the other grades.

The Kruskal–Wallis test found significant differences by grade for "I send email" ($\chi^2(3, N = 210) = 21.29, p < 0.001$); "I send text messages" ($\chi^2(3, N = 211) = 19.77, p < 0.001$); "I send instant messages" ($\chi^2(3, N = 195) = 9.69, p < 0.02$); and "I play online games" ($\chi^2(3, N = 195) = 11.15, p < 0.01$). The difference by grade on the Parental Control scale was also significant: ($\chi^2(3, N = 211) = 15.30, p < 0.002$). The Mann–Whitney tests revealed that sixth graders were significantly more likely to send email ($p < 0.001$), send text ($p < 0.03$), and play online games ($p < 0.004$) than fifth graders; seventh graders were more likely to send email ($p < 0.001$), send text ($p < 0.001$), go to social networking sites ($p < 0.03$), and use IM ($p < 0.004$) than fifth graders; and eighth graders were more likely to send email ($p < 0.001$) and use IM ($p = 0.01$) than fifth graders. Between sixth and seventh graders, significant differences were found for sending texts ($p < 0.02$) and playing online games ($p < 0.02$) with seventh graders sending more text messages and using IM more often. There were no significant differences between sixth and eighth graders on any of the variables, and seventh and eighth graders differed only on sending email ($p < 0.04$), with eighth graders having the higher mean rank. Although the difference for going to social networking sites was not significant, a trend towards increasing use with higher grades was observed.

Other analyses

In order to understand more about cyberbullying and victimization in this sample, a series of chi-square analyses were conducted. Cyberbullies ($\chi^2(1(N = 150) = 4.20, p = 0.04$) and cybervictims ($\chi^2(1(N = 150) = 6.71, p = 0.009$) were almost four times more likely to report that their caregivers did *not* have all their passwords than their peers who were not classified as cyberbullies. The correlation between the two variables (cyberbullying and cybervictimization) was 0.79 ($p < 0.001$).

Regression analyses were conducted to determine which variables would predict involvement in cyberbullying. A model with cyberbullying as the dependent variable was significant ($F(2,192) = 230.914, p = 0.001$) and accounted for 70% of the variance in the score on the Cyberbully scale. Both predictor variables were statistically significant, with the following beta values: risky online behaviors = 0.14, $p < 0.002$; cybervictimization, beta = 0.77, $p < 0.001$.

A similar analysis was conducted with level of cybervictimization as the dependent variable. The final model was significant, $F(1,196) = 404.48, p < 0.001$, explaining 67% of the variance in cybervictimization, with only cyberbullying being the significant predictor (beta = 0.82, $p < 0.001$).

To investigate whether the level of self-blaming attributions predicted the degree of distress (negative affect) in response to the cyberbullying scenario, a hierarchical linear regression analysis was conducted. The overall model with self-blaming attributions as the predictor (after controlling for the influence of gender) was significant, $F(2,197) = 31.58$, $p < 0.001$, explaining 24% of the variance. Gender was entered in Step 1, accounting for 3% of the variance in distress in response to the scenario. Self-blaming attribution was added in Step 2, explaining an additional 21% of variance. Beta values were −0.15 for gender ($p < 0.02$), and for self-blaming attribution was 0.46 ($p < 0.0001$).

A similar analysis was conducted to examine the degree to which the levels of moral disengagement and self-blaming attributions predicted the level of acting out (hitting, throwing, yelling) in response to the scenario after controlling for gender. Gender was entered in Step 1, and explained less than 1% of the variance. After entering the level of moral disengagement in Step 2, the model was significant, $F(3,186) = 20.25$, $p < 0.001$, explaining 23% of the variance in acting out. The beta value for self-blaming attributions was −0.23, $p = 0.001$, and moral disengagement, beta = 0.43 ($p < 0.001$).

Discussion

In the sample, 78% were uninvolved in cyberbullying. This is similar to the overall rate of 72% reported by Kowalski and Limber (2007) in their large sample of sixth through eighth grade (3% rural) students in two areas of the US. Juvonen and Gross (2008) noted that rates for experiencing at least one incident of victimization by cyberbullying range from 9–49%. The percentage of victims in the current study is at the low end of that range.

Students in this rural school reported home Internet access rates similar to national estimates for comparable communities. Although the majority reported that access was in a public area of the home—which is recommended as a strategy to reduce inappropriate use of the internet, including cyberbullying—it is notable that 22% of these intermediate students who had Internet access indicated that their computer was in their bedroom. This means that adult supervision is difficult at best, and that caregivers may not be aware of the need to supervise their child's Internet activities. Further indications of this problem were detected. Students did not perceive that caregivers exercised a great deal of control of their activities online; the mean on that scale was slightly less than "sometimes." Again, the adults may not be aware of the importance of strategies to oversee their youth's behaviors in cyberspace. Additional evidence of the lack of adult oversight was that participants involved as cyberbullies and cybervictims were four times more likely than uninvolved students to say that their caregivers did not have all their passwords. It is possible that youth provide parents with a password to sites they keep for that purpose (showing to parents), and use other sites for less restricted activities (such as cyberbullying). If students are not providing parents with their passwords, it is more likely that they are concealing activities of which their parents would disapprove. These findings underscore the importance of educating parents about cyberbullying and the ways in which they can both protect and supervise their children to reduce their involvement in harmful activities. Mason (2008) observed that the absence of parental monitoring of their children's Internet use contributes to the cyberbullying problem. Some parents may not even request their child's passwords, which gives free rein to the student to post harmful or inappropriate material without worrying about parental censure. Additional cause for concern is that many students were uncertain whether or disagreed that the school made efforts to curb cyberbullying. It could be that students are unaware of those efforts, or that because of the low rate at which these events occur, the school, like many others, has not made this problem a priority.

Findings related to cell phone use are interesting. Almost half the participants reported having their own phone. Given the rural location, this may be a safety precaution in many families even when cost is a concern. It is notable that 35% only indicated they spend no time on the cell phone per day; this suggests that students may be sharing cell phones. If 50% have cell phones, but 65% are using one daily, at least some of those additional 15% may be using friends' phones. There are anecdotal reports from school staff that this is the case. One concern about this practice is that a student may use another's phone to cyberbully another child, but when adults confront the phone's owner about the incident, he or she may be accurate in saying they were not the perpetrator. They also could be advised that they will be accountable for cyberbullying that originates from their phone, regardless of who actually sent the harmful message. Such a policy may help youth who are reluctant to say "no" to friends who ask (or demand) to use their cell phones. Youth need to be aware of the dangers of allowing others to use their cell phones, in the same way we caution them not to share their passwords, even with best friends.

Students in the sample reported using a variety of forms of technology: email, text messages, instant messaging, online games, etc. Although none of these forms is specifically linked to cyberbullying, all of them can be appropriated for that purpose. The fact that more than a third of participants (39%) believed that students know how to circumvent filters and blocks is further indication of the relative sophistication of these young users of technology. Turow (2001) noted that adolescents are quite adept at circumventing these restraints of their online activities. Further, 62% indicated that their caregivers never used filters or blocks, which may or may not be accurate. Turow found that many parents who were not technologically adept were reluctant to use these tools. In any case, adults may believe that by installing such programs on computers, they are ensuring that their children do not have access to prohibited sites, but their sense of security may be unfounded.

Students' reports of how they would respond if cyberbullied also highlighted the need for more focused attention on this problem. The most common response was to retaliate (bully back)—which is likely to escalate the situation. Ignoring the problem, the second most frequently selected option, may be wise in cases in which the incident occurs only once; for repeated incidents, that strategy is unlikely to be effective. Similar findings were reported by researchers in the Netherlands (Dehue, Bolman, & Völlink, 2008); in their sample of 1211 upper primary and lower secondary students, pretending to ignore it was the most common response, followed by talking to others, actually ignoring it, and retaliating toward the cyberbully. Patchin and Hinduja (2006) asked the 115 adolescents in their sample who had been cyberbullied how they responded: the most common response, reported by 57% of the sample, was to tell an online friend. Doing nothing was reported by 25%, bullying others was reported by less than 3%, and 20% said they would tell parents. Of greater concern is that only 12% of students in the current study indicated they would tell an adult at school, and only 9% said they would tell parents. This pattern is similar to that found by Mishna, Saint, and Solomon (2009) and suggests that either pressure not to "snitch," "narc," etc. is quite strong, or that youth fear the adult solution to the problem might be to limit access to technology. Some children might prefer to tolerate cyberbullying rather than be excluded from the cyber-community. However, in another study carried out by students in grades six through nine, researchers found that 47% would tell school personnel, and 57% would tell their parents (Cassidy, Jackson, & Brown, 2009). Of those in the Cassidy, Jackson, and Brown sample who would not tell school personnel if they were cyberbullied, 30% would fear retribution, 27% believed that the staff could not stop the bullying, 26% worried about getting friends into trouble, 24% feared their parents would restrict access to technology, and 20% worried about being labeled an informer.

The strong relationship between cyberbullying and victimization, and the finding that the largest group of involved students was cyberbully-victims, raises the possibility that at least a portion of what is labeled cyberbullying may in fact be reciprocal aggression. The three characteristics of the subset of aggression we call bullying are that the harm is intentional, repeated, and characterized by a power imbalance between the perpetrator and the target of the aggressive actions. In some cases of cyberbullying, we may be seeing a case of youth trading insults or having a conflict that does not have the element of power imbalance. While the findings here do not allow for any definitive conclusion, they suggest that perhaps we need to be more precise in the questions we ask about experiences with cyberbullying,

The fact that about 50% of respondents report not knowing the identity of the cyberbully also makes the classification of the behavior problematic. By comparison, this is the same rate reported by Kowalski and Limber (2007). There are technological tools that can be used to identify many who commit these offenses, even when efforts have been made to conceal one's identity.

Gender and grade differences were few but illuminating. Despite the small number of students involved in cyberbullying, girls were found to be almost three times as likely to be involved in cyberbullying in various ways as boys. This was the case although there were no differences in the proportion of boys and girls who had access to technology. We found a small difference in the time spent on the Internet on weekends, and time on cell phones, with girls spending slightly more time. It seems that our results are consistent with those of Kowalski and Limber (2007) who found greater involvement of girls in cyberbullying and as cybervictims, but contrary to those reported by Li (2006) or Hinduja and Patchin (2008), who found no gender differences for involvement in cyberbullying at the middle school level.

However, Hinduja and Patchin (2009) observed that girls appear to be involved in cyberbullying at least as much as boys. They note that as cyberbullying is more similar to indirect or relational bullying, in which girls have been found to be more engaged than boys, so greater involvement by girls is not contrary to expectations.

Because there was a fifth grade included in this school, there was an opportunity to examine patterns over a larger range than is typical for middle schools. It is interesting that the pattern reveals that even though the fifth grade was part of the school, there were notable increases (in sending email, text messages, playing online games) beginning in sixth grade. Thus, it was not the transition to a new school that is sometimes linked to increases in bullying behaviors (Pellegrini, 2004; Williams & Guerra, 2007). Fifth graders engaged in all cyber-activities less often than the other grades, and their parents also did less supervising of their cyber-activities. In the Kowalski and Limber (2007) study, sixth graders were the youngest in the school, and they reported lower rates of victimization and bullying via instant messaging and text messaging than their older schoolmates. There is nothing in the dataset to provide an explanation for this finding, so future research should focus on this dynamic. However, the increase detected in sixth grade suggests that prevention and intervention efforts should occur prior to that time. Perhaps fourth and fifth grade are when more intensive prevention efforts should be implemented.

The two cognitive scales—self-blaming attributions and moral disengagement—were not predictive of either cyberbullying or cybervictimization. Studies by Hymel, Rocke Henderson, & Bonanno (Hymel, Rocke Henderson, & Bonanno, 2005; Hymel, Schonert-Reichl, Bonnano, Vaillancourt, & Rocke Henderson, 2010) found that students who bullied others had higher rates of moral disengagement, but in this study, that was not the case. However, the cognitive variables were predictive of how one might respond when victimized. It appears that self-blaming attributions were predictive of distress (internalizing) in response to being cyberbullied. This can be very useful for designing both prevention and intervention. If cognitive strategies to reduce self-blaming attributions were to be used, perhaps the distress associated with victimization could be ameliorated. Along with self-blaming attributions, moral disengagement predicted acting out (externalizing). Including components that address these strategies in prevention efforts might help reduce problem behavior when cyberbullying does occur.

Study 2: Cyberbullying Among Deaf Students and Their Hearing Peers

Among deaf and hard of hearing students, conventional bullying is at least as common as among hearing students (McCrone, 2004). Research on bullying in the deaf/HOH population is rare (Weiner & Miller, 2006). The highest rate of both bullying and victimization among special needs students was found in those who were hearing-impaired (Whitney, Smith, & Thompson, 1994); a more recent qualitative study was conducted in a school for hearing impaired students who used spoken English, and did not communicate using sign language (Dixon, Smith, & Jenks, 2004). Technological advances such as text messaging and Internet use have been lauded as great communication tools for deaf and hard of hearing students (Chen-See, 2009). However, these tools are also commonly used for cyberbullying in the deaf community (Sticks and Stones, 2006). Deaf students are encouraged to use technology to communicate; anecdotal reports suggest that this communication may include cyberbullying. No previous research on cyberbullying among deaf students was located. However, it is likely that deaf students, who are at increased risk of being bullied, may feel empowered to retaliate using technological means.

Based on the little research available, I hypothesized that rates of cyberbullying and victimization would be greater in the deaf/HOH students than in the hearing group, and that cyberbullying and victimization would be strongly related to conventional bullying and victimization.

Method

School context

The setting in which this study was completed is unique. The School for the Deaf is a charter school, with 30 students in the secondary level (beginning with grade 7). Students in the secondary school are between 12 and 19 years of age. The language of instruction and communication in the deaf school is American Sign Language (ASL). Another charter school for hearing students shares the same campus. The two schools share grounds, and students share the same recess and lunch facilities. The survey was administered in November of the fall semester, which begins in August, so students were reporting on the previous three months.

Participants

Thirty deaf/HOH (100% of eligible participants) and 22 hearing students (73% of eligible participants) completed the survey. All participants were in grades 7–12; the percentages in each grade were determined by the enrollment at the deaf school. Note that the deaf/HOH students represented 100% of the school population; for the hearing school, the 30 students invited to participate were selected to match the grade, gender, and ethnicity of the deaf/HOH, and were only a sample of the 400 students enrolled in the school.

Procedure

The survey used in Study 1 was modified for use in this study, with two additional items: a demographic item regarding hearing status, and an additional option under "who was the bully?" that asked whether the perpetrator was a deaf or hearing student. Items assessing conventional bullying and victimization were added, and some sections were removed to reduce the total time needed for survey completion. For the deaf/HOH students, the researcher read items aloud with the aid of a certified interpreter, and three bilingual teachers assisted with the translation of questions from students and answers from the researcher. Several of the older students proceeded to read items on their own. With the hearing students, students preferred to read the survey independently, and had assistance from the researcher and a staff member with logistics and responding to questions.

Results

Internal consistency coefficients (alpha) for scales on the questionnaire were computed for the sample. They are as follows: Conventional victimization, 0.66; Conventional bullying, 0.91, Cybervictimization, 0.86, Cyberbullying, 0.76, Risky online behavior, 0.60, Parental oversight of Internet use, 0.60, Self-blaming attributions, 0.73, and Moral disengagement, 0.83.

Regarding the use of technology, deaf/HOH students were more likely to have Internet access at home, while hearing students were more likely to have a cell phone.

Although small sample and cell sizes prohibited inferential statistical analyses, descriptive data increase our understanding of the phenomenon under investigation. Among deaf/HOH students, 22% ($n = 6$) reported being victimized by conventional bullying, compared to 5% of hearing students. Seventeen percent ($n = 5$) of the deaf/HOH group acknowledged bullying others by conventional means; 9% of the hearing students did so. Being a victim of cyberbullying was acknowledged by 17% ($n = 3$) of the deaf/HOH participants and no hearing participants. While no deaf/HOH students said they had cyberbullied others, one hearing student did.

In responses to an item inquiring about the identity of the cyberbully, 14% of deaf/HOH students reported that the cyberbully was deaf/HOH, and 7% said the cyberbully was hearing. No hearing students acknowledged they had been cyberbullied. Respondents were asked what they would do if they were cyberbullied in the future: 24% of deaf/HOH and 17% of hearing students indicated they would tell their parents, 28% deaf/HOH and 8% of hearing students would tell an adult at school, and 19% deaf/HOH and 17% hearing would tell a friend.

Correlation analyses revealed several notable relationships. Table 8.4 shows the non-parametric correlation tables for selected variables. Conventional bullying and victimization were strongly correlated, as were cyberbullying and cybervictimization. Conventional victimization and bullying were associated with being a cyberbully, but conventional victimization and cybervictimization were not correlated. Moral disengagement was related to conventional bullying, but not cyberbullying.

Self-blaming attributions were associated with distress in response to the scenario; distress and acting out were also correlated, but moral disengagement was not correlated with either variable.

Rates at which adults and parents would be told of incidents were higher than those found in previous research (Mishna, Saint, & Solomon, 2009). It may be that the small school environment encourages a sense of trust in adults to be helpful in these situations.

Table 8.4 Correlations Among Selected Variables.

		Con. Victim	*Con. Bully*	*Cybervictim*	*Cyberbully*	*Moral Disengage*
Kendall's tau	Con. Victim	1.00	.472**	.285	.426**	.104
Sig. (2-tailed)			.000	.051	.003	.339
N		48	47	29	30	45
Kendall's tau	Con. Bully		1.00	.314*	.310*	.309**
Sig. (2-tailed)				.034	.031	.004
N			51	29	31	48
Kendall's tau	Cybervictim			1.00	.682**	.231
Sig. (2-tailed)					.000	.109
N				30	29	29
Kendall's tau	Cyberbully				1.00	.209
Sig. (2-tailed)						.137
N					32	30
Kendall's tau	Moral Disengage					1.00
Sig. (2-tailed)						
N						49

Note: *significant at 0.05 (2-tailed), **significant at 0.01 (2-tailed). Con = conventional.

Discussion

The advantages of technological communication for deaf/HOH students are numerous (see Akamatsu, Mayer, & Farrelly, 2006; Chen-See, 2009) but these students may also be more vulnerable to cyberbullying and cybervictimization. The results of this study were hardly definitive, but nevertheless suggested that cybervictimization and cyberbullying are problems for this population, perhaps more so than for hearing students. Although it might be expected that the deaf/HOH students who had been victimized by hearing students in the past might retaliate using electronic means, the findings suggest otherwise. It appears that much of the cyberbullying and victimization in this sample was within-group, and it could be that what is being termed "cyberbullying" is in reality reciprocal hostility among peers, which occurs face-to-face as well.

Limitations

In the first study, the survey was administered by school personnel, so there is no way to ensure that students were given sufficient assurances of anonymity to encourage honest responding. Further, there is no information on those students who did not take the survey (were they absent? Did some teachers choose not to participate?). Thus, there is no way to determine whether the sample was representative of the school population. However, with the exception of the eighth grade, a high percentage of students completed the survey, and the findings are nevertheless useful in advancing this area of research.

Sample sizes were relatively small in both studies, and the small number of students involved in cyberbullying contributed to the violation of some assumptions and necessitated the use of non-parametric analyses, which are less powerful. This has been true of the research on this topic to date. Thus, the findings must be interpreted with caution, and may not be generalizable to other settings.

The settings of these studies were unique, and while that may limit external validity, it also provides an opportunity to examine this phenomenon in the early stages of its development. Findings demonstrated that those students with greater access to technology are more likely to engage in these practices. In addition, students are reluctant to report problems to teachers and caregivers, so educating adults as well as students will be an essential strategy to prevent an increase in cyberbullying. However, we must also consider whether most of the cyberbullying events are bullying, or whether we are looking at another form of interpersonal conflict, in which two persons are equally engaged in a reciprocal loop of relational aggression.

Conclusion

These studies do much to advance our knowledge of cyberbullying. We learned that cyberbullying occurs even in locations where access to technology is somewhat limited. We provided evidence that suggests that girls might be more involved in cyberbullying and victimization than boys. We also found that an increase in use of technology at sixth grade was associated with an increase in cyberbullying at that age, even when sixth grade was not associated with a move to middle school. This is useful information for determining optimal timing for prevention and intervention efforts.

Implications of the Research

Practice

Both studies make it clear that cyberbullying is a problem that is not restricted to affluent or non-disabled youth. While rates of cyberbullying lag behind those of conventional bullying, these events are not trivial and need to be addressed. A focused effort–supported by sufficient funding–to identify prevention and intervention strategies whose effectiveness can be empirically tested needs to be a high priority for educators. Counselors need to understand the problem in order to be able to provide appropriate support to victims. One important aspect of practice is direct teaching of technological options: blocking senders, reporting infractions to site owners, tracking caller numbers, saving evidence, etc.

Policy

Although legislation to prevent or punish cyberbullying appears to be proliferating at a state level, legislation alone is unlikely to have a major impact. Although some have suggested that criminalizing the behavior will have a deterrent effect, the relative size of the US prison population is evidence of the absence of a deterrent effect on most behavior. The US Department of Education is in a position to mandate certain actions to schools receiving federal monies (which is the case for the vast majority of public schools). Promising practices such as requiring teacher training about cyberbullying, supporting funded research to identify effective prevention practices, etc., need to have the force of a major national agency to make much progress. Even adding items regarding bullying and cyberbullying to major national health monitoring surveys would be an important step. For example, the Youth Risk Behavior Survey (YRBS) is developed by the Center for Disease Control (CDC) and made available to all states. The sampling practices ensure a large nationally representative sample is obtained, and data are weighted so that researchers can apply correct analytic procedures to reflect the sampling strategy. The YRBS now has optional bullying items that states may select to include, up to a certain maximum number of items. Cyberbullying items need to be added as well. Making those items part of the standard survey would be a simple but very helpful step in understanding the extent and dynamics of the problem. With a national dataset, the problem of small numbers of victims, for example, can be overcome and the data can yield valuable information.

The Federal Office of Safe and Drug Free Schools in the US Department of Education is arguably the agency most interested in reducing violence in schools, but its scope is quite broad and includes drug prevention and other challenging areas. The current list of rigorous evaluation studies funded by this agency (30) includes no mention of bullying or cyberbullying. While drug and violence prevention may include these topics, it seems a more specific effort would bring together researchers and practitioners on this crucial problem.

I recently attempted to contact the sponsor and co-sponsors of proposed federal legislation, hoping to inquire about other efforts to combat cyberbullying, and all of the legislator's websites restricted email correspondence to residents of the legislator's home district. These problems are clearly not local—with technology, they are truly international—and garnering national support for initiatives is critical. The tradition of local control of schools in the US appears to hamper efforts to initiate major efforts to address the problem.

Theory

The major theoretical question at this point seems to be whether cyberbullying is a subtype of traditional bullying, which means that the same prevention and intervention strategies would likely apply. I believe my findings, reported above, suggest that we have no definitive answers yet, and I believe this is a central issue that will drive not only research but practice. Like Wolak, Mitchell, and Finkelhor (2007), but perhaps for different reasons, I suspect that not all of the behaviors being classified as cyberbullying constitute "bullying" in cyberspace.

Future research

Future research would be most useful if large nationally representative samples could be obtained in order to get an accurate picture of the extent and dynamics of the problem of cyberbullying (as for example provided by Salmivalli and Pöyhönen, this volume, for Finland). Although some websites (such as iSafe.org) collect data from large national samples, the participants are limited to persons who visit their website and choose to participate. Such participants may not represent the broad spectrum of people using the technology. In addition, researchers should attempt to understand *how* these events cause psychological harm (for example, through attribution style, moral disengagement, lack of empathy, impulsivity, etc.) in order to design and test specific cyberbullying prevention programs for youth and adults. Further research is also needed to understand the unique needs of Deaf/HOH students with respect to cyberbullying so that appropriate interventions can be designed and evaluated. In addition, efforts to reach a targeted population of those already involved in cyberbullying to add to the knowledge base and drive intervention efforts also seems needed. There is no lack of areas for researchers to pursue in this important and growing problem.

Appendix: Student survey (modified for use with Deaf/HOH middle school students)

Student survey: Technology

Please tell us the following about you:

Grade: ☐ 6 ☐ 7 ☐ 8 **Gender:** ☐ Male ☐ Female
Race/Ethnicity: ☐ African-American/Black ☐ Asian American
☐ Caucasian/White ☐ Hispanic/Latino ☐ Native American ☐ Biracial/bi-ethnic (Two races/ethnicities) ☐ Other _____
Are you: ☐ Deaf or Hard of Hearing ☐ Hearing

1. Do you have the **Internet at home**? ☐ Yes ☐ No **If you marked NO, skip to 2 now.**
   a. If yes, where is the computer you **usually** use at home located?

☐ in a public area (living room, family room) or ☐ in your bedroom
☐ in your brother or sister's room ☐ in your parents' room

b. If yes, do your parents have **ALL** your **passwords**, screen names, and email addresses? ☐ Yes ☐ No

2. Do you have your own **cell phone**? ☐ Yes ☐ No **If you marked NO, go to 3 now.**
   a. If yes, does it have a camera? ☐ Yes ☐ No
   b. If yes, do you have unlimited text messaging? ☐ Yes ☐ No
3. a. Do you have a **Sidekick?** ☐ Yes ☐ No
   b. Do you have a phone or a **PDA with Internet access?** ☐ Yes ☐ No
4. Do you go to an after-school program (or day care) where you can access the Internet? ☐ Yes ☐ No
5. About how many hours do you spend on the Internet on a typical **school day**? _____
   ☐ None ☐ Less than 1 hour ☐ 1–2 hours ☐ 3–4 hours ☐ 5–6 hours ☐ 7–8 hours
6. On a **weekend** or day you are not in school? _____
   ☐ None ☐ Less than 1 hour ☐ 1–2 hours ☐ 3–4 hours ☐ 5–6 hours ☐ 7–8 hours
7. About how much time do you spend on your **cell phone** each day? _____
   ☐ None ☐ Less than 1 hour ☐ 1–2 hours ☐ 3–4 hours ☐ 5–6 hours ☐ 7–8 hours
8. How many brothers and sisters do you have? _____ How many are older than you?_____ **If you answered 0, go to 11 now.**
9. Do your older sisters and brothers have **MySpace** accounts? _____ ☐ Yes ☐ No
   If yes, have you seen their MySpace page? ☐ Yes ☐ No
10. Do your older sisters and brothers have **Facebook** accounts? _____ ☐ Yes ☐ No
    If yes, have you seen their Facebook page? ☐ Yes ☐ No
11. Are you a member (free) of **Club Penguin?** ☐ Yes ☐ No
12. Are you a member (paid) of **Club Penguin**? ☐ Yes ☐ No **If you said No to 11 and 12, go to 13 now. If you said Yes, answer a–c.**
    a. About how many buddies do you have on **Club Penguin?**
       ☐ 1–5 ☐ 6–10 ☐ 11–15 ☐ 16–20 ☐ 21–25 ☐ more than 25
    b. How many of your **Club Penguin** buddies do you know in real life?
       ☐ 1–5 ☐ 6–10 ☐ 11–15 ☐ 16–20 ☐ 21–25 ☐ more than 25
    c. How much time do you spend on **Club Penguin** each day?
       ☐ None ☐ Less than 1 hour ☐ 1–2 hours ☐ 3–4 hours ☐ 5–6 hours ☐ 7–8 hours
13. Are you a member (free) of **Kidzworld**? ☐ Yes ☐ No
14. Are you a member (paid) of **Kidzworld**? ☐ Yes ☐ No **If you said no to 13 and 14, go to 15 now. If you said yes, answer a–c.**
    a. About how many friends do you have on **Kidzworld**?
       ☐ 1–5 ☐ 6–10 ☐ 11–15 ☐ 16–20 ☐21–25 ☐ more than 25
    b. How many of your **Kidzworld** friends do you know in real life?
       ☐ 1–5 ☐ 6–10 ☐ 11–15 ☐ 16–20 ☐21–25 ☐ more than 25

c. How much time do you spend on **Kidzworld** each day?
☐ None ☐ Less than 1 hour ☐ 1–2 hours ☐ 3–4 hours ☐ 5–6 hours ☐ 7–8 hours

15. Put an X in the box next to the sites you go to at least **once a week**:
☐ Tagged
☐ Friendster
☐ HI 5
☐ Xanga
☐ Chamber of Chat
☐ Runescape
☐ Bebo
☐ IMVU
☐ There
☐ Tickle
☐ Stardoll
☐ Imbee
☐ Sanriotown
☐ Neopets
☐ Boom Bang
☐ Awol
16. Have you ever visited **YouTube**.com? ☐ Yes ☐ No
17. Have you ever posted a video on **YouTube**.com? ☐ Yes ☐ No
18. Have you ever visited **MySpace**.com? ☐ Yes ☐ No
19. Do you have an account on **MySpace**.com? ☐ Yes ☐ No **If no, skip to 20 now.**
a. Do you have a personal profile on MySpace.com? ☐ Yes ☐ No
b. Do you have a photo on your profile? ☐ Yes ☐ No
c. Do you have a blog on your **MySpace** page? ☐ Yes ☐ No
d. Do you post photos on your page? ☐ Yes ☐ No
Are your photos ☐ Public or ☐ Private?
e. How much time do you spend on **MySpace** each day?
☐ None ☐ Less than 1 hour ☐ 1–2 hours ☐ 3–4 hours
☐ 5–6 hours ☐ 7–8 hours
f. About how many **friends** do you have on MySpace?
☐ 1–5 ☐ 6–10 ☐ 11–15 ☐ 16–20 ☐ 21–25 ☐ more than 25
g. How many of your MySpace friends do you know in real life?
☐ 1–5 ☐ 6–10 ☐ 11–15 ☐ 16–20 ☐ 21–25 ☐ more than 25
20. Have you ever visited **Facebook**.com? ☐ Yes ☐ No
21. Do you have an account on **Facebook**? ☐ Yes ☐ No **If no, skip to 22 now. If yes, answer a–f first.**
a. Do you have a personal profile on **Facebook**.com? ☐ Yes ☐ No
b. Do you have a photo on your profile? ☐ Yes ☐ No
c. Do you have a blog on your **Facebook** page?
d. Do you post photos on your page? ☐ Yes ☐ No
Are your photos ☐ Public or ☐ Private?

e. How much time do you spend on **Facebook** each day?
☐ None ☐ Less than 1 hour ☐ 1–2 hours
☐ 3–4 hours ☐ 5–6 hours ☐ 7–8 hours

f. About how many friends do you have on **Facebook**?
☐ 1–5 ☐ 6–10 ☐ 11–15 ☐ 16–20 ☐ 21–25 ☐ more than 25

g. How many of your **Facebook** friends do you know in real life?
☐ 1–5 ☐ 6–10 ☐ 11–15 ☐ 16–20 ☐ 21–25 ☐ more than 25

We all have different experiences in school. Based on your experiences, please mark an X in the box that shows how often each has happened SINCE SCHOOL STARTED THIS YEAR.

How often	*Never*	*1 or 2 times*	*A few times*	*Weekly*	*Daily*
1. has another kid teased you in a mean way?	☐	☐	☐	☐	☐
2. has another kid hit, kicked, or pushed you in a mean way?	☐	☐	☐	☐	☐
3. has a another kid spread rumors or said nasty things about you?	☐	☐	☐	☐	☐
4. has another kid threatened you with physical violence?	☐	☐	☐	☐	☐
5. has another kid grabbed, held, or touched you in a way you didn't want?	☐	☐	☐	☐	☐
6. has another kid left you out of an activity you wanted to do?	☐	☐	☐	☐	☐
7. has another kid scared you into giving up money or other things?	☐	☐	☐	☐	☐
8. has another kid chased you to try to hurt you?	☐	☐	☐	☐	☐
9. has another kid played a mean trick to hurt or scare you?	☐	☐	☐	☐	☐
10. has another kid damaged, destroyed, or hidden your things?	☐	☐	☐	☐	☐

We all have different experiences in school. Based on your experiences, please mark an X in the box that shows how often each has happened SINCE SCHOOL STARTED THIS YEAR.

	Never	*1 or 2 times*	*A few times*	*Weekly*	*Daily*
1. have you teased another kid in a mean way?	☐	☐	☐	☐	☐
2. have you hit, kicked, or pushed a another kid in a mean way?	☐	☐	☐	☐	☐
3. have you spread rumors or said nasty things about another kid?	☐	☐	☐	☐	☐
4. have you threatened another kid with physical violence?	☐	☐	☐	☐	☐
5. have you grabbed, held, or touched another kid in an undesired manner?	☐	☐	☐	☐	☐
6. have you kept another kid out of an activity he or she wanted to join?	☐	☐	☐	☐	☐
7. have you scared another kid into giving up money or other things?	☐	☐	☐	☐	☐
8. have you chased another kid so you could hurt him or her?	☐	☐	☐	☐	☐
9. have you played a mean trick to hurt or scare a another kid?	☐	☐	☐	☐	☐
10. have you damaged, destroyed, or hidden another kid's things?	☐	☐	☐	☐	☐

We all have different experiences in school. Based on your experiences, please mark an X in the box that shows how often each has happened SINCE SCHOOL STARTED THIS YEAR.

	Never	*1 or 2 times*	*A few times*	*Weekly*	*Daily*
1. Have you seen a another kid teased in a mean way?	☐	☐	☐	☐	☐
2. Have you seen a another kid hit, kick, or push another student in a mean way?	☐	☐	☐	☐	☐
3. Have you seen another kid spread rumors or lies about another student?	☐	☐	☐	☐	☐
4. Have you seen another kid threaten another student with physical violence?	☐	☐	☐	☐	☐
5. Have you seen another kid grab, hold, or touch another student in an undesired manner?	☐	☐	☐	☐	☐
6. Have you seen another kid exclude another student from something he or she wanted to do?	☐	☐	☐	☐	☐
7. Have you seen another kid scare another student into giving up money or other things?	☐	☐	☐	☐	☐
8. Have you seen another kid chase another student with the intent to harm him or her?	☐	☐	☐	☐	☐
9. Have you seen another kid play a mean trick to hurt or scare another student?	☐	☐	☐	☐	☐
10. Have you seen another kid damage, destroy, or hide another kid's things?	☐	☐	☐	☐	☐

THESE QUESTIONS ARE ABOUT YOUR PARENTS AND TECHNOLOGY. PLEASE MARK AN X IN THE BOX THAT SHOWS YOUR OPINION.

About how often do you think **your parents** do each of these activities:

	Never	*Monthly*	*Weekly*	*Daily*	*I don't know*
Send or receive emails	☐	☐	☐	☐	☐
Send or receive text messages	☐	☐	☐	☐	☐
Play online games	☐	☐	☐	☐	☐
Look up things online	☐	☐	☐	☐	☐
Visit social networking sites (MySpace, Facebook, Bebo)	☐	☐	☐	☐	☐
Shop online	☐	☐	☐	☐	☐
Design websites or profiles	☐	☐	☐	☐	☐
Keep a blog	☐	☐	☐	☐	☐
Comment on other blogs	☐	☐	☐	☐	☐
Instant message (IM)	☐	☐	☐	☐	☐
Visit chatrooms	☐	☐	☐	☐	☐
Restrict the amount of time you spend on the computer	☐	☐	☐	☐	☐
Review the history of websites you visit	☐	☐	☐	☐	☐
Install filters or blocks on your home computer	☐	☐	☐	☐	☐
Talk with you about right and wrong behaviors using technology	☐	☐	☐	☐	☐

About how often do your parents **communicate with you** by:

	Never	*Monthly*	*Weekly*	*Daily*
Email	☐	☐	☐	☐
Text message	☐	☐	☐	☐
Cell phone calls	☐	☐	☐	☐

PLEASE MARK THE BOX THAT IS CLOSEST TO YOUR OPINION ON THESE STATEMENTS.

	Strongly disagree	*Disagree*	*Unsure*	*Agree*	*Strongly agree*
The Internet and cell phones make it easier for me to communicate with others	☐	☐	☐	☐	☐
I have more friends because of the Internet and other technology (cell phones, Sidekicks, etc.)	☐	☐	☐	☐	☐
I do better in school because of the Internet	☐	☐	☐	☐	☐
I feel safer because I have a cell phone	☐	☐	☐	☐	☐
The Internet and cell phones cause too many problems	☐	☐	☐	☐	☐
I like texting because it is a way I can have private conversations with someone	☐	☐	☐	☐	☐

THESE QUESTIONS ARE ABOUT YOU AND TECHNOLOGY. PLEASE PUT AN X IN THE BOX THAT SHOWS ABOUT HOW OFTEN YOU DO EACH ACTIVITY:

	Never	*Monthly*	*Weekly*	*Daily*
Send or receive emails	☐	☐	☐	☐
Send or receive text messages	☐	☐	☐	☐
Play online games	☐	☐	☐	☐
Look up things online for school (homework, reports)	☐	☐	☐	☐
Write a blog	☐	☐	☐	☐
Comment on other blogs	☐	☐	☐	☐
Instant message (IM)	☐	☐	☐	☐
Visit chatrooms	☐	☐	☐	☐
Go to social networking sites (MySpace, Facebook, Imbee, Kidzworld, etc.)	☐	☐	☐	☐

PLEASE MARK AN X IN THE BOX THAT SHOWS YOUR OPINION:

At my school:	*Strongly disagree*	*Disagree*	*Not sure*	*Agree*	*Strongly agree*
There is a clear policy about cyberbullying	☐	☐	☐	☐	☐
Teachers are well informed about cyberbullying	☐	☐	☐	☐	☐
Teachers take steps to stop cyberbullying	☐	☐	☐	☐	☐
The school keeps parents informed about cyberbullying	☐	☐	☐	☐	☐
Cyberbullying is a big problem	☐	☐	☐	☐	☐

PLEASE MARK AN X IN THE BOX THAT SHOWS HOW OFTEN THESE THINGS HAVE HAPPENED:

How often have you:	*Never*	*1 or 2 times*	*3–5 times*	*More than 5 times*
Talked with your parents about your online activities	☐	☐	☐	☐
Showed your profile (MySpace, for example) to your parents	☐	☐	☐	☐
Changed or added to your profile on a website	☐	☐	☐	☐
Given a friend your password	☐	☐	☐	☐
Gotten more than one email address or screen name	☐	☐	☐	☐
Been in an online fight	☐	☐	☐	☐
Received online messages that made you feel afraid	☐	☐	☐	☐
Received mean or nasty email messages	☐	☐	☐	☐
Received mean or nasty text messages	☐	☐	☐	☐
Sent mean or nasty messages online	☐	☐	☐	☐
Sent mean or nasty text messages	☐	☐	☐	☐
Sent a text message to scare someone	☐	☐	☐	☐

PLEASE MARK AN X IN THE BOX THAT SHOWS HOW OFTEN THESE THINGS HAVE HAPPENED:

How often have you:	*Never*	*1 or 2 times*	*3–5 times*	*More than 5 times*
Received a scary text message	☐	☐	☐	☐
Had someone post bad or embarrassing things about you on the Internet	☐	☐	☐	☐
Had someone send lies about you via text message to other kids	☐	☐	☐	☐
Sent an embarrassing photo of someone via cell phone	☐	☐	☐	☐
Found out someone had sent an embarrassing photo of you to friends	☐	☐	☐	☐
Had someone pretend to be you and send an email or text message that damaged your reputation or friendships	☐	☐	☐	☐
Pretended to be someone else on the Internet	☐	☐	☐	☐
Had someone tell your secrets on the Internet or by cell phone without your permission	☐	☐	☐	☐
Told someone else's secrets online or by cell phone without their permission	☐	☐	☐	☐
Had someone spread a rumor about you on the Internet	☐	☐	☐	☐
Spread a rumor about someone on the Internet	☐	☐	☐	☐
Been excluded (left out) of a chat group or IM buddy list	☐	☐	☐	☐
Excluded someone else from an online chat or IM buddy list	☐	☐	☐	☐
Seen mean things about a teacher online	☐	☐	☐	☐
Posted mean things about a teacher online	☐	☐	☐	☐
Read something online or in a text message in which someone said they were going to kill someone else or kill themselves	☐	☐	☐	☐

How often have the following things happened to **you**?

	Never	*Once a month*	*Once a week*	*More than once a week*
I stayed home from school because of something that happened online or by cell phone	☐	☐	☐	☐
I confronted someone at school because of something that happened online or by cell phone	☐	☐	☐	☐
I had trouble concentrating because of something that happened online or by cell phone	☐	☐	☐	☐
I got in trouble at school for something that happened online or by cell phone	☐	☐	☐	☐

Cyberbullying means using technology (the Internet, cell phones) to threaten or harass someone, or to damage their reputation or their friendships (by spreading rumors, excluding them from groups, embarrassing, or humiliating them).

Have you ever been cyberbullied? If yes, how often has this happened to you?
☐ I have never been cyberbullied
☐ It only happened once
☐ It happened two or three times
☐ It happened two or three times **a month**
☐ It happened once a week or more often

If you have been cyberbullied, how much did it upset you?
☐ I wasn't upset at all
☐ I was only a little annoyed
☐ I was upset
☐ I was very upset

If so, who was the bully? **Check all that apply.**
☐ I have never been cyberbullied
☐ I don't know who did it
☐ Someone in one of my classes
☐ My friend
☐ My brother or sister

☐ Someone at school that I don't know at all
☐ Someone I dislike
☐ A Deaf or Hard Of Hearing student
☐ A hearing student

What did you do when you were cyberbullied? (Check all that apply)
☐ I bullied the person back
☐ I told the bully to stop
☐ I didn't do anything
☐ I told my friends
☐ I told a teacher or adult at school
☐ I told my parents

Which of the following would you be **MOST** likely to do **IF** you were cyberbullied in the future?
☐ Bully back online
☐ Beat up the bully at school
☐ Just ignore it
☐ Tell the bully to stop
☐ Tell an adult at school about it
☐ Tell my parents
☐ Tell my friends
☐ Print the material to show to an adult
☐ Do nothing

What would you be **MOST** likely to do if you **saw someone else** being cyberbullied?
☐ Join in
☐ Tell the bully(ies) to stop
☐ Leave the situation (chatroom, website, hang up phone)
☐ Tell my friends about it
☐ Tell the victim privately about it
☐ Report the situation to an adult at school
☐ Report the situation to my parents
☐ Attack the bully
☐ Stick up for the victim online
☐ Do nothing

What would you be **MOST** likely to do if you discovered a hate page about a **student** at your school?
☐ Post my opinion on it
☐ Leave the page
☐ Tell my friends
☐ Tell the "victim"

☐ Tell an adult at school
☐ Tell my parents
☐ Do nothing

What would you be **MOST** likely to do if you discovered a hate page about a **teacher** at your school?
☐ Post my opinion on it
☐ Leave the page
☐ Tell my friends
☐ Tell the teacher
☐ Tell another adult at school
☐ Tell my parents
☐ Do nothing

IMAGINE THAT YOU NOTICED OTHER KIDS LAUGHING AT YOU AND TALKING ABOUT YOU IN SCHOOL, BUT YOU DIDN'T KNOW WHY. THEN YOU DISCOVERED THAT SOMEONE HAS POSTED AN EMBARRASSING PHOTO OF YOU ON THE INTERNET AND SENT IT OUT BY CELL PHONE TO LOTS OF KIDS.

Here are some things other kids say they would **THINK** in this type of situation. Would you think this?

	Definitely	*Probably*	*Not sure*	*Probably would NOT*	*Definitely would NOT*
"I must have done something to cause them to do this to me."	☐	☐	☐	☐	☐
"These kids do this to me because other kids treat me this way too."	☐	☐	☐	☐	☐
"They do this to me because they know I won't get them in trouble."	☐	☐	☐	☐	☐
"These kids do this to everyone, not just me."	☐	☐	☐	☐	☐
"They do this to me because they know I won't do it back."	☐	☐	☐	☐	☐

"This kind of thing happens to me more than it does to other kids."	☐	☐	☐	☐	☐
"If I was cooler, this wouldn't happen."	☐	☐	☐	☐	☐
"I need to figure out what to do about this."	☐	☐	☐	☐	☐
"I know this will happen again."	☐	☐	☐	☐	☐
"Kids at this school are mean."	☐	☐	☐	☐	☐

Here are some things that other kids say they would **FEEL** if this happened. Would you FEEL this way?

	Definitely	*Probably*	*Not sure*	*Probably would NOT*	*Definitely would NOT*
I would be mad at the kids who did it	☐	☐	☐	☐	☐
I would be scared	☐	☐	☐	☐	☐
I would feel like crying	☐	☐	☐	☐	☐
I would feel helpless	☐	☐	☐	☐	☐
I would feel as though it's no big deal	☐	☐	☐	☐	☐
I would feel amused.	☐	☐	☐	☐	☐
I would feel put down	☐	☐	☐	☐	☐

Here are some things that other kids say they would **DO** if this happened. Would you DO this?

	Definitely	*Probably*	*Not sure*	*Probably would NOT*	*Definitely would NOT*
Try to ignore it	☐	☐	☐	☐	☐
Tell a teacher or another adult	☐	☐	☐	☐	☐

Try to forget the whole thing	☐	☐	☐	☐	☐
Do something to get even	☐	☐	☐	☐	☐
Keep quiet	☐	☐	☐	☐	☐
Tell a close friend	☐	☐	☐	☐	☐
Do something to take my mind off it	☐	☐	☐	☐	☐
Try to think about something that makes me happy	☐	☐	☐	☐	☐
Get upset and not talk to anyone	☐	☐	☐	☐	☐
Ask someone else who had this happen what they think I should do	☐	☐	☐	☐	☐
Worry about it a lot	☐	☐	☐	☐	☐
Yell and scream out loud	☐	☐	☐	☐	☐
Throw something or hit something	☐	☐	☐	☐	☐
Ask a family member for advice	☐	☐	☐	☐	☐
Feel sorry for myself	☐	☐	☐	☐	☐
Pretend it didn't happen	☐	☐	☐	☐	☐

Please check the box that is **closest to your opinion** about these statements:

	Strongly disagree	*Disagree*	*Not sure*	*Agree*	*Strongly agree*
Cyberbullying obnoxious classmates teaches them a lesson	☐	☐	☐	☐	☐
Kids don't really mind being cyberbullied because it shows others are interested in them	☐	☐	☐	☐	☐

It's okay to treat someone badly if they behave like a jerk	☐	☐	☐	☐	☐
If people give out their passwords to others, they deserve to be cyberbullied	☐	☐	☐	☐	☐
It's okay to get revenge if someone cyberbullies one of your friends	☐	☐	☐	☐	☐
It's okay to spread nasty rumors about someone because it's not as bad as beating them up	☐	☐	☐	☐	☐
Someone who cyberbullies another kid because their friends push them to do it should not be blamed for what they do	☐	☐	☐	☐	☐
If kids cyberbully others in school, it's the teacher's fault for not stopping it	☐	☐	☐	☐	☐
I know how to protect myself against cyberbullying	☐	☐	☐	☐	☐

If you know how to protect yourself from cyberbullying, HOW DID YOU LEARN to protect yourself?

☐ I figured it out on my own
☐ I learned from teachers at school
☐ I learned from friends at school
☐ I learned from my parents

☺ THANK YOU FOR DOING THIS SURVEY ☺

References

Akamatsu, C. T., Mayer, C., & Farrelly, S. (2006). An investigation of two-way text messaging use with deaf students at the secondary level. *Journal of Deaf Studies and Deaf Education, 11*, 120–131.

Alexander, S. (2008, Spring 25). *More cell phone users hanging up land lines for good. Star Tribune.* Retrieved December 14, 2008 from www.highbeam.com/DocPrint.aspx?DocID=1G1:179495620

Bandura, A., Barbaranelli, C., Caprara, G. V., & Pastoretti, C. (1996). Mechanisms of moral disengagement in the exercise of moral agency. *Journal of Personality and Social Psychology, 71*, 364–374.

Bauman, S. (2010). Cyberbullying in a rural intermediate school: An exploratory study. *Journal of Early Adolescence, 30*, 803–833.

Bauman, S., & Pero, H. (2011). Bullying and cyberbullying among Deaf and hard of hearing students and their hearing peers. *Journal of Deaf Studies and Deaf Education, 16*, 236–253.

Beckstrom, D. C. (2008). State legislation mandating school cyberbullying policies and the potential threat to students' free speech rights. *Vermont Law Review 33*, 283–321.

Cassidy, W., Jackson, M., & Brown, K. N. (2009). Sticks and stones can break my bones, but how can pixels hurt me?: Students' experiences with cyberbullying. *School Psychology International, 30*, 383–402.

Chen-See, S. (2009). *The Internet: Breaking down barriers to communication for deaf teens.* Retrieved July 18, 2011 from www.aboutkidshealth.ca/En/News/NewsAndFeatures/Pages/The-Internet-Breaking-down-barriers-to-communication-for-deaf-teens.aspx

Dehue, F., Bolman, C., & Völlink, T. (2008). Cyberbullying: Youngsters' experiences and parental perception. *CyberPsychology & Behavior, 11*, 217–223.

Dixon, R., Smith, P. K., & Jenks, C. (2004). Bullying and difference. *Journal of School Violence 3*, 41–58.

Harris Interactive. (2008). *A generation unplugged*. Rochester, NY.

Hinduja S., & Patchin, J. (2008). Cyberbullying: An exploratory analysis of factors related to offending and victimization. *Deviant Behavior, 29*, 129–156.

Hinduja, S. & Patchin, J. W. (2009). *Bullying beyond the schoolyard: Preventing and responding to cyberbullying*. Thousand Oaks, CA: Sage Publications (Corwin Press).

Hymel, S., Rocke Henderson, N., & Bonanno, R. A. (2005). Moral disengagement: A framework for understanding bullying among adolescents. *Journal of Social Sciences, 8*, 1–11.

Hymel, S., Schonert-Reichl, K. A., Bonnano, R. A., Vaillancourt, T., & Rocke Henderson, N. (2010). Bullying and morality. In S. Jimerson, S. M. Swearer, & D. L. Espelage (Eds,), *Handbook of bullying in schools: An international perspective* (pp. 101–118). New York & London: Routledge.

Juvonen, J., & Gross, E. F. (2008). Extending the school grounds? Bullying experiences in cyberspace. *Journal of School Health, 78*, 496–505.

Kowalski, R., & Limber, S. (2007). Electronic bullying among middle-school students. *Journal of Adolescent Health, 41*, S22–S30.

Li, Q. (2006). Cyberbullying in schools: A research of gender difference. *School Psychology International, 27*, 157–170.

Mason, K. L. (2008). Cyberbullying: A preliminary assessment for school personnel. *Psychology in the Schools, 45*, 323–348.

McCrone, W. P. (2004). School bullying: A problem for deaf and hard of hearing students? *Odyssey, 5*, 4–9.

Mishna, F., Saint, M., & Solomon, S. (2009). Ongoing and online: Children and youth's perceptions of cyberbullying. *Children and Youth Services Review, 31*, 1222–1228.

National Telecommunications and Information Administration. (2008). *Households using the Internet in and outside the home, by selected characteristics*. Retrieved June 19, 2008 from www.ntia.doc.gov/reports/2008/NetworkedNation.html

Patchin, J., & Hinduja, S. (2006). Bullies move beyond the schoolyard: A preliminary look at cyberbullying. *Youth Violence and Juvenile Justice, 4*, 148–169.

Pellegrini, A. D. (2004). Bullying during the middle school years. In C. E. Sanders & C. D. Phye (Eds.), *Bullying: Implications for the classroom* (pp. 177–202). London: Elsevier.

Sticks and Stones. (2006, August 30). *Sticks and stones: Bullying and deaf people*. Retrieved July 28, 2011 from www.ascdeaf.com/blog/?cat=24&paged=3

Surdin, A. (2009, January 1). In several states, a push to stem cyberbullying. *Washington Post*, from http://washingtonpost.com/wp-dyn/content/article/2008/12/31/A03.html

Turow, J. (2001). Family boundaries, commercialism, and the Internet: A framework for research. *Applied Developmental Psychology, 22*, 73–86.

Weiner, M. T., & Miller, M. (2006). Deaf children and bullying: Directions for future research. *American Annals of the Deaf, 151*, 61–70.

Whitney, I., Smith, P. K., & Thompson, D. (1994). Bullying and children with special educational needs. In P. K. Smith & S. Sharp (Eds.), *School bullying: Insights and perspectives* (pp. 213–240). London & New York: Routledge.

Willard, N. (2006). *Cyberbullying and cyberthreats*. Eugene, OR: Center for Safe and Responsible Internet Use.

Williams, K. R., & Guerra, N. G. (2007). Prevalence and predictors of internet bullying. *Journal of Adolescent Health, 41*, S14–S21.

Wolak, J., Mitchell, K. J., & Finkelhor, D. (2007). Does online harassment constitute bullying? An exploration of online harassment by known peers and online only contacts. *Journal of Adolescent Health, 41*, 851–858.

Part V

Studies in the Pacific Rim

9

Cyberbullying in Japan

Cases, Government Reports, Adolescent Relational Aggression, and Parental Monitoring Roles

Ikuko Aoyama, Shoka Utsumi, and Motohiro Hasegawa

In this chapter we discuss the increase in awareness of cyberbullying in Japan, along with several relevant government reports and legislation on Internet use and cyberbullying among children. We also discuss cyberbullying cases reported by the media, and the information gap between parents and children of the technology-savvy generation. Then, two studies are presented to exemplify research on cyberbullying in Japan. The first study examines the relationship between parental monitoring, relational aggression, Internet use, and cyberbullying involvement among junior-high school students in Tokyo ($N = 487$). The second study is a cross-cultural comparison between Japanese and US high school students ($N = 275$), which aimed to investigate cultural differences between these two countries in terms of cyberbullying, parental monitoring, and help-seeking behaviors.

Internet and Mobile Phone Use Among Children and Adolescents

Spam and phishing emails were first noticed and seen as a negative use of the Internet in Japan in 2005. Then, between 2006 and 2007, the media picked up and sensationalized several bullying incidents carried out via the Internet and mobile phones as new types of peer victimization. However, at that time, it was not known how prevalent cyberbullying was; thus, the government started to examine the phenomenon. Cyberbullying in Japan has attracted more public attention as the use of "unofficial school websites" (*gakko ura site*) has been steadily increasing. Unofficial

Cyberbullying in the Global Playground: Research from International Perspectives, First Edition.
Edited by Qing Li, Donna Cross, and Peter K. Smith.

school websites are created by students to enjoy hanging out without adult supervision, because access to those unofficial school websites is often secured by ID and password (Yasukawa, 2008). Initially, student websites were used as harmless communication tools similar to social networking sites (SNS) (Ogiue, 2008, cited in Tagawa, 2010). However, some students started posting offensive information online, including hurtful false rumors and nudity pictures. According to the report issued by the Ministry of Education, Culture, Sports, Science, and Technology (MEXT, 2008), there were more than 38,000 unofficial school websites, and half of them contained inappropriate postings.

Taking into account that students often access such websites through their mobile phones, schools drew attention to the importance of teaching students how to use mobile phones safely and appropriately. A subsequent national study by MEXT (MEXT, 2009a) surveyed 5000 public schools and found that approximately half of junior and high schools and 17% of elementary schools worked on school-based education programs focused on proper mobile phone use. Even though the annual governmental research on students' problematic behaviors demonstrates a slight reduction in cyberbullying incidents among students (in first to twelfth grades), there were still 4520 cases reported (MEXT, 2009b). Moreover, the reported prevalence can be biased towards underestimation, because the voluntary survey was filled out by school administrators, not by students; often, school administrators do not want to admit there are problems at their schools. Thus, it is highly likely that incidents of cyberbullying are much more frequent than was estimated and that many cases of bullying are not recognized by teachers.

When the government released several reports on alarming trends in cyberbullying, the media attention increased dramatically as well. While in 2005 there were no news articles about unofficial school websites, in 2009 about 100 articles were printed in the *Asahi* newspaper alone (Yamagata, 2009). As the media reported cyberbullying more frequently, it has been increasingly recognized as a serious educational and social problem; however, scholarly works on this topic are scarce in Japan. Currently, government reports are the key source of information on technology use and cyberbullying among children. A national study has only begun in the last few years; thus, more rigorous research is needed to gain a deeper understanding of cyberbullying behavior.

Legal Issues and Problems for Intervention

To encourage adolescents' safe and appropriate Internet use, the government enforced some legislation. The Act on Developing an Environment that Provides Safe and Secure Internet Use for Young People (Act No. 79 of 2008) was introduced with the purpose of minimizing occasions for children to be exposed to harmful information on the Internet. In addition, the Act outlined obligations of national and regional public agencies, mobile phone companies, Internet providers, and parents to keep children away from inappropriate content online. Under this Act, guardians are encouraged to monitor children's Internet usage and use filtering software. Guardians are also expected to assume responsibility for educating children on appropriate Internet use, while mobile phone companies are obliged to embed a filtering function in mobile phones sold to children aged under 18. In reality, however, only 6% of parents are aware of the obligation, and 45% have never heard of these new requirements (Keio Univ. & Digital Arts Inc., 2010). Further, Otani, Kagawa, and Honma (2010) found that none of the sales personnel in mobile phone shops mentioned the Act to parents. Moreover, 68% of sales personnel did not even know about or understand the Act. Thus, parents have to actively seek information from mobile phone companies and service providers to protect children from the harm associated with inappropriate use of the Internet through mobile devices.

While the government enforces legislation to increase the safety of Internet use, some of the new laws undermine the effectiveness of school monitoring efforts. For example, the Act on the Prohibition of Unauthorized Computer Access prohibited the disclosure of another person's password, in order to prevent unauthorized access to personal data. This Act is effective in preventing impersonation, when perpetrators make up fake profiles on social networking sites (SNS) to damage someone's reputation, or pretend to be somebody else to make a victim look bad by posting negative messages or comments (Willard, 2007). However, the Act can prevent schools from intervening in cyberbullying incidents. When a teacher intervenes in a cyberbullying situation on unofficial school websites or bulletin boards where access is often restricted by passwords, they must obtain the passwords through legal avenues. If a teacher finds a password to enter such a website without legal permission, his action is considered as unauthorized access, regardless of his intentions. (However, helping cybervictims can be prioritized in case immediate interventions are necessary; for more information, see Hasegawa, Otake, & Otani, 2008). In addition to monitoring the actions of individual school teachers, several private companies also check websites that have the potential for cyberbullying, and report any problems to their clients. Even though many schools use these services, the fact that unofficial websites require a password lessens the effectiveness of such services.

A Cyberbullying Case From a Legal Standpoint

In May 2010, a junior-high school girl was bullied by five students from the same school, in the Chubu region of Japan. The victim was bullied at several locations, and the perpetrators took off her clothes as part of their bullying actions. The abuse incidents were recorded with a mobile phone camera, and the videos were sent as email attachments to other students (*Chuichijoshi*, 2010). The victimized student consulted her homeroom teacher, and the parents of the abusers were contacted on the same day and asked to come to the school for a meeting. The perpetrators and their guardians apologized to the victim. The students who had received the videos were also sought out and made to delete the records. In addition, the City Board of Education prepared several workshops for parents and children to learn more about appropriate mobile phone use. Both the school and the Board of Education devoted their full attention to prevent similar occurrences of cyberbullying in the future. However, the parents of the victimized student filed a claim with the police, and one of the perpetrators, who was 14 years old at the time, was sent to the criminal prosecutor's office for indecent assault and violating the Act on Punishment of Activities Relating to Child Prostitution and Child Pornography, and the Protection of Children. The other the perpetrators, 13-year-old students, were transferred to the family court (*Kani no ijime,* 2010). The Act was originally passed to prevent pedophiles from exploiting children's sexuality, but it was applied to children themselves; thus, the decision was controversial.

The incident also indicates the difficulty of intervening with cyberbullying, and the limitations of educational efforts provided only by schools. Japanese schools often take responsibility not only for academic education, but also for social and life education. Schools often share class problems with a whole class (Akiba, 2004), and a homeroom is designed for students to develop a sense of belonging with homeroom teachers and classmates (Kanetsuna, Smith, & Morita, 2006). Thus, teachers try to solve *ijime* (bullying) problems without punishing or excluding the bullies. Similarly, schools also avoid informing the police or outside agencies of bullies as much as possible (Akiba, 2004). For this reason, it is rare for Japanese parents to file a lawsuit for traditional bullying in schools. In the case of cyberbullying, however, the objective evidence (for example, videos of a victim) would make it easier for them to take judicial action. If so, the impact of cyberbullying would be huge to the community and family as well. Because cyberbullying often occurs outside of schools, it is impossible for schools to deal with these problems and to take sole responsibility. Thus, parents and the community need to work along with schools on cyberbullying prevention and intervention.

Psychological Concerns

As more children and adolescents use technological devices on a daily basis, new problems are starting to emerge. The negative psychological influences of cyberbullying on children are one of the most critical concerns in today's society. The Japanese mass media has reported that victims of cyberbullying often internalize their problems and become upset and socially withdrawn. For example, a male junior-high school student was diagnosed with clinical depression after being cyberbullied. He was a transfer student and created a website to make friends in his new school, but the outcome was unexpected. Numerous verbal attacks online and through emailing to his mobile phone escalated from troubling behaviors to felonious assault. The press reported that this student was so emotionally devastated that he could not go to school (*Kyoto no*, 2007).

When internalizing problems become severe, victims may commit suicide or harm themselves physically. Recently, the media reported an incident that happened to a female junior-high school student who was attacked on a number of Internet sites. The girl left a final message stating, "So scary, I'm going to die!" on an Internet bulletin board before she lay down on a railway track (*Okayama*, 2007). Another junior-high school girl, who complained about insomnia, and hated her new classmates, was found hanged, with a suicide note by her side which read, "Sorry Mom and Dad, I got tired of living," "I hate that school," and "I will retaliate against my friends [adding their real names] who wrote lies about me" (*Jisatsushita*, 2010). As Patchin and Hinduja (2006) mentioned, mean text messages and hurtful pictures can easily be distributed in cyberspace. Experiences of being cyberbullied may damage the self-esteem of adolescents who need social acceptance for their emotional and social development.

While the tragedies of cyberbullied children are highlighted in the media, the psychological aspects of the cyberbullies and the contextual nature of cyberbullying are seldom considered. Research is needed to understand the characteristics of both victims and perpetrators, as well as environmental factors influencing children at this time.

A Family Issue: The Information Gap Between Parents and Their Technology-Aware Children

In Japan, for the past few years, new regulations have been enforced to protect children from harmful experiences on the Internet, but familial effort is still essential to ensure safe online environments for children. To help parents prevent Internet-related problems, government officials drafted handouts focusing on intervention methods to address cyberbullying concerns, and have distributed them. Reports on tragic outcomes of cyberbullying have caught parents' attention and increased awareness of the issue. According to recent government surveys (Cabinet Office, Government of Japan (COGJ), 2007; MEXT, 2009a), parents now seek more information about Internet software filtering and are more likely to lay down rules for their children's usage of the Internet, compared to before. A report showed that 95% of parents have heard of and 73% recognized the benefits of filtering software; however, the reported rate of software implementation at home was low, at 33% (Keio Univ. & Digital Arts Inc., 2010). Parents need to be more aware of the importance of filtering software to protect their children.

Various Western researchers have pointed out that parents underestimate bullying and cyberbullying incidents (Holt & Keyes, 2004; Dehue, Bolman, & Völlink, 2008). Matsunaga (2009) called this tendency an "information gap" between children and their parents and argued that this gap may prevent parents from providing support to their victimized children. Furthermore, this information gap applies to rules on Internet use at home. McQuade, Colt, and Meyer (2009) reported that 93% of US parents said they have established Internet rules for their children; however, 37% of children reported no rules were set by their parents for online activities. Similar findings were published by a government report in Japan: 57% of parents of junior-high school students confirmed that they restricted Internet use for their children, but the corresponding finding was 40% among students; moreover, 54% of high school and 29% of junior-high school students reported no Internet rules at home (MEXT, 2009a). These findings indicate insufficient communication between parents and children on Internet use.

Parental Monitoring Roles

With a wide generation and information gap between parents and children, the parental monitoring role is critical in preventing cyberbullying, which occurs at home in many cases. However, parental monitoring strategies may not be effective enough. Many parents are unsure what their children do online; only 35% of Japanese high school students said that their parents have talked with them about how to behave with others in an online environment, while 36% of them stated that their parents have never looked at what they were doing online (Aoyama & Talbert, 2009). Thus, parents' education is as important as students' education. In fact, parents who have learned about the possible risks of mobile phone and the Internet use are more likely to install filtering software and monitor their children more carefully (MEXT, 2009a). The above findings suggested that effective prevention and intervention programs aimed to minimize instances of cyberbullying should encourage parental participation and facilitate cooperation between schools and homes.

Research

We have emphasized the importance of parental monitoring in discussing cyberbullying; thus, it is useful to explore how parental monitoring practices are related to Internet use and cyberbullying among children. The following section presents two studies. The first study explores the relationship between parental monitoring, Internet use, and cyberbullying involvement among Japanese junior-high school students. The second study provides a cross-cultural comparison between Japanese and US high school students, examining differences in terms of cyberbullying, parental monitoring, and help-seeking behaviors.

Study 1: Cyberbullying Among Junior-High School Students: Its Association With Children's Perception of Parental Control and Relational Aggression

One of the typical problems derived from adolescents' use of the Internet is cyberbullying, or online harassment, which can be defined as an overt intentional act of aggression towards another person online (Ybarra & Mitchell, 2004b). To lessen the undesirable effects of the Internet, parental control, such as specific rules on the Internet or mobile phone use, might be necessary (Wartella & Jennings,

2000). Parental monitoring would be also an effective protective factor to keep young people from destructive behaviors (Soenens, Vansteenkiste, Luyckx, & Goossens, 2006) and to prevent them from becoming victims or offenders. If so, how do these controls lessen the chance of children's involvement in cyberbullying?

Shields and Behrman (2000) assert that parents should set a limit on children's use of computers and mobile phones, because too much time in front of screens and monitors displaces physical and social activities in real life, which are very important for their healthy development. The longer children devote to Internet activities, the more frequently they will encounter opportunities for cyberbullying. Ybarra and Mitchell (2007) report that aggressive behavior problems, as well as infrequent parental monitoring, have a significant association with youths' experiences of cyberbullying.

The amount of Internet use has bidirectional associations with other aspects of adolescents' aggression, such as hostility, physical offence, assertion, and belittlement (Takahira, Ando, & Sakamoto, 2006). General aggression, which has been one of the major deleterious factors in youths' development, might be a third variable that explains the relationship between cyberbullying and the use of the Internet. Crick and Grotpeter (1995) suggest that not only physically overt aggression but also covert (relational) aggression, such as ostracizing and excluding classmates, makes children's adjustment difficult. Because cyberbullying occurs in a communication context and may include telling secrets or sharing confidential information, gossiping, and verbal attacks on the appearance of victims (Ponsford, 2007), it would be reasonable to assume that relational aggression has a strong relationship with cyberbullying.

Aims

The main aim of this study was to create a hypothetical model, which delineates associations among parental controls, the amount of time children spend on the Internet, and their experiences of cyberbullying. First, it was hypothesized that more Internet-related control at home has an association with less Internet use, which leads in turn to fewer experiences of cyberbullying and victimization. Second, it was hypothesized that youths' relational aggression is a mediator between the amount of Internet use and experiences of cyberbullying and victimization. In addition, gender differences in Internet activities were examined, because some previous studies have reported gender differences in hours of Internet use (Gross, 2004; COGJ, 2007) and in cyberbullying (Ybarra & Mitchell, 2004a; Li, 2006; Smith et al., 2008).

Method

Participants and data collection

Participants were randomly selected from five public junior-high schools in a metropolitan city in Japan (N=551). The sample consisted of 487 junior-high students (7th–9th grade, 13–15 years old; male=51%, female=49%) who were

Internet users either via PCs at home, or via mobile phones, or both. With the passive consent procedure, students participated voluntarily and provided information pertaining to protection of privacy. (Some interview- or experiment-type studies need to obtain parental consent in Japan. However, currently parental consent is not required for questionnaire-type surveys for students in Japanese schools.) Hasebe, Nucci, and Nucci (2004) describe this convention as "following the customary procedures in Japan, the school principals acted in loco parentis and granted permission for students to participate in the research," p. 819). Student refusal rate was only 0.4%. The questionnaires were given to students by classroom teachers during August and September, 2007. It took about 20 minutes for the students to fill out the questionnaire.

Measures

Unless otherwise indicated, the survey required respondents to score items on four-point Likert scales, from 1 (none), 2 (seldom), 3 (sometimes), to 4 (frequently). Key variables are outlined below.

Internet use: Participants were asked how many hours on average they used the Internet via PCs and mobile phones during a typical day. Items were scored ranging from 0 (none), 1 (less than 1 hour), 2 (1–2 hours), 3 (2–3 hours), 4 (3–4 hours), 5 (4–5 hours), to 6 (more than 5 hours), separately for PC and mobile phone. The scores for the two items were combined.

Perceptions of Internet protection measures, parental monitoring, and free access to the Internet: These three constructs were tapped from exploratory factor analysis. (1) Perception of Internet control was based on six items, such as "My parents warn me to be careful about the risks of the Internet;" (2) Perception of Internet monitoring covered five items, such as "My parents usually know what I am doing with my mobile phone;" and (3) Perception of free access to the Internet including four items, for example "My parents allow me to access any website." Cronbach alphas for this sample ranged from 0.87 to 0.65.

Relational aggression: Seven items were adapted from the PRAQ-C (Proactive and Reactive Aggression Questionnaire; Sakai & Yamasaki, 2004). For example, "I have intentionally excluded someone from my peer group," "I have gossiped about someone in order for him/her to be disliked by other peers," and "I have ignored someone when I make arrangement with peers to meet up after school." Sakai and Yamasaki (2004) previously reported adequate Cronbach alpha reliability of this relational aggression scale, and for this sample it was 0.88.

Experience of being a cyberbully/cyberbullied: Two equivalent items were used to measure the experience of being a cyberbully, and of being cyberbullied. These were, "I have posted name-calling messages to Internet bulletin boards or blogs," and "I have been mean to some peers using the Internet" (for cyberbullies), and "Someone has posted negative information about me on Internet bulletin boards or blogs," and "Someone has been mean to me using the Internet" (or cybervictims). Response choice was from 1 (none) to 4 (frequently) as mentioned earlier. Limited channels were chosen for this study because at the time (2007), bulletin boards on student-made websites and personal blogs were popular among junior-high school students, and social networking sites were not as popular as in some Western countries. The most popular SNS, mixi, was not available for individuals aged under 18 at that time. Cronbach's alpha reliabilities were 0.87 and 0.89 for cyberbullies and cybervictims respectively.

Data analysis

Model testing was performed by structure equation analysis, with missing data treated with Full Information Maximum Likelihood. AMOS 17.0 was used.

Results

Descriptive statistics

The survey revealed that 12% of respondents spent over five hours a day using the Internet. Almost one third (33%) of the participants reported some involvement in cyberbullying (the time period was not specified). Eighteen percent were cyberbullies or cybervictims, 8% were cyberbullies only, 7% were victims only, and 67% were uninvolved. No gender difference was observed for the classification.

The relationships between parental monitoring, aggression level, Internet use, and cyberbullying

Because the structural coefficients of paternal and maternal Internet controls were almost the same, items of both parents' controls were combined. Relational aggression was expected to serve as a mediator between hours of Internet use and experiences of cyberbullying, accounting for 15% of total variances of cyberbullying and 7% of those of being cyberbullied. Two models that assumed all paths between variables were tested, first for the experiences of cyberbullying and then for being cyberbullied, and then nonsignificant paths were deleted one by one. The models with only significant paths showed a good fit. Further, an exploratory multigroup analysis was performed to examine the consistency of these two models across gender. The final two models are presented together in Figure 9.1. The models produced statistically nonsignificant chi-square and excellent fit indices both for predicting the experience of cyberbullying ($\chi^2(8)=2.46$, $p=0.77$, CFI = 1.00, RMSEA = 0.01) and of being cyberbullied ($\chi^2(8)=4.40$, $p=0.82$, CFI = 1.00, RMSEA = 0.01).

The analysis showed that youths' perception of Internet control from their parents was positively related to perceived monitoring which, in turn, negatively correlated with hours of Internet use. On the other hand, perception of free access to the Internet, which had a negative relationship with perceived control practice, was also negatively related to hours of Internet use. While the amount of Internet use could be directly correlated with more experience of cyberbullying adding to its indirect effect through relational aggression, none of the perceptions of Internet control had a significant direct path to either experiences of cyberbullying or being

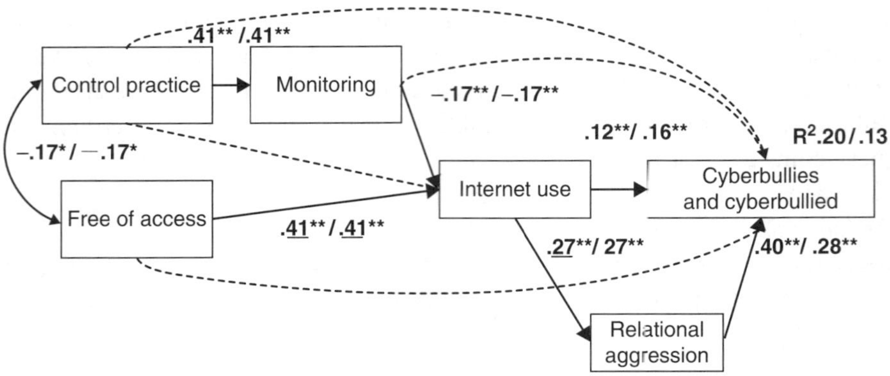

Figure 9.1 Standardized Path Coefficients for the Models Predicting Relationships Among Youths' Perceptions of Parental Internet Controls, Hours on the Internet, and the Experiences of Cyberbullies/Cybervictims. Based on Utsumi (2010), pp. 12–22. Reprinted with permission.

Note: The first coefficients shown are for the best-fitting model for the experiences of cyberbullies, and the second coefficients for cybervictims. Underlined figures show significant differences in path between boys and girls. Dashed lines indicate assumed nonsignificant paths. $^*p < 0.05$, $^{**}p < 0.01$.

cyberbullied. Gender differences are shown on the underlined coefficients in the two models. The relationship between free access and Internet use among girls was much stronger than that among boys (boys, $\beta = 0.28, p < 0.01$; girls, $\beta = 0.52, p < 0.01$; $z = 2.66, p < 0.01$). The relationship between Internet use and relational aggression was much stronger for boys in the experience of cyberbullies model only (boys, $\beta = 0.31, p < 0.01$; girls, $\beta = 0.25, p < 0.01$; $z = 1.96, p < 0.05$).

Discussion

The results indicate that more than 30% of junior-high school students have harassed peers, have been harassed, or both, via the Internet, which is comparable to the prevalence rates discovered by previous researchers (for example, Ybarra & Mitchell, 2004b; Patchin & Hinduja, 2006; Smith et al., 2008). Thus, cyberbullying might be considered a serious social problem with its roots in poor control of teenagers' Internet use.

The main aim of this study was to explain how youths' perception of parental Internet control are related to their Internet use and involvement in cyberbullying, either as a victim or a perpetrator. We hypothesized that three Internet-related parental controls (practices, parental monitoring, and free access to the Internet) would have relationships with both the amount of Internet use and experiences of cyberbullying, and also that relational aggression would be a mediator between adolescents' Internet use and experiences of cyberbullying.

Regarding the Internet controls practiced by parents, no direct effects were observed on time spent on the Internet. However, the perceptions of free access to the Internet, especially by female students, and of parental monitoring, were related indirectly to cyberbullying involvement through Internet use (time), in line with previous studies (Ybarra & Mitchell, 2004a; Smith et al., 2008). Unlike traditional behavioral problems (such as delinquency or substance use), youths' perceptions of parental Internet controls do not predict cyberbullying experiences. As Csikszentmihalyi and Larson (1984) stated, it is difficult for parents to track all of their children's activities during adolescence. Moreover, cyberbullying did not exist in the childhood years of parents, due to the absence of the Internet at that time. Therefore, parents may lack sufficient knowledge about effective Internet controls. To address cyberbullying concerns, parents should be empowered with knowledge to educate their children on the safe use of the Internet.

The results also identified an association between relational aggression and the tendency to cyberbully. The level of relational aggression had significant associations with experience of cyberbullying as well as being cyberbullied. Like Japanese traditional bullying, *ijime*, in which a key aspect is indirect aggression (Taki et al., 2008), cyberbullying might offer a tactical vehicle for relationally aggressive adolescents to ventilate frustrations about peers by gossiping and posting lies. Thus, intervention programs to prevent cyberbullying should pay attention to adolescent aggression.

This cross-sectional study cannot identify causal relationships. In particular, it is possible to assume that the more adolescents become involved with cyberbullying, the more they relationally retaliate. Thus, it is necessary to gather data over time to examine longitudinal relationships. Second, general parental practices vary across cultural groups (Harkness & Super, 1995). Therefore, cross-cultural perspectives are necessary to ensure the generalizability of the study. Future research should investigate proximate factors of cyberbullying other than hours of the Internet use and relational aggression. Regardless of these limitations, this study adds a unique perspective to the cyberbullying literature in Japan, where little empirical work is available.

Study 2: A Comparison of Cyberbullying Among High School Students in Japan and the United States

Bullying patterns and peer dynamics can vary across different cultures. Besides actual behaviors, the nomenclature is also important. The English term "bullying" often has no equivalent word to describe exactly the same idea in other languages (Smith, Cowie, Olafsson, & Liefooghe, 2002). In Western culture, bullying may include physical behaviors such as hitting, punching, and spitting, as well as non-physical aggression such as verbal assault, teasing, ridicule, sarcasm, and scapegoating (Campbell, 2005; Kanetsuna et al., 2006). However, the word *ijime,* which has a similar meaning to bullying, often takes psychological and indirect forms, such as ostracism/exclusion and systematic ignoring by a peer group (Morita, Soeda, Soeda, & Taki, 1999). Sometimes, an entire class is involved in bullying and multiple perpetrators target one victim (Maeda, 1999; Akiba, 2004). In fact, one study found that over 90% of Japanese students believed that only group-to-one harassments are *ijime* (Maeda, 1999). In sum, the definition and perception of traditional bullying varies greatly among different cultures. However, little is known about cultural differences in the perception and practice of cyberbullying. Because cyberbullying can happen internationally, it is important to examine cultural characteristics.

Aim

Does children's engagement in cyberbullying vary in different cultures? To give an answer to this question, in 2008 we explored how cyberbullying is different among high school students in one school in Japan and one school in the United States. The research question is: Are there any cultural differences between these Japanese and American students in terms of (a) cyberbullying behavior patterns, (b) parental monitoring, and (c) help-seeking behaviors?

Method

Participants and data collection

Participants were 275 high school students; 142 from Japan (mean age = 17.2, *SD* = 0.41, male = 98.6%, female = 1.4%), and 133 from the United States (mean age = 15.7, *SD* = 1.25, male = 52.7%, female = 47.3%). The Japanese participants were recruited from one school in Tokyo, and the US participants from one school in Texas. The Japanese school was a private school; thus, the socioeconomic status of the students' family was relatively high. The US school was located in a suburban area, and most of the students were from middle class families.

A self-report online survey was administered during class time at each site. The participants were provided with a URL to access the online survey. The survey was modified from Willard (2007) and Smith et al. (2008), and consisted of 55 multiple-choice and open-ended questions. The Japanese version of the survey was translated by the researcher, and cyberbullying was translated as "*Net ijime*." The online survey was conducted during April and June in 2008 and took about 20 minutes to complete.

Measures

Cyberbullying offending behaviors: These were measured by two questions, "In the last six months, have you sent mean or nasty [email/text] messages to someone?" and, "In the last six months, have you put down someone online by sending or posting cruel messages, gossip, rumors, or other harmful materials?" Response choices were "No" (coded as 0), "Yes, 1 to 4 times" (coded as 1), and "Yes, more than 5 times" (coded as 2). The scores of the two questions were combined.

Cyberbullying victimization: This was measured by two corresponding questions, "In the last six months, have you received mean or nasty messages from someone?" and "In the last six months, have you been put down online by someone who has sent or posted cruel messages, gossip, rumors, or other harmful materials?" Response choices and scoring were the same as for cyberbullying offending.

Parental monitoring: This was measured by one question, "How often do you discuss what you are doing online with your parents?" Response choices were "Frequently" (coded as 3), "Occasionally" (coded as 2), and "Never" (coded as 1).

Help-seeking pattern: This was measured by one question, "If you were cyberbullied, would you tell your parents?" Response choices were "Very likely" (coded as 5), "Somewhat likely" (coded as 4), "Somewhat unlikely" (coded as 3), "Very unlikely" (coded as 2), and "Not sure" (coded as 1).

Data analyses

Missing data were handled by using the Multiple Imputation (MI) method, as each question had missing data (0.7–3.3%). Then, *t*-tests were performed to identify significant group differences (Japan versus the US) in students' cyberbullying experiences, parental monitoring, and help-seeking. SPSS 18.0 was utilized for quantitative analysis.

Results

Descriptive data

Descriptive statistics are summarized in Table 9.1. Overall, the results indicated that the US participants were more involved in cyberbullying, both as victims and bullies, than the Japanese participants.

Cyberbullying patterns

Japanese participants ($M=0.15$, $SD=0.46$) reported being victims of cyberbullying less often than US participants ($M=0.43$, $SD=0.83$); $t(273)=3.39$, $p<0.01$), $d=0.41$. Similarly, fewer Japanese respondents (M=0.14, SD=0.57) reported being cyberbullies than US students ($M=0.45$, $SD=0.93$); $t(291)=3.11$, $p<0.01$), $d=0.40$. Cohen's *d*s indicated moderate effects both for victimization and offending.

Parental monitoring

Japanese participants' parents monitored their children's online behaviors less often ($M = 1.34$, $SD = 0.50$) than US parents ($M = 1.68$, $SD = 0.62$); $t(268) = 4.95$, $p < 0.01$, $d = 0.6$. Cohen's d indicated a moderate effect.

Help-seeking from parents

Japanese participants reported they were less likely to seek help from their parents ($M = 2.86$, $SD = 1.49$) than the US participants ($M = 3.04$, $SD = 1.16$); $t(271) = 1.06$, $p < 0.01$, $d = 0.14$. The effect size is small; thus, in practice this group difference may be considered to be small.

Discussion

Overall, the Japanese participants reported less experience of cyberbullying than was found in the US. Because cyberbullying is indirect, it was hypothesized that the Japanese students were more likely to be involved with cyberbullying than US

Table 9.1 Responses to Cyberbullying Questions, in Japanese and US Samples.

Questions	*Response choice*	*Japanese responses*	*US responses*
In the last six months, have you received mean or nasty messages from someone?	Yes, 1 to 4 times	8.6%	20.0%
	Yes, more than 5 times	0.7%	4.6%
	No	90.6%	75.4%
In the last six months, have you sent mean or nasty messages to someone?	Yes, 1 to 4 times	4.3%	14.5%
	Yes, more than 5 times	0.7%	6.9%
	No	95.0%	78.6%
In the last six months, have you been put down online by someone who has sent or posted cruel gossip, rumors, or other harmful materials?	Yes, 1 to 4 times	5.0%	9.9%
	Yes, more than 5 times	0%	1.5%
	No	95.0%	88.5%
In the last six months, have you put down someone else online by sending or posting cruel gossip, rumors, or other harmful materials?	Yes, 1 to 4 times	2.9%	6.3%
	Yes, more than 5 times	1.4%	4.0%
	No	95.7%	89.7%
How often do you discuss what you are doing online with your parents?	Frequently	1.4%	8.3%
	Occasionally	30.4%	51.9%
	Never	68.1%	39.8%
If you were being cyberbullied would you tell your parents?	Very likely	3.6%	35.3%
	Somewhat likely	20.7%	15.8%
	Somewhat unlikely	35.0%	10.5%
	Very unlikely	18.6%	30.8%
	Not sure	22.1%	7.5%

students; however, the results did not support this hypothesis. It is likely that the age difference between the two country samples is a factor; the mean age of the Japanese participants was about two years older than the US participants. Thus, the observed cultural difference may be, in part, an age difference. Another possible factor is translation issues. The questionnaire to measure cyberbullying was developed by Western researchers, and the Japanese version was translated from the original questionnaire. Nevertheless, the lower experience of cyberbullying in Japan is consistent with past research which found that traditional bullying is a major peer victimization practice and the prevalence of cyberbullying is still very low in Japan (less than 5% of total bullying incidents) (MEXT, 2009b). The corresponding figure is 32% among nationally representative adolescents in the US (Lenhart, 2007). However, the prevalence reported by the Japanese government may be an underestimate, because the Japanese government surveys were filled out by school principals, while the US surveys were answered by adolescents. Therefore, the real gap between the two cultures may be different.

As for parental monitoring, the US parents in this sample were more interested in their children's Internet activity than Japanese parents, as they discussed Internet use with their children more often than Japanese parents. This finding is consistent with results of research by Webroot Software Inc. (2007): The number of US parents who use filtering software to block harmful sites is about triple that of Japanese parents. It is reasonable to assume that the higher prevalence of cyberbullying among US children may trigger parents' awareness and motivate them to monitor their children's Internet use. In Japan, the media reported several incidents when Internet users were illegally charged large amounts of money by fraudulent companies for visiting adult sites, playing online games, and downloading music. Therefore, Japanese parents may be more concerned about the practice of fraudulent charging than their children's involvement in cyberbullying. Another explanation of this finding is in the way the level of parental monitoring was measured. The question, "How often do you discuss what you are doing online with your parents?" was the indicator of parental monitoring, but monitoring of mobile phone use was not included. It is possible that Japanese parents monitor their children's mobile phone use as often as US parents do.

Regarding help-seeking from parents, Japanese participants were less likely to seek help from their parents than US participants. Because the US parents in this sample discussed online activities with their children quite often, children may have had more opportunities to share the problems they face online. This result suggests that parental monitoring may help to increase communication between parents and children. Moreover, the US participants had more experiences of cyberbullying than their Japanese counterparts; thus, they might have more opportunity to need help from their parents than Japanese participants. Second, cultural backgrounds may explain the difference. In a collectivist culture like Japan, people try not to bother each other even within the family, with the aim of not damaging their family reputation. Japanese children may believe that online victimization embarrasses their parents, and they are reluctant to tell them about any cyberbullying incidents.

A limitation of this study is the small sample size—only one school in each culture. In addition, Japanese participants were from a metropolitan area and US participants from a suburban area. Also, the Japanese participants were about two years older than the US participants. Japanese children attend high school for three years while US children attend for four years. Thus, the observed difference between groups could be explained by regional and age differences as well. The cross-sectional nature of the study is another limitation because it cannot infer a causal relationship. Thus, the generalizability of the findings is limited. Finally, only limited cyberbullying behaviors were measured in this study. There are many ways to cyberbully others (for example, via YouTube and Photoshop); thus, future research should investigate cultural differences in each type of cyberbullying. A longitudinal study is also necessary to understand the cyberbullying phenomenon more deeply. As technological devices become smaller and more ubiquitous, new types of cyberbullying will emerge. Researchers need to keep up with new ways to use technology among children and to establish collaborative relationships to work on effective intervention/prevention strategies across cultures.

General Implications and Future Research

Scholarly works on cyberbullying are still scarce in Japan. As cyberbullying research advances internationally, Japanese policy makers and educators should actively seek practical intervention strategies from Western researchers. However, Japanese traditional bullying, *ijime*, is very different from Western bullying (Morita et al., 1999; Taki et al., 2008). Thus, future studies need to collect more qualitative and quantitative data to address the complexity of this phenomenon and identify culture-specific characteristics. To date, no nationwide intervention program has been implemented in Japan, and prevention efforts are limited to the school-district context. Some factors, such as schools' exclusiveness to outsiders, excessive concern for personal information protection, and the heavy workload of school teachers (Sakai, 2009), hinder efforts of researchers from collect sufficient data. Despite many difficulties, it is vital for schools to work with parents, guardians, researchers, and the community to create effective educational policies, guidelines, and programs to combat bullying and cyberbullying.

Acknowledgments

The first study in this chapter was adapted from S. Utsumi (2010) Cyberbullying among middle school students: Association with children's perception of parental control and relational aggression [in Japanese]. *Japanese Journal of Educational Psychology*, *58*(1), 12–22. We thank and acknowledge the Japanese Association of Educational Psychology for permission to reproduce text from the original article. We would also like thank Dr. Smith and Dr. Willard for letting us use parts of their questionnaires to measure cyberbullying among youth for the second study.

References

Act on Developing an Environment that Provides Safe and Secure Internet Use for Young People (Act No. 79 of 2008). Retrieved September 20, 2010 from www8.cao.go.jp/youth/youth-harm/pdf/neteng.pdf

Akiba, M. (2004). Nature and correlates of ijime [bullying] in Japanese middle school. *International Journal of Educational Research*, *41*, 216–236.

Aoyama, I., & Talbert, L. T. (2009, April). *A cross-cultural study on cyberbullying among high school students in the Unites States and Japan*. Paper presented at the meeting of the American Educational Research Association (AERA), San Diego, CA.

Cabinet Office, Government of Japan. (2007). *Dai 5-kai Jouhouka Shakai to Seishounen ni Kansuru Ishikichousa ni Tsuite* [*The Fifth Survey on Information Society and Youth*]

(in Japanese). Retrieved August 25, 2010 from www8.cao.go.jp/youth/kenkyu/jouhou5/index.html

Campbell, M. A. (2005). Cyberbullying: An old problem in a new guise? *Australian Journal of Guidance and Counseling, 15*, 68–76.

Chuichijoshi no hadaka satsuei Kani 2-nennsei 5nin ga ijime mail soushinnmo [Cyberbullying in Kani city: Five junior-high school second-graders took nude photos of a first-grade girl and sent them by email to other students] (in Japanese). (2010, June 29). *Chunichi Simbun*, p. 13.

Crick, N. R., & Grotpeter, J. K. (1995). Relational aggression, gender, and social-psychological adjustment. *Child Development, 66*, 710–722.

Csikszentmihalyi, M., & Larson, R. (1984). *Being adolescent*. NY: Basic Books.

Dehue, F., Bolman, C., & Völlink, T. (2008). Cyberbullying: Youngsters' experiences and parental perception. *CyberPsychology & Behavior, 11*, 217–223.

Gross, E. F. (2004). Adolescent Internet use: What we expect, what teens report. *Applied Developmental Psychology, 25*, 633–649.

Harkness, S., & Super, C. M. (1995). Culture and parenting. In M. H. Bornstein (Ed.), *Handbook of parenting* (pp. 211–234). Hillsdale, NJ: Erlbaum.

Hasebe, Y., Nucci, L., & Nucci, M. (2004). Parental control of the personal domain and adolescent symptoms of psychopathology: A cross-national study in the United States and Japan. *Child Development, 75*, 815–828.

Hasegawa, M., Otake, T., & Otani, T. (2008). A suggestion to the educational and legal problems of school teachers' response to cyberbullying and their tasks: Through a public lower secondary school's case (in Japanese). *Information Network Law Review, 7*, 104–113.

Holt, M. K., & Keyes, A. M. (2004). Teachers' attitudes toward bullying. In D. L. Espelage & S. M. Swearer (Eds.), *Bullying in American schools* (pp. 121–139). Mahwah, NJ: Lawrence Erlbaum.

Jisatsushita joshiseito no tsukue kara mitsukatta isho to shirusareta okigaki [Suicide note and memo by the dead junior high school girl found in her desk drawer]. (2010, January 19). *The Asahi Newspaper*, p. 39.

Kanetsuna, T., Smith, P. K., & Morita, Y. (2006). Coping with bullying at school: Children's recommended strategies and attitudes to school-based interventions in England and Japan. *Aggressive Behavior, 32*, 570–580.

Kani no ijime 14sai chu2 o shoruisoukenn 13sai 4nin kasaishouchi handan e. [A 14 year-old junior high school second-grader was charged and four 13-year-old students are to be transferred to family court.] (August 6, 2010). *Chunichi (newspaper)*, p. 13.

Keio Univ., & Digital Arts Inc. (2010). *Seishounen no Internet Keitaidenwa Riyou ni Kansuru Ankeito* [*Survey on adolescents' use of the Internet and mobile phones*] (in Japanese). Retrieved August 25, 2010 from www.daj.jp/company/release/data/reference_r012601_2010.pdf

Kyoto no chu3 dannshi, net-ijime de utsubyou-ni [A junior high school third-grade boy suffered from severe depression after being cyberbullied] (2007, November 1), *Yomiuri* (evening paper), p. 18.

Lenhart, A. (2007). *Cyberbullying and online teens*. Washington, DC: Pew Internet and Life Project. Retrieved August 25, 2010 from http://pewinternet.org/~/media//Files/Reports/2007/PIP%20Cyberbullying%20Memo.pdf.pdf

Li, Q. (2006). Cyberbullying in schools: A research of gender differences. *School Psychology International, 27*, 157–170.

Maeda, R. (1999). *Ijime: An exploratory study of a collective form of bullying among Japanese students*. ERIC Document Reproduction Service No. ED438015. Retrieved October 5, 2007 from the ERIC database, http://eric.ed.gov:80/PDFS/ED438015.pdf

Matsunaga, M. (2009). Parents don't (always) know their children have been bullied: Child–parent discrepancy on bullying and family-level profile of communication standards. *Human Communication Research, 35*, 221–247.

McQuade, C. S., Colt, P. J., & Meyer, B. N. (2009). *Cyberbullying. Protecting kids and adults from online bullies*. Westport, CT: Praeger.

Ministry of Education, Culture, Sports, Science, and Technology. (2008). *Seisyonen ga riyo suru gakko hikousiki site nado ni kansuru cyousa (Gaiyo)* [*Research on adolescents' use of unofficial school websites and other websites*] (in Japanese). Retrieved August 25, 2010 from www.mext.go.jp/b_menu/houdou/20/04/08041805/001.htm

Ministry of Education, Culture, Sports, Science, and Technology. (2009a). *Kodomono keitaidenwa tou no riyouni kannsuru chousa: chousakekka no gaiyou* [*Research on adolescents' use of mobile phones: Overview*] (in Japanese). Retrieved August 25, 2010 from www.mext.go.jp/component/b_menu/houdou/__icsFiles/afieldfile/2009/05/15/1266544_1_1.pdf

Ministry of Education, Culture, Sports, Science, and Technology. (2009b). *Heisei 20 nendo jidouseito no mondai koudou nado seitosido jo no syomondai ni kansuru cyousa* [*Research on problematic behaviors and related problems among adolescents*] (in Japanese). Retrieved August 25, 2010 from www.mext.go.jp/b_menu/houdou/21/11/__icsFiles/afieldfile/2009/11/30/1287227_1_1.pdf

Morita, Y., Soeda, H., Soeda, K., & Taki, M. (1999). Japan. In P. K. Smith, Y. Morita, J. Junger-Tas, D. Olweus, R. Catalano, & P. Slee (Eds.), *The nature of school bullying: A cross-national perspective* (pp. 309–323). New York & London: Routledge.

Okayama chu3 joshi jisatsu net-ijime musume no sakebi oitsuzukeru haha [Mother of cyberbullying victim, junior-high school third-grade girl who committed suicide in Okayama city, is seeking redress for her daughter's suffering] (in Japanese). (2007, December 28), *The Sanyo Newpaper*, p. 31.

Otani, Y., Kagawa, S., & Honma, F. (2010). Research to explore explanations when mobile phone shops sell mobile phones to children (in Japanese). *Bulletin of the Faculty of Education, 103*, 85–93.

Patchin, J. W., & Hinduja, S. (2006). Bullies move beyond the schoolyard: A preliminary look at cyberbullying. *Youth Violence and Juvenile Justice, 4*, 148–169.

Ponsford, J. (2007). *The future of adolescent female cyberbullying: Electronic media's effect on aggressive communication*. Retrieved August 20, 2008 from http://ecommons.txstate.edu/honorprog/64

Sakai, A. (2009). Chousa field to shiteno gakkou: Access no konnannsa to action research heno kitai [Schools as locations of field research: Difficulties in accessing schools and expectations from research] (in Japanese). *Advances in Social Research, 2*, 13–19.

Sakai, A., & Yamasaki, K. (2004). Development of the Proactive and Reactive Aggression Questionnaire for elementary school children. *Japanese Journal of Psychology, 75*, 254–261.

Shields, M. K., & Behrman, R. E. (2000). Children and computer technology: Analysis and recommendations. *Future of Children, 10*, 4–30.

Smith, P. K., Cowie, H., Olafsson, R., & Liefooghe, A. P. D. (2002). Definitions of bullying: A comparison of terms used, and age and sex differences, in a 14-country international comparison. *Child Development, 73*, 1119–1133.

Smith, P. K., Mahdavi, J., Carvalho, M., Fisher, S., Russell, S., & Tippett, N. (2008). Cyberbullying: its nature and impact in secondary school pupils. *Journal of Child Psychology and Psychiatry, 49*, 376–385.

Soenens, B., Vansteenkiste, M., Luyckx, K., & Goossens, L. (2006). Parenting and adolescent problem behavior: An integrated model with adolescent self-disclosure and perceived parental knowledge as intervening variables. *Developmental Psychology, 42*, 205–318.

Tagawa, T. (2010). Net Ijime no atarashi sa [The novelty of cyberbullying] (in Japanese). In M. Fukaya, K. Fukaya, & M. Takahata (Eds.), *Ubiquitous syakai deno kodomo no seicyo* [Children's growth and development in ubiquitous society] (in Japanese) (pp. 45–55). Tokyo: Harvest-sha Inc.

Takahira, M., Ando, R., & Sakamoto, A. (2006). Estimation of causal effects through longitudinal study: An example of Internet use and aggression (in Japanese). *Japanese Journal of Personality, 15*, 87–102.

Taki, M., Slee, P., Hymel, S., Pepler, D., Sim, H., & Swearer, S. (2008). A new definition and scales for indirect aggression in schools: Results from the longitudinal comparative survey among five countries. *International Journal of Violence and School, 7*, 3–19.

Utsumi, S. (2010). Cyberbullying among middle-school students: Association with children's perception of parental control and relational aggression. *Japanese Journal of Educational Psychology, 58*, 12–22.

Wartella, E. A., & Jennings, N. (2000). Children and computers: New technology—old concerns. *Future of Children, 10*, 31–43.

Webroot Software Inc. (2007). *State of Internet security: Protecting children online*. Retrieved August 25, 2010 from www.webroot.com/pdf/Webroot_SoIS_Q0207.pdf

Willard, N. (2007). *Cyberbullying and cyber-threats: Responding to the challenge of online social aggression, threats, and distress*. Champaign, IL: Research Press.

Yamagata, F. (2009). *Nihon kodomo syakai kodomo gakkai* [*Research on unofficial school websites*] (in Japanese). Retrieved August 25, 2010 from http://js-cs.jp/research/09_urasaito_B.pdf

Yasukawa, M. (2008). *Gakko ura site kara kodomo o mamoru* [How to protect children from unofficial school websites] (in Japanese). Tokyo: Chukei Publishing Company.

Ybarra, M. L., & Mitchell, K. J. (2004a). Online aggressor/targets, aggressors, and targets: A comparison of associated youth characteristics. *Journal of Child Psychology and Psychiatry, 45*, 1308–1316.

Ybarra, M. L., & Mitchell, K. J. (2004b). Youth engaging in online harassment: Associations with caregiver–child relationships, Internet use, and personal characteristics. *Journal of Adolescence, 27*, 319–336.

Ybarra, M. L., & Mitchell, K. J. (2007). Prevalence and frequency of Internet harassment instigation: Implications for adolescent health. *Journal of Adolescent Health, 41*, 189–195.

10

Cyberbullying in South Korea

Neil Tippett and Keumjoo Kwak

Over the last decade, the use of mobile phones, the Internet, and other forms of Information and Communication Techologies (ICTs) has increased rapidly, especially among young people. While most of this use has been positive, instances of abuse have also increased, bringing the issue of cyberbullying to international attention. Given the amount of time children are now able to spend online, often unsupervised, cyberbullying has grown into a real threat which can affect any child who has access to the Internet and mobile phones. This study seeks to add to the knowledge being gathered worldwide on the subject of cyberbullying by examining the prevalence and nature of cyberbullying among a sample of South Korean adolescents.

Although cyberbullying has received increasing attention over recent years, much of this comes from Western countries, predominantly the UK, the US, and Australia; there has been much less study of cyberbullying in Eastern cultures. For South Korea in particular, traditional bullying among children and adolescents is only now becoming widely documented, and at present studies of cyberbullying are somewhat sparse.

In terms of public consciousness around the issue, cyberbullying has begun to garner increased attention in recent years due to media reports of high-profile cyberbullying cases. In 2008, the South Korean actress Choi Jin Sil committed suicide, supposedly in the face of unrelenting harassment by Internet users (*Time* Magazine, 2008), and throughout 2010, the South Korean singer Tablo endured a malicious online cyberbullying campaign directed at him by Internet users who doubted his academic credentials (*The Korea Times*, 2010). Despite well publicized police intervention, and

Cyberbullying in the Global Playground: Research from International Perspectives, First Edition.
Edited by Qing Li, Donna Cross, and Peter K. Smith.

national and international media reports, the campaign still continues at the time of writing. Reports such as these have been widely circulated in South Korean media, bringing to prominence the issue of cyberbullying, and raising questions as to the extent to which it affects both children and adults in South Korea.

The widespread use of technology within South Korea is one of the key reasons meriting the need for research into cyberbullying. South Korea is a world leader in the use of the Internet, and was one of the first countries in the world to implement a national broadband network. The International Telecommunication Union (ICU, 2010) reported that, as of 2010, 81.1% of the population was using the Internet and that, by 2005, 96.8% of mobile phones in the country were already being used to access the Internet.

According to a report by the Ministry of Information and Communication and National Internet Development Agency of Korea (2008), 26.3% of elementary school students, 81.8% of middle school students, and 93.3% of high school students use a mobile phone. A similar report on Internet usage in South Korea found 58.7% of 3–5-year-olds, 77.1% of 6–12-year-olds, and 99.9% of teenagers used the Internet (Korea Communications Commission and National Internet Development Agency of Korea, 2008). Sung, Kim, Lee, and Lim (2006) in a survey of 1382 10–19-year-olds, showed that a large proportion of South Korean children's free time was spent online. The average amount of free time each child had on a weekday was three hours, of which almost two thirds (111 minutes) was spent online; on weekends, children reported 392 minutes of free time each day, of which over half (215 minutes) was spent online. In late 2010, the issue of Internet addiction was widely discussed within the South Korean media, raising concerns over the amount of time spent by children and adolescents on the Internet, and the safety and welfare of those who use it for long periods of time.

Despite such pervasive use of the communication technologies among children and young people in Korea, the issue of cyberbullying has to date received little attention from researchers. One comparative survey of traditional bullying from four countries during 2004–2005 (International Symposium on Educational Reform, 2005) included data on being victimized by computer/mobile phone. Rates for being cyberbullied "sometimes or more often" were highest in Canada (17.9%), followed by Australia (8.0%), and Japan (5.8%), with the lowest prevalence being reported in South Korea (5.2%).

Further research which specifically concerns South Korea is harder to come by, although a small number of studies have been published in Korean language journals which either discuss children's online behavior, or make some reference to the concept of cyberbullying. While not focused solely on children, Jung (2005) estimated the degree of cyber-violence taking place in South Korea by analyzing the number of requests made to the Korea Internet Safety Commission for corrections to be made to online information. In the first half of 2005, 17,247 incidents were reported; the greatest proportion of these incidents concerned sexually inappropriate behavior, libellous comments, and privacy infringements. Similarly, Park (2008) analyzed records collected by the National Statistics Office between 2001–2007;

from 2001 to 2005 the total number of cases of cyber-violence rose sharply, from 1054 to 8406 respectively. This same increase was reflected in the majority of subtypes of cyber-violence, including online libel, insults, sexual violence, and stalking. It appears that this cyber-violence reached a peak in 2005, as in the following two years there was a decrease in both the total number of reported incidents, and those within the subcategories of online violence.

These two studies did not specifically address cyberbullying, but outlined different types of violence commonly found to occur online, and appears to have set a framework for future studies. Rather than using the concept of cyberbullying, South Korean researchers have instead tended to use the terms *cyber-pokryuk* (cyber-violence) or *ak-peul* (malicious comments) when investigating online aggression among children. These terms cannot be considered directly comparable to cyberbullying, as they concern differing forms of behavior, but the studies in which they are used do provide an initial indication of aggressive and harassing behaviors which are experienced by children who access the Internet.

A brief study by Han (2001) gave an account of cyber delinquency among 823 adolescents aged 12 to 18 years. The main purpose of the study was to examine the relationship between adolescent cyber delinquency and socio-relational factors, but the results showed that 34% of participants could be classified as cyber delinquents (44% of boys, and 14% of girls).

Sung, Kim, Lee, and Lim's (2006) study of 1382 teenagers (above) defined cyber-violence as the online equivalents of insults, damaging reputations, stalking, sexual violence, privacy infringement, and rumor spreading. Cyber insults were the most commonly reported form of cyber-violence, with 39% of participants having experienced them; 14% had encountered online privacy infringement or rumor spreading, 13% had experienced reputation damaging cyber behaviors, and 11% had been victims of cyber sexual violence. For each of these types of online violence, victims were asked to disclose their relationship to the antagonist; for insults and sexual violence the perpetrator was most often unknown to the victim, or hid their identity; but for rumor spreading and reputation damaging, just under one third of victims said that a friend had been responsible. Males were more likely to have carried out any form of cyber-violence, although gender differences were less pronounced for victims.

Hwang (2006) reported on forms of cyber-violence experienced by 576 middle school students (262 male, 314 female), attending five schools within Seoul. Cyber-violence was examined through five different media: Internet message boards, chatting and instant messaging programs, online messages, emails, and text messages. Figures are reported for each form of online aggression: abuse, slander, rumor spreading, personal threats, bomb messaging, and sexual harassment. Abuse was the most commonly experienced form of cyber-violence, with 23% through chatting and messaging, 15–20% through Internet boards, online messages, and text messages, but only 4% through emails. Other forms of cyber-violence were reported by only around 5% of participants. The majority of participants who reported being victimized in any way stated that the incidents had occurred once or twice a year, while smaller numbers reported being targeted once a month, or once a week.

Cheon (2000) examined the underlying reasons as to why young people engage in violent behaviors online, and the characteristics that can instigate this. In line with suggestions in Western research (Vandebosch & van Cleemput, 2009) on the relationship between traditional victims and online bullies, Cheon discussed how the apparent anonymity of the Internet and other forms of ICT, and the ability to communicate without using face-to-face interaction, allows Internet users to harass others or express their grievances without fear of discovery or repercussions. In addition, the Internet provides a place through which young people are able to separate from their parents and families, thereby expressing their feelings and developing their own identities. The author suggested that this freedom encourages individuals to continue using the Internet, therefore they spend more and more time online, and when combined with the anonymity, the combination of these factors may encourage cyber deviance.

These reports of cyber-violence in South Korea provide an understanding of children's experience of aggression through the Internet and mobile phones, but do not directly address cyberbullying which, given the behaviors involved and the effect on the victim, can be considered as a separate issue to cyber-violence. Therefore the present study aims to give a detailed account of the prevalence and nature of cyberbullying among children in South Korea, which is in line with contemporary accounts from Western research.

Method

Participants

The present study was conducted in January 2009, using a quantitative questionnaire presented to 416 South Korean children attending two secondary schools in Seoul. The sample comprised pupils from grades 7 to 9 in the South Korean educational system, an age range of 12 to 15 years (mean age 14.00 years), with a gender split of 198 boys (47.8%) and 216 girls (52.2%). There were 46 participants from grade 7 (17 boys, 29 girls), 233 from grade 8 (107 boys, 126 girls), and 137 from grade 9 (74 boys, 63 girls). All pupils who participated in this study resided in South Korea, and spoke Korean as their first language.

The two secondary schools had existing connections with the Developmental Psychology Department at Seoul National University, therefore providing an opportunistic sample. Both schools were located in urban areas close to the center of Seoul. Parents had a good standard of education, with 97.2% of mothers and 97.8% of fathers having graduated from high school.

Instruments and procedure

The questionnaire used was adapted from that used in the cross-national DAPHNE-funded project, "An investigation into forms of peer–peer bullying at school in preadolescent and adolescent groups: new instruments and preventing strategies" (see Genta, Berdondini, Brighi, & Guarini, 2009, and Chapter 2 in this book). The English language version of the questionnaire had been validated over the course of several UK studies, albeit with slight revisions. Translation of the questionnaire was conducted by research staff and students from the Department of Psychology at Seoul National University.

The questionnaire was divided into three sections. The first, entitled "About you," requested demographic information concerning the children's age, gender, ethnicity, and background of their parents (highest level of education, current occupation). The second section, "About your school," asked for basic information regarding the participant's current educational situation, using a series of statements designed to represent children's feelings regarding their school. The third and most substantial section of the questionnaire was entitled "About bullying and cyberbullying," in which participants were asked to detail their experiences of four forms of victimization: direct bullying, indirect bullying, mobile phone bullying, and Internet bullying. For each of these categories, participants were presented with a short definition, which included examples of the behaviors each entailed. Respondents were asked to state whether they had experienced any of these forms of bullying as either a victim or bully in the last two months, using a five-point scale which ranged from 0 ("have not experienced") to 4 ("experienced several times a week"). This scale was also used to measure bystander involvement in bullying, by asking participants whether they had "seen or heard" of each form of bullying in the last two months.

Children who reported that they had been bullied at least "once or twice" for any form of bullying were then asked to complete a series of multiple choice questions. These asked "how long did the bullying last?" using a four-point scale from 0 ("one to two weeks"), to 3 "more than one year," "who bullied you?" (with responses relating to age and gender of perpetrators), "how did the bullying make you feel?," and "what did you do about the bullying?," in order to ascertain children's perceptions and coping strategies for the differing forms of bullying. In addition, participants who had witnessed any form of traditional bullying or cyberbullying taking place were asked how they had responded to the incident, using three multiple choice questions which examined bystander responses and participant roles in bullying.

To test the validity of the questionnaire, a pilot study was conducted with 54 elementary school pupils (28 boys, 26 girls) in Incheon and 139 middle school pupils (80 boys, 59 girls) in a suburb of Seoul. The questionnaire was distributed by two trained instructors who visited the classes and assisted pupils in responding to the survey.

Results from this pilot raised a number of issues; in order to make the questionnaire more suitable for South Korean school children, some of the language was modified to make it more understandable, and three questions regarding bystander behavior were combined into a single question. The largest part of the revision concerned the inclusion of a separate section which asked participants about their experiences of bullying and harassment in online computer games. The pilot study indicated that a large proportion of reported cyberbullying taking place online occurred through the medium of online games, so it was decided to add a separate category to further explore this form of bullying. The questions used in this section corresponded with those used for other forms of traditional bullying and cyberbullying; therefore the participants were asked whether they had experienced online game bullying as victims, perpetrators, or bystanders. Victims of online game bullying were then asked further questions relating to how long it had lasted, who they were bullied by, how they felt, and what coping strategies they had used.

After these revisions, the questionnaires were then posted to schools taking part in the main study, along with an instruction sheet for the class teacher. The questionnaires were completed during regular class sessions, under the supervision of a class tutor. Using the information sheet provided, staff instructed pupils to fill out the questionnaire alone and in silence. The pupils were given up to one hour to fill out the form. 416 questionnaires were returned in a complete state. Responses were coded and analyzed using SPSS v.15. Frequencies were obtained for questions regarding each type of bullying. For comparisons between groups, chi-square, ANOVAs and correlations were used.

Results

Prevalence of bullying and cyberbullying

Victims

The number of respondents who reported being victimized through each of the five types of bullying is illustrated in Figure 10.1. Around 12% of pupils reported being either directly or indirectly bullied "once or twice" or more often in the last two months. Victims of direct bullying gave varying responses regarding how long they had been bullied for, with most reporting it had occurred either once or twice (37% of victims) or several times per week (29%). In contrast, the majority of victims who had experienced indirect bullying in the last two months reported that it had occurred only once or twice (69%).

Around 10% of all pupils reported having been bullied by mobile phones. Of these, 77% had been victimized only once or twice within the last two months, while 13% had been targeted once a week or more often. Internet bullying was the least prevalent, reported by 6.3% of all pupils, the majority being targeted just once or twice over the previous two months (73%), while five pupils were harassed online once a week or more often (5%).

By far the most prevalent form of any bullying was victimization through online games, with 43% of all pupils reporting that they had experienced this in the last two

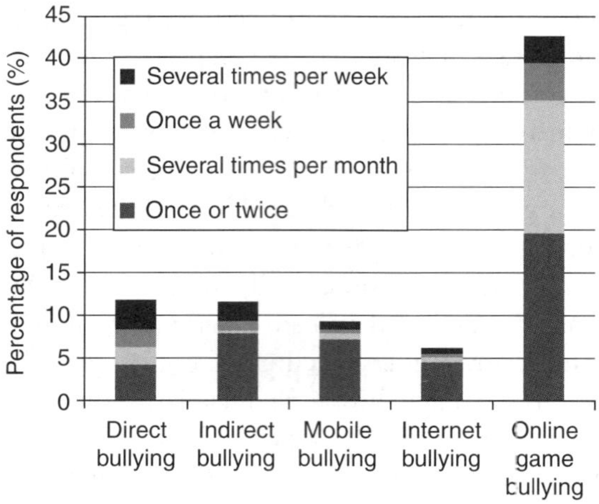

Figure 10.1 Rates of Victimization for Five Types of Bullying. Created by Neil Tippett and Keumjoo Kwak.

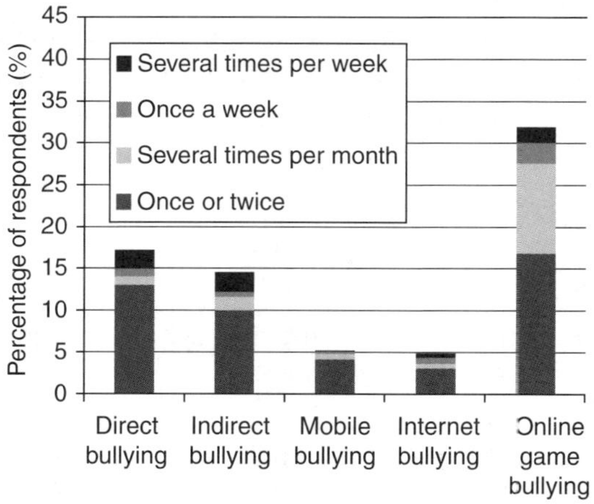

Figure 10.2 Rates of Bullying Others for Five Types of Bullying. Created by Neil Tippett and Keumjoo Kwak.

months. Among these, 46% had been bullied just once or twice over the previous months, but 30% had experienced online game bullying on a regular basis, at least once a week or more often.

Bullies

Figure 10.2 shows the proportion of pupils who had victimized others, according to each form of bullying. Around 15% of all participants admitted to having bullied other children either directly or indirectly. This was mostly once or twice within the last two months, 75% among pupils who bullied others directly, and 69% for indirect bullies; but around 15% of those who had bullied others either directly or indirectly admitted doing this once a week or more often.

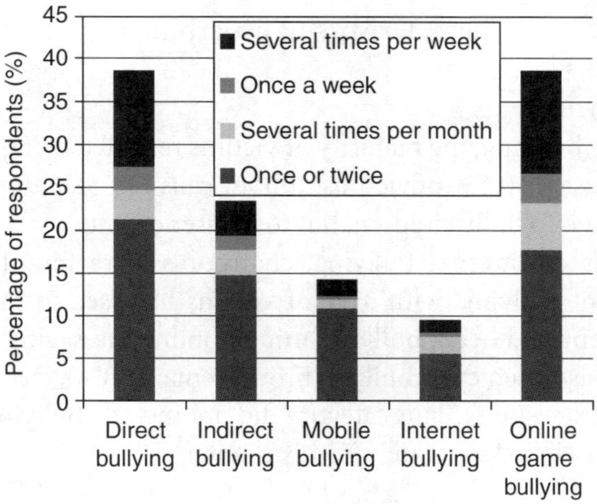

Figure 10.3 Rates of Witnessing the Five Types of Bullying. Created by Neil Tippett and Keumjoo Kwak.

For cyberbullying, around 5% of respondents had bullied other people using either mobile phones or the Internet. The majority of these had bullied others only once or twice in the past two months (77% for mobile bullying, 65% for Internet bullying), although a small number did so on a weekly basis. Just 20 pupils (4.9%) admitted to carrying out Internet bullying, and 22 (5.3%) mobile bullying. Online game bullying was by far the most prevalent form of bullying reported; over 30% of pupils admitted to this in the last two months, and of these, 47% bullied other online game users at least two to three times a month or more often.

Bystanders

In contrast to self-reports regarding being victimized or bullying others, a much larger proportion of the sample had seen either direct or indirect bullying taking place. Figure 10.3 illustrates the number of pupils who had witnessed each form of bullying. Over one fifth of pupils had observed direct bullying in the last two months, while just under 10% had seen it happen several times each week. Indirect bullying had been observed by just under a quarter of all participants, with most having witnessed it once or twice over the previous two months.

The number of bystanders for mobile and Internet bullying was lower than that for traditional bullying. For mobile bullying, around 15% had seen it occur within the last two months, although in most cases this had only been a rare occurrence. Only 11 pupils (3%) had seen mobile bullying taking place more than two or three times per month. Internet bullying revealed slightly lower figures, with fewer than 10% of participants having seen it occur, and most reporting that it had happened only once or twice.

Online game bullying was the most prevalent form of cyberbullying witnessed by bystanders, with 38% of students having seen it occur within the previous two months. Of these, the largest percentage (17%) said it had only taken place once or twice, while 12% reported witnessing online game bullying taking place several times a week.

Characteristics of cyberbullying

Types of cyberbullying

For mobile phone bullying, the majority of victims reported being targeted through the use of text messages (67% of victims). Phone calls (28%) and picture/video texts (8%) were also used to bully children, but to a lesser extent.

Among victims of Internet bullying, chatrooms were found to be the most common source of bullying, with 31% of victims harassed in this way. A further 15% of victims reported being bullied through online messaging sites, while small proportions had also been cyberbullied through emails (8%), chatrooms (8%), and social networking sites (4%). This category did not include bullying through online games, which is discussed separately in this chapter.

Duration of cyberbullying

According to the reports by victims, cyberbullying was generally short in duration, mostly lasting for one and two weeks among both mobile and Internet victims (64% and 52% of victims, respectively). Of those who had been bullied for a longer period of time, 24% of mobile victims reported being targeted for a month or more, while 13% of Internet victims had been bullied for over a year.

Identity of perpetrators

Asking participants to identify the person who had bullied them revealed that, in most cases, the identity of the attacker was unknown. Half of mobile victims and 46% of Internet victims did not know who had bullied them. However, among the victims who were aware of the protagonists' identity, mobile victims were reported as more likely to attend the same school as the bully; 53% of mobile victims said they attended the same school as the bully, and in 37% of cases were in the same class as them. In comparison, only 23% of Internet victims attended the same school as the bully.

Victims of mobile and Internet bullying were asked if they knew the gender of the bully or bullies who had targeted them in the last two months. Again, most respondents did not know their attacker's identity (37% of victims for mobile bullying, 39% for Internet bullying). Among those who knew the protagonist, victims of both mobile and Internet bullying most often stated that they had been attacked by one boy (32% and 19% respectively). Mobile victims also reported being harassed by just one girl (16%), several girls (13%), several boys (10%), and groups of mixed gender (5%). For Internet victims, several boys, and both boys and girls were equally likely to have been the bullies (12%), while being bullied by one girl or several girls occurred to a much lesser degree (4%).

Coping strategies

Victims of cyberbullying outlined the variety of strategies they had employed in response to victimization; these findings are shown in Table 10.1. Differing strategies

Table 10.1 Most Common Responses Shown by Children After Being Cyberbullied.

Victims/strategy	*Mobile bullying (n = 26)*	*Internet bullying (n = 26)*
Told friends	11 (28.9%)	3 (12.0%)
Ignored it	10 (26.3%)	4 (16.0%)
Blocked	8 (21.1%)	8 (32.0%)
Tried to retaliate	3 (7.9%)	6 (24.0%)
Turned mobile off/logged off	6 (15.8%)	1 (4.0%)

Table 10.2 Most Commonly Reported Feelings by Victims of Bullying and Cyberbullying.

Direct bullying	*Indirect bullying*	*Mobile bullying*	*Internet bullying*	*Online game bullying*
Anger 27 (55.1%)	Anger 23 (47.9%)	Anger 13 (34.2%)	Anger 11 (42.3%)	Not worried 59 (45.0%)
Stress 22 (44.9%)	Stress 18 (37.5%)	Not worried 11 (28.9%)	Stress 6 (23.1%)	Anger 56 (42.7%)
Upset 8 (16.3%)	Depression 11 (22.9%)	Stress 6 (15.8%)	Not worried 5 (19.2%)	Stress 17 (13.0%)

were used by victims depending on whether they had experienced mobile or Internet bullying. The most common coping strategy for mobile bullying was to report the incident to a friend, parent, or teacher, which was used by over 50% of victims. Among Internet victims, only 24% had chosen to report the bullying to another person. Internet victims were slightly more likely to retaliate against bullies than mobile victims (24% and 8% respectively), while around a quarter of mobile victims and 16% of Internet victims had simply chosen to ignore the bully in the hope that the cyberbullying would stop.

Feelings about being cyberbullied

Victims of cyberbullying were asked to describe how they felt about their experiences; the findings are shown in Table 10.2. The most common response to all forms of bullying, except through online games, was feeling anger; this was reported by around a third to a half of all victims. Similarly, feeling stress was a commonly reported reaction by victims to all forms of bullying, while depression was reported less but still mentioned by a significant proportion of all victims.

There were some small but noticeable differences between forms of bullying. Feeling embarrassed was only reported by victims of traditional forms of bullying. Feeling afraid and scared was only reported by victims of mobile phone bullying. Almost one half of online game victims did not feel worried about having been bullied, compared to 29% of mobile victims, and 19% of Internet victims.

Online game bullying

On the basis that online game bullying appears to occur much more frequently than both traditional bullying and cyberbullying (either mobile or Internet-based), it seems pertinent that these findings should be discussed separately.

Victims of online game bullying most commonly reported that they experienced aggressive language, such as swearing or insults (reported by 64%). Also prevalent was name calling, through which 44% of online game victims had been victimized. Other forms included violence against one's character or avatar (16%), threats (12%), rumor spreading (4%), and social exclusion (2%).

Victims of online game bullying were asked about their relationship to the person who bullied them. This was divided on the basis of whether the victim knew the bully within the online or offline world. The most common response (70%) was that the bully was someone whom the victim did not know either online or offline. Of victims who did know the identity of their attacker, 18% knew the bully online, but only as an acquaintance, and did not consider the bully a friend; some had been bullied in online games by friends they knew offline (10%), while a few had been bullied by online friends (6%), or people they knew offline, but did not consider as friends (5%).

Age and gender effects for bullying and cyberbullying

Initial examination showed age and gender to have only minor effects on direct, indirect, mobile, and Internet forms of bullying. Among pupils who had experienced being bullied, gender revealed significant differences only for mobile bullying, with boys more likely to have been targeted than girls ($M = 1.14$, $F = 8.374$, $p < 0.005$). Using the same analysis by age groups, only direct bullying showed any significant result, with the youngest pupils, those aged 12 and 13, having experienced more direct bullying than children in older age groups ($M = 1.28$, $F = 3.562$, $p < 0.05$).

Among children who had bullied others either traditionally or electronically, significant differences by gender were only observed for direct bullying, in which boys were more likely to bully others than girls ($M = 1.27$, $F = 4.128$, $p < 0.05$). Age showed a greater impact. The eldest group of pupils was found to be significantly less likely than the younger groups to take part in direct ($M = 1.27$, $F = 6.279$, $p < 0.005$) or indirect bullying of others ($M = 1.23$, $F = 6.890$, $p < 0.005$).

Among bystanders who had witnessed the four types of bullying, no significant differences were found according to gender. However, pupils aged 14, the middle group, were significantly more likely to have witnessed direct and indirect bullying taking place than 13- or 15-year-olds ($M = 1.78$, $F = 12.287$, $p < 0.001$, and $M = 1.42$, $F = 6.426$, $p < 0.005$ respectively).

For online games, although age showed no effect for victims, bullies, or bystanders, gender was highly significant within each category. Boys were significantly more

Table 10.3 Notable Correlations Between Victims and Bullies Among the Five Types of Bullying.

Types of bullying	*Number of respondents (N)*	*Correlation (Pearson's)*	*Significance level*
Direct victim–indirect victim	411	0.36	0.005
Direct victim–direct bully	402	0.33	0.005
Indirect victim–indirect bully	409	0.32	0.005
Direct bully–indirect bully	401	0.47	0.005
Internet bully–Internet victim	408	0.42	0.005
Mobile bully–Indirect bully	405	0.33	0.005
Internet victim–mobile victim	413	0.19	0.005
Internet bully–mobile bully	405	0.10	0.5 (NS)
Game bully–game victim	321	0.61	0.005

likely to be online game victims ($M = 1.37$, $F = 58.722$, $p < 0.001$), online game bullies ($M = 1.24$, $F = 64.181$, $p < 0.001$), and to have seen or heard of online game bullying ($M = 1.49$, $F = 4.343$, $p < 0.001$).

Relationship between bullying and cyberbullying

Correlations were conducted between children's involvement as bullies or victims in each of the differing forms of bullying. Table 10.3 shows the key correlations observed between victims and perpetrators for all five forms of bullying and cyberbullying. For traditional victimization a correlation of 0.36 was observed between direct and indirect victims. Conversely, a solely bullying group was identified by a correlation of 0.47 between direct bullies and indirect bullies. Correlations of 0.33 and 0.32 were reported between direct victims and direct bullies, and indirect victims and indirect bullies respectively. For cyberbullying, only small correlations were found between Internet victims and mobile victims (0.19), and Internet bullies and mobile bullies (0.10). However, Internet bullies and Internet victims showed a correlation of 0.42. A high correlation of 0.61 was found between online game bullies and online game victims.

Discussion

This study provides a baseline assessment of the prevalence and nature of cyberbullying in South Korea. Having been based on previously validated methodologies used in the UK and Europe, the findings from this study provide an account of cyberbullying in South Korea which is comparable to contemporary Western research.

The overall findings on the prevalence of bullying and cyberbullying show that it occurs among a significant proportion of children living in South Korea. Consistent with research in the UK and Europe generally (for example, Smith et al., 2008; Genta et al., 2009) traditional bullying was more likely to occur than cyberbullying. In this study, the prevalence of traditional forms of bullying was slightly higher than reported in previous research (Lee & Kwak, 2000; Koo, Kwak, & Smith, 2008), but the nature of traditional bullying appears consistent with the findings of Koo et al. (2008), who reported that a greater number of South Korean children admitted bullying others than being victims themselves. While this may relate to the nature of traditional bullying in South Korea, which shows a greater tendency towards group-based forms of bullying, an alternative explanation for this finding could be children's reluctance to report being a victim of bullying. Although respondents were assured the questionnaires were anonymous, it is conceivable that children may have felt ashamed or embarrassed in reporting that they were a victim of bullying, and therefore they were reluctant to admit this on the questionnaire.

With regard to the prevalence of cyberbullying, while low when compared to the rate of traditional bullying, cyberbullying is a worrying concern for a significant minority of South Korean children. In the two months prior to this study, approximately 10% of children had been bullied through mobile phones and around 6% through the Internet. The majority of pupils reported experiencing cyberbullying once or twice per month; however, some were bullied on a weekly basis, which suggests these children may need help in order to avoid experiencing further harassment.

The effects of age and gender in involvement in traditional bullying and cyberbullying reveal interesting findings. In line with general research on bullying, males were more likely to take part in direct bullying of other students, and younger pupils were more likely to be both traditional victims and bullies. In the case of cyberbullying, boys reported more often than girls that they had been the victim of mobile phone bullying, while no differences were reported in relation to Internet bullying. This contrasts with the findings of Ortega, Calmaestra, and Mora-Merchan (2008) and Genta et al. (2009), who report that among samples of Italian and Spanish adolescents, girls were more likely to experience mobile phone bullying than boys. There were no significant differences in the experience of being cyberbullied or of cyberbullying others between different age groups.

The characteristics of South Korean cyberbullying show some similarities with cyberbullying found in the UK and elsewhere in Europe. Among mobile victims, text messages were the most commonly used method of bullying reported, while chatrooms and instant messaging programs were the most prominent sources for cybervictimization through the Internet. For both groups of victims, the bullying was often short-lived, lasting for one or two weeks, while only a small minority were victimized for a period of several months or more. This finding could be expected given that the majority of pupils who experienced cybervictimization reported that it occurred on an infrequent basis.

The majority of victims were unaware of the identity of their attacker, although it is not clear whether this is because the identity was hidden, or simply that there was no relationship between the victim and attacker. The anonymity afforded by new communication technologies may be one of the key reasons that children choose to target others online or through mobile phones. In examining this, the relationship between traditional bullying and cyberbullying is important to consider. Smith et al. (2008) reported a correlation between cyberbully and traditional victim status, suggesting that children who are victimized at school may retaliate via electronic forms of communication, possibly to overcome the imbalance of power that has led to them being bullied. No such correlation was found in this study, suggesting that victims were targeted by someone to whom they had no connection, or that cyberbullies were more adept at hiding their true identity online.

The coping strategies of Internet and mobile victims give an insight into how children respond to these differing forms of cyberbullying. Mobile victims showed a stronger tendency to report the incident to another person, such as a parent, friend, or teacher, while Internet victims appeared more prepared to fight back. Considering the nature of each technology, the Internet affords a greater variety of means through which a victim could retaliate, which may encourage children to seek revenge rather than request help or report their experiences. The most common response of Internet victims, however, was to block the bully, an encouraging finding which suggests that there are a variety of methods available throughout all forms of ICT which allow children to protect themselves from abuse and harassment.

Evidence of the effect of cyberbullying on children who are involved comes from victims' reports of how they felt after the incident—many Internet and mobile victims reported feeling either angry or stressed. Stress can have a profound effect on the child, affecting their health, self-esteem, enjoyment at school, and academic attainment. Feelings of anger can give rise to similar effects, and research acknowledges that both stress and anger can be causally linked. However, a potential result of the feelings of anger displayed by victims could be a tendency to retaliate against their aggressor. This is reflected in the proportion of Internet victims who chose to fight back against their aggressor. In retaliating, the child only serves to deepen their involvement in cyberbullying, creating a cycle of bullying others, and being bullied in return, thereby falling into the classification of cyberbully-victim. Support for this is found through the significant correlation observed between Internet bullies and Internet victims.

Online game bullying

An interesting aspect of this study concerns children's experiences of online game bullying. No study to date was found which directly examined bullying through online games, but after analysing the results of the pilot study, and considering the high proportion of South Korean children who participate in online games, it was decided that this would be incorporated as part of the study. It was anticipated that the results would generally resemble those observed for mobile and Internet bullying; but the findings led to a surprising insight. Of all children surveyed, 46% of participants reported being bullied while playing online games and 37% admitted to having bullied others. These figures are far higher than the number of pupils involved in both traditional and cyber forms of bullying. This finding suggests that bullying in online games may be a regular experience and an often encountered risk of playing computer games online.

There was a highly significant gender difference in victims' reports of online game bullying. Boys were significantly more likely to be online game victims, online game bullies, and to have seen or heard of online game bullying. While there is little previous research to compare this to, it could be argued that the culture of online games is more male-orientated, and therefore it may be expected that boys would be more greatly involved in any bullying that takes place in this area.

As the inclusion of online game bullying in the questionnaire was only on an exploratory basis, less detailed information on its nature and characteristics was collected compared to that for mobile and Internet bullying. However, reports from victims indicated that bullying behaviors experienced through online games most typically involved aggressive and insulting language or name-calling. Relational behaviors or physical aggression towards a player's avatar were also reported, but to a lesser degree. While these findings give an indication of the behaviors experienced online, the degree of interaction available to players varies according to the games they play and the extent to which they involve themselves in the gaming community. More detailed research is required into the interactions and behaviors that take place through online gaming.

In regard to other forms of cyberbullying, the majority of victims of online games reported that the bully was someone they did not know either online or offline. Online games allow players to form social groups within a virtual setting, sometimes referred to as "clans" or "guilds" depending on the game being played. Through this, players are able to establish a network of friends who they may not necessarily know in real life. The finding that victims most often did not know the bully suggests that these experiences of victimization may be the result of casual encounters with players outside of one's social group. The degree to which a player is able to monitor and target another player through a game can vary greatly, and thus without a clearer understanding of the games through which bullying took place, these results cannot be fully explored.

The correlation between online game bullies and victims was highly significant, suggesting that many of these children could be considered "cyberbully/victims." This might result from a similar pattern to that reported for Internet bullying, whereby children retaliate against initial harassment, thereby developing a bully–victim schema. Alternatively, the very nature of online games may encourage aggressive behaviors, given the competitive environment of the game and the rivalries which exist between differing online social groups.

These findings show that online game bullying is experienced by a substantial proportion of South Korean children, and also indicate the need for further research in this area. Whether the findings are unique to children living in South Korea is unknown, as research on cyberbullying has not yet focused on the issue of online game bullying. While online gaming appears to be less popular in Western countries than in South Korea, the establishment of faster and more widely available Internet access across the world has led to a sharp rise in the number of children who spend time playing games online. Further research is required to gain a clearer understanding of bullying in online games, so that children who experience it can take preventative measures and be better equipped to respond to this form of victimization when it occurs.

Limitations of the research

This study provides an account of the nature and prevalence of cyberbullying in South Korea, but there are several limitations which need to be considered. First, the survey used only a moderately sized sample of just over 400 participants. As the data was cross-sectional, no casual inferences can be made regarding the wider population, therefore the results are specific to pupils attending the two schools visited in this study. Second, there were some concerns over the translation of the questionnaire from English into Korean, mainly centering on the definition of the various forms of bullying. Until recently, terms such as *gipdan-ttadolim* (group isolation), *gipdan-gogphim* (group harassment), and *hakkyo-pokryuk* (school violence) were used to define bullying in South Korea, but Smith, Kanetsuna, and Koo (2007) argued that these are poor equivalents to the English term "bullying." More recently the term *wang-ta*, traditionally perceived as slang used by children, has been used by researchers due to its closer resemblance to the Western concept of bullying. This raises some questions over the accuracy of the definitions used in this study, and it may be that terms used in previous research on Internet violence, such as *cyber-pokryuk* or *ak-peul,* may be more appropriate for describing cyberbullying. Third, the questions asked in relation to online game bullying were included in the questionnaire in response to the findings from the pilot study, and only provide a starting point for any future studies into cyberbullying that occurs in the online gaming community. While the results from these questions provide an insight into this form of bullying, a better understanding of the social interactions that occur online is required to fully understand the nature of bullying that takes place through online games.

Conclusion

The findings from this research provide an initial assessment of cyberbullying in South Korea. The methodologies used, having been based on large-scale studies carried out in the UK and Europe, provide support for previous findings, and add to the knowledge of cyberbullying being gathered across the world. The fact that a small but significant proportion of South Korean children have experienced cyberbullying, some frequently, merits the need for more detailed and representative research to be carried out, so the nature of cyberbullying can be as well documented as it is in Western countries. In addition, the findings concerning online game bullying address an issue which has yet to be explored, but is deserving of further attention, and suggests the need for the development of specific intervention strategies, not just within Korea, but also among the wider international community. While the findings provide an initial insight into cyberbullying among South Korean children, the limitations of the study, such as the small number of participants and the concerns surrounding children's definitions of bullying, necessitate the need for further research which examines the concept of cyberbullying more extensively. If these concerns are addressed, a clearer understanding of cyberbullying in South Korea can be gained, thereby assisting in the development of interventions which can be used to prevent its occurrence, and help children who are at risk, or already victims of cyberbullying.

Acknowledgments

This study was in part supported by a PMI2 Connect research cooperation award: "Preventing school bullying: Cross-national perspectives on intervention between UK and South Korea" from the British Council, which is gratefully acknowledged. The authors would also like to thank Peter K. Smith from Goldsmiths, University of London, and Jisun Han, Jeeyeon Kim, and Jungah Seo, from the Developmental Psychology Laboratory at Seoul National University, for their valuable input and assistance.

References

Cheon, J. (2000). A study on the characteristics of youth deviance in cyberspace. *Korean Journal of Youth Studies, 7*, 97–116.

Genta, M. L., Berdondini, L., Brighi, A., & Guarini, A. (2009). Il fenomeno del bullismo elettronico in adolescenza [The phenomenon of cyberbullying in adolescence]. *Rassegna di Psicologia, 26*, 141–161.

Han, J. K. (2001). A study on the social relationship variables of cyber delinquent juveniles. *The Korean Journal of Police Institute, 3*, 357–384.

International Symposium on Educational Reform. (2005). *Symposium Report*. Tokyo: National Institute for Educational Policy Research of Japan, and Ministry of Education, Culture, Sports, Science, and Technology.

International Telecommunication Union. (2010). *World Telecommunication/ICT Indicators Database 2010*. Retrieved July 26, 2011 from www.itu.int/ITU-D/ict/publications/world/world.html

Jung, W. (2005). Status of victims of cyber-violence and countermeasures. *Victim Studies, 13*, 329–360.

Koo, H., Kwak, K., & Smith, P. K. (2008). Victimization in Korean schools: The nature, incidence, and distinctive features of Korean bullying or wang-ta. *Journal of School Violence, 7*, 119–139.

Korea Communications Commission and National Internet Development Agency of Korea. (2008). *Internet users and penetration in South Korea, by age, December 2007 & June-July 2008*. Seoul: NIDA.

The Korea Times. (2010). *Tablo-bashing website shutdown*. Retrieved June 29, 2011 from www.koreatimes.co.kr/www/news/nation/2010/10/117_75055.html

Lee, C., & Kwak, K. (2000). *Bullying at school: Actual condition and characteristics*. Seoul: Gibmoondang.

Ministry of Information and Communication and National Internet Development Agency of Korea. (2008). *Mobile phone users in South Korea, by gender and age, December 2007*. Seoul: NIDA.

Ortega, R., Calmaestra, J., & Mora-Merchan, J. (2008). Cyberbullying. *International Journal of Psychology and Psychological Therapy, 8*, 183–192.

Park, J. H. (2008). *Hatyisyu: Current status and countermeasures of cyber-violence*. Seoul: Korea Region Information Institute.

Smith, P. K., Kanetsuna, T, & Koo, H. (2007). Cross-national comparison of "bullying" and related terms: Western and Eastern perspectives. In K. B. Österman & K. Björkqvist (Eds.), *Contemporary research on aggression: School violence. Proceedings of the XVI World Meeting of the International Society for Research on Aggression, Santorini, Greece* (pp. 3–9, Vol. 1). Åbo: Åbo Academy University Press.

Smith, P. K., Mahdavi, J., Carvalho, M., Fisher, S., Russell, S., & Tippett, N. (2008). Cyberbullying: Its nature and impact in secondary school pupils. *Journal of Child Psychology and Psychiatry, 49*, 376–385.

Sung, D. K., Kim, D. H., Lee, Y. S., & Lim, S. W. (2006). A study on the cyber-violence induction factors of teenagers: Focused on individual inclination, cyber-violence damage experience, and moral consciousness. *Cyber Communication Gazette, 19*, 79–129.

Time Magazine. (2008). *South Koreans are shaken by a celebrity suicide*. Retrieved June 29, 2011 from www.time.com/time/world/article/0,8599,1847437,00.html

Vandebosch, H., & van Cleemput, K. (2009). Cyberbullying among youngsters: prevalence and profile of bullies and victims. *New Media & Society, 11*, 1–23.

Part VI

The Psychological Context of Cyberbullying

11

Virtual but not Less Real

A Study of Cyberbullying and Its Relations to Moral Disengagement and Empathy

Ana Almeida, Isabel Correia, Sylvie Marinho, and D'Jamila Garcia

Cyberbullying is still a relatively unexplored research topic in Portugal, but it is receiving increasing attention from researchers in psychology, education, sociology, and information and communication technology (ICT) areas. Following a traditional line of epidemiological studies initiated in other European countries (see Smith et al., 2008), two cross-sectional surveys have been conducted in junior high (Almeida, Marinho, Esteves, Gomes, & Correia, 2008) and secondary schools (Almeida et al., 2009; Almeida, Correia, Marinho, Garcia, & Lourenço, 2010). Additionally, as part of an ongoing study of health behavior in school-age children (HBSC), the most recently surveyed sample (2009) answered items on cyberbullying (Matos et al., 2010). These three first studies give us a snapshot of prevalence rates for cyberbullies (CB), cybervictims (CV), and cyberbully/victims (CBV), developmental trends related to age and gender, comorbidity rates for traditional bullying and cyberbullying, as well as other data concerning time spent online and cyberbullying experiences, where these experiences have taken place and which resources were used (mobile phones or the Internet).

The first survey on cyberbullying, carried out in 2008, was based on a sample of 934 students enrolled in the seventh, eighth, and ninth grades in junior high schools. Some 11% of students reported incidents of cyberbullying via mobile phones and 10% via the Internet. No significant differences were found between the three age levels; however, gender was significant, with a higher number of girls reporting being cyberbullied, or having been involved simultaneously as victims and bullies, and a higher number of boys reporting having bullied others, supposedly contributing to the heightened number of female victims.

Cyberbullying in the Global Playground: Research from International Perspectives, First Edition.
Edited by Qing Li, Donna Cross, and Peter K. Smith.

The second survey was launched within a year and extended the inquiry to 800 secondary students in three consecutive years from tenth to twelfth grade. Gender and other socio-demographic variables were assessed, as in the first study, to allow for comparisons. Older students compared to younger ones spent more time connected to the web, fostering a higher involvement in Internet activities that, in turn, was significantly associated with an increase of cyberbullying incidents through the Internet. Indeed, cyberbullying via the Internet increased, with a significant rise in being bullied and bullying others occurring through social networking, a practice that doubled in frequency between junior high and secondary school. Cyberbullying via mobile phones maintained identical rates for involved and non-involved students in junior school, but the percentage of mobile phone bullying doubled from junior to high school.

A comorbidity rate of 32% for traditional bullying and cyberbullying, calculated as the number of students who reported having had experiences of both traditional and cyberbullying, either as bully, victim, bully/victim, or any matched pair of roles (corresponding to 547 participants from a total of 1734) indicated that experiences with bullying in school and cyberbullying are enmeshed together. The overlap of these experiences is quite high. Some 47% of students involved in traditional bullying were involved in cyberbullying, against 13% of students who experienced cyberbullying without prior experience of bullying (Almeida et al., 2010).

The data on gender showed that boys were more frequently involved in cyberbullying as bullies and bully/victims, and girls were more frequently involved as victims. Additionally, there was a gradual increase in time spent on the Internet between junior high and secondary school; this was particularly significant for the group of bullying others.

Another area of work on cyberbullying with promising challenges for research is linked to psycho-educational intervention in school communities and, through school, in the familial context. Similar to cases of traditional bullying, severe, defamatory, and injurious situations of cyberbullying in Portugal are connected to school relationships and are carried out back and forth with students, staff, and teachers. Therefore, dissemination of guidelines to students, parents, teachers, and schools, as well as training manuals addressing beliefs, practices, and possible solutions are important developments for prevention and intervention. Gathering of relevant information to develop resources that prove helpful and empowering to adults in educational roles have essentially been the focus of the Portuguese team participating in "CyberTraining—A Research-based Training Manual on Cyberbullying," a project funded by European Union (EU) programs in the fields of education and training, active citizenship, youth, audiovisual resources, and culture (EACEA), and developed between 2008 and 2010. The products of this partnership include the collection of best practices in a manual edited in printed and electronic versions and disseminated via forums of specialists, educators, and the wider community (Matos, Pessoa, Amado, & Jäger, 2009; Amado, Matos, & Pessoa, 2010).

A second national cyberbullying project with a strong international component is COST Action IS0801 (http://sites.google.com/site/costis0801/), which aims to share expertise on cyberbullying in educational settings. The Portuguese team is particularly involved in its workgroups on policy development and coping strategies. Through this project a number of initiatives are planned to take forward research, training, and dissemination of best practice guidelines involving young career and research mentors, policy-makers, practitioners' associations, governmental, and non-governmental institutions.

Another line of research that focuses on cyberbullying experience is a study of the uses and influences of new technologies and issues related to cyber-safety. Portugal has participated in the EU Kids Online project network (www2.lse.ac.uk/media@lse/research/EUKidsOnline/Home.aspx) since 2006, providing information to chart, characterize, and reflect on the uses and opportunities of the Internet, but also to enhance knowledge of the risks to children and their families that the Internet can represent for personal and social development (Ponte & Vieira, 2008). This project, funded by the EU Safer Internet Plus program, has enabled the grouping of projects and studies that contribute to an extensive and comprehensive coverage of questions, experiences, and practices related to cyber-safety and, consequently, to cyberbullying.

Children and adolescents have acquired a reputation for expertise and skill in using various electronic gadgets and have thus been given greater autonomy in e-learning and digital entertainment. Being born in the digital era has led to early familiarity with various forms of technology and thus a close relationship with the world of technology, which has seen a significant increase in the use of ICTs and time spent online by children and adolescents (Livingstone & Haddon, 2009). Responding to youth demands, products and services have addressed specific interests surrounding connectivity and communication with others, as well as access to valuable information and advice (Ybarra, Diener-West, & Leaf, 2007). However, opportunities do not mean there are no risks (Hasebrink, Livingstone, Haddon, & Ólafson, 2009).

Access to and use of ICTs by children and adolescents in Portugal share a number of commonalities with other European countries; nonetheless, a few distinctive features are worth mentioning. According to the latest series of reports by EU Kids Online (Hasebrink et al., 2009), between late 2005 and 2008 the percentage of children aged 6 to 17 in Portugal who had access to and used the Internet increased significantly. Drawing on figures presented at the Eurobarometer survey conducted in late 2005/early 2006, in under two years Portugal moved from 38% of young people having Internet access to 68%, considerably decreasing the difference in the range of averages in EU countries (from between 38% and 70% in 2005/2006, to between 68% to 75% in 2008).

It is worth noting that the reported data came from parents or carers, and other sources of information conducted at around the same time point to much higher ICT usage for Portuguese children. A considerable discrepancy is shown by the WHO survey (Currie et al., 2008) carried out from 2005–2006. This report positioned Portugal at a much higher level regarding children's and adolescents' use of the Internet, when they themselves were the respondents.

Despite the fact that there are expected differences in data reported by parents and children about children's online activities, the above disparity gains added value considering that the comparison of children's and parents' use of the Internet places Portugal in the small group of countries where children have more access to the Internet than their parents. In most countries in Europe, the proportion of parents using the Internet is higher than the proportion of children, but within the Portuguese family households surveyed, some 22% of children are not able to count on parental advice and depend less on family support to access and use the Internet (Hasebrink et al., 2009). For many Portuguese children the status of "digital native" means not only being born in the digital era, but at a time when immersion in computers and online activities was much less monitored due to a lack of parental surveillance and media awareness of possible problems that could occur on the Internet.

The National Technological Plan

These shortcomings were challenged through Portugal's National Technological Plan (Zorrinho, 2008). The relative delay in Portuguese society entering the technology domain led to a wake-up call in vital sectors for the country's development, in late 2005, through the National Technological Plan announced by the government. This constituted a massive effort to surmount serious barriers of access to the global society of knowledge and information. Presented as a pillar for growth and competitiveness, it promoted and supported projects that fostered radical improvements in technological modernization, knowledge, and innovation in education, administration, services, and other sectors of production. Through programs such as "Ligar Portugal" (Connecting Portugal; see www.infosociety.gov.pt/) the government managed to achieve an impressive diffusion of technology. By 2008, 87% of public institutions, 76% of companies, and 30% of households had fixed access to a broadband connection, where prior to the implementation of the program, these figures were 53%, 49%, and 12% respectively (Zorrinho, 2008). For public schools, this program had a tremendous impact, representing a move from a coverage of 18% to 100% with a fixed broadband connection. Additionally, the Technological Plan for Education (www.escola.gov.pt) meant a heightened ratio of computers to students in the school context, increasing to one computer for every two students; and 90% of teachers received certified ICT training.

To overcome the consequences of prolonged e-exclusion in society in general and, in particular, in more impoverished groups, the Technological Plan for Education gave cheap access to laptops and mobile broadband for students, teachers, and adults who wished to retrain. The launch of this e-school initiative was extremely popular and the "Magalhães" laptop reached 750,000 students in primary education; as a result, Portugal was recognized as an example of international good practice. Safety and privacy issues were included in the plan and constituted one of its strategic orientations. Recognizing the importance of raising awareness and empowering ICT users to make use of and fully benefit from these utilities safely and responsibly, the Internet Segura program, the national counterpart of the EU Safer Internet (1999) and Safer Internet Plus (2005) programs, included a number of initiatives to minimize abuse and illegalities that might occur in the use of ICTs, as well as appealing for global action for their safe and responsible use. In the scope of this program, under the Ministry of Education, the Department for Innovation and Curricular Development (ERTE/PTE, Direcção Geral de Inovação e Desenvolvimento Curricular, 2008) created the Computers, Networks, and Internet Mission Group, which became responsible for the Seguranet project. This project targeted students, parents, teachers, and schools, making available crucial information and relevant guidelines. In addition to this, the project involved students, families, and schools in team-building and networking activities. An arm of this action on behalf of safety is the mission group of the Ministry of Education Escola Segura, commissioned to work together with the Criminal Investigation Police (www.policiajudiciaria.pt) to prevent negative or criminal acts committed through ICT.

In Portugal, safety concerns have created a context for addressing and discussing the risks related to the use of ICT. A search through the above official websites and other popular portals, such as Miúdos Seguros na Net (www.miudossegurosna.net/) or Jovens Seguros Online (http://jovensonline.net/html/default.htm), shows that cyberbullying is mentioned several times, in terms of the importance of informing about its manifestations, harmful consequences for the victims, approaches used by cyberbullies, and some practical hints on how to prevent and to cope with bullying situations through the Internet and mobile phones. Some of these sites have extended information on cyberbullying for parents, carers, and teachers, recommending some basic steps that include reporting bullies to the website provider or the telecommunications operator or contacting the police; saving cyberbullying messages as evidence; encouraging children to change the account under which the abuse has occurred (online chatrooms, social networks, email, blog or other), or to keep the old account to help catch cyberbullies, and inform children and adolescents how to behave on the Internet.

National research on risks on the Internet is inconclusive about how much these recommendations regarding cyberbullying activities are echoed by the concerns of parents, children, and young people (Ponte & Vieira, 2008; Ponte & Simões, 2009). Interestingly, when questioned in general about common risks that children encounter online either as victim, bully, or bystander, Portuguese parents worry about their child being bullied; concerns about cyberbullying are at the same level as other concerns about possible contact with strangers and "grooming" online. However, when it comes to behavior problems online, parents exclude cyberbullying from their concerns and worry that their child may become isolated from others if they are spending too much time online or that their child may give out personal/private information online. In contrast, parents, children, and young people themselves point to the risk of being exposed to sexual content (pornographic and unwelcome sexual content) and to aggressive content (violent or hateful content). For Portuguese parents and young people, the negative consequences and the impact that cyberbullying might have are only seriously considered when the child is actually being cyberbullied. In this respect Portuguese parents are the same as parents in other European countries (Hasebrink et al., 2009).

Considering the prominence of the recommendations on cyberbullying and the outcomes of the above empirical studies, it might be argued that policy development should emphasize the risks to the child as victim and participant, in order to encourage parents and young people to be more proactive and develop self-agency. But stressing the risk of being bullied can activate both parents' and youngsters' fears, their restrictive and inhibitory attitudes, or even encourage retaliatory behaviors. To counter the shortcomings of common false beliefs and misinformation mentioned earlier, it is important that public guidelines, either governmental or private, are based on evidence-based research.

Attitudes and Socio-Emotional Competence: A Study of Cyberbullying and Its Relations With Moral Disengagement and Empathy

To understand cyberbullying and prevention efforts, it is important to identify the sociocognitive variables that are associated with attitudes towards bullying. Moral disengagement and empathy are two of these variables. Particularly, studying moral disengagement and empathy allows us to assess the self-reported attitudes and beliefs of bullies and victims, using a sociocognitive frame that we claim is fundamental for intervention, as we stress in the last section of this chapter.

Moral disengagement

In his sociocognitive theory of moral agency, Bandura (1986, 1999) describes moral disengagement as the sociocognitive processes through which normal people can commit horrible actions against other people. These are the cognitive restructuring of inhumane behavior into being benign or even worthy by means of moral justification, euphemistic labeling, and advantageous comparison; diffusion or displacement of personal responsibility; distortion of consequences; and blaming or dehumanization of victims. In the context of bullying, a higher level of moral disengagement has been found in bullies (Menesini et al., 2003; Hymel, Rocke-Henderson, & Bonnano, 2005), and a lower level has been found for victims and outsiders (Menesini et al., 2003).

Empathy has been considered a factor that can inhibit antisocial behavior (Miller & Eisenberg, 1988). Empathy is generally considered to be a two-dimensional construct (Davis, 1980) with an affective/emotional dimension (the ability to share another's emotional state) and a cognitive dimension (the ability to understand another's emotional state). There is more agreement about the lack of emotional empathy of bullies (Arsenio & Lemerise, 2001) than that bullies lack cognitive empathy (see Crick & Dodge, 1999; Sutton, Smith, & Swettenham, 1999 for discussion). Previous studies have found that emotional empathy significantly predicted fewer bullying behaviors and more defending behavior (Gini, Albiero, Benelli, & Altoe, 2007; Correia & Dalbert, 2008); one study found that cognitive empathy is negatively associated with bullying behavior, but was not significantly associated with defending behavior (Gini et al., 2007).

In a previous study in Portugal regarding the prediction of attitudes towards the bully role and the defender role (Almeida, Correia, & Marinho, 2010), more positive attitudes regarding the bully role were predicted by higher levels of moral disengagement, whereas more positive attitudes regarding the defender role of the victim were predicted by lower levels of moral disengagement. Low levels of affective and cognitive empathy also endorsed positive attitudes towards the bully role. Both cognitive and affective empathy and higher empathy correlated with positive attitudes towards the defender role, but these empathy dimensions did not contribute additionally when socio-demographic characteristics and moral disengagement were accounted for. This previous study was limited to traditional bullying. However, cyberbullying gives additional grounds for exploring the influence of sociocognitive factors in bullying relationships in a virtual forum, and can add to our knowledge about the strength of these relations in a comparison between the two types of bullying.

In the present study we investigate whether moral disengagement and empathy (cognitive and affective) differ among adolescents who report being engaged in cyberbullying. We consider four roles: cyberbullies, cybervictims, cyberbully/victims, and cyber non-involved. We also compare cyberbullying through the Internet with cyberbullying through mobile phones.

Method

Participants

Over 1700 (1751) adolescents attending seventh to twelfth grades in 34 public urban schools in Portugal (Lisbon and Braga) participated in the study conducted between 2008 and 2009. The sample was reasonably balanced across grade levels, with (in junior high schools) 331 in the seventh grade, 318 in the eighth, 292 in the ninth, and (in secondary schools) 325 in the tenth, 209 in the eleventh, and 276 in the twelfth grade. Ages varied from 11 to 20 ($M = 15.15$ years, $SD = 1.94$); 822 were boys (47.5%) and 907 (52.5%) girls.

Measures

Roles in bullying

A 36-item self-report measure adapted from Smith et al. (2008) that assesses participants' experiences with traditional bullying and cyberbullying by mobile phone and the Internet. Participants considered to be cyberbullies through mobile phones were those who answered the question, "Have you bullied others through text messages in the past couple of months in school?" with, "It has only happened once or twice," "Two or three times a month," "About once a week," and "Several times a week," and simultaneously answered, "I haven't been bullied through texts messages in the past couple of months" to the question "How often have you been bullied through text messages in the past couple of months in school?" The answers to both these questions served to create the other three groups: cybervictims through mobile phones answered that they had been bullied in this way at least once or twice but did not bully others; cyberbully/victims through mobile phones have both bullied and been bullied in this way; and non-involved students are those that have neither bullied or been bullied through mobile phones. Similar questions were asked regarding bullying by the Internet.

Moral disengagement

The Moral Disengagement Regarding School Bullying Scale (Hymel et al., 2005) includes 18 items that assess moral disengagement mechanisms, identified by Bandura (1999) and applied to bullying situations (for example, "bullying is just a normal part of being a kid"). With younger participants in the seventh to ninth grades we used a four-point Likert response scale for items: (1) strongly disagree, (2) disagree, (3) agree, and (4) strongly agree ($\alpha = 0.79$). Older participants answered on a six-point Likert scale: (1) strongly disagree, (2) disagree, (3) slightly disagree, (4) slightly agree, (5) agree, and (6) strongly agree ($\alpha = 0.81$).

Empathy

With younger adolescents in seventh to ninth grades, empathy was assessed using the Basic Empathy Scale (BES; Jolliffe & Farrington, 2006), with 20 items and a five-point Likert scale: (1) strongly disagree, (2) disagree, (3) neither agree nor disagree, (4) agree, and (5) strongly agree. The scale has two factors: a *cognitive dimension* (nine items, for example, "I can understand my friend's happiness when he does well at something," $\alpha = 0.60$ for the present study), and an *affective dimension* (11 items, for example, "I get caught up in other people's feelings easily," $\alpha = 0.71$ for the present study). For older adolescents, empathy was measured using the Interpersonal Reactivity Index (Davis, 1980), a 28-item measure that has seven items related to cognitive empathy (for example, "I sometimes try to understand my friends better by imagining how things look from their perspectives," $\alpha = 0.68$], and seven items related to emotional empathy (such as, "I often have tender, concerned feelings for people less fortunate than me," $\alpha = 0.73$). The response scale had six points: (1) strongly disagree, (2) disagree, (3) slightly disagree, (4) slightly agree, (5) agree, and (6) strongly agree.

Procedure

Authorization for the administration of the questionnaire was obtained from the Portuguese Ministry of Education and the school boards. Permission from the parents of the students who participated was requested, and students were

Table 11.1 Percentages of Students Who Reported Cyberbullying Through Mobile Phones and the Internet Across School Grades (N = 1751).

Mode	*School grades*	*Non-involved*	*Victim*	*Bully*	*Bully/victim*
Mobile	7–9	89.1 (828)	4.8 (45)	3.9 (36)	2.2 (20)
	10–12	85 (630)	6.6 (49)	5.1 (38)	3.2 (24)
Internet	7–9	90.3 (840)	5.2 (48)	2.8 (26)	1.7 (16)
	10–12	82.9*** (647)	7.6*** (59)	6.2*** (48)	3.3*** (26)

Note: $^{***}p < 0.001$. Frequencies are in brackets. Due to missing data group size slightly varies across variables, therefore valid percentages are presented.

invited to participate in a research study about school life and completed the questionnaires during class time. It was stressed that participation was anonymous and voluntary.

Results

Descriptive statistics by grade level

At a descriptive level, the prevalence rates presented in Table 11.1 show an increase in cyberbullying victimization and perpetration across school levels. Specifically, 10.9% (n = 101) in the younger cohort and 14.9% (n = 111) in the older cohort reported involvement in cyberbullying situations with mobile phones, whereas for the Internet these rates were 9.7% (n = 90) and 17.1% (n = 133), respectively. These grade changes did not reach statistical significance for mobile phones ($X^2 = 6.39$, $df = 3$, $p = 0.09$), but for the Internet we found a clear association with status across all three groups with significant increases in the bully, victim, and bully/victim groups ($X^2 = 22.11$, $df = 3$, $p = 0.001$).

For gender differences, the statistical analyses were performed entering only those adolescents who reported involvement in cyberbullying through mobile phones (see Table 11.2) and the Internet (see Table 11.3), in order to control for the effect size of the non-involved group. The percentages in Tables 11.2 and 11.3 represent the different ratios of boys and girls who reported involvement in cyberbullying through mobile phones and the Internet, according to school level. Girls were significantly more involved as victims regardless of grade level or type of cyberbullying. In contrast, boys were more likely than girls to bully others through mobile phones in grades 7 to 9, and to bully others through the Internet in secondary schools. Also, younger boys were more involved as bully/victims. The comparisons shown in Tables 11.2 and 11.3 were significant for mobiles in both the younger ($X^2 = 13.58$, $df = 2$, $p = 0.001$) and older ($X^2 = 10.85$, $df = 2$, $p = 0.004$) cohort. Similar results were found for the Internet, respectively for younger ($X^2 = 6.64$, $df = 2$, $p = 0.03$) and older ($X^2 = 6.05$, $df = 2$, $p = 0.05$) cohorts.

Table 11.2 Percentages of Students Involved in Cyberbullying Through Mobile Phones, in Roles of Victim, Bully, or Bully/Victim, by School Grade and Gender (N = 209).

		School grade			
		7–9 (N = 101)		*10–12 (N = 108)*	
		Boys	*Girls*	*Boys*	*Girls*
Mobile	Victim	27.8 (15)	63.8** (30)	33.9 (19)	55.8** (29)
	Bully	44.4** (24)	25.5 (12)	33.9 (19)	36.5 (19)
	Bully/victim	27.8** (15)	10.6 (5)	32.1 (18)	7.7 (4)
	n	54	47	56	52

Note: $^{**}p < 0.01$, frequencies in brackets.

Table 11.3 Percentages of Students Involved in Cyberbullying Through the Internet, in Roles of Victim, Bully, or Bully/Victim, by School Grade and Gender (N = 221).

		School grade			
		7–9 (N = 89)		*10–12 (N = 132)*	
		Boys	*Girls*	*Boys*	*Girls*
Internet	Victim	41.3 (19)	67.4 * (29)	35.3 (24)	54.7 * (35)
	Bully	34.8 (16)	23.3 (10)	45.6 * (31)	26.6 (17)
	Bully/victim	23.9 (11)	9.3 (4)	19.1 (13)	18.8 (12)
	n	46	43	68	64

Note: $^{*}p < 0.05$, frequencies in brackets.

Relationship to sociocognitive measures

To allow for comparisons between different scaling in empathy and moral disengagement measures we standardized the results of these two variables and performed separate analysis of variance (ANOVA) for each of the dependent variables (cognitive empathy, affective empathy, and moral disengagement), considering "role in bullying" to be the dependent variable. Significant effects were examined further by post-hoc Tukey tests. For easier interpretation of the results we present the means and standard deviations using the non-standardized values in Table 11.4 (seventh to ninth grades) and Table 11.5 (tenth to twelfth grades).

Younger pupils (seventh to ninth grade)

There were significant differences in all three sociocognitive measures as a function of status in cyberbullying; all three for mobile phones and one for the Internet; see Table 11.4.

Table 11.4 Mean Differences of Cyberbullying Statuses in Empathy and Moral Disengagement in Junior High School (Grades 7–9).

		Non-involved	*Victims*	*Bullies*	*Bully/victims*		
		Mean (SD)	*Mean (SD)*	*Mean (SD)*	*Mean (SD)*	*F-value*	P
Cognitive empathy	Mobile	3.48 (0.44)	3.70 (0.39)	3.56 (0.53)	3.32 (0.38)	4.40**	0.004
	Internet	3.49 (0.44)	3.56 (0.53)	3.40 (0.50)	3.53 (0.48)	7.87	0.501
Affective empathy	Mobile	3.45 (0.60)	3.68 (0.65)	3.32 (0.67)	3.39 (0.41)	2.69*	0.045
	Internet	3.46 (0.60)	3.60 (0.61)	3.31 (0.61)	3.50 (0.59)	1.38	0.246
Moral disengagement	Mobile	1.99 (0.36)	2.01 (0.40)	2.32 (0.48)	2.36 (0.47)	14.93***	0.000
	Internet	1.98 (0.36)	2.02 (0.37)	2.33 (0.35)	2.34 (0.50)	11.38***	0.000

Note: $^{*}p < 0.05$; $^{**}p < 0.01$; $^{***}p < 0.001$.

Mobile phones: For cognitive empathy, victims scored significantly higher than both non-involved participants and bully/victims, whereas bullies did not significantly differ from the other three roles (Tukey $p \leq 0.05$). For affective empathy, victims scored significantly higher than bullies, whereas non-involved participants and bully/victims did not differ significantly from the other roles (Tukey $p \leq 0.045$). For moral disengagement, non-involved and victims scored significantly lower than cyberbullies and bully/victims (Tukey $p \leq 0.05$).

The Internet: Here, the only significant effect was for moral disengagement, where non-involved and victims had significantly lower scores than bullies and bully/victims (Tukey, $p \leq 0.05$).

Older pupils (tenth to twelfth grade)

There were significant differences on two sociocognitive measures as a function of status in cyberbullying; both for mobile phones: See Table 11.5.

Mobile phones: For cognitive empathy, non-involved and victims showed significantly higher scores than bully/victims, and, as for the younger sample, bullies did not differ significantly from the other three roles (Tukey $p \leq 0.05$). For affective empathy, victims scored significantly higher than bully/victims; all other differences were not significant. For moral disengagement there was no significant effect.

Internet: There were no significant effects.

Discussion

The prevalence rates in Internet- or mobile-based cyberbullying evidenced in the present study appear to be low for Portugal. Comparisons between school levels show some consistency throughout adolescence and the time range under study (between 11 and 20 years old), although with an increase in involvement in cyberbullying through the Internet. Gender differences are worth noting. Girls are over-represented in the victim group whether we consider mobile or Internet cyberbullying, while in the bully group the younger are more prone to cyberbullying via mobile phone and the older ones are more active in cyberbullying via the Internet.

As a first epidemiological survey on cyberbullying these prevalence rates should be interpreted carefully, taking into consideration the relative lack of knowledge about which factors influence how adolescents report their practices of cyberbullying with mobile phones and the Internet. In Portuguese society, cyberbullying is still considered a new phenomenon, not easily recognized and generally viewed as an atypical usage of online interactions. Other contextual factors such as a lesser penetration of computers and the Internet in Portuguese family households in comparison to other European countries (Hasebrink et al., 2009) might also help to explain the incipient extent of the phenomenon in Portugal. Just as in other

Table 11.5 Mean Differences of Cyberbullying Statuses in Empathy and Moral Disengagement in Secondary Schools (Grades 10–12).

		Non-involved	*Victims*	*Bullies*	*Bully/victims*		
		Mean (SD)	*Mean (SD)*	*Mean (SD)*	*Mean (SD)*	*F-value*	p
Cognitive empathy	Mobile	4.09 (0.76)	4.07 (0.81)	3.32 (0.74)	3.32 (0.73)	3.68*	0.012
	Internet	4.08 (0.81)	4.04 (0.89)	3.93 (0.96)	3.63 (0.90)	1.50	0.214
Affective empathy	Mobile	4.29 (0.81)	4.60 (0.76)	4.13 (0.81)	3.76 (0.69)	3.09*	0.027
	Internet	4.26 (0.81)	4.42 (0.84)	4.19 (0.54)	4.05 (0.81)	0.97	0.406
Moral disengagement	Mobile	2.62 (0.63)	2.66 (0.60)	2.74 (0.64)	2.30 (0.57)	1.57	0.196
	Internet	2.62 (0.57)	2.60 (0.68)	2.91 (0.66)	2.76 (0.85)	1.77	0.152

Note: $^{*}p < 0.05$.

European countries (see, for example, Gradinger, Strohmeier, & Spiel, 2008; Steffgen & König, 2009; Genta, Brighi, & Guarani, 2009) the phenomenon is seldom carried out in Portugal.

In addition to the general prevalence and trends by grade shown in Table 11.1, there are important individual differences in sociocognitive markers, specifically cognitive and affective empathy and moral disengagement. The findings in this study of differences by role (bully, victim, bully/victim, non-involved) corroborate and extend the results reported for traditional bullying (Almeida, Correia, & Marinho, 2010). In the previous study we examined how moral disengagement, empathy, belief in a just world, and the perception of normative beliefs of the peer group were associated with attitudes about the roles of bully and defender of the victim. In fact, only moral disengagement and the perception of normative beliefs of the peer group predicted attitudes regarding roles in bullying. However, if lower empathy measures (both cognitive and affective) predicted positive attitudes towards the bully role, the pattern was not so consistent towards the victim role or the defender.

Some consistency in patterns suggests that these sociocognitive processes play a significant role in the development and maintenance of bullying across different relational scenarios. In this study, both cognitive and affective empathy differed according to status, the most striking finding being that victims showed a higher level of sensitiveness and were significantly higher on both types of empathy than either bully/victims and/or bullies across grades. For cyberbullying through mobile phones, for seventh through to twelfth grades, cognitive and affective empathy showed differences by role, but not for Internet bullying.

These findings are relevant to the controversy about empathic skills and emotional competence (Eisenberg & Miller,1987; Miller & Eisenberg, 1988; Mehrabian, 1997; Arsenio & Lemerise, 2001). Our results only partially confirm the deficits of empathic skills of adolescents who bully their peers; although there scores were (in seven out of eight comparisons) lower than for non-involved pupils, these differences were not statistically significant. Focusing on cyberbullying through mobile phones and taking the victim's perspective, a clear positive association is in favor of the victims' cognitive and affective empathic skills in cyberbullying. Thus, the negative association of cyberbullying behavior and empathy is not confirmed in this study. Other differences show a negative association between empathic skills and cyberbullying behavior of the bully/victim group. Besides pointing to the need to differentiate the roles of bully/victims from the pure victims and their possible motives for engaging in cyberbullying (Gradinger et al., 2009), our results can be understood as an incentive to further explore the controversial relationship between empathy dimensions and aggression and its externalized manifestations, specifically in cyberbullying situations.

As far as moral disengagement is concerned, the pattern of results differs between grades rather than by type of cyberbullying. For those in seventh to ninth grades, bullies and bully/victims show higher moral disengagement than both victims and non-involved participants, both for cyberbullying through the

Internet and through mobile phones. For those in the tenth to twelfth grades, moral disengagement did not differ according to roles in either type of cyberbullying.

It is interesting that the differences in moral disengagement detected in the junior high (grades 7 to 9) study were moderated at the secondary school level (grades 10 to 12). In the junior high (which enrolls students aged between 13 and 15), bullies scored significantly higher than the other three statuses. At the secondary school level, role differences were leveled; despite the relative higher moral disengagement score of the bully group in comparison to other groups, this did not reach statistical significance. Considering that this group represents a non-normative sample it is not totally surprising to find an increase in moral disengagement values. However, globally, our findings deviate from the normative developmental trajectories of moral disengagement (Pacciello, Fida, Tramontano, Lupinetti, & Caprara, 2008), which show a decline with age normally linked with lower levels of aggressive and violent behavior in late adolescence.

It will be important in future research, whether cross-sectional or longitudinal, that we seek for age trends, as well as look at which groups accentuate different mechanisms of moral disengagement, controlling for levels of cyberbullying across school levels. Longitudinal studies can also permit us to examine Bandura's hypothesis (2001) that mechanisms of moral disengaging result in considerable tolerance of harmful behaviors and heighten the level of indifference to self-censure, creating the psychological conditions to practice minor and less minor detrimental actions as routine. Thus, to undertake an individual differences perspective and even a personality approach can help to disentangle how particular cognitive, emotional, and socio-psychological processes strengthen some young people's dispositions to engage and sustain different forms of negative acts against their peers.

The results on empathy and moral disengagement together stress the importance of further exploring individual differences to understand and explain the interactions between cognitive, affective, and moral dimensions of human behavior and their relative weight during adolescence.

Implications

As highlighted in previous studies on peer bullying (Menesini et al., 2003; Hymel et al., 2005; Gini et al. 2007; Correia & Dalbert, 2008), including our own research (Almeida, Correia, & Marinho, 2010), in the present study we gathered evidence that moral disengagement and empathy are related to adolescents' cyberbullying behavior. Possible implications of these processes entail concerns about moral disengagement mechanisms, from subtle forms of moral disengaging through to serious derogatory ones, as well as empathic responsiveness, distinguishing its cognitive and affective dimension and its relations to behavior of both bullies and victims in adolescence.

Practice

Our research draws attention to the status differences in moral disengagement levels shown in the younger group attending junior high (13–15 years) and in the older adolescent group in the secondary school (16–20 years). We also address the role of empathy in cyberbullying, and consider the uses of ICTs and the risks associated with the extensive dissemination of these among young people.

The widest effect of moral disengagement mechanisms was noticed in early adolescence, a period where a normative decrease in moral disengagement levels should be noted. As expected, compared to the non-involved pupils, the levels of moral disengagement were significantly higher for bullies in junior high, a pattern comparable to the pathway of the so-called "later desister group." According to the developmental data on moral disengagement trajectories in adolescence, this later desister group has been identified as youngsters who show high levels of antisocial and aggressive behavior during adolescence and whose problematic behavior only decreases late in adolescence (Moffitt, Caspi, Harrington, & Milne, 2002; Paciello, Fida, Tramontano, Lupinetti, & Caprara, 2008). Additionally, the decline of moral disengagement in adolescence has been associated with the development of cognitive and emotional skills, the influence of moral reasoning processes, and the development of the moral self (Blasi, 2004).

Our findings do not support the stated developmental trend, but corroborate the inter-individual variations in the two age groups. This has implications for the practice and prevention of cyberbullying as a phenomenon that can have serious and damaging consequences for young adolescents—either the bully, the victim, or the witness. Throughout adolescence there are increased challenges for interpersonal development in private and public life domains, but mainly because online interactions call for rapid and early maturing of cognitive, affective, and moral structures throughout adolescence.

In theory and in reality, adolescence is a time of increasing autonomy and exploration. Given the tremendous popularity and impact that ICTs have in the lives of young adolescents, a world of potential opportunities and risks is embedded in the uses that are made of these new tools of communication and social affiliation in a virtual environment. The novelty, diversity, and still ascending status of technological items as progress and wealth symbols (that is, new types and increasing numbers of social networks, devices, and interactions) make ICTs particularly attractive to adolescents, due to the exploratory nature of young people's behavior. Therefore, adolescence brings a number of questions related to the uses, skills, and maturing psychological competencies in the interpersonal domain. The enlarging and emerging net of online relationships not only transfers important experiences, but increasingly gives way to events and relationships that have their origin and are lived largely in a virtual world. As such, it can be said that this virtual world is progressively gaining added symbolic value in the lives of adolescents. These reflections about the scope and meaning attached to ICTs, combined with the specified results discussed above relating to moral disengagement and empathy skills in early and late adolescence, are reasonable motives to realize the importance of making specific use of the Internet to raise early adolescents' awareness of cyberbullying, its manifestations, and consequences, as well as addressing this period as particularly important in terms of prevention programs.

Policy

Relating research to policy development is an enduring concern for scientists, who have increasingly felt the need to make society more aware of the importance of science for progress and innovation. This argument is not only true in general, but is especially relevant for cyberbullying studies. This idea has proven to be a good source of inspiration for studies on aggression and bullying (Bandura, 1999, 2001; Correia & Dalbert, 2008).

As regards cyberbullying, our understanding has evolved from epidemiological studies aiming at determining its incidence, manifestations, who is involved, and how they are affected, to psychological studies that address the mediating role of cognitive, emotional, and behavioral factors in the phenomenon. Psychologists and mental health scientists have long believed that beliefs, attitudes, and emotions are powerful motives for action and, therefore, a good reason to affirm that knowing more (and let others know more) about different people's motivations will make us all more capable of responding to individual and social needs, and also more knowledgeable, to make assertions about possible positive ways to overcome difficulties. This rationale applies to the development of policies related to cyberbullying prevention. In fact, a lot has been learned through research on school bullying, but cyberbullying presents specific difficulties that deserve to be studied in isolation (Ybarra & Mitchell, 2004; Ybarra, Diener-West, & Leaf, 2007; Li, 2007; Raskauskas & Stoltz; 2007; Cross et al., 2008).

In Portuguese society, studies on cyberbullying can bring valuable data to inform policies and guidelines. Whether this information comes from studies on epidemiological features or correlates of cyberbullying behaviors, research can help to establish useful criteria for the development of guidelines. For instance, addressing adolescents as a focus group, raising awareness of false beliefs about cyberbullying, countering the idea that cyberbullying is fun and has a lesser impact on early adolescents. As far as policy development goes, it will also be important to encourage youth organizations and governmental and educational authorities, such as schools and parent associations, to involve adolescents in prevention and promotional campaigns for safety and positive relations online. Empowering adolescents through increasing their participation in prevention activities is not only a capacity-building experience, but an appropriate way to ensure the provision of rights and responsibilities.

Theory

Two findings of our present study are relevant for theory development. The first relates to the results on moral disengagement and role differences in adolescents in junior high school. Confirming reported data on developmental trajectories in adolescence, these findings bring to attention inter-individual variations and the influence of beliefs, attitudes, and underlying psychological factors on behavior. We agree with Paciello et al.'s (2008) thoughts about the social growth opportunities that adolescents have, to see others' perspective, to engage in moral dilemmas, and to reason about possible consequences of their actions to themselves and to others. In line with Hart and Atkins (2002) and Hart, Atkins, Markley, and Youniss (2004), these are challenging and indispensable resources for building up moral structures and, subsequently, a moral life in adolescence, and to help prevent moral disengagement now and later on. Besides, as Bandura argued (1999, 2001), socio-moral reasoning is a foundational vector of moral agency.

A second finding with interesting, yet puzzling, implications for theory development relates to our results on cognitive and affective empathy. Our findings differ from results found by other authors that have highlighted a negative relation between aggressive behavior and empathy (Miller & Eisenberg, 1988; Davis, 1994; Jolliffe & Farrington, 2004). Despite the controversy about bullies lacking cognitive empathic responsiveness (Crick & Dodge, 1999; Sutton, Smith, & Swettenham, 1999), there is more agreement about the lack of emotional empathy (Arsenio & Lemerise, 2001). Studies on peer bullying have corroborated this relation (Endresen & Olweus, 2001; Gini et al., 2007) and Correia and Dalbert (2008) obtained the same pattern of results for emotional empathy because it significantly predicted fewer bullying behaviors and more defensive behavior. Fewer studies of cyberbullying and empathy have been conducted. Nevertheless, Steffgen and Konig (2009) have reported a greater lack of empathy for cyberbullies than for others being victimized.

Yet, a distinctive aspect of our findings is that across cognitive and affective empathy measures, the group of cyberbullied adolescents have significantly higher levels of empathy. Without having a strong theoretical assumption on this finding, we would draw attention to the possibility that adolescents victimized through mobile phones and the Internet do not fit the socio-psychological pattern of the typical victim of peer bullying studies. Further studies will be welcome.

Future Research

The attention paid to children and young people's experiences online is leading researchers to study the complex nature of communicating and relating to others in the virtual world. An increasing amount of time spent online has become part of the daily routine of youngsters, and being connected represents an important interactional mode that should not be viewed as imaginary or fantasy, since it is real to young people (Almeida et al., 2007; Rivers & Noret, 2010). However, it is recognized that the virtual world creates an ambience that combines proximity and distance, a mixture of closeness and aloneness which might give way to greater power to engage in abusive behaviors. Cyberbullying raises intriguing questions about social and personal development in adolescence, among which are issues concerned with the psychological factors that strengthen moral agency and sensitivity to others.

Acknowledgment

The research discussed in this chapter was partially supported by the grant PDCT/PSI/55709/2004 from the Portuguese Science and Technology Foundation to the first two authors of this manuscript.

References

Almeida, A., Correia, I., Garcia, D., Marinho, S., Gomes, S., & Esteves, C. (2009). *Are moral disengagement and empathy related to cyberbullying practises?* Paper presented at the XIVth European Conference on Developmental Psychology, Vilnius.

Almeida, A., Correia, I., & Marinho, S. (2010). Moral disengagement, normative beliefs of peer group and attitudes regarding roles in bullying. *Journal of School Violence, 9*, 23–36.

Almeida, A., Correia, I., Marinho, S., Garcia, D., & Lourenço, J. (2010). *As práticas de cyberbullying na perspectiva dos alunos do 3° ciclo e secundário*. Paper presented at the VII Simpósio Nacional de Investigação Psicológica, Braga.

Almeida, A., Marinho, S., Esteves, S., Gomes, C., & Correia, I. (2008). *Virtual but not less real: a study of cyberbullying and its relations with moral disengagement and empathy*. Paper presented at the XX Biennial Meeting of the International Society for the Study of Behavioral Development, Wurzburg.

Amado, J., Matos, A., & Pessoa, T. (2010). *Cyberbullying: um novo campo de investigação e de formação*. Paper presented at the Congresso Galego Português de Psicopedagogia. Universidade do Minho, Braga, Portugal, September 9–12. *Proceedings of the Congresso Galego Português de Psicopedagogia* (pp. 262–273). Braga: CIEd-Universidade do Minho.

Arsenio, W. F., & Lemerise, E. A. (2001). Varieties of childhood bullying: Values, emotion processes and social competence. *Social Development, 10*, 59–73.

Bandura, A. (1986). *Social foundations of thought and action: A social cognitive theory*. Englewood Cliffs, NJ: Prentice Hall.

Bandura, A. (1999). Moral disengagement in the perpetration of inhumanities. *Personality and Social Psychology Review, 3*, 193–209.

Bandura, A. (2001). Social cognitive theory: An agentic perspective. *Annual Review of Psychology, 52*, 1–26. Palo Alto, CA: Annual Review.

Blasi, A. (2004). Moral functioning: Moral understanding and personality. In D. Lapsley & D. Narvaez (Eds.), *Moral development, self, and identity* (pp. 335–349). Mahwah, NJ: Lawrence Erlbaum.

Correia, I., & Dalbert, C. (2008). School bullying: Belief in a personal just world of bullies, victims and defenders. *European Psychologist, 13*, 248–254.

Crick, N. R., & Dodge, K. A. (1999). 'Superiority' is in the eye of the beholder: A comment on Sutton, Smith, and Swettenham. *Social Development, 8*, 128–131.

Cross, D., Shaw, T., Hearn, L., Epstein, M., Monks, H., Lester, L., & Thomas, L. (2009). *Australian Covert Bullying Prevalence Study (ACBPS)*. Retrieved June 4, 2009 from www.deewr.gov.au/Schooling/NationalSafeSchools/Pages/research.aspx

Currie, C., Gabhainn, S., Godeau, E., Roberts, C., Smith, R., Currie, D., Pickett, W., Richter, M., Morgan, A., & Barnekow, V. (Eds.). (2008). *Inequalities in young people's health: HBSC International Report from 2005/2008 Survey*. Copenhagen, WHO Regional Office for Europe, 2008. (Health Policy for Children and Adolescents, No. 5).

Davis, M. H. (1980). A multidimensional approach to individual differences in empathy. *JSAS Catalog of Selected Documents Psychology, 10*, 85.

Davis, M. H. (1994). *Empathy: A social psychological approach*. Madison, WI: Brown & Benchmark.

Eisenberg, N., & Miller, P. (1987). The relation of empathy to prosocial and related behaviours. *Psychological Bulletin, 101*, 91–119.

Endresen, I. M., & Olweus, D. (2001). Self-reported empathy in Norwegian adolescents: Sex differences, age trends, and relationship to bullying. In A. Bohart & D. Stipek (Eds.), *Constructive and destructive behavior: Implications for family, school, and society* (pp. 147–165). Washington, DC: American Psychological Association.

Equipa de Recursos e Tecnologias Educativas (ERTE/PTE). (2008). *Direcção-Geral de Inovação e Desenvolvimento Curricular. Lisboa: Ministério da Educação*. Retrieved March 1, 2010 from www.crie.min-edu.pt/

Genta, M., Brighi, A., & Guarini, A. (2009). *Il bullismo elettronico*. Rome: Carocci.

Gini, G., Albiero, P., Benelli, B., & Altoè, G. (2007). Does empathy predict adolescents' bullying and defending behavior? *Aggressive Behavior, 33*, 467–476.

Gradinger, P., Strohmeier, D., & Spiel, C. (2009). Traditional bullying and cyberbullying: Identification of risk groups for adjustment. *Zeitschrift für Psychologie/Journal of Psychology, 217*, 205–213.

Hart, D., & Atkins, R. (2002). Civic competencies in urban youth. *Applied Developmental Science, 6*, 227–236.

Hart, D., Atkins, R., Markley, P., & Youniss, J. (2004). Youth bulges in communities: The effect of age structure on adolescent civic knowledge and civic participation. *Psychological Science, 15*, 591–597.

Hasebrink, U., Livingstone, S., Haddon, L., & Ólafsson, K. (2009). *Comparing children's online opportunities and risks across Europe: Cross-national comparisons for EUKids online* (2nd ed.). London: LSE. EUKids Online. Retrieved July 28, 2011 from http://eprints.lse.ac.uk/24368/

Hymel, S., Rocke-Henderson, N., & Bonnano, R. A. (2005). Moral disengagement: A framework for understanding bullying among adolescents. *Journal of Social Sciences, 8*, 1–11.

Jolliffe, D., & Farrington, D. P. (2004). Empathy and offending: A systematic review and meta-analysis. *Aggression and Violent Behavior*, 9, 441–476.

Jolliffe, D., & Farrington, D. P. (2006). Development and validation of the Basic Empathy Scale. *Journal of Adolescence, 29*, 589–611.

Li, Q. (2007). New bottle but old wine: A research of cyberbullying in schools. *Computers in Human Behaviour, 23*, 1777–1791.

Livingstone, S., & Haddon, L. (2009). Opportunities and risks for European children. In Carlsson, U. (Ed.), *Young people in the European digital media landscape: A statistical overview* (pp. 15–26). Gothenburg: Nordicom.

Matos, A., Pessoa, T., Amado, J., & Jäger, T. (2009). *Cyberbullying: o desenvolvimento de um manual para formadores.* Paper presented at the National Conference EU Kids Online Portugal, Universidade Nova de Lisboa, Lisboa, Portugal. *Proceedings of the National Conference EU Kids Online Portugal*, pp. 16–33. Retrieved July 28, 2011 from www2.fcsh.unl.pt/eukidsonline/docs/LivroActas.pdf

Matos, M., Simões, C., Tomé, G., Gaspar, T., Camacho, I., Diniz, J., & Equipa da Aventura Social. (2010). *A Saúde dos Adolescentes Portugueses—Relatório do Estudo do HBSC 2010.* Retrieved August 1, 2011 from http://aventurasocial.com/arquivo/1303144700_Relatorio_HBSC_adolescentes.pdf

Mehrabian, A. (1997). Relations among personality scales of aggression, violence, and empathy: Validational evidence bearing on the Risk of Eruptive Violence scale. *Aggressive Behavior, 23*, 433–445.

Menesini, E., Sanchez, V., Fonzi, A., Ortega, R., Costabile, A., & Lo Feudo, G. (2003). Moral emotions and bullying: A cross-national comparison of differences between bullies, victims and outsiders. *Aggressive Behavior, 29*, 515–530.

Miller, P. A., & Eisenberg, N. (1988). The relationship of empathy to aggressive and externalizing/antisocial behavior. *Psychological Bulletin, 103*, 324–344.

Moffitt, T., Caspi, A., Harrington, H., & Milne, B. (2002). Males on the life-course persistent and adolescence-limited antisocial pathways: follow-up at age 26. *Developmental Psychopathology, 14*, 179–207.

Paciello, M., Fida, R., Tramontano, C., Lupinetti, C., & Caprara, G. (2008). Stability and change of moral disengagement and its impact on aggressive and violent behavior in late adolescence. *Child Development, 79*, 1288–1309.

Ponte, C., & Simões, J. (2009). *Parental perspectives about children's Internet use. Exploring ways of asking questions.* Paper presented at the 2009 Annual Conference of the International Association for Media and Communication Research, Mexico City. Retrieved August 1, 2011 from www2.lse.ac.uk/media@lse/research/EUKidsOnline/Presentations/PonteAudienceParentalPerspective.pdf

Ponte, C., & Vieira, N. (2008). Crianças e Internet, riscos e oportunidades. Um desafio para a agenda de pesquisa nacional. In M. Martins & M. Pinto (Orgs.), *Comunicação e Cidadania. Proceedings of the 5° Congresso da Associação Portuguesa de Ciências da Comunicação*, (pp. 2732–2741). Braga: Centro de Estudos de Comunicação e Sociedade (Universidade do Minho). Retrieved February, 28, 2010 from http://lasics.uminho.pt/ojs/index.php/5sopcom/article/viewFile/236/255

Raskauskas, J., & Stoltz, A. D. (2007). Involvement in traditional and electronic bullying among adolescents. *Developmental Psychology, 43*, 564–575.

Rivers, I., & Noret, N. (2010). "Ih8u": Findings from a five-year study of text and e-mail bullying. *British Educational Research Journal, 36*, 643–671.

Smith, P. K., Mahdavi, J., Carvalho, M., Fisher, S., Russell, S., & Tippett, N. (2008). Cyberbullying: its nature and impact in secondary school pupils. *Journal of Child Psychology and Psychiatry, 49*, 376–385.

Steffgen, G., & König, A. (2009). Cyberbullying: the role of traditional bullying and empathy. In B. Sapio, L. Haddon, E. Mante-Meijer, L. Fortunati, T. Turk, & E. Loos (Eds.),

Conference Proceedings, Vol. 1, The good, the bad and the challenging (pp. 1041–1047). Ljubljana: Copis.

Sutton, J., Smith, P. K., & Swettenham, J. (1999). Social cognition and bullying: Social inadequacy or skilled manipulation? *British Journal of Developmental Psychology, 17*, 435–450.

Ybarra, M., Diener-West, M., & Leaf, P. (2007). Examining the overlap in Internet harassment and school bullying: Implications for school intervention. *Journal of Adolescent Health, 41*, S42–S50.

Ybarra, M., & Mitchell, K. (2004). Online aggressor/targets, aggressors, and targets: a comparison of associated youth characteristics. *Journal of Child Psychology and Psychiatry, 45*, 1308–1316.

Zorrinho, C. (2008). *A country better prepared to confront the global economic conjuncture. Presidency of the Council of Ministers, Cabinet of the National Coordinator of the Technological Plan and the Lisbon Strategy*. Retrieved February 27, 2010 from http://www.planotecnologico.pt/document/GCNELPT_paper2008_en.pdf

12

Cyberbullying and Traditional Bullying

Unique, Additive, and Synergistic Effects on Psychological Health Symptoms

Ersilia Menesini, Pamela Calussi, and Annalaura Nocentini

The extraordinary diffusion of new communication technologies has been a global phenomenon over the last few years. Virtual and electronic communication have become a major component of adolescents' social life (Williams & Guerra, 2007). Technological tools, such as mobile phones and personal computers, provide a new type of person-to-person communication, by transforming interactions from face-to-face to virtual. These tools, although they can expand and strengthen communication, can also be used for negative purposes such as bullying—a phenomenon known as *cyberbullying*, which includes bullying through email, instant messaging, in a chatroom, on a website, or through messages or pictures sent to a mobile phone or posted on the Internet (Smith et al., 2008).

In Italy, the term "cyberbullying" first appeared in the media in 2006, somewhat later than in other countries, where the first reports appeared around 2000. Similarly, scientific research is just beginning to describe the phenomenon of cyberbullying in Italy. No Italian studies have been published to date, whereas the first international contributions date back to 2000 (Finkelhor, Mitchell, & Wolak, 2000).

One reason for this delay is the difference in the diffusion of the new technologies in Italy relative to other countries, in particular the use of the Internet. A Europe-wide comparative study *Children and their Changing Media Environment* (Livingstone & Bovill, 2001), classified Italy (together with France and Spain) in a cluster with a strong focus on national television and relatively low dissemination of new technologies. For example, in the US in 2003, 97% of youth (12–18 years old) used the Internet (Ybarra & Mitchell, 2004) whereas in Italy, between 2003 and 2007 young people aged 14–29 years who used the Internet once or twice a week increased from

Cyberbullying in the Global Playground: Research from International Perspectives, First Edition.
Edited by Qing Li, Donna Cross, and Peter K. Smith.

61% to 83%. Despite the slower uptake than other countries, usage rates in Italy are increasing, especially for more frequent use: the percentages of youth aged 14–29 years using the Internet at least three times a week rose from 22% in 2001 to 39% in 2003 and to 74% in 2007 (CENSIS/UCSI, 2005, 2008). The most frequent online activities included chatrooms, forums, newsgroups, blogs, and messaging.

In relation to mobile phone use, the Italian Institute of Statistics (ISTAT, 2008) reported that in 2006 80% of adolescents aged 11–14 and 93% of adolescents aged 15–19 used a mobile phone—up from 41% and 74% respectively in 2000. These usage rates are consistent with other European countries, such as Sweden and the UK, where percentages are 96% and 91% respectively (Slonje & Smith, 2008).

Given the very recent diffusion of new information and communication technologies in Italy, it is easy to understand why few scientific studies on cyberbullying have been published yet. Although this area of research is growing rapidly, most studies are still in progress and can be found on the Internet, in project reports and conference communications.

Research

Cyberbullying in Italy was described for the first time by the DAPHNE project, a European project financed between 2007–2009 with the aim of supporting knowledge of traditional and new types of bullying. Specifically, this cross-sectional project was intended to investigate the problem in preadolescents and adolescents by comparing results from different countries including England, Spain, Italy, Finland, and Bosnia (see Chapters 2 and 3 in this book). In Italy the study included a sample of 1945 students, aged 12–17 years, selected from 27 middle and secondary schools in the region of Emilia Romagna, northern-central Italy (Genta, Brighi, Guarini, & Berdondini, 2008; Genta, Brighi, & Guarini, 2009).

Other exploratory cross-sectional studies in Italy have been carried out by several research groups during the last two years. For example, Bartolo and Palermiti (2007) conducted a study involving 320 high school students aged 13–15 in a city in southern Italy. Menesini, Calussi, and Nocentini (2008) surveyed Tuscany, in central Italy, using a sample of 708 students from middle and secondary schools. Furthermore, Saturno and Pisano (2008) examined cyberbullying among 1047 students, aged 11–20, selected from middle and secondary schools in seven regions across Italy.

Most of these studies used the questionnaire (with some modifications) developed by Smith and colleagues (2008) to measure cyberbullying. Overall, prevalence rates of cyberbullying perpetration ranged from 7–12% and cyberbullying victimization ranged from 7–16%. The most common cyberbullying behaviors on mobile phones are silent calls and SMS. On the Internet the most common cyberbullying behaviors include insults on instant messaging, chat, and email. Results across studies reported a higher prevalence for high school students than for younger students. Furthermore, females reported being victimized more often than males. Finally, in relation to cyberbullying perpetration, studies showed contrasting results in relation to gender differences, with some suggesting no overall gender difference while others reported significant gender differences related to specific types of behavior.

Popular Reports

Moving from scientific studies to more popular reports, there are many web pages and blogs concerning bullying and cyberbullying. These websites give information about bullying and cyberbullying, provide guidelines for interventions at different levels (family, school, peer, and community), and support victims of bullying and cyberbullying and share expertise on these issues. For example, www.smontailbullo. It was developed by the Italian Ministry of Education to support a national project against bullying in 2007. Other informative websites include www.bullismo.it, a site offering guidelines and advice to students, parents, and to people directly or indirectly involved in bullying; www.bullismo.info, where experts in the educational and health fields provide projects, studies, events, suggested reading, and strategies to address the problem of violent behavior; www.cyberbullismo.com, a website specifically dedicated to the real and virtual bullying among students and providing advice and information for parents, teachers, and students; www.bullismo.com, managed by an independent non-profit agency ("SOSBULLISMO") and dedicated to supporting victims and their families and to awaken public opinion to the problem of bullying; www.stopalbullismo.it, a website created by a team of psychologists working for the Public Health Service in Milan to prevent, oppose, and reduce bullying in schools. Importantly, the most recent initiative supported by the city of Lucca is a website created for young people (www.squarciagola.net/cyberbullismo), which has a special section on cyberbullying. In this section a space called "noncadiamointrappola" (Let's not fall in the trap), is managed by a group of young students from high schools and it is devoted to preventing these behaviors by raising awareness about traditional and cyberbullying. In particular, the students who act as peer educators also act as moderators in two forums and provide counseling and support to other students.

Public Awareness

Although Italian research on cyberbullying is in its early stages, public awareness of this kind of behavior has increased dramatically in recent years as events are frequently reported by Italian media. Some of these can be referred to as cyberbullying, whereas others as cyber-stalking. In some cases they are related to sexual interactions or harassment, especially in the case of sending compromising or embarrassing photos to other people to see.

The first shocking news was in November 2006: In Ancona, in central Italy, a videoclip showing a group of boys aged 14–16 victimizing a 13-year-old girl was circulated to other friends by mobile phone. A similar event occurred in December of the same year in Naples (southern Italy) where six boys, aged between 15 and 16 years, filmed a rape of a schoolmate. In Reggio Emilia a 16-year-old student attempted suicide because she discovered that some pictures of her having sex with her boyfriend had been sent to schoolmates by mobile phone. In the same year in Turin, northern Italy, some boys distributed a video (which was later posted on YouTube) in which a disabled student was insulted and hit by a classmate. All of these cases involve a violation of norms for both the aggressive behaviors perpetrated and for the public diffusion of private scenes.

Other examples of cyberbullying behaviors can involve sending nasty messages or insults. For example, in Bologna in 2009, a 16-year-old student sent messages to the whole class threatening to kill a schoolmate. In Florence, in June 2009, an 18-year-old girl was threatened by text messages and phone calls from her 16-year-old ex-boyfriend, who had not accepted the end of their relationship.

There is some evidence that mobile phones seem to be the principal means for such acts; however, newspapers and televisions also highlight the dangers of the web and the safe use of the Internet. For example, in Bari, in December 2007, a 15-year-old boy received threats on a chatline where he posted photos and information about his habits, friendships, and school, after which he was attacked outside his school. More recently, in Venice in May 2010, five males aged 20 created a fake profile on a social networking site so they could post sarcastic, mean, and offensive comments about another male. In June 2010 in Rome, a group of seven girls threatened some classmates via the Internet; they were subsequently beaten and had their property stolen.

After the first events reported by the media in February 2007, the Minister for Public Education issued a directive (Direttiva n.5) regarding prevention and intervention programs to combat bullying. A National Project was set up to alert students, parents, teachers, principals, and school personnel and to find specific strategies according to the different levels of education. Twenty permanent Observatories on bullying were developed in several regions which were funded by the Ministry of Education. These services included a free phone number to get information or to ask for assistance and support, and a new website to improve awareness on bullying. Subsequently, to address cyberbullying, a legislative note (N. 30/dip./segr.) was issued on March 15, 2007. In this case the Minister tried to regulate the use of technological tools at school, as most of the cases reported by the media implied they were the legal responsibility of schools. Severe sanctions were put in place to discourage the use of mobile phones during class lessons. Schools' own regulations were recommended by the Minister to monitor students' use of school computers; in particular when the students are minors. One strategy that was adopted required students to identify themselves using a username and password, instead of having free access to the Internet. These aspects could enable the monitoring of students' online actions and find illegal acts perpetrated by or directed towards minors online. The same legislative note introduced the "Social Pact of Co-Responsibility," where not only the students but also their parents are held responsible for actions carried out by children in schools. Finally, another document

(Directive n.104, November 30, 2007) stated that it is necessary to have written consent for the diffusion of personal pictures, audio, or video records inside schools, according to Privacy Law Code no.7 (D. L. 196 del 2003). If the transgressor is aged between 14 and 18, the jurisdiction belongs to the Juvenile Court, however, if he/she is younger than 14, any crimes are not prosecutable.

Recently, the new Minister of Public Education proposed two different approaches through which schools can act against bullying and violence (Resolution n.137, September 2009). The first one introduces a new subject to the curriculum, "Education to Citizenship" (Educazione alla cittadinanza), which aims to promote the knowledge of rules and legal conventions. The second approach redefines evaluation criteria of the students' behavior, using discipline, negative marks, sanctions, and school duties for students behaving badly or illegally.

Our Research

Our research on the topic of cyberbullying had three initial objectives:

1. to analyze the prevalence of cyberbullying in Tuscany, Italy (Calussi & Menesini, 2008),
2. to investigate the associations between traditional bullying and cyberbullying (Menesini, Calussi, & Nocentini, 2008), and
3. to examine the issues relating to measuring cyberbullying (Menesini & Nocentini, 2009; Menesini, Nocentini, & Calussi, 2011).

Within this framework the current study focused on psychological health symptoms related to cyberbullying and cybervictimization and on the association between traditional bullying and cyberbullying in relation to externalizing and internalizing symptoms.

Several studies have addressed the interpersonal difficulties related to traditional bullying and victimization (Craig, 1998; Nansel et al., 2001; Roland, 2002; Raskauskas & Stoltz, 2007). Bullying others has been associated with school problems, such as absenteeism from school and low academic competence (Rigby, 1997) and with externalizing behaviors, such as aggressive or delinquent conduct (Kupersmidt, Coie, & Dodge, 1990; Nansel et al., 2001). Being victimized has been associated with the development of general psychological distress, increased levels of depression, anxiety, and psychosomatic symptoms (O'Moore & Kirkham, 2001; Kochenderfer-Ladd & Skinner, 2002).

Similar psychological health symptoms have been reported for cyberbullying and cybervictimization (Ybarra & Mitchell, 2004; Mitchell, Ybarra, & Finkhelor, 2007). Cyberbullying is reported to have negative psychological and emotional effects on its victims, leaving them angry, frustrated, and depressed (Hinduja & Patchin, 2008). However, some people have suggested that the cyber context might produce more serious consequences than the traditional bullying context, because of its special characteristics (e.g., Kowalski & Limber, 2007), such as spreading information to a wide audience, hiding responsibility through anonymity, the more permanent nature of written words and the ability to reach the target at any time and in any place. The increased level of anxiety in the victims is not surprising given the often unknown status of the perpetrator (Kowalski, Limber, & Agatston, 2008). It has also been postulated that because perpetrators do not see their victim's immediate reaction, they may increase the intensity of the attacks and continue for longer than they would do face-to-face (Conn, 2004). Slonje and Smith (2008) suggest that, while the impact may be more serious for the reasons described above, those victimized could simply avoid attacks by shutting down their computer or deleting a phone message or an email. Among the few studies which have examined the relationship between psychological outcomes and cybervictimization, Finkelhor et al. (2000) found that nearly one third of people who were harassed through electronic means reported one symptom of stress. Further, Ybarra (2004) reported an association between cybervictimization and depressive symptoms. In extreme cases, being a victim of cyberbullying has been linked to suicidal behavior in adolescents (Bramwell & Mussen, 2003).

In relation to the association between cyberbullying and externalizing symptoms, only one study has been published (Gradinger, Strohmeier, & Spiel, 2009). Menesini et al. (2008) considered the double involvement in traditional and cyberbullying given the low number of youth who were involved in cyberbullying only. Results from these studies showed that youth who bully using traditional and cyber strategies showed higher levels of aggressive and delinquent behaviors compared to those who bullied using traditional methods only. Similar results were found for victims in both traditional and cyber contexts. These students showed higher levels of internalizing symptoms than did only traditional victims (Menesini et al., 2008).

In order to further understand this effect (i.e., whether it is cumulative or interactive), the present study aims to analyze different models representing the association between traditional and cyberbullying in the development of negative psychological outcomes. In particular, using a variable-centered approach, we aim to test three models evaluating the independent and interactive effects of the traditional and cyber context on psychological health (and ill health) symptoms. The first model (*unique effects*) states that traditional and cyberbullying or victimization will influence the externalizing or internalizing symptoms separately. The second model (*additive effects*) postulates that each context contributes uniquely to the presence of the externalizing and internalizing symptoms. The third model (*synergistic effects*) postulates a synergistic interaction between traditional and cyberbullying in order to explain externalizing and internalizing symptoms.

Method

Participants in the study were 707 adolescents, 347 males (49%) and 360 females (51%), enrolled in the seventh to tenth grades of four junior schools and six high schools in Tuscany, Italy. The age of participants ranged from 11 to 21: the mean age was 14.6 years (SD = 1.5 years). With regard to the high school sample (70.5% of the students), 21.4% of students attended lyceum high schools (this type of school comprises grammar and high schools), 33.6% of students attended technical institutes (divided into industrial technical institutes and technical institutes of tourism), and 44.9% of students attended vocational colleges to learn a trade. The schools were selected using a self-selection inclusion process and classes were selected by the school staff. Self-report questionnaires were administered in class during school time by trained researchers. The consent procedure for the research consisted of approval by the schools and a consent form provided by the parents. Due to the prolonged collaboration with these school districts, 100% of the families agreed to their children's participation in the research. Data were collected in 2008.

Consistent with the self-report questionnaire developed by Smith and colleagues (2008), after a definition of bullying and cyberbullying, the perception of involvement in different typologies of traditional and cyberbullying was measured by four scales, two for each context, one for perpetration and one for victimization (Menesini et al., 2008). The cyberbullying acts could happen anywhere; that is, inside or outside school. For traditional bullying, each scale comprised 11 behavioral items (for example, teasing, threatening, leaving out, calling names), and asked how often adolescents had experienced the listed behaviors in the past couple of months using a five-point Likert scale ranging from never to several times a week. For cyberbullying, each scale comprised 10 items and asked how often adolescents experienced the following behaviors: nasty text messages, phone pictures/photos or videoclips of violent scenes, phone pictures/photos or videoclips of intimate scenes, silent/prank phone calls, nasty or rude emails, insults on websites, insults on instant messaging, insults in a chatroom, insults on a blog, and unpleasant pictures/photos on websites in the past couple of months. Participants were asked to respond to items using a five-point Likert scale ranging from never to several times a week. For all the four scales we calculated a dichotomous cyberbullying prevalence using two thresholds: threshold 1, where the prevalence was from only once or twice to always in the last couple of months, and threshold 2, where the prevalence ranged from two or three times a month to always (see Table 12.1). Furthermore, regression analyses were performed using the continuous scales computed by the mean scores of the items. Given the asymmetry of the scales (ranging from 1.15 to 2.44), we used the logarithm transformation to normalize the data.

In previous work (Menesini et al., 2008), we confirmed the factorial structure of the four scales. Reliability coefficients showed acceptable values: for traditional bullying and victimization alphas were 0.76 and 0.70, for cyberbullying and cybervictimization alphas were 0.75 and 0.76. Furthermore, although the two phenomena (traditional and cyberbullying) were highly correlated (0.71 for bullying and 0.57 for victimization), they maintained their own specificity. Additional psychometric characteristics about the Cyberbullying Scale (CS) can be found in Menesini et al. (2011).

Table 12.1 Endorsement of Items by Gender and by Threshold. Numbers, With Percentages in Brackets.

		Perpetration (% yes)				*Victimization (% yes)*			
	Threshold	*Male*	*Female*	*Total*	χ^2	*Male*	*Female*	*Total*	χ^2
(a) nasty text messages	1	31 (10%)	16 (4.6%)	47 (7.2%)	7.049**	18 (5.6%)	41 (11.8%)	59 (8.8%)	8.052**
	2	5 (1.6%)	3 (0.9%)	8 (1.2%)		5 (1.5%)	6 (1.7%)	11 (1.6%)	n.s.
(b) phone pictures/ photos or videoclips of violent scenes	1	23 (7.1%)	0	23 (3.4%)		18 (5.5%)	4 (1.1%)	22 (3.3%)	
	2	5 (1.6%)	0	5 (0.7%)		4 (1.2%)	0	4 (0.6%)	
(c) phone pictures/ photos or videoclips of intimate scenes	1	20 (6.7%)	5 (1.8%)	25 (4.3%)	8.721**	31 (9.6%)	10 (2.9%)	41 (6.1%)	13.133***
	2	3 (1%)	0	3 (0.5%)		14 (4.3%)	0	14 (2.1%)	
(d) silent/prank phone call	1	126 (38.9%)	120 (34.4%)	246 (36.6%)	n.s.	125 (38.1%)	177 (50.6%)	302 (44.5%)	10.645**
	2	35 (10.8%)	16 (4.6%)	51 (7.6%)	9.275**	33 (10.1%)	49 (14%)	82 (12.1%)	n.s.
(e) nasty or rude email	1	18 (5.6%)	7 (2%)	15 (3.7%)	5.923*	22 (6.8%)	26 (7.4%)	48 (7.2%)	n.s.
	2	5 (1.6%)	3 (0.9%)	8 (1.2%)		7 (2.2%)	9 (2.6%)	16 (2.4%)	n.s.
(f) insults on websites	1	32 (9.9%)	14 (4%)	46 (6.9%)	9.151**	29 (9%)	27 (7.8%)	56 (8.4%)	n.s.
	2	8 (2.5%)	1 (0.3%)	9 (1.3%)		13 (4%)	5 (1.4%)	18 (2.7%)	4.326*
(g) insults on instant messaging	1	80 (24.8%)	74 (21.2%)	154 (22.9%)	n.s.	50 (15.5%)	88 (25.3%)	138 (20.6%)	9.740**
	2	17 (5.3%)	17 (4.9%)	34 (5.1%)	n.s.	16 (5%)	25 (7.2%)	41 (6.1%)	n.s.
(h) insults in a chatroom	1	25 (7.7%)	12 (3.5%)	37 (5.5%)	5.878*	18 (5.6%)	20 (5.7%)	38 (5.7%)	n.s.
	2	9 (2.8%)	2 (0.6%)	11 (1.6%)		7 (2.2%)	5 (1.4%)	12 (1.8%)	n.s.
(i) insults on a blog	1	26 (8%)	30 (8.6%)	56 (8.3%)	n.s.	23 (7.1%)	46 (13.2%)	69 (10.3%)	6.618*
	2	9 (2.8%)	9 (2.6%)	18 (2.7%)	n.s.	5 (1.6%)	14 (4%)	19 (2.8%)	n.s.
(j) unpleasant pictures/photos on websites	1	17 (5.2%)	1 (0.3%)	18 (2.7%)		19 (5.9%)	12 (3.5%)	31 (4.7%)	n.s.
	2	6 (1.8%)	0	6 (0.9%)		5 (1.6%)	3 (0.9%)	8 (1.2%)	

Note: $^{***}p < 0.001$, $^{**}p < 0.01$, $^{*}p < 0.05$. The chi-squared statistics are not reported for cells where the number of subjects was lower than 5. Threshold 1: the prevalence ranged from only once or twice to always in the last couple of months. Threshold 2: the prevalence ranged from two or three times a month to always.

Externalizing symptoms were measured by the scales of aggressive behaviors and delinquent conduct (Youth Self-Report: Achenbach & Edelbrock, 1991; Pastorelli et al., 2002). The scales were composed respectively by the sum of 19 and 11 items and their reliability coefficients were 0.79 and 0.70. Any transformation was used given that asymmetry indices were acceptable.

Internalizing symptoms were measured by the scales of anxious-depressive symptoms, somatic complaints, and social withdrawal symptoms (Youth Self-Report: Achenbach & Edelbrock, 1991; Pastorelli et al., 2002). The scales were composed respectively by the sum of 15, 9, and 7 items and their reliability coefficients were 0.83, 0.65, and 0.68. Any transformation was used given that asymmetry indices were acceptable.

Results

Prevalence rates of cyberbullying perpetration and victimization

Table 12.1 shows the dichotomous prevalence of cyberbullying perpetration and victimization in relation to both males and females and to the different thresholds considered. Consistent with previous literature (e.g., Campbell, 2005), the most common forms of cyberbullying were silent phone calls (for threshold 1, 36.6%; for threshold 2, 7.6%) and insults on instant messaging (for threshold 1, 22.9%; for threshold 2, 5.1%). Similar perpetration rates for these two behaviors were found for males and females using threshold 1; males made higher levels of silent phone calls using threshold 2. For all the other cyberbullying behaviors, a higher level of prevalence was found for males than for females using both thresholds, except for the item "insults on blog" where percentages of involvement are the same across gender.

In relation to victimization, the most common forms were silent phone calls (for threshold 1, 44.5%; for threshold 2, 12.1%) and insults on instant messaging (for threshold 1, 20.6%; for threshold 2, 6.1%). Considering threshold 1, females reported higher levels of victimization for insults on blogs, instant messaging, silent or prank calls, and nasty text messages, but no differences exist considering threshold 2. At a descriptive level, males reported higher rates of distributing photos and videos than females. For the other three items the rates of involvement were similar between the two genders using both thresholds, except for the item "insults on websites," which is higher for males than females using threshold 2.

What are the effects of traditional and cyberbullying on externalizing and internalizing symptoms?

In order to evaluate the unique and multivariate effect of the two bullying contexts on health symptoms, we tested three regression models. In the first model we considered the independent effect of each context on externalizing and internalizing symptoms for perpetration and victimization respectively, controlling for age. In the

Table 12.2 Standardized Regression Coefficients and Explained Variance (R^2) for the Univariate Effects of Bullying on Externalizing Symptoms.

		Aggressive behaviors		*Delinquent behavior*	
		Male	*Female*	*Male*	*Female*
Traditional context	Age	n.s.	n.s.	0.15**	0.23***
	R^2			0.03	0.04
	Traditional bullying	0.41***	0.49***	0.42**	0.38***
	R^2	0.17	0.24	0.20	0.18
Virtual context	Age	n.s.	n.s.	0.15**	0.24***
	R^2			0.04	0.04
	Cyberbullying	0.36***	0.36***	0.42***	0.23***
	R^2	0.12	0.12	0.21	0.09

Note: ***$p < 0.001$, **$p < 0.01$, *$p < 0.05$.

second model, the additive hypothesis was tested examining the effects of traditional bullying while controlling for the effects of the cyberbullying, and vice versa. Finally, to test the synergistic model, we assumed that not only could traditional and cyberbullying explain the unique variance of psychological outcomes, as predicted by the additive model, but they do so in a multiplicative (or non-additive) way. The dependent variables in each analysis are the two externalizing symptoms for the perpetrated forms of bullying and the three internalizing symptoms for the victimization. The analyses were conducted separately for gender. In order to take into account the school-level clustering, we conducted some preliminary analyses on all the variables considered in the study. Results showed that school has an effect on traditional bullying for males and on traditional victimization for females. Comparing the 10 schools, we found only two schools significantly different for males, and four schools significantly different for females. Given their relevance, we controlled regression analysis for this variable (school) and for its interaction with the traditional bullying for males and with traditional victimization for females. No significant interactional effects were found for either males and females, thus we dropped these interactive factors from the results.

Tables 12.2 and 12.3 show the regression coefficients and the portion of explained variance for the unique effect of bullying and victimization on externalizing and internalizing symptoms, respectively.

For bullying behavior, results showed a significant effect for age only for delinquent behavior in both contexts (traditional and cyber), with older youth presenting higher levels of these outcomes. The effects of traditional and cyberbullying on externalizing problems was strong and significant in males and in females, both in terms of the magnitude of the regression coefficients and of the explained variance by the single models. Higher levels of traditional and cyberbullying are associated

Table 12.3 Standardized Regression Coefficients and Explained Variance (R^2) for the Univariate Effects of Victimization on Internalizing Symptoms.

		Somatic symptoms		*Anxious and depressive symptoms*		*Withdrawal*	
		Male	*Female*	*Male*	*Female*	*Male*	*Female*
Traditional context	Age	−0.13*	n.s.	n.s.	n.s.	n.s.	n.s.
	R^2	0.01					
	Traditional victimization	0.26***	0.24***	0.45***	0.33***	0.28***	n.s.
	R^2	0.08	0.05	0.20	0.10	0.07	
Virtual context	Age	−0.13*	n.s.	n.s.	n.s.	n.s.	n.s
	R^2	0.01					
	Cyber-victimization	0.28***	0.20***	0.30***	0.21***	0.17**	n.s.
	R^2	0.09	0.03	0.09	0.04	0.02	

Note: ***$p < 0.001$, **$p < 0.01$, *$p < 0.05$.

with higher levels of aggressive and delinquent behaviors. In relation to externalizing symptoms, for females the contribution of traditional bullying seems to be more consistent in term of explained variance than cyberbullying (aggressive behaviors, 24% versus 12%; delinquent behaviors, 18% versus 9% respectively). For males, the contribution of traditional context was higher than that of the cyber context in relation to aggressive scale (17% versus 12%), but for delinquent behaviors comparable data were found (20% versus 21%).

With regard to the effects of victimization on internalizing symptoms, we found strong and positive associations between independent and the dependent variables. In particular, for males and females the contribution of traditional and cybervictimization is similar in relation to somatic complaints (respectively, for males, 8% and 9%; for females, 5% and 3%). Regarding anxious-depressive symptoms, traditional victimization explained more variance than cybervictimization for both genders (respectively, for males, 20% and 9%; for females, 10% and 4%). Finally, for withdrawal symptoms cybervictimization and traditional victimization have a significant effect in males and a non-significant effect in females. The effect of age was significant only for males in relation to somatic complaints; younger adolescents reported higher levels of somatic complaints than did older adolescents.

With regard to the multivariate effect of bullying and victimization in traditional and cyber contexts, we found strong evidence in support of additive effects. For

Table 12.4 Standardized Regression Coefficients and Explained Variance (R^2) for the Additive and Synergistic Effects of Bullying on Externalizing Symptoms.

	Aggressive behaviors		*Delinquent behaviors*	
	Male	*Female*	*Male*	*Female*
Age	n.s.	n.s.	0.15**	0.23***
R^2	−0.003	−0.003	0.03	0.04
Traditional bullying	0.34**	0.43**	0.32**	0.39**
Cyberbullying	0.21**	0.12*	0.29**	n.s.
R^2	0.21	0.25	0.29	0.19
Traditional bullying x Cyberbullying	n.s.	n.s.	0.27**	n.s.
R^2			0.31	

Note: ***$p < 0.001$, **$p < 0.01$, *$p < 0.05$.

externalizing symptoms (see Table 12.4), additive effects were found for both aggressive and delinquent behaviors in males: The regression coefficients are similar for both contexts, supporting the independent contribution of each form of bullying. For females, there is no additive effect on delinquent behavior, given that the weight of cyberbullying on these symptoms is clearly weak.

Similar patterns of additive effects were found for internalizing symptoms (Table 12.5). For somatic complaints and anxious-depressive symptoms we found a significant additive effect of both bullying contexts in males and females. For social withdrawal no additive effect was found in either males or females: Cybervictimization did not contribute to higher levels once we had controlled for traditional victimization.

With regard to the interaction effect, the findings provide limited support for the hypothesis of a synergistic effect of the traditional and cyber contexts (Tables 12.4 and 12.5). The significant interaction effect occurred between traditional and cyberbullying in predicting delinquent behavior in males. In this model, the interaction effect of the two contexts is statistically significant and the explained variance is slightly higher than the additional model (31% versus 29%). In order to explain the interaction, we calculated the significance of the traditional bullying regression coefficient on delinquent behavior in males at different levels of cyberbullying (lower and higher than 50th percentile). The results showed that for low levels of cyberbullying, the association between traditional bullying and the psychological outcome is weaker than for high levels of this behavior, both in terms of the magnitude of the regression coefficients and of the overall explained variance. These results underline the interactive effect of traditional and cyber contexts on delinquent behaviors.

Table 12.5 Standardized Regression Coefficients and Explained Variance (R^2) for the Additive and Synergistic Effects of Victimization on Internalizing Symptoms.

	Somatic symptoms		*Anxious and depressive symptoms*		*Withdrawal*	
	Male	*Female*	*Male*	*Female*	*Male*	*Female*
Age	−0.14*	n.s.	n.s.	n.s.	n.s.	n.s
R^2	0.02					
Traditional victimization	0.16**	0.22**	0.39**	0.30**	0.27**	n.s.
Cybervictimization	0.23**	0.13*	0.15**	0.12*	n.s.	n.s.
R^2	0.11	.08	0.21	0.11	0.08	
Traditional victimization x Cybervictimization	n.s.	n.s	n.s.	n.s	n.s.	n.s
R^2						

Note: ***$p < 0.001$, **$p < 0.01$, *$p < 0.05$.

Discussion and Conclusions

The present study aimed to extend our knowledge of cyberbullying in Italy, with particular attention being paid to the prevalence of different behaviors perpetrated and received. An additional aim concerned the multivariate effect of traditional and cyberbullying in relation to self-reports of externalizing and internalizing symptoms.

Our results provided evidence that the most common forms of cyberbullying and cybervictimization are silent or prank phone calls and insults on instant messaging. In relation to gender differences, the results emphasized the need to consider the type of cyberbullying behaviors perpetrated or received and the repetition across time for each behavior. In fact, males presented higher levels of bullying through text messages, photos, and videoclips of intimate scenes, insults on websites and chatrooms for both thresholds (that is, either the act was done only once or twice or more often). Silent or prank phone calls, insults on instant messaging, and insults on blogs are equally perpetrated by males and females, although considering a higher threshold (from two or three times a month) males reported higher levels of silent/prank calls than females. In contrast, females were more likely to be victims of nasty text messages, silent phone calls, insults on instant messaging, and on blogs considering a lower threshold (only experienced once or twice), but no differences exist considering a higher frequency across time. Males are more likely to be victimized through photos and videos than females. Overall, it seems that cyberbullying and victimization through photos and videos characterizes mainly males for both perpetrated and received behaviors. It is interesting that females report perpetrating cyberbullying through IM and blogs at the same level as males, regardless of frequency. On the contrary, the frequency and repetition across time of the action is a relevant index to consider for victimized behaviors. In fact, although higher levels of victimization for females were reported in relation to a lower threshold, gender differences were still not present at the higher threshold of bullying.

According to the literature, there is no agreement about the gender differences (Li, 2006; Raskauskas & Stoltz, 2007; Smith et al., 2008). Some authors suggest that cyberbullying is similar in some aspects to indirect forms of traditional bullying, so girls could be more involved than boys, but, at the same time, technological devices may be more attractive to males, which may explain the higher involvement of males (Smith et al., 2008). Furthermore, there is also evidence that girls and boys engage with technologies differently; for example, girls send more IMs than boys.

Regarding the association between traditional bullying and cyberbullying on psychological health symptoms, we found both a unique and a multivariate effect. The first model (*unique effect*) showed that both types of bullying and victimization (traditional and cyber) contribute significantly to explain externalizing and internalizing symptoms respectively, with the exception of self-reported social withdrawal in females. With regard to males, the significant effect of traditional victimization on social withdrawal symptoms may be due to negative face-to-face interactions, which are likely to contribute to a sense of loneliness. The effect of cybervictimization on self-reported symptoms of social withdrawal in males may be related to males reporting higher levels of visual forms of cyberbullying victimization, such as being the object of phone pictures/photos or videoclips of intimate scenes. This particular kind of victimization is related to the negative experiences of self-exposure and we suppose it may elicit shame or the need to withdraw socially. For females we did not find this kind of relationship, probably because the nature of the received acts (that is, nasty text messages, insults on the web, on a blog, or in a chatroom) is less associated to negative exposure of the self. On the whole, the experience of victimization seems to be more serious for boys than for girls.

Of particular significance is the effect of cyberbullying on delinquent behaviors in males, which is equally strong as the effect of traditional bullying. On the other hand, for aggressive behaviors the traditional context seems to be stronger than cyber context. This finding shows that youth involved in cyberbullying behaviors are likely to exhibit the same level of rule-breaking and socially transgressive behaviors as those involved in traditional bullying, but lower levels of general aggressive acts.

The second model (*additive effect*), evaluating the multivariate effect of the two forms of bullying and victimization on externalizing and internalizing symptoms, was supported, with the exception of self-reported social withdrawal (for males and females) and for delinquent behavior in females. These results illustrate that, although there is a strong association between traditional bullying and cyberbullying, each is characterized by specific features that may have a differential impact on health and psychological symptoms. We did not find an additive effect on delinquent behavior in females, which is likely due to the low frequency of cyberbullying behavior in this group.

The synergistic effect was found only for delinquent behavior in males, which may be due to the consistent association between cyberbullying and delinquent behaviors found by the unique effect analysis. The interaction between the two types of bullying seems to have a propulsive effect on the symptoms. In particular, a stronger association between traditional bullying and delinquent behavior was found only if the reported cyberbullying was high. Thus, it was not only the sum of the two types of bullying that amplified the effect on delinquent behaviors, but it was also the interaction between high levels of both cyber and traditional bullying that influenced the level of maladjustment.

Implications

In terms of prevention and intervention strategies, these findings provide some important suggestions. In fact, even if the two types of bullying (traditional and cyber) are strictly related, they also maintain specific features and explain unique variance in psychological symptoms. This was supported by the results of the additive and synergistic models, which demonstrated that cyberbullying behaviors have specific effects on externalizing and internalizing symptoms over and above the effects of traditional bullying behaviors. Some specific differences between traditional and cyberbullying include the important role of technology in students' lives, the various ways through which cyberbullying occurs, the anonymous nature of cyberbullying, and the many and insidious digital ways through which cyberbullying can reach the victim at any time. It is possible that some or all of these characteristics can explain the differential impact that cyberbullying has on adolescents' well-being. Therefore in terms of prevention and intervention strategies, school and educational programs should focus not only on traditional bullying but also more specifically on cyberbullying.

Although cyberbullying can occur outside school, often without the use of school computers, schools have a significant role to play in preventing and responding to these problems since they may begin in school contexts and can have negative effects on students' well-being and education. Using an educational approach, schools need to establish clear policies regarding cyberbullying. Rules should be introduced regarding the use of the school's Internet as well as the use of personal mobile phones. In this sense we find the Minister's Directive of 2007 regulating this specific aspect very appropriate.

The present study also presents some limitations which can be addressed in future studies. First, starting from the cyber-context effects, there is a need to further examine the effect of the different typologies of electronic devices (mobile phones, the Internet) as well as the type of behavior (sending IMs, posting personal photos) on psychological health. Second, longitudinal studies are needed to evaluate the direction of the association between symptoms and bullying behaviors. For example, is delinquent behavior an antecedent or a consequence of traditional bullying and cyberbullying? Third, aside from the symptoms used in this study, a more complex definition of health conditions should be considered, comprising other aspects such as self-esteem or emotion regulation. Fourth, there is a need to evaluate whether the specific characteristics of cyberbullying (that is, anonymity, wide audience, possibility of reaching the victims anywhere and anytime) can affect the degree of the psychological symptoms reported. Finally, the generalizability of the results is limited because of the self-selection sampling and the restricted location considered: Tuscany's sample needs to be extended to a larger and more representative national sample.

References

Achenbach, T. M., & Edelbrock, C. (1991). *Manual for the youth self-report and profile.* Burlington, VT: Department of Psychiatry, University of Vermont.

Bartolo, M. G., & Palermiti, A. (2007). *Il cyberbullying: Prepotenze elettroniche [Cyberbullying: Bullying through electronic means]*. Symposium XXI International Congress AIP, Bergamo, Italy, September 20–22.

Bramwell, S., & Mussen, D. (2003, November 20). Boy text bullied to death. *Star Times,* p. 1.

Calussi, P., & Menesini, E. (2008). *Cybervictimization in adolescents: A preliminary investigation of types, actors and incidence.* Poster symposium, XI EARA Congress, Turin Italy, May 7–10.

Campbell, M. A. (2005). Cyberbullying: An old problem in a new guise? *Australian Journal of Guidance and Counselling, 15*, 68–76.

CENSIS/UCSI (2005). *Quinto rapporto sulla comunicazione in Italia. Cinque anni di evoluzione e rivoluzione nell'uso dei media (2001–2005) [5th report on communication in Italy. Five years of evolution and revolution in media use]*. Rome.

CENSIS/UCSI (2008). *Settimo rapporto sulla comunicazione in Italia. L'evoluzione delle diete mediatiche giovanili in Italia e in Europa [7th report on communication in Italy. The evolution of youth media diets in Italy and Europe]*. Rome.

Conn, K. (2004). *Bullying and harassment: A legal guide for educators.* Alexandria, VA: Association for Supervision and Curriculum Development.

Craig, W. M. (1998). The relationship among bullying, victimization, depression, anxiety, and aggression in elementary school children. *Personality and Individual Differences, 24*, 123–130.

Finkelhor, D., Mitchell, K. J., & Wolak, J. (2000). *Online victimization: A report on the nation's youth* (NCMEC 6–00–020). Alexandria, VA: National Center for Missing and Exploited Children.

Genta, M. L., Brighi, A., & Guarini, A. (Eds.) (2009). *Bullismo elettronico. I fattori di rischio delle nuove tecnologie [Cyberbullying. Risk factors of new technologies]*. Rome: Carocci.

Genta, M. L., Brighi, A., Guarini, A., & Berdondini, L. (2008). *Cyberbullying: A new context for bullying.* Poster workshop, XX ISSBD conference, Würzburg, Germany, July 13–17.

Gradinger, P., Strohmeier, D., & Spiel, C. (2009). Traditional bullying and cyberbullying: Identification of risk groups for adjustment problems. *Journal of Psychology, 217*, 205–213.

Hinduja, S., & Patchin, J. W. (2008). Cyberbullying: An exploratory analysis of factors related to offending and victimization. *Deviant Behavior, 29*, 129–156.

ISTAT (Italian Institute of Statistics). (2008). *La vita quotidiana nel 2007* [*Everyday life in 2007*]. Rome: ISTAT.

Kochenderfer-Ladd, B., & Skinner, K. (2002). Children's coping strategies: moderators of the effects of peer victimization? *Developmental Psychology, 38*, 267–278.

Kowalski, R. M., & Limber, S. P. (2007). Electronic bullying among middle school students. *Journal of Adolescent Health, 41*, S22–S30.

Kowalski, R. M., Limber, S., & Agatston, P. (2008). *Cyberbullying: Bullying in the digital age.* Malden, MA: Blackwell.

Kupersmidt, J. B., Coie, J. D., & Dodge, K. A. (1990). The role of poor peer relationships in the development of disorder. In S. R. Asher & J. D. Coie (Eds.), *Peer rejection in childhood* (pp. 274–308). New York: Cambridge University Press.

Li, Q. (2006). Cyberbullying in schools: A research of gender differences. *School Psychology International, 27*, 157–170.

Livingstone, S., & Bovill, M. (Eds.) (2001). *Children and their changing media environment: A European comparative study*. Hillsdale, NJ: Lawrence Erlbaum.

Menesini, E., Calussi, P., & Nocentini, A. (2008). *Cyberbullying and psychological health symptoms.* Poster workshop, XX ISSBD conference, University of Würzburg, Germany, July 13–17.

Menesini, E., & Nocentini, A. (2009). Cyberbullying definition and measurement: Some critical considerations. *Journal of Psychology, 217*, 230–232.

Menesini, E., Nocentini, A., & Calussi, P. (2011). The measurement of cyberbullying: Dimensional structure and relative item severity and discrimination. *Cyberpsychology & Behavior, 14*(5), 267–274.

Mitchell, K. J., Ybarra, M. L., & Finkelhor, D. (2007). The relative importance of online victimization in understanding depression, delinquency, and substance use. *Child Maltreatment, 12*, 314–324.

Nansel, T. R., Overpeck, M., Pilla, R. S., Ruan, W. J., Simon-Morton, B., & Scheidt, P. (2001). Bullying behavior among US youth: Prevalence and association with psychological adjustment. *Journal of the American Medical Association, 285*, 2094–2100.

O'Moore, M., & Kirkham, C. (2001). Self-esteem and its relationship to bullying behavior. *Aggressive Behavior, 27*, 269–283.

Pastorelli, C., Gerbino, M., Vecchio, G. M., Steca, P., Picconi, L., & Paciello, M. (2002). L'insuccesso scolastico: Fattori di rischio e di protezione nel corso della preadolescenza [School failure: Risk and protective factors during adolescence]. *Età Evolutiva, 71*, 84–91.

Raskauskas, J., & Stoltz, A. D. (2007). Involvement in traditional and electronic bullying among adolescents. *Developmental Psychology, 43*, 564–575.

Rigby, K. (1997). *Bullying in schools, and what to do about it.* London: Jessica Kingsley.

Roland, E. (2002). Bullying, depressive symptoms and suicidal thoughts. *Educational Research, 44*, 55–67.

Saturno, M. E., & Pisano, L. (2008). *Cyberbullismo: indagine esplorativa sul fenomeno delle prepotenze on line* [*Cyberbullying: an explorative analysis of bullying online*]. IFOS: Cagliari.

Slonje, R., & Smith, P. K. (2008). Cyberbullying: Another main type of bullying? *Scandinavian Journal of Psychology, 49*, 147–154.

Smith, P. K., Mahdavi, J., Carvalho, M., Fisher, S., Russell, S., & Tippett, N. (2008). Cyberbullying: Its nature and impact in secondary school pupils. *Journal of Child Psychology and Psychiatry, 49*, 376–385.

Williams, K. R., & Guerra, N. G. (2007). Prevalence and predictors of Internet bullying. *Journal of Adolescent Health, 41*, S14–S21.

Ybarra, M. L. (2004). Linkages between depressive symptomatology and Internet harassment among young regular Internet users. *Cyberpsychology & Behavior, 7*, 247–257.

Ybarra, M. L., & Mitchell, K. J. (2004). Online aggressor/targets, aggressor and targets: A comparison of associated youth characteristics. *Journal of Child Psychology and Psychiatry, 45*, 1308–1316.

13

Motives for Bullying Others in Cyberspace

A Study on Bullies and Bully-Victims in Austria

Petra Gradinger, Dagmar Strohmeier, and Christiane Spiel

While traditional bullying and victimization is well researched in Austria (see for overviews Atria & Spiel, 2003; Strohmeier & Spiel, 2009), studies related to cyberbullying and cybervictimization are rather limited. The main focus of these studies was on the use of online and mobile technologies in children and youth (Bildungsmedien Zentrum, 2007, 2008; European Commission, 2007, 2008). For instance, in 2004, 2006, 2007, and 2008 Austria participated in the Eurobarometer studies that were conducted in the context of the Safer Internet Program of the European Commission (European Commission, 2004, 2006, 2007, 2008). In 2007, the Eurobarometer also examined cyberbullying and cybervictimization. Seventeen girls and nineteen boys aged 9 to 14 were interviewed. The summary of these qualitative interviews indicated that cyberbullying and cybervictimization were relevant issues for some of the participants (European Commission, 2007, p. 21). In 2008, the Eurobarometer study focused on parents' views. Five hundred Austrian parents participated in telephone interviews. About half of them were worried that their children could be bullied online or via mobile phones (54% versus 51%, respectively). Only one study reported prevalence rates of cyberbullying and cybervictimization in 761 adolescents aged 14 to 19 attending schools in Vienna (Gradinger, Strohmeier, & Spiel, 2009). Seven percent of youth reported that they have cyberbullied others and 5% reported that they have been victims of cyberbullying at least once.

The lack of research in Austria is alarming given the fact that the distribution of mobile phones, computers, and the Internet in Austrian youth is very high: 93% of househoulds with parents and children below the age of 15 have computers, 85% have Internet access, and 98% have mobile phones (Statistik Austria, 2008).

Cyberbullying in the Global Playground: Research from International Perspectives, First Edition.
Edited by Qing Li, Donna Cross, and Peter K. Smith.

Context

Violence prevention in kindergartens and schools as well as safe Internet use by children and youth are issues of public concern in Austria. Like many other European countries, Austria ratified the UN Convention of the Rights of the Child, committing itself to safeguarding children and adolescents from all forms of physical or psychological violence (Article 18). Furthermore, in 2007, a national strategy plan for violence prevention in kindergartens and schools was developed and has since been rolled out nationwide (Spiel & Strohmeier, 2007, in press). For instance, a national homepage on the topic of violence prevention has been set up (www.gemeinsam-gegen-gewalt.at), the application of evidence-based practice programs has been promoted in kindergartens and schools, and teacher training courses have been implemented.

Austria is also part of the Safer Internet Program, a European Commission initiative aimed at empowering and protecting children and young people online by awareness-raising and by fighting illegal and harmful online content and conduct. Within this program, a wide variety of projects are funded, such as the "Safer Internet Day," a conference which brings together representatives of industry, law enforcement authorities, child welfare organizations, and policy-makers. The Safer Internet Program also supports an information website (www.saferinternet.at/). Austria is also involved in the COST Action IS0801 on cyberbullying. This Action is supported by the EU RTD framework program, and aims to share expertise on cyberbullying in educational settings, coping with negative uses, and enhancing positive uses of new technologies.

In July 2006, an anti-stalking law became operative in Austria. Since then there has been heightened public awareness that repeated persecution, which might also include harassment via phones and the Internet, is a criminal offence. Although this law does not apply to children and youth it helps to raise awareness that cyberbullying in general is a harmful and antisocial behavior.

Underlying Motives for Bullying Others in Cyberspace: A Study on Bullies and Bully-Victims in Austria

Although many studies focus on the underlying motives of aggressive behavior (Dodge & Coie, 1987; Dodge, 1991; Vitaro & Brendgen, 2005; Card & Little, 2006; Vitaro, Brendgen, & Barker, 2006) and bullying (e.g., Roland & Idsøe, 2001; Salmivalli & Nieminen, 2002; Fandrem, Strohmeier, & Roland, 2009), the question why students bully others in cyberspace has not been adequately addressed in research. Some evidence suggests that cyberbullying, traditional bullying, cybervictimization, and traditional victimization co-occur (Ybarra & Mitchell, 2004; Kowalski & Limber, 2007; Li, 2007a, 2007b; Raskauskas & Stoltz, 2007; Solberg, Olweus, & Endresen, 2007; Ybarra, Diener-West, & Leaf, 2007; Juvonen & Gross, 2008; Smith et al., 2008; Gradinger et al., 2009; Katzer, Fetchenhauer, & Belschak, 2009). Therefore, to not bias results it is crucial to also consider traditional forms when studying cyberbullying or cybervictimization. The present study investigates whether students belonging to particular groups of bullies (traditional, cyber or combined) and bully-victims (i.e., students who are involved in bullying and victimization, either traditional, cyber or combined) differ regarding their motives for bullying others.

Two motive systems of aggressive behavior: Reactive and instrumental aggression

Two concepts are often described as underlying mechanisms, functions, or motive systems[1] for aggressive behavior: Reactive and instrumental aggression (e.g., Dodge & Coie, 1987; Dodge, 1991; Little, Jones, Henrich, & Hawley, 2003; Vitaro & Brendgen, 2005; Card & Little, 2006; Vitaro et al., 2006). The concept of reactive aggression has its roots in frustration-anger theory (e.g., Dollard et al., 1939; Berkowitz, 1989, 1993). To harm somebody else occurs as a "reaction" to a (perceived) provocation, threat, or frustration and is usually accompanied by strong feelings of anger. Thus, reactive aggression is triggered by goal blocking and its main motive is to react to the anger-frustration stimulus and to hurt the perpetrator of the provocation or the threat (Vitaro & Brendgen, 2005, p. 178). In contrast, the concept of instrumental aggression is based on social learning theory (Bandura, 1973, 1983). To harm somebody else is a premeditated, calculated behavior that is used as an "instrument" to reach particular goals. The dominant emotions involved in this type of aggression are pleasure and stimulation. Reactive and instrumental aggression were found to be highly correlated but distinct constructs (e.g., Poulin & Boivin, 2000). About half of the children who display aggressive behavior were found to be both reactively and instrumentally aggressive, about one third were usually found to be only reactively aggressive and only a minority (about 15%) of children were found to be only instrumentally aggressive (e.g., Dodge, Lochman, Harnish, Bates, & Pettit, 1997). Usually, boys score higher in both reactive and instrumental aggression than girls (e.g., Little et al., 2003).

The underlying motives of bullying

Bullying behavior is usually considered to be a subcategory of aggressive behavior and instrumental aggression is considered by several researchers to be the underlying mechanism (e.g., Dodge, 1991; Berkowitz, 1993; Olweus, 1993; Sutton, Smith, & Swettenham, 1999). However, very few studies have empirically studied the associations between reactive and instrumental aggression and bullying behavior (e.g., Roland & Idsøe, 2001; Salmivalli & Nieminen, 2002; Fandrem et al., 2009).

Roland and Idsøe (2001) investigated how bullying others was related to reactive and instrumental aggression. If a student uses aggressive behavior to react to an anger-frustration stimulus, this behavior was defined as reactive aggression. To put it succinctly, the motive or underlying function of reactive aggression is to cope with an anger reaction. If a student uses aggressive behavior as an "instrument" to reach a particular goal, this behavior was defined as instrumental aggression. More specifically, Roland and Idsøe (2001) distinguished two goals—power and affiliation—which a perpetrator wants to achieve. A student who exerts aggressive behavior with a power motive wants to dominate others. A student who uses aggressive behavior with an affiliation motive wants to establish good relationships [with other perpetrators]. Both power and affiliation have also been distinguished in the literature dealing with children's social goals (Buhrmeister, 1996; Ojanen, Aunola, & Salmivalli, 2007). In total, 1801 fifth grade pupils and 2083 eighth grade pupils in Norway were studied. The two instrumental motives, power and affiliation, were found to be related, but distinct, constructs. Among eighth graders, Roland and Idsøe (2001) found that bullying others was positively associated with both power and affiliation, but not with anger reactions. Among fifth graders, power, affiliation, and anger reactions were associated with bullying others. This latter finding is in line with Salmivalli and Nieminen (2002) who also found high levels of instrumental and reactive aggression in bully-victims and bullies in the same age group (10–12 years). Roland and Idsøe (2001) also reported gender differences indicating higher associations between bullying others and the affiliation motive in girls compared with boys in both fifth and eighth graders. Among eighth graders the power motive was found to be more important for boys than for girls.

The underlying motives of cyberbullying

Only a few studies have investigated the motives for bullying others in cyberspace. Raskauskas and Stoltz (2007) in a US study asked for the reason why electronic perpetrators choose to cyberbully. From the 84 participants aged 14 to 18 years, 18 were identified as cyberbullies, and 16 of them answered the question concernings the reason behind cyberbullying. Six respondents did it for fun, four respondents out of anger or for retaliation ("to get back at someone they're mad at"), and one adolescent did it because of a bad feeling about himself or herself. Five respondents did not know the motives for their electronic bullying behavior.

Gradinger and colleagues (2009) surveyed 761 adolescents aged 14 to 19 years in Austria and compared levels of reactive and instrumental aggression in bullies and victims of bullies. The authors differentiated groups of bullies depending on their involvement in traditional bullying and cyberbullying. Students who bullied others both traditionally and in cyberspace were defined as combined bullies. Those students who were being bullied and actively bullied others both traditionally and in cyberspace were categorized as combined bully-victims. Only those students who were neither involved in traditional bullying, cyberbullying, traditional victimization, or cybervictimization were categorized as totally uninvolved. Combined bullies showed the highest levels of reactive and instrumental aggression compared to traditional bullies, cyberbullies, and non-bullies. Combined bully-victims showed the highest levels of reactive and instrumental aggression compared to traditional bully-victims and totally uninvolved adolescents.

Co-occurences of cyberbullying and traditional bullying

Considerable evidence suggests that cyberbullying and traditional bullying co-occur, as do cybervictimization and traditional victimization (Li, 2007a, 2007b; Raskauskas & Stoltz, 2007; Juvonen & Gross, 2008; Smith et al., 2008; Katzer et al., 2009). There is also a substantial overlap between traditional bullying and traditional victimization (Solberg et al., 2007) as well as between cyberbullying and cybervictimization (Ybarra & Mitchell, 2004; Kowalski & Limber, 2007; Li, 2007a). However, the combination of all four forms has so far been investigated in only one study.

Gradinger, Strohmeier, and Spiel (2009) reported patterns of co-occurence between traditional bullying, cyberbullying, traditional victimization, and cyber-victimization in 761 adolescents aged 14 to 19 years in Austria. Controlling for traditional bullying, only 1% of students were identified as cyberbullies only using the most inclusive criterion possible (all students who did not state explicitly "no involvement" during this term were included). On the contrary, controlling for cyberbullying and using the same inclusive criterion, 61% of students were identified as traditional bullies only.[2] Five percent of students were identified as combined bullies, because they bullied others both traditionally and in cyberspace. Thus, when using the most inclusive criterion possible a very low number of students were identified as cyberbullies, and nearly all of them were also traditional bullies. Considering gender, boys were found to be over-represented in the combined bully group; girls were found to be under-represented in the cyberbully-only group. Furthermore, when additionally controlling for traditional victimization and cybervictimization, more students than expected by chance were identified in the following groups: Totally uninvolved students (24%), traditional bully-victims (33%), and combined bully-victims (traditional and cyber, 1%). Fewer students than expected by chance were found to be traditional bullies only (and not victims, 25%), traditional victims only (and not bullies, 8%), or combined bullies (but not victims, 0.4%). To summarise, the Gradinger et al. (2009) study highlights the overlapping nature of being involved in cyberbullying and cybervictimization with traditional bullying and traditional victimization. Because cyberbullying and cybervictimization were such rare phenomena, a very inclusive criterion had to be used for categorization.

Overall, it seems to be important to control for involvement in traditional bullying and traditional victimization in studies on cyberbullying and cybervictimization in order to not misattribute findings to cyberbullying and cybervictimization, when in fact they might reflect involvement in traditional bullying and victimization. Therefore, the present study uses the same procedure as described in Gradinger et al. (2009) to identify particular bully and bully-victim groups.

Thus, the aims of this chapter are to

1. identify empirically relevant groups of bullies (traditional, cyber, or combined) and bully-victims by considering traditional bullying, cyberbullying, traditional victimization, and cybervictimization.
2. analyze whether students belonging to these groups of bullies and bully-victims differ regarding the motives of power, affiliation, anger, and fun. Because the sample consists of preadolescent students, we predict all four motives will be important.

Method

Sample and procedure

We used the pre-test data from the pilot phase of a national intervention evaluation study, ViSC, in Austria (Spiel & Strohmeier, in press), with 1461 students (712 girls, 749 boys), in fifth to eighth grades, from 11 different schools located in three different federal states (Carinthia, Salzburg, and Vienna) participating in the study. The students were aged 10–15 ($M = 12.31$, $SD = 1.20$). This sample is totally distinct from that of Gradinger et al. (2009). The sample was culturally diverse and represents the population well; 81.2% of the students were born in Austria; the students not born in Austria are from 39 different countries.

Participation was voluntary and based on active parental consent; 90% of eligible students participated in the study. The data were collected in November and December 2008 through Internet-based questionnaires which were completed during one regular school hour in the school's computer lab under the supervision of one or two trained research assistants. The order of the items within scales was counterbalanced to avoid ordering effects.

Instruments

Bullying and victimization

Bullying and victimization were measured by modified items of the Olweus bully-victim questionnaire (Olweus, 1996). Because no exact translation of the term "bullying" exists in the German language, the term was avoided in the questionnaire. Instead, "bullying" was described as "hurting or insulting" (in German, "beleidigen oder verletzen"). The combination of these two German terms have a similar connotation to "bullying" or "harassing" in English and are easily understood by preadolescents. The frequency of bullying and victimization during the last two months was measured. The response format of the items ranged from 0 (never) through 1 (one or two times), 2 (two or three times a month), 3 (once a week), to 4 (nearly every day).

We think that, with this procedure, two out of three bullying criteria (intent to harm and repetition) are captured. While intent to harm is captured in the terms, repetition is captured in the rating scale. Power imbalance is usually not directly integrated in the (English) bullying items, but is present within the definition of bullying given before the items. Because there is evidence that adolescents underestimate being victimized when a standard definition of bullying is given (Vaillancourt et al., 2008), and given the very low frequency of cyberbullying in Austria found in a prior study (Gradinger et al., 2009), we did not provide a definition in the questionnaire.

Cronbach alpha reliabilities are based on the data from this study.

Traditional bullying ($\alpha = 0.68$). Three specific forms of bullying behavior were measured:

1. How often have you insulted or hurt other students by verbally harassing them during the last two months? (verbal)
2. How often have you insulted or hurt other students by physically harassing them during the last two months? (physical)
3. How often have you insulted or hurt other students by socially excluding them during the last two months? (exclusion)

Cyberbullying was measured by one newly developed item which covers four different electronic means to hurt others. "How often have you insulted or hurt other students by sending mean text messages, emails, videos, or photos to them during the last two months?"

Traditional victimization ($\alpha = 0.73$). Corresponding to traditional bullying, three specific forms of victimization were measured:

1. How often have you been insulted or hurt by being verbally harassed by others during the last two months? (verbal)
2. How often have you been insulted or hurt by being physically harassed by others during the last two months? (physical)
3. How often have you been insulted or hurt by being socially excluded during the last two months? (exclusion)

Cybervictimization was measured by one newly developed item which covers four different electronic ways of hurting others. "How often have you been insulted or hurt by receiving mean text messages, emails, videos, or photos during the last two months?"

Underlying motives

Four underlying motives of bullying behavior were measured: power, affiliation, anger, and fun. These motives were measured separately after each bullying item. The Internet-based questionnaire allowed us to ask only those students actually involved in particular forms of bullying about their motives. All students who indicated being involved in bullying at least once were presented with the following question and answering alternatives:

Why did you hurt or insult another student by .... during the last two months?

Depending on the respective bullying item, one of the following text phrases was included in the sentence: verbally harassing/physically harassing/socially excluding/sending mean text messages, emails, videos, or photos (to) them.

I did this

1. to show that I am more powerful. (power)
2. to be accepted by my friends. (affiliation)
3. because it was fun. (fun)
4. because I was angry. (anger)

The response format for the four items ranged from 0 (not at all true) through 1 (somewhat true), 2 (fairly true), to 3 (very true). For each underlying motive a sum score was computed and divided by the number of items answered (ranging between 0 and 3).

Results

First, we built bully and bully-victim groups by systematically combining traditional bullying, cyberbullying, traditional victimization, and cybervictimization and checked for frequency distribution. Contingency tables of ascending complexity are computed and Configural Frequency Analyses (CFA) were applied to check for systematic patterns. Then, we analyzed whether students belonging to particular groups of bullies (traditional, cyber, or both) and bully-victims differ regarding their underlying motives for bullying others, using MANOVAs.

Identification of bully and bully-victim groups

In the first step, the frequency of the different forms of bullying and victimzation was explored. Because of very low cell sizes in the the answer categories "two or three times per month," "once a week," and "nearly every day," we collapsed these to one category "at least two or three times per month." The percentages of students reported being involved in the different forms—as well as the frequency of these forms—are shown in Table 13.1 (for bullying) and Table 13.2 (for victimization).

Cyberbullying is reported comparatively rarely. While 43.3% of girls and 47.1% of boys reported being involved in verbal bullying, only 6.9% of students reported being involved in cyberbullying at least once or twice during the last two months. Therefore, to be able to make any comparisons between traditional bullying and cyberbullying we had to use the most inclusive criterion. When using the standard criterion of frequency rates above once or twice, only 1.1% of boys and 1.8% of girls would have been identified as being involved in cyberbullying (see Table 13.1).

To explore gender differences, a chi-square test was applied for each form of bullying separately. Boys outperformed girls in frequent verbal and physical bullying

Table 13.1 Frequency of Different Forms of Bullying, and Gender Differences.

Forms of bullying	*Girls (N = 712)* *Boys (N = 749)*	*Never*	*Once or twice*	*At least two or three times per month*	χ^2 *(df)*	p
Cyberbullying	girls %	93.1	5.8	1.1	1.66 (2)	0.435
	boys %	93.1	5.1	1.8		
Traditional bullying						
Verbal	girls %	56.7	35.4	7.9	17.47 (2)	0.000***
	boys %	52.9	32.3	14.8		
Exclusion	girls %	77.5	18.8	3.7	1.83 (2)	0.401
	boys %	76.9	18.0	5.1		
Physical	girls %	87.9	9.0	3.1	54.00 (2)	0.000***
	boys %	72.6	21.5	5.9		

Note: Percentages of girls and boys; * $p < 0.05$, ** $p < 0.01$, *** $p < 0.001$.

Table 13.2 Frequency of Different Forms of Victimization, and Gender Differences.

Forms of victimization	*Girls (N = 712)* *Boys (N = 749)*	*Never*	*Once or twice*	*At least two or three times per month*	χ^2 *(df)*	p
Cybervictimization	girls %	86.9	10.5	2.6	14.40 (2)	0.001**
	boys %	92.1	5.2	2.7		
Traditional victimization						
Verbal	girls %	41.0	39.3	19.7	12.36 (2)	0.002**
	boys %	49.8	31.8	18.4		
Exclusion	girls %	64.9	25.1	10.0	16.32 (2)	0.000***
	boys %	74.5	17.6	7.9		
Physical	girls %	78.9	14.2	6.9	27.27 (2)	0.000***
	boys %	66.8	22.4	10.8		

Note: Percentages of girls and boys; * $p < 0.05$, ** $p < 0.01$, *** $p < 0.001$.

(see Table 13.1). While girls show higher percentages in verbal bullying (one or two times), boys show higher percentages in frequent verbal bullying. Concerning physical bullying, for all response alternatives higher percentages were observed in boys. No gender differences were found for cyberbullying.

Cybervictimization is reported also comparatively rarely. While 59% of girls and 50.2% of boys reported being verbally victimized, only 13.1% of girls and 7.9% of boys reported being cybervictimized at least once or twice during the last two months. Again we had to use the most inclusive criterion for classification to be able to make any comparisons between traditional victimization and cybervictimization. To explore gender

Table 13.3 Co-occurrence of Traditional Bullying and Cyberbullying: Results of the First Order CFA, Bonferroni Adjusted $\alpha = 0.006$.

		Variable patterns	*Frequencies*		*Statistics*
Bully groups	*Gender*	$B_T B_C G$	*observed*	*expected*	*p (z)*
Non-bully	girl	111	347	306.67	0.011
	boy	112	317	322.60	0.378
Cyberbully only	girl	**121**	**7**	**22.77**	**0.000**[A]
	boy	**122**	**5**	**23.96**	**0.000**[A]
Traditional bully only	girl	211	316	356.11	0.017
	boy	212	380	374.62	0.391
Both (traditional and cyberbully)	girl	**221**	**42**	**26.45**	**0.001**[T]
	boy	**222**	**47**	**27.82**	**0.000**[T]

Note: Variable patterns represent the systematic combination of three categorical variables: B_T = being a traditional bully (1 = no, 2 = yes), B_C = being a cyberbully (1 = no, 2 = yes), and G = gender (1 = girl, 2 = boy). Superscripts mark types (T) and antitypes (A).

differences, chi-square tests were applied for each form of victimization separately. Girls mainly exceeded boys in cybervictimization, and in the verbal and exclusion forms of victimization. Boys exceeded girls in physical victimization (see Table 13.2).

In the second step, we prepared data to identify bully and bully-victim groups. A student was considered to be a traditional bully if he or she reported being involved in at least one form of traditional bullying (answering options "one or two times" and "at least two or three times per month"). A student was considered to be a traditional victim if he or she reported being involved in at least one form of traditional victimization (answering options "one or two times" and "at least two or three times per month"). Accordingly, a student was considered to be a cyberbully or cybervictim if he or she reported being involved in cyberbullying or cybervictimization (answering options "one or two times" and "at least two or three times per month"), respectively.

Identification of bully groups

For this analysis, a contingency table comprising three categorical variables, namely being a traditional bully (no/yes), being a cyberbully (no/yes), and gender (girl/boy) was computed (see Table 13.3). The systematic combination of these three variables resulted in eight cells. Each cell is characterized by a certain variable pattern (for example, pattern 222: Being a traditional bully, being a cyberbully, and being a boy). To investigate whether certain variable patterns occur more or less often than expected by chance or, in other words, whether local relations between these three variables exist, first-order Configural Frequency Analysis (CFA) was applied. CFA (Lienert, 1969; von Eye, 2002) is a multivariate method of analysis which checks for local relations in categorical data. CFA compares the observed cell frequency with the expected frequency estimated under a chance model. A chance model is contradicted if variable relationships assumed not to exist do exist (for a description of methodology and examples see, for example, Spiel & von Eye, 2000; von Eye, Mun, & Bogat, 2008). Variable patterns that are, relative to some expectations, more frequent are termed "types," while less frequent variable patterns are termed "antitypes."

As shown in Table 13.3, the base model of independence of the three variables was contradicted, $\chi^2 = 58.29$, df = 4, $p < 0.001$, and the existence of two types (pattern 221 and 222) and two antitypes (pattern 121 and 122) was suggested. The patterns 221 and 222 indicate that there are more female (221) and male (222) combined bullies (traditional and cyber) than expected. The patterns 121 and 122 indicate that there are fewer females (121) and males (122) who are only cyberbullies than expected.

Identification of bully-victim groups

For this analysis, a contingency table comprising four categorical variables, namely being a traditional bully (no/yes), being a cyberbully (no/yes), being a traditional victim (no/yes), and being a cybervictim (no/yes) was computed (see Table 13.4). The systematic combination of these four variables resulted in sixteen cells. Again, first-order CFA was applied to check for types and antitypes. Gender could not be included in the analyses because of very low cell frequencies in some cells (see the descriptive information in Table 13.4). The base model of independence of the four variables was contradicted, $\chi^2 = 226.7$, df = 9, $p < 0.001$. Results suggest the existence of three types (patterns 1111, 2121, 2222) and three antitypes (patterns 1121, 1122, 2111).

The pattern 1111 indicates that there are more students than expected who are totally uninvolved (neither a bully nor a victim). Pattern 2121 suggests that there are more students than expected who are traditional bully-victims; pattern 2222 reveals that there are more students than expected who are combined bully-victims of both traditional and cyberbullying. The three antitypes indicate that fewer students than expected traditional victims but not bullies (pattern 1121), combined victims but not bullies (pattern 1122), and traditional bullies but not victims (pattern 2111).

Motives for bullying in bully groups and bully-victim groups

Motives for bullying in bully groups

To check for differences between the bully groups (cyberbully only, traditional bully only, and combined bully) in motives for bullying, a MANOVA with bully group and gender as factors and the four motives for bullying (power, affiliation, anger, and fun) as dependent variables was conducted.[3] The application of a multivariate test using Pillai's criterion revealed a significant effect for the bully group, $F(8, 1562) = 7.93$, $p < 0.001$, $\eta^2 = 0.04$. Subsequent univariate analyses showed an

Table 13.4 Co-occurrence of Traditional Bullying, Cyberbullying, Traditional Victimization, and Cybervictimization. Results of the First Order CFA, Bonferroni Adjusted $\alpha = 0.003$.

Bully groups	*Victim groups*	*Gender distribution (descriptive information)*	*Variable patterns* $B_T B_C V_T V_C$	*Frequencies* *observed*	*expected*	*Statistics* p
Non-bully	non-victim	164 girls; 180 boys	**1111**	**344**	**233.60**	**0.000** ^{T}
	cybervictim only	4 girls; 2 boys	1112	6	7.27	0.319
	traditional victim only	162 girls; 124 boys	**1121**	**286**	**361.31**	**0.000** ^{A}
	combined victim	17 girls; 11 boys	**1122**	**28**	**61.81**	**0.000** ^{A}
Cyberbully only	non-victim	1 girl; 2 boys	1211	3	4.22	0.276
	cybervictim only	1 girl; 0 boys	1212	1	0.13	0.008
	traditional victim only	2 girls, 3 boys	1221	5	6.53	0.275
	combined victim	3 girls; 0 boys	1222	3	1.12	0.037
Traditional bully only	non-victim	62 girls; 85 boys	**2111**	**147**	**244.86**	**0.000** ^{A}
	cybervictim only	2 girls; 4 boys	2112	6	7.62	0.278
	traditional victim only	205 girls; 263 boys	**2121**	**468**	**378.73**	**0.000** ^{T}
	combined victim	47 girls; 28 boys	2122	75	64.79	0.102
Combined bully	non-victim	5 girls; 15 boys	2211	20	31.31	0.022
	cybervictim only	1 girl, 2 boys	2212	3	0.98	0.020
	traditional victim only	18 girls; 18 boys	2221	36	48.43	0.037
	combined victim	18 girls; 12 boys	**2222**	**30**	**8.29**	**0.000** ^{T}

Note: Variable patterns represent the systematic combination of four categorical variables: B_T = being a traditional bully (1 = no, 2 = yes), B_C = being a cyberbully (1 = no, 2 = yes), V_T = being a traditional victim (1 = no, 2 = yes), V_C = being a cybervictim (1 = no, 2 = yes). Superscripts mark types (T) and antitypes (A).

Table 13.5 Motives for Bullying in Bully Groups and by Gender.

Bully groups	*Power* *M (SD)*	*Affiliation* *M (SD)*	*Anger* *M (SD)*	*Fun* *M (SD)*
Cyberbully only (N = 12)	0.25 (0.62)$_a$	0.42 (0.79)	1.33 (1.37)	0.83 (1.27)
Traditional bully only (N = 696)	0.33 (0.73)$_a$	0.30 (0.68)$_a$	1.68 (1.19)	0.37 (0.73)$_a$
Combined bully (traditional and cyber) (N = 89)	0.86 (1.10)$_b$	0.76 (1.07)$_b$	1.81 (1.10)	0.96 (1.13)$_b$
Gender				
girl (N = 432)	0.28 (0.66)	0.28 (0.67)	1.58 (1.20)	0.33 (0.72)
boy (N = 365)	0.48 (0.89)	0.42 (0.80)	1.78 (1.17)	0.55 (0.88)

Note: Standard deviations (SD) are reported in parentheses; column means with different subscripts are significantly different, at least at $p < 0.05$. Motive scales range from 0 to 3.

effect on *power*, $F\,(2, 783) = 19.02, p < 0.001, \eta^2 = 0.05$, on *affiliation*, $F\,(2, 783) = 15.72, p < 0.001, \eta^2 = 0.04$, and on *fun*, $F\,(2, 783) = 23.44, p < 0.001, \eta^2 = 0.06$.

Alpha-corrected Bonferroni post hoc tests showed that combined bullies (traditional and cyber) scored higher in the three motives power, affiliation, and fun compared to traditional bullies only. Means and standard deviations are shown in Table 13.5.

Motives for bullying in bully-victim groups

We selected three groups of pupils for these analyses: traditional bullies only, traditional bully-victims and combined bully-victims. To check for differences between these three groups in the underlying motives of bullying, a MANOVA with bully-victim group and gender as factors and the four motives for bullying (power, affiliation, anger, and fun) as dependent variables was conducted (see endnote 3). Application of a multivariate test using Pillai's criterion revealed a significant effect on bully-victim group, $F\,(8, 1260) = 4.02, p < 0.001, \eta^2 = 0.03$, and on gender, $F\,(4, 629) = 2.45, p < 0.05, \eta^2 = 0.02$.

Subsequent univariate analyses showed an effect for bully-victim groups on all four motives: *power*, $F\,(2, 632) = 3.28, p < 0.05, \eta^2 = 0.01$; *affiliation*, $F\,(2, 632) = 5.75, p < 0.01, \eta^2 = 0.02$; *anger*, $F\,(2, 632) = 7.20, p < 0.01, \eta^2 = 0.02$; and *fun*, $F\,(2, 632) = 3.81, p < 0.05, \eta^2 = 0.01$. Subsequent univariate analyses showed an effect for gender on two motives: *power*, $F\,(1, 632) = 3.79, p < 0.10, \eta^2 = 0.01$, and *fun*, $F\,(1, 632) = 6.94, p < 0.01, \eta^2 = 0.01$. Alpha-corrected Bonferroni post hoc tests revealed that that combined bully-victims (traditional and cyber) scored higher in the motives of power, affiliation, and fun compared to traditional bully-victims. Moreover, traditional bully-victims scored higher on the anger scale compared to traditional bullies. In addition, boys scored higher in power and fun than girls. Means and standard deviations are shown in Table 13.6.

Table 13.6 Motives for Bullying in Bully-Victim Groups and by Gender.

Bully-victim groups	*Power* *M (SD)*	*Affiliation* *M (SD)*	*Anger* *M (SD)*	*Fun* *M (SD)*
Traditional bully only (N=147)	0.37 (0.83)	0.24 (0.65) $_{a}$	1.33 (1.20) $_{a}$	0.45 (0.85)
Traditional bully-victims only (N=468)	0.32 (0.71) $_{a+}$	0.30 (0.66) $_{a}$	1.76 (1.18) $_{b}$	0.35 (0.72) $_{a+}$
Combined bully-victims (traditional and cyber) (N = 30)	0.65 (1.05) $_{b+}$	0.73 (1.13) $_{b}$	1.59 (1.26)	0.67 (1.03) $_{b+}$
Gender				
girl (N=285)	0.24 (0.62) $_{a+}$	0.24 (0.64)	1.54 (1.22)	0.25 (0.63) $_{a}$
boy (N=360)	0.43 (0.85) $_{b+}$	0.35 (0.73)	1.74 (1.18)	0.50 (0.85) $_{b}$

Note: Standard deviations (SD) are reported in parentheses; column means with different subscripts are significantly different at least at $p < 0.05$. Marginal differences are additionally indicated with +. Motive scales range from 0 to 3.

Discussion

Our intention was to investigate whether students belonging to particular groups of bullies (traditional, cyber, or combined) and bully-victims differed regarding their motives for bullying others. Extending the existing literature, this was the first quantitative study focusing on the motives behind cyberbullying. Based on the literature on instrumental and reactive aggression, we investigated four potentially relevant motives: power, affiliation, anger, and fun. Furthermore, we considered cyberbullying to potentially co-occur with traditional bullying, traditional victimization, and cybervictimization. Therefore, we controlled for these variables in the analyses and compared different bully-groups (traditional, cyber, or combined) and bully-victim groups regarding their motives.

Identification of bully and bully-victim groups

In line with previous studies (Li, 2006; Raskauskas & Stoltz, 2007; Smith et al., 2008; Gradinger et al., 2009), we found cyberbullying and cybervictimization to occur infrequently compared to traditional forms. Frequency rates of students involved in cybervictimization (10%) and cyberbullying (7%) were even lower than findings from other countries, ranging between 11% and 49% for cybervictimization and 10% and 22% for cyberbullying. This is an interesting result because we used the most inclusive criterion possible to identify cyberbullies and cybervictims, and included all students who had been bullied or bullied others in cyberspace at least once during the last two months. Because cyberbullying and cybervictimization were such rare phenomena, we used this very inclusive criterion to be able to make any comparisons with traditional bullying and victimization. Moreover, in Austria the distribution of mobile phones, computers, and the Internet in young people is high, and prevalence rates of traditional bullying and traditional victimization are also high in cross-national comparative studies (Currie et al., 2008; Statistik Austria, 2008).

The low frequency of cyberbullying and cybervictimization may be due to some country-specific characteristics which cannot be determined as long as cross-national studies are lacking. Interestingly, the rates of cyberbullying and cyber-victimization in the present study were slightly higher than in a previous study conducted in Austria about one year earlier (Gradinger et al., 2009). In this previous study, 7% of adolescents aged 14 to 19 years were found to be involved in cybervictimization and 5% were found to be involved in cyberbullying. It is difficult to say whether these figures represent a real increase in cyberbullying and cyber-victimization in Austrian youth without systematic, nationwide studies conducted on a regular basis.

Gender differences in cyberbullying and cybervictimization also remain unclear in Austria, because no consistent patterns could be revealed compared with the previous study (Gradinger et al., 2009). In the present study, more girls (13%) than boys (8%) were found to be involved in cybervictimization; however, no gender differences were found in cyberbullying. In the previous study, more boys (8%) than girls (5%) were found to be involved in cyberbullying and no gender differences were found in cybervictimization (Gradinger et al., 2009). These inconsistencies concerning gender differences have also been found in international studies. Some studies report more girls than boys being cybervictims (Kowalski & Limber, 2007; Ybarra et al., 2007; Smith et al., 2008), but not all studies have found these results. Thus, gender effects might remain unclear until systematic, cross-national studies are conducted.

To identify different bully and bully-victim groups we applied the same procedure as described in Gradinger et al. (2009). By systematically combining traditional bullying, cyberbullying, traditional victimization, and cybervictimization we were able to identify all groups of bullies, bully-victims, and victims described in the previous study. Given the many inconsistencies in research on cyberbullying, we regard this as a remarkable result. Looking at bully groups and confirming results presented in Gradinger et al. (2009), we found more students than expected by chance being combined bullies (traditional and cyber) and fewer students than expected by chance being cyberbullies. In other words, students rarely behaved exclusively as cyberbullies, but were mostly also traditional bullies, thus forming the "combined bully" group.

Looking at bully-victim groups, we were also able to confirm the results reported in Gradinger et al. (2009). Compared with a chance model, students were over-represented in the traditional bully-victim group, the combined bully-victim groups (traditional and cyber), and the uninvolved group. These consistencies in results highlight the importance of simultaneously looking at both traditional and cyber forms of bullying and victimization to be able to appropriately identify at-risk groups of students. Therefore, research on cyberbullying should take these co-occurences seriously in order to not misattribute findings to cyberbullying and cybervictimization, when in fact they might reflect involvement in traditional bullying and victimization.

Motives for bullying in bully groups and bully-victim groups

We used these bully and bully-victim groups for further analyses. In the first analysis, we looked at bully groups (traditional, cyber or combined). For cyberbullies only, the main motive to bully others was anger, followed by fun, followed by relatively low levels of affiliation and power. For traditional bullies only, the main motive behind bullying others was anger. The other three motives were mentioned comparatively rarely. Anger was also mentioned most often as a motive by combined bullies. However, in this group fun, power, and affiliation were also often mentioned. Interestingly, the three bully groups did not differ from each other regarding anger; however, combined bullies had higher levels of power, affiliation, and fun compared with traditional bullies.

The relatively high importance of anger as a motive in the three groups confirms a developmental pattern already found in other studies (Roland & Idsoe, 2001; Salmivalli & Niemenen, 2002). Preadolescents bully others both out of anger and to reach particular goals like dominance or power. Our study also shows that for cyberbullies or combined bullies anger is an important motive. However, combined bullies also pursue very strong instrumental motives (power, affiliation, and fun) compared with traditional bullies. Exactly the same result was also found in our previous study (Gradinger et al., 2009). This suggests that combined bullies are very aware of their actions. They bully others not only to cope with their anger, but also to reach particular goals. In this sense, they are goal oriented and teachers, counsellors, parents, victims, or observers need to be aware of that.

In a second step, we looked at bully-victim groups. We compared three groups: combined bully-victims, traditional bully-victims, and traditional bullies. Again, for all three groups anger was the most important motive for bullying others. However, there were differences between the groups. Traditional bully-victims had higher levels of anger than tradional bullies. Combined bully-victims did not differ in anger from the other two groups; however, they scored higher in the power, acceptance, and fun motives than traditional bully-victims. Furthermore, we detected gender differences. Boys more often chose motives of power and fun than did girls. While there is also evidence in traditional bullying and aggression research that boys of that age group score higher in power motives than girls (Roland & Idsøe, 2001; Little et al., 2003), there is not enough knowledge regarding gender differences regarding the fun motive.

Our research demonstrates how important it is to consider both traditional and cyber forms of bullying and victimization simultaneously to be able to draw appropriate conclusions about associated aspects, such as motives for bullying.

Limitations of the present study

Despite the benefits of our study we also want to discuss some limitations. First, for the measurement of cyberbullying and cybervictimization, we relied on single item measurements. Although both items comprised all relevant forms of cyberbullying others and being cybervictimized discussed in the literature (e.g., text messages, email, videos, or photos) we believe these forms should be measured separately in future studies (as in Smith et al., 2008). The single item measurement might have resulted in a systematic underestimation of frequency rates of involvement in cyberbullying and cybervictimization. A related issue and possible shortcoming of the present study is that we had to use the most inclusive criterion for categorizations. As a consequence we systematically neglected the repetitive nature of cyberbullying and cybervictimization proposed in several definitions (e.g., Smith et al., 2008). In future studies, multiple item measurements for cyberbullying and cybervictimization should be used and frequent cyberbullies and cybervictims should be distinguished from occasional cyberbullies and cybervictims in the analyses.

Furthermore, although the fun motive is somehow neglected in the literature, it turned out to be important, especially for cyberbullying behavior (e.g., Raskauskas & Stoltz, 2007). Thus, we suggest including some more instrumental motives (such as boredom or loneliness) to better understand why some students bully others.

Implications

To date, only two large-scale studies have been conducted on cyberbullying in Austria. In the first study, 761 adolescents aged 14 to 19 years participated (Gradinger et al., 2009), while in the present study 1461 preadolescents aged 10 to 15 years were surveyed. Although both studies comprised large samples, there is still an urgent need to conduct further studies on cyberbullying in Austria to better understand this new phenomenon. Nevertheless, we believe that these two studies clearly demonstrate that cyberbullying and cybervictimization co-occur with traditional bullying and traditional victimization. We regard this as an important result which has important implications for practice, policy, theory, and research.

Practice

Our research demonstrated that virtually no student can be labelled as a "pure" cyberbully or "pure" cybervictim. Out of 1461 students we only found 7 girls and 5 boys who harassed others exclusively using mobile phones or on the Internet. On the other hand, 89 students (6%) were identified as bullying others both traditionally *and* in cyberspace. Both in adolescents and preadolescents, these combined groups of bullies and victims showed the highest levels in both externalizing and internalizing problems. Thus, our research identified these combined groups as risk groups for adjustment problems.

Thus when dealing with cases of cyberbullying or cybervictimization we advise practitioners to also find out about involvement in traditional forms of harassment. In most cases, the involvement in cyberbullying or cybervictimization will turn out to be the tip of the iceberg, because the student will also be involved in several other forms of bullying and victimization. Therefore, cyberbullying should be dealt with in the same way as traditional bullying. All measures applicable for dealing with traditional bullying can be recommended to tackle cyberbullying. Effective approaches include school-level, class–level, and individual-level measures and should focus on both intervention and prevention. Generally speaking, we recommend the application of evidence-based programs which have undergone rigorous evaluations and proven their effectiveness (Spiel, 2009).

Policy

In Austria, both violence prevention and safe Internet use by children and young people are issues of public concern. In 2007, a national strategy to prevent violence in kindergartens and schools was developed and has been implemented step by step. Cyberbullying is also covered in the national action plan. Information, guidelines, and other resources to tackle cyberbullying can be found on a national website (www.gemeinsam-gegen-gewalt.at). Although rates of cyberbullying are currently comparatively low in Austria, our data indicate that they may be increasing. In a study conducted in 2007, 7% of adolescents were found to be involved in cybervictimization and 5% were found to be involved in cyberbullying at least once. In a study conducted in 2009, 10% of preadolescents were found to be involved in cybervictimization and cyberbullying, while 7% were found to be involved in cyberbullying at least once in the last two months. Systematic, nationwide studies which are conducted on a regular basis are needed to determine whether there has been an increase in cyberbullying and cybervictimization in Austrian youth or not.

Theory

Our studies might contribute to theory building in two important ways. First, to identify risk groups of students we applied a person-centered approach to data analyses. Given the huge overlap between cyberbullying, cybervictimization, traditional bullying, and traditional victimization we consider this an appropriate approach for studying bullying in cyberspace. Also, when applying variable centered approaches to data analyses, we strongly recommend controlling for traditional forms of bullying and victimization in all studies on cyberbullying, so as not to misattribute findings. Second, our research contributes to a better understanding of instrumental aggression in youth. We suggest that research should not be restricted to status goals (such as power), but should also include affiliation goals and fun when studying bullying or cyberbullying. Based on our study and on the study conducted by Raskauskas and Stoltz (2007), fun seems to be a particularly important motive for bullying others via mobile phone or the Internet.

Future research

There is an urgent need to conduct further studies on cyberbullying. Country-comparative, representative studies would be very important to better understand basic issues such as the age and gender effects of cyberbullying. Moreover, it is necessary to replicate our findings on the co-occurrence of cyberbullying, cybervictimization, traditional bullying, and traditional victimization in other countries. Furthermore, it is worthwhile investigating further the combined groups identified as being at risk of adjustment problems. In our studies we did not distinguish students according to the severity of their involvement in bullying and victimization, but instead used an inclusive criterion for classification. Thus, it is possible that there is an even more at-risk group within the combined groups which we have overlooked with our approach.

Last, but not least, we consider the static view of present studies on cyberbullying as a severe limitation. Although bullying and cyberbullying are defined as processes that unfold over a certain period of time, longitudinal studies are notably lacking. Therefore, we recommend conducting short-term longitudinal studies by which it is possible to investigate processes unfolding over a certain period of time. Such a design could help to answer the important question of how traditional bullying and cyberbullying are acted out simultaneously.

Notes

1 The terminology is not consistent in the literature. Instead of the term "mechanisms" the terms "functions" or "motive systems" are used synonymously. To avoid confusion for the reader, in this chapter the term "motive" is used.

2 The very high number of traditional bullies in this study is comparable to the WHO study on Health Behavior in School-aged Children (Craig & Harel, 2004), which reported bullying rates in Austria ranging between 29.9% and 65.7%.

3 Because developmental effects are still unclear in research on cyberbullying, we also conducted a MANCOVA with age as the covariate. Age could not be determined as being of significance. Multivariate and univariate results were identical to the results of the MANOVA.

References

Atria, M., & Spiel, C. (2003). The Austrian situation: Many initiatives against violence, few evaluations. In P. K. Smith (Ed.), *Violence in schools: The response in Europe* (pp. 83–99). London: Routledge/Falmer.

Bandura, A. (1973). *Aggression: a social learning analysis*. Englewood Cliffs, NJ: Prentice-Hall.

Bandura, A. (1983). Psychological mechanisms of aggression. In R. G. Green & E. I. Donnerstein (Eds.), *Aggression: Theoretical and empirical views* (Vol. 1, pp. 1–40). New York: Academic Press.

Berkowitz, L. (1989). Frustration–aggression hypothesis: Examination and reformulation. *Psychological Bulletin, 106*, 59–73.

Berkowitz, L. (1993). *Aggression: Its causes, consequences, and control*. New York: McGraw-Hill.

Bildungsmedien Zentrum. (2007). *1. Oberösterreichische Kinder-Medien-Studie. Das Medienverhalten von Kindern aus dem Blickwinkel von Kindern im Alter von 6 bis 10 Jahren sowie Eltern von Kindern im Alter von 3 bis 10 Jahren und PädagogInnen [First upper Austrian children media study. Children's media behavior from the children's, parents,' and educators' perspective]*. Retrieved July 28, 2011 from www.bimez.at/uploads/media/pdf/medienpaedagogik/jugend_medien_studie09/bericht_eltern.pdf

Bildungsmedien Zentrum. (2008). *1. Oberösterreichische Jugend-Medien-Studie. Das Medienverhalten der 11- bis 18-jährigen in OÖ [First upper Austrian children media- study. Media behavior of adolescents]*. Retrieved July 28, 2011 from www.bimez.at/uploads/media/pdf/medienpaedagogik/jugend_medien_studie09/bericht_jugendliche.pdf

Buhrmeister, D. (1996). Need fulfillment, interpersonal competence, and the developmental contexts of early adolescent friendship. In W. M. Bukowski, A. F. Newcomb & W. Hartup (Eds.), *The company they keep: Friendship in childhood and adolescence* (pp. 158–185). New York: Cambridge University Press.

Card, N. A., & Little, T. D. (2006). Proactive and reactive aggression in childhood and adolescence: A meta-analysis of differential relations with psychosocial adjustment. *International Journal of Behavioral Development, 30*, 466–480.

Craig, W. M., & Harel, Y. (2004). Bullying, physical fighting and victimization. In C. Currie (Ed.), *Health behavior in school-aged children: A WHO cross-national study* (pp. 133–144). Geneva: WHO.

Currie, C., Gabhainn, S., Godeau, E., Roberts, C., Smith, R., Currie, D., Pickett, W., Richter, M., Morgan, A., & Barnekow, V. (2008). *Inequalities in young people's health. HBSC international report from the 2005/2006 survey*. Copenhagen: World Health Organization.

Dodge, K. A. (1991). The structure and function of reactive and proactive aggression. In D. Pepler & K. Rubin (Eds.), *The development and treatment of childhood aggression* (pp. 201–218). Hillsdale, NJ: Erlbaum.

Dodge, K. A., & Coie, J. D. (1987). Social information processing factors in reactive and proactive aggression in children's playgroups. *Journal of Personality and Social Psychology, 53*, 1146–1158.

Dodge, K. A., Lochman, J. E., Harnish, J. D., Bates, J. E., & Pettit, G. S. (1997). Reactive and proactive aggression in school children and psychiatrically impaired chronically assaultive youth. *Journal of Abnormal Psychology, 106*, 37–51.

Dollard, D. J., Doob, L. W., Miller, N. E., Mowrer, O. H., & Sears, R. R. (1939). *Frustration and aggression*. New Haven, CT: Yale University Press.

European Commission. (2004). *Special Eurobarometer. Illegal and harmful content on the Internet*. Retrieved July 28, 2011 from http://ec.europa.eu/information_society/activities/sip/docs/eurobarometer/eurobarometer_2003_15_ms.pdf

European Commission. (2006). *Special Eurobarometer. Safer Internet*. Retrieved July 28, 2011 from http://ec.europa.eu/information_society/activities/sip/docs/eurobarometer/eurobarometer_2005_25_ms.pdf

European Commission. (2007). *Eurobarometer 2007. Safer Internet for children—a children's perspective. National Analysis: Austria*. Retrieved July 28, 2011 from http://ec.europa.eu/information_society/activities/sip/docs/eurobarometer/qualitative_study_2007/austria.pdf

European Commission. (2008). *Flash Eurobarometer. Towards a safer use of the Internet for children in the EU—a parents' perspective*. Retrieved July 28, 2011 from http://ec.europa.eu/information_society/activities/sip/docs/eurobarometer/analyticalreport_2008.pdf

Fandrem, H., Strohmeier, D., & Roland, E. (2009). Bullying and victimization among Norwegian and immigrant adolescents in Norway: The role of proactive and reactive aggressiveness. *Journal of Early Adolescence, 29*, 898–923.

Gradinger, P., Strohmeier, D., & Spiel, C. (2009). Traditional bullying and cyberbullying: Identification of risk groups for adjustment problems. *Zeitschrift für Psychologie/Journal of Psychology, 217*, 205–213.

Juvonen, J., & Gross, E. F. (2008). Extending the school grounds? Bullying experiences in cyberspace. *Journal of School Health, 78*, 496–505.

Katzer, C., Fetchenhauer, D., & Belschak, F. (2009). Cyberbullying in Internet chatrooms—Wer sind die Täter? *Zeitschrift für Entwicklungspsychologie und Pädagogische Psychologie, 41*, 33–44.

Kowalski, R. M., & Limber, S. P. (2007). Electronic bullying among middle school students. *Journal of Adolescent Health, 41*, 22–30.

Li, Q. (2006). Cyberbullying in schools. A research of gender differences. *School Psychology International, 27*, 157–170.

Li, Q. (2007a). Bullying in the new playground: Research into cyberbullying and cyber victimisation. *Australasian Journal of Educational Technology, 23*, 435–454.

Li, Q. (2007b). New bottle but old wine: A research of cyberbullying in schools. *Computers in Human Behavior, 23*, 1777–1791.

Lienert, G. A. (1969). Die "Konfigurenzfrequenzanalyse" als Klassifikationsmethode in der Klinischen Psychology [Configural frequency analyses as classification method in clinical psychology]. In M. Irle (Ed.), *Bericht über den 26. Kongress der Deutschen Gesellschaft für Psychologie* (S. 244–253) [*Report about the 26th congress of the German Society for Psychology*] (pp. 244–253). Gottingen: Hogrefe.

Little, T. D., Jones, S. M., Henrich, C. C., & Hawley, P. H. (2003). Disentangling the "whys" from the "whats" of aggressive behavior. *International Journal of Behavioral Development, 27*, 122–133.

Ojanen, T., Aunola, K., & Salmivalli, C. (2007). Situation-specificity of children's social goals: Changing goals according to changing situations? *International Journal of Behavioral Development, 31*, 232–341.

Olweus, D. (1993). *Bullying at school: What we know and what we can do*. Oxford: Blackwell.

Olweus, D. (1996). *The Revised Olweus Bully-Victim Questionnaire*. Mimeo Bergen, Norway: Research Center for Health Promotion (HEMIL Center), University of Bergen.

Poulin, F., & Boivin, M. (2000). Reactive and proactive aggression: Evidence of a two-factor model. *Psychological Assessment, 12*, 115–122.

Raskauskas, J., & Stoltz, A. D. (2007). Involvement in traditional and electronic bullying among adolescents. *Developmental Psychology, 43*, 564–575.

Roland, E., & Idsøe, T. (2001). Aggression and bullying. *Aggressive Behavior, 27*, 446–462.

Salmivalli, C., & Nieminen, E. (2002). Proactive and reactive aggression among school bullies, victims, and bully-victims. *Aggressive Behavior, 28*, 30–44.

Smith, P. K., Mahdavi, J., Carvalho, M., Fisher, S., Russell, S., & Tippett, N. (2008). Cyberbullying: Its nature and impact in secondary school pupils. *Journal of Child Psychology and Psychiatry, 49*, 376–385.

Solberg, M. E., Olweus, D., & Endresen, I. M. (2007). Bullies and victims at school: Are they the same pupils? *British Journal of Educational Psychology, 77*, 441–464.

Spiel, C. (2009). Evidenzbasierte Bildungspolitik und Bildungspraxis—eine Fiktion? Problemaufriss, Thesen, Anregungen [Evidence-based education policy and educational practice—a fiction? Problem, theses, and suggestions]. *Psychologische Rundschau, 60*, 255–256.

Spiel, C., & Strohmeier, D. (2007). *Generalstrategie zur Gewaltprävention an österreichischen Schulen und Kindergärten [National strategy for violence prevention in Austrian schools and kindergarten]*. Vienna: University of Vienna.

Spiel, C., & Strohmeier, D. (in press). National strategy for violence prevention in Austrian schools and kindergarten: Development and implementation. *International Journal of Behavioral Development.*

Spiel, C., & von Eye, A. (2000). Application of Configural Frequency Analysis in educational research. *Psychologische Beitrage, 42*, 515–525.

Statistik Austria. (2008). *IKT-Einsatz in Haushalten [Use of information and communication technologies within households]*. Vienna: Statistik Austria.

Strohmeier, D., & Spiel, C. (2009). Gewalt in der Schule: Vorkommen, Prävention, Intervention [Violence at school: Prevalence, prevention, intervention]. In W. Specht (Ed.), *Nationaler Bildungsbericht. Österreich 2009. Band 2: Fokussierte Analysen bildungspolitischer Schwerpunktthemen [National report of education. Austria 2009. Volume 2]* (pp. 269–286). Graz: Leykam.

Sutton, J., Smith, P. K., & Swettenham, J. (1999). Bullying and "theory of mind": A critique of the "social skills deficit" view of antisocial behavior. *Social Development, 8*, 117–127.

Vaillancourt, T., McDougall, P., Hymel, S., Krygsman, A., Miller, J., Stiver, K., & Davis, C. (2008). Bullying: Are researchers and children/youth talking about the same thing? *International Journal of Behavioral Development, 32*, 486–495.

Vitaro, F., & Brendgen, M. (2005). Proactive and reactive aggression: A developmental perspective. In R. E. Tremblay, W. W. Hartup, & J. Archer (Eds.), *Developmental origins of aggression* (pp. 178–201). New York: Guilford Press.

Vitaro, F., Brendgen, M., & Barker, E. D. (2006). Subtypes of aggressive behaviors: A developmental perspective. *International Journal of Behavioral Development, 30*, 12–19.

von Eye, A. (2002). *Configural Frequency Analysis—Methods, models, and applications.* Mahwah, NJ: Erlbaum.

von Eye, A., Mun, E. Y., & Bogat, G. A. (2008). Temporal patterns of variable relationships in person-oriented research: Longitudinal models of configural frequency analysis. *Developmental Psychology, 44*, 437–445.

Ybarra, M. L., Diener-West, M., & Leaf, P. J. (2007). Examining the overlap in Internet harassment and school bullying: Implications for school intervention. *Journal of Adolescent Health, 41*, 42–50.

Ybarra, M. L., & Mitchell, K. J. (2004). Online aggressor/targets, aggressors, and targets: A comparison of associated youth characteristics. *Journal of Child Psychology and Psychiatry, 45*, 1308–1316.

Part VII

Research and Intervention in Cyberbullying

14

Understanding and Preventing Cyberbullying

Where Have We Been and Where Should We Be Going?

Donna Cross, Qing Li, Peter K. Smith, and Helen Monks

This book contributes to an understanding of cyberbullying, its nature, harmful effects, and correlates of this behavior as it affects young people. Many previous publications on cyberbullying have focused on studies in North America. However, in this book we have presented findings from eleven countries: Australia, Austria, Canada, England, Finland, Italy, Japan, Portugal, Spain, South Korea, and the United States. By providing a range of cultural perspectives, this collection of research aims to contribute new knowledge about the cross-cultural issues relevant to cyberbullying, and the generality or specificity of findings. Beyond that, we hope to develop more effective strategies to prevent and reduce harm from cyberbullying. This chapter discusses some issues arising from the research presented in the twelve empirical studies in this book, and considers the implications of this and other relevant research for the design, development, and evaluation of cyberbullying interventions.

Cross-Cultural Issues

Cyberbullying is clearly an important issue in all the countries represented in this book. It may vary in importance according to country, however. Thus in Finland (Chapter 4, Figure 4.1), involvement in cyberbullying appears to be relatively minor compared to traditional bullying. In Austria too (Chapter 13, Table 13.1), traditional bullying is considerably more frequent than cyberbullying. Nonetheless, other studies have found cyberbullying to account for perhaps a quarter to a third of all bullying (Smith et al., 2008; Tokunaga, 2010). In South Korea, cyberbullying

Cyberbullying in the Global Playground: Research from International Perspectives, First Edition.
Edited by Qing Li, Donna Cross, and Peter K. Smith.

accounts for a similar fraction of all bullying (Chapter 10, Figure 10.1), or indeed exceeds traditional bullying if online game bullying is taken into account.

Two chapters in this book provide direct cross-cultural comparisons. Genta et al. (Chapter 2, Table 2.4) compare rates of mobile phone and Internet victimization and bullying in Italy, England, and Spain. While the differences are not huge, cyberbullying is generally lower in Spain, and in three out of four comparisons is highest in Italy. Aoyama et al. (Chapter 9, Table 9.1) compared two measures of cyberbullying victimization, and corresponding measures of cyberbullying, in Japan and the US. In all cases, rates in Japan were considerably lower than in the US.

What might account for these cultural differences, where exactly corresponding methodology was used? Two methodological issues need to be borne in mind first. Language issues may be important. Terms such as "bullied" or "cyberbullied" (Chapter 2) and even terms such as "mean" or "nasty" (Chapter 9) have to be translated, and meanings in different languages may not be exactly equivalent (Smith, Cowie, Olafsson, & Liefooghe, 2002). Also, for realistic country comparisons, samples must be adequate; samples were acknowledged to be small, and thus the cross-cultural comparisons only provisional, in Aoyama et al. (Chapter 9).

If the cross-cultural differences are real, then what can account for them? Obviously, one aspect may be the availability and use of new technologies. However, this cannot account for the apparently low rates of cyberbullying in Finland, or in South Korea, where ICT use is very widespread. Local and national policies on bullying and on cyberbullying may be important—an explanation invoked by Genta et al. (Chapter 2) to explain high rates in Italy, where there is no national policy in place. The nature of educational systems and the extent of personal and social education in the curriculum may be a factor. At the societal level, there are relevant aspects such as the extent of violence in the media, and the extent to which bullying-like or abusive behaviors are tolerated in everyday life. The Hofstede categories, especially those of individualism–collectivism, power distance, and masculinity–femininity, may also provide useful insights; for example, the individualism–collectivism dimension has been invoked to understand aspects of bullying in Eastern cultures such as Japan and South Korea (Kanetsuna, Smith, & Morita, 2006).

The differences in frequency of cyberbullying between cultures may be appreciable, but the types of phenomenon appear similar, as do many correlates and consequences, as reviewed below. As indicated in the title of our book, cyberbullying takes place in a "global playground," and this, arguably, lessens the impact of national boundaries. Nevertheless, there are also likely to be cultural differences beyond simply the overall frequency of cyberbullying. The incidence of online game bullying in South Korea (Chapter 10) is one example from this book.

Overlap of Traditional Bullying and Cyberbullying

One of the most well established findings in the literature on cyberbullying so far is the substantial—but not complete—overlap between involvement in traditional and in cyber forms (e.g., Beran & Li, 2007; Raskauskas & Stoltz, 2007;

Hinduja & Patchin, 2008; Smith et al., 2008; Cross et al., 2009; Vandebosch & van Cleemput, 2009). This is also reported in this book, by Salmivalli and Pöyhönen (Chapter 4), Cross et al. (Chapter 5), Holfeld and Grabe (Chapter 7), and Gradinger et al. (Chapter 13). For instance, the Australian Covert Bullying Prevalence Study (ACBPS) found that most (87%) of those students who were victimized via technology also reported being bullied in other ways, and likewise, most (77%) of those students who cyberbully others also report they bully students in other ways (Cross et al., 2009). However, Tippett and Kwak (Chapter 10) found no significant correlation between traditional and cyber-involvement behaviors in their sample of South Korean young people.

The high overlap of these behaviors in many cultures suggests that research on interventions to reduce traditional school-based bullying may also be useful to reduce cyberbullying—something established empirically in the KiVa project in Finland (Chapter 4).

Gender Differences and Other Personal Characteristics

Unlike the clear patterns of gender-related traditional bullying behavior, gender differences in cyberbullying are less clear. This was remarked on in reviews by Tokunaga (2010) and Smith (2011). Some studies report no gender differences (Ybarra & Mitchell, 2004; Hinduja & Patchin, 2008). Salmivalli and Pöyhönen (Chapter 4) report that Finnish boys are more likely to be cyberbullied and cyberbully others than girls. Genta et al. (Chapter 2, Table 2.2) generally find little difference in being a victim of cyberbullying, but boys were more involved in perpetration. Gradinger et al. (Chapter 13) found that, in Austria, girls were more involved as occasional victims, and boys more involved as frequent perpetrators. Cross et al. (Chapter 5) found that Australian girls were more likely to be cyberbullied and less likely to perpetrate cyberbullying than boys. But in the US, Holfeld and Grabe (Chapter 7) and Bauman (Chapter 8, Figure 8.1) report more females perpetrating and being targets of cyberbullying. These inconsistent findings may reflect sample differences, and also which types of cyberbullying are occurring; there is some evidence of girls being more involved in social networking sites than boys, in recent years, and hence being more exposed to potential abusive acts in that domain (Smith, 2011).

Research on cyberbullying also needs to consider other more specific sub-populations which may be at greater risk, such as young people who are hearing impaired, as described by Bauman in Chapter 8. Almeida et al. (Chapter 11) demonstrate that (at least in some categories) involvement is predicted by a lack of cognitive and affective empathy, and greater moral disengagement.

The Impact of Cyberbullying

The negative effects of traditional bullying have long been established (Hawker & Boulton, 2000). For victims these include lowered self-esteem, greater risk of psychosomatic symptoms and depression, and lack of trust in relationships. There are issues about cause and effect—for example, does being victimized cause lower self-esteem, or does lower self-esteem make becoming a victim more likely? But longitudinal studies have suggested that victimization has some definite causal effects or consequences, even if the possibility of some bi-directional influence is acknowledged (Arseneault, Bowes, & Shakoor, 2009).

Previous research has found being cyberbullied to be associated with greater likelihood of depressive symptomatology (Ybarra, 2004), psychosomatic problems (headaches, recurring abdominal pain, difficulty sleeping), emotional and peer problems, and high levels of perceived difficulties (Sourander et al., 2010), as well as conduct and behavior problems such as substance use, stealing, school disciplinary problems, and assault (Hinduja & Patchin, 2007; Sourander et al., 2010).

But how do effects of involvement in cyberbullying compare with the effects of involvement in traditional bullying? The research reported by Brighi et al. (Chapter 3, Tables 3.5 and 3.6) suggests a strong association between being cyberbullied and its effects on self esteem and loneliness, especially when one's reputation is attacked online. Yet on seven out of ten measures, those only cyberbullied were less affected than those only traditionally bullied (Table 3.7); some additive or synergistic effects were also found (i.e. those active in both traditional and cyber domains were most affected). Correspondingly, Menesini et al. (Chapter 12, Tables 12.2–12.5) found that cybervictimization was associated with internalizing symptoms, while cyberbullying was associated with externalizing symptoms. Again, an interesting aspect of Menesini et al.'s chapter is the comparison with the effects of traditional bullying. By and large, the effects of cybervictimization and cyberbullying, while significant, were less than those of traditional bullying, although there were a few additive or synergistic effects. These findings (from Italy, England, and Spain) are very much in line with findings from Austria reported by Gradinger, Strohmeier, and Spiel (2009), in relation to depression and psychosomatic symptoms. They are also in line with student estimates of effects, reported by Smith et al. (2008) in England. Hinduja and Patchin (2010) found that being a victim of cyberbullying was significantly associated with suicidal thoughts; but again at a comparable level to the association with traditional bullying.

The many characteristics of cyberbullying, described in Chapter 1, might lead one to suppose that the effects of cyberbullying involvement would be particularly great; for example, the breadth of potential audience and the difficulty of getting respite. However, the evidence seems to suggest that, by and large, the effects are not greater than for traditional bullying, and sometimes less. This may be because young people do ultimately see this as a virtual world, such that they are not "really" hurt. However, such a conclusion invites a number of cautionary comments. First, young people vary: Some can take a blasé attitude to cyberspace, but others (perhaps more often girls, to whom social networking can often be more important than to boys) are more affected (Ortega, Elipe, Mora-Merchán, Calmaestra, & Vega, 2009). Second, the type of cyberbullying is important; it is easier to shrug off some nasty emails, than it is to ignore "happy slapping" where degrading video clips are circulated around many of one's peers (Smith et al., 2008). Third, methods of cyberbullying are continually developing, so (as in many other areas) judgments about the relative impact of cyberbullying may change from one year to the next.

The negative effects of involvement in both traditional and cyberbullying present challenges to schools, parents, and others concerned with the welfare of children and young people. In the remainder of this chapter we focus on what can be done to reduce cyberbullying. While the special nature of cyberbullying means that some more specialized actions may be necessary, the long history of work on traditional bullying, and the high overlap of involvement (in most studies) means that methods for dealing with bullying generally are very relevant (see also Chapter 4).

School-Based Bullying Interventions

Bullying is a systemic problem with multiple factors associated with its manifestation. Accordingly, single-level programs such as classroom curriculum only, or targeted interventions engaging only higher risk young people, while necessary, are not sufficient to provide an effective and sustainable response (Smith, Schneider, Smith, & Ananiadou, 2004; Vreeman & Carroll, 2007). Consequently multidimensional (systemic) whole-school programs incorporating both prevention and intervention elements are more likely to be effective (Vreeman & Carroll, 2007; Rigby & Slee, 2008). A whole-school approach is collaborative and systematic, targeting bullying prevention and reduction at all levels of a school's ecology, including students, parents, teachers, and other school staff, as well as the wider community (Rigby & Slee, 2008). Such an approach is consistent with ecological frameworks of human development (Bronfenbrenner, 1977), which propose that bullying behaviors are influenced by a broad range of individual and contextual factors, including both the immediate and more distal settings in which young people engage.

Farrington and Ttofi (2009b) analyzed 44 high-quality evaluations of school-based bullying programs conducted from 1983 to May 2009. This review (and a subsequent one; see Ttofi and Farrington, 2011) concluded that school-based bullying programs, especially those that provide a comprehensive approach, are effective in reducing bullying perpetration and victimization, achieving on average a 20–23% reduction in rates of perpetration, and a 17–20% reduction in rates of victimization.

Effective Strategies Within a Whole-School Anti-Bullying Intervention

The meta-analyses and reviews of anti-bullying programs undertaken to date (Rigby, 2002; Smith et al., 2004; Baldry & Farrington, 2007; Farrington & Ttofi, 2009a; Ttofi & Farrington, 2011) have augmented our understanding of how to enhance program effectiveness. Until recently, largely because research reports may lack sufficient detail to allow for reanalyses of data, it was difficult to disentangle the effects of each component of the multilevel whole-school approach (Baldry & Farrington, 2007). In their meta-analysis, Farrington and Ttofi (2009a) sought to identify the effective components of school-based bullying programs by correlating these program components with weighted mean effect sizes for victimization and perpetration. Some reservations are in order with their conclusions. As the programs reviewed span a 20-year period, there are historical limitations—program components change and develop over time, and some interventions, such as restorative justice, have only been applied in the school context in recent years. There are also issues around how terms such as "disciplinary measures" are defined. Nevertheless, to date this provides the best indication of which program components are most important, and we take them as a starting point for analysis and discussion.

The program components that they found to be most highly associated with a decrease in victimization were the use of: (1) videos, (2) disciplinary methods, (3) work with peers, (4) parent training, and (5) cooperative group work (Farrington & Tolfi, 2009a). Similarly, the program components most highly associated with a decrease in perpetration were: (1) parent training, (2) improved playground supervision, (3) disciplinary methods, (4) school assemblies, (5) videos, (6) information for parents, (7) classroom rules, and (8) classroom management (Farrington & Ttofi, 2009a).

Although we have an understanding of the effectiveness of school-based anti-bullying programs, evidence describing how to effectively prevent and intervene in cyberbullying is virtually absent, despite the intense public interest and media attention on this topic. While cyberbullying shares many similarities with traditional bullying, some important differences exist, as discussed in Chapter 1. With these cyber-differences considered, there is an urgent need to provide current evidence-based practice in bullying including cyberbullying prevention to schools and families and to provide the most effective yet parsimonious models of intervention. Here we overview components that may need to be considered by schools and families to reduce all forms of bullying in schools, including cyberbullying. We review these components using a set of Informed Practice Guidelines for School Bullying Prevention and Management (Cross, Pintabona, Hall, Hamilton, & Erceg, 2004; Pearce, Cross, Monks, Waters, & Falconer, 2011) based on current research evidence, and discuss the relevance of these for preventing and intervening in bullying in the cyber context.

Intervention strategies are classified into six domains that are considered fundamental elements to promote health in schools (International Union for Health Promotion and Education, 2009): (1) key understandings and competencies for staff, parents and families, and young people; (2) proactive policies, plans, and practices; (3) supportive social environment; (4) protective physical environment; (5) collaborative school–family–community partnerships; and (6) building capacity for action. In the following section each of the six domains is discussed in detail. Where appropriate, this discussion is connected to findings described in earlier chapters.

Key Understandings and Competencies for Staff, Students, and Families

One of the key strategies to help reduce cyberbullying in schools is raising awareness and educating the whole school community about bullying. This includes staff training, explicit student learning through the curriculum, as well as improving key family understandings and skills (Cross et al., 2004; Pearce et al., 2011).

All school staff, parents, and families

In their meta-analysis, teacher training was identified as a program element significantly associated with reducing the prevalence of bullying (Farrington & Ttofi, 2009b). Given the generation gap between "digitally native" young people and their teachers (Tapscott, 1998; Palfrey & Gasser, 2008) and evidence that suggests teachers do not have a sufficient understanding of the extent to which cyberbullying directly and indirectly impacts on students' learning (Beran & Li, 2005; Li, 2008), adequate training and support for all staff (including auxiliary staff such as school bus drivers), is necessary (Espelage & Swearer, 2003; Vernberg & Gamm, 2003). Furthermore, during their university training many Canadian teachers have reported not feeling confident identifying or managing this behavior in schools (Li, 2008). Hence, it is essential to provide professional learning for pre-service teachers and those currently teaching about cyberbullying, along with ways to prevent and manage this and other forms of bullying behavior among young people (Hanewald, 2008).

Providing bullying-related information to parents appears to be an important factor in reducing the perpetration of bullying (Farrington & Ttofi, 2009b) and is also seemingly useful in reducing cyberbullying, especially given cyberbullying is generally more likely to occur outside of school than in school (Slonje & Smith, 2008; Smith et al., 2008). Interestingly, Aoyama, Utsumi, and Hasegawa (Chapter 9) found that Japanese youth perceptions of parental Internet controls did not predict cyberbullying experiences. Conversely, they did find that young people's perceptions of having free access to the Internet, especially among females, was related to their Internet involvement. In their research comparing Japanese and US students' perceptions of parental monitoring and help-seeking behavior responses, Aoyama et al. suggest that the Japanese young people in their sample perceived their parents were less likely to monitor and communicate with their children about their Internet use, which subsequently may be related to Japanese young people being less likely to seek help from their parents than US respondents. While the small sample in this study limits generalization, it is reasonable to assume that if parents have established communication with their children about Internet use and cyberbullying, their children may be more willing to talk with their parents about cyberbullying related behaviors. This may be especially true if parents have knowledge of these behaviors and ways to prevent them, as well as some knowledge about information communication technology

(ICT). Significantly, parent education will also help adults deal with their exposure to harm from new technologies (Patchin & Hinduja, 2006).

Importantly there is not just a need to increase teachers' and families' knowledge and skills with regards to the relational issues of bullying (although this needs to remain the focus); there is also a need to provide education around technology use. It will be necessary for the whole school community to remain updated with new technologies and how they are used positively (Costabile & Spears, 2011), as well as the potential for such technologies to be misused (Genta et al., Chapter 2). Cyber safety skills will need to be a component of any cyberbullying prevention program, and technical skills about how to prevent and respond to cyberbullying in different online environments will need to be taught (e.g., how to protect privacy online, how to block senders, report abuse or bullying). For example, findings from Tippett and Kwak (Chapter 10) suggest that multi-player online gaming for South Korean young people is a major source of online cyberbullying, especially for boys. Hence imparting knowledge about ways to respond effectively to cyberbullying in different environments will be important via a variety of online and offline formats (e.g., podcasts, SMS tips, online self-help tools).

Young people

Whereas improving young people's understandings and skills seems important to reducing both bullying and cyberbullying, providing such a curriculum for students was not associated with reductions in bullying in Farrington and Ttofi's (2009b) meta-analysis. Instead more interactive multimedia methods to educate students through the use of anti-bullying videos to raise students' awareness about bullying was associated with a reduction in students being bullied (Farrington & Ttofi, 2009b). Given young people's fascination with multimedia, the use and quality of video or online games as a platform for bullying prevention programs is likely to increase in the coming years. For instance, the KiVa program (Salmivalli & Pöyhönen, Chapter 4) which incorporated a virtual learning environment through an anti-bullying computer game, has achieved some success as part of a whole-school program in reducing cyberbullying among students in third to fifth grades.

Although young people are usually very proficient at using all forms of technology, they still require the technical knowledge necessary to effectively prevent and reduce cyberbullying. For instance, while young people do cite strategies for dealing with cyberbullying including blocking the sender or ignoring the bullying, they do not appear to know how to remove harmful websites or how to respond positively as a bystander to cyberbullying (Agatston & Limber, 2007). Interestingly in Bauman's study (Chapter 8), the most common responses in her US sample of young people to being cyberbullied was to retaliate by bullying back or to ignore the behavior. Tippett and Kwak (Chapter 10) found that their sample of South Korean young people responded differently to cyberbullying according to the form of technology used to bully them. Those bullied using the Internet were more likely to seek revenge or fight back than seek help, whereas those cyberbullied by mobile phone were more likely to seek help than fight back.

Juvonen and Gross (2008) found that only a minority of young people reported using positive electronic tactics such as blocking the sender, changing their screen name, or sending warnings to respond to cyberbullying. Thus, it would appear to be important to provide young people with some specific technical skills, including how to contact Internet Service Providers (ISPs) and mobile phone companies, as well as how to report bullying when they experience or witness this, and what support they can expect to receive. A challenge for future research is to examine how young people can be encouraged to report cyberbullying, and what support, including online support, needs to be provided to young people who are bullied. Holfeld and Grabe (Chapter 7) found that nearly a third of cyberbullied students did not report the incident, most commonly because they felt they could handle the bullying on their own, but a significant proportion of others didn't tell anyone because they were scared, or believed reporting would exacerbate the problem. Interestingly, this study also found that the chances of the cyberbullying stopping were about the same whether it was reported to peers or adults, and suggested that neither group is particularly effective in supporting students who are being cyberbullied.

Li and Fung (Chapter 6) suggest that attitudes and beliefs about cyberspace are highly influential factors in determining young people's online and offline behaviors, and they found that more positive beliefs about cyberspace were associated with a reduced likelihood of cyberbullying others. Further, these attitudes were associated with a greater likelihood of taking positive action when cyberbullied, such as telling the perpetrator to stop, removing themselves from the situation (e.g., by logging off), or telling an adult or peer. Conversely, young people with more negative beliefs about cyberspace were more likely to respond by doing nothing, or bullying or cyberbullying other young people. Positive beliefs about cyberspace were also associated with more positive reactions when witnessing cyberbullying, including trying to help or befriend the student being bullied, reporting the cyberbullying, or leaving the online environment. Hence, enabling young people to develop positive attitudes to cyberspace and good "digital citizenship" skills may be a vital component in reducing cyberbullying.

Young people also need to be given opportunities to develop their social skills, and be educated about their own and others' rights and responsibilities, and how to show respect for others online and offline. Educating young people about appropriate and inappropriate ways to interact with other young people and how to resolve relationship conflicts are necessary for both cyber and non-cyber environments. This is particularly important given findings concerning motives for cyberbullying. Holfeld and Grabe (Chapter 7) found that young people reported they cyberbullied mostly for revenge, followed by their dislike for the person being bullied, for fun, and because others were doing it. The findings from Gradinger et al. (Chapter 13, Table 13.5) especially highlighted the "for fun" motive for cyberbullying, as well as anger (the latter was also a main reason for traditional bullying). Given many young people's moral approval of bullying (Williams & Guerra, 2007) and the findings by Bauman (Chapter 8) and Almeida et al. (Chapter 11) that moral disengagement is associated with young people's engagement in both bullying and cyberbullying others, it would seem appropriate that digital morality be considered a key component of programs to reduce cyberbullying.

Proactive policies, plans, and practices

According to Farrington and Ttofi's (2009b) meta-analysis, an important program element associated with a reduction in bullying others was the organization of school assemblies where students' awareness of bullying is raised and when anti-bullying initiatives are formally announced. The presence of a formal whole-school anti-bullying policy was also strongly associated with a reduction in students' bullying behavior. Clear and consistent policy and practices related to bullying behavior send a strong message to the whole school community about the school's commitment to sustain a safe and supportive school environment, and provides the school with a framework to guide school action for the prevention, early response, and case management of all bullying behaviors (Cross et al., 2004; Pearce et al., 2011). The school's policy is also an important place to outline the responsibilities of staff, students, and families with regards to preventing and intervening in bullying. This may be especially important for cyberbullying, which largely occurs outside of school; however, the incident and its effects tend to spread quickly into the school (Bhat, 2008; Smith et al., 2008) making it the responsibility of bystanders and other members of the school community to protect targets from this behavior.

Clear and consistent plans and practices to deal with bullying incidents are an important component of bullying prevention programs (Cross et al., 2004; Pearce et al., 2011). Farrington and Ttofi (2009b) suggested that disciplinary methods are associated with a reduction in both bullying and victimization. The results of their meta-analyses should be interpreted with caution, as "disciplinary methods" can suggest quite punitive actions; but in fact this finding was related to the large effects of the Olweus Program (which appeared several times in the analyses), of which a component was firm methods (but not necessarily "punitive") for addressing bullying. Evaluation of the KiVa program (Salmivalli & Pöyhönen, Chapter 4) is providing additional information about the effectiveness of punitive versus non-punitive methods. The use of only punitive strategies such as banning the use of ICT as a consequence for cyberbullying may result in the under-reporting of the behavior, and little change to this behaviour, as it takes place largely outside the school and in many cases the perpetrator is anonymous or may be from another school.

Developing a sound procedure for responding to incidents of cyberbullying documented in the whole-school policy is essential. Case management is likely to be especially important in countering cyberbullying, because of the potential for an incident to escalate in a short period of time. It may also be important to consult with IT professionals who can help to remove inappropriate content and save evidence of cyberbullying.

Supportive social environment

A positive school climate or ethos that builds student connectedness to school, provides safety, and encourages open communication, can be beneficial in protecting young people from the risks of bullying (Cross et al., 2004; Pearce et al., 2011). Not feeling safe at school has been identified as a risk factor for being cyberbullied, and/or cyberbullying others (Sourander et al., 2010). Similarly, Holfeld and Grabe (Chapter 7) found that 45% of students who were cyberbullied reported feeling safe at school only "sometimes." Williams and Guerra (2007) also found that students who reported greater connectedness to school and a positive school climate were less likely to be cyberbullied and to cyberbully others.

Li and Fung (Chapter 6) found that participation in extracurricular activities was associated with young people being more likely to inform their peers when they were cyberbullied, and less likely to respond to being cyberbullied by bullying other young people. Extracurricular activities, such as sport, recreation, music, arts, and voluntary work, are an important way that school connectedness and social networks can be increased (McBride, Midford, & James, 1995; McNeely, Nonnemaker, & Blum, 2002; Hamilton, Cross, Hall, & Townsend, 2003). Therefore, creating a supportive social environment, including the provision of extracurricular activities may be an important strategy in reducing cyberbullying.

Some studies have examined family and parental factors. Ybarra and Mitchell (2007) associated Internet harassment with greater caregiver–child conflict, and Wang, Iannotti, and Nansel (2009) found that lower parental support of adolescents predicted greater involvement in all kinds of bullying, including cyber. Law, Shapka, and Olsen (2010) linked adolescent online aggression to lack of communication with parents, but it was unrelated to attempts to limit time on the Internet, or sites visited.

Cyberbullying has also been associated with family composition, specifically not living with two biological parents (for example, having a single parent, or parents who have remarried, adoptive parents, or living with grandparents or in foster care) (Sourander et al., 2010). Likewise, perpetrators of cyberbullying are more likely to report a poor emotional bond with their caregiver, as well as more frequent discipline and less frequent monitoring on the part of their caregiver (Ybarra & Mitchell, 2004; Vandebosch & van Cleemput, 2009).

These findings suggest parents need to be encouraged to employ strategies to effectively communicate with their child about their use of communication technology and cyberbullying and shown ways they can appropriately supervise and protect their children online (Aoyama et al., Chapter 9). This strategy, however, would need to be coupled with youth-targeted education and intervention for those young people who do not receive this parent/carer support.

Protective physical environment

Improved playground supervision and grounds have been associated with a reduction in perpetration of traditional bullying (Smith & Sharp, 1994; Farrington & Ttofi, 2009b). Not surprisingly, students' greater access to, more frequent use of, greater dependency on, and greater proficiency with technology has been linked to a higher risk of involvement in cyberbullying (Bauman, Chapter 8; Genta et al., Chapter 2; Holfeld & Grabe, Chapter 7; Li & Fung, Chapter 6; Ybarra & Mitchell, 2004; Hinduja & Patchin, 2008; Smith et al., 2008; Vandebosch & van Cleemput, 2009). Genta et al. (Chapter 2) for example, found that young people who have access to the Internet in their own room were both more likely to be cyberbullied and more likely to cyberbully others.

Importantly, there are factors within the physical environment that can promote or inhibit cyberbullying behaviors. The school (and home) environment can encourage, through education, the safe use of technology (both at home and at school) as well as the suitable location of computers and other technical equipment available to students; and provide adequate supervision (in addition to filters) to students using technology in the classroom (Patchin & Hinduja, 2006). Further, schools need to promote the positive uses of technology for both educational purposes and social interaction, given that students' attitudes and beliefs about cyberspace are related to their online and offline behaviors, as a victim, perpetrator, or bystander to cyberbullying (Li & Fung, Chapter 6).

Collaborative school–family–community partnerships

Schools need to encourage consultation and participation between the school and students' families, and clearly project that reducing bullying is a responsibility of the whole school and wider community (Cross et al., 2004; Pearce et al., 2011). A coordinated approach between school staff and parents is crucial to address cyberbullying, given that young people potentially have unlimited access to technology outside school hours and therefore, not surprisingly, cyberbullying incidents occur largely outside of school (Smith et al., 2008). Open communication with schools and families means that schools can identify those students who may be most at risk of cyberbullying, and enable the family to support the school's efforts and interventions to reduce cyberbullying, and conversely the school can support the family when incidents of cyberbullying occur.

Parent training (such as information nights and parent–teacher meetings) is identified as an important program element associated with a decrease in both the incidence of students being bullied and bullying others (Farrington & Ttofi, 2009b), and this is becoming particularly evident for cyberbullying. Families report needing help to support their child prevent or deal with cyberbullying, more so than with traditional bullying, likely due to their lack of proficiency with social communications technology, but also because the behavior often occurs at home and not necessarily at school.

Part of a comprehensive and coordinated approach to bullying prevention includes working to create linkages with community service providers in order to reduce bullying (Cross et al., 2004; Pearce et al., 2011). Cooperation among interdisciplinary professionals in working with students directly involved in bullying has been shown to be an important element of anti-bullying programs, associated with a reduction in both students' bullying others and being bullied (Farrington & Ttofi, 2009b). There is a need to form partnerships with professionals in the areas of mental health and learning support, as well as with doctors, drug, and alcohol counsellors. These linkages will help to ensure that quality support is provided to students involved in all forms of bullying.

Several additional partnerships may also be important in reducing cyberbullying among young people, including access to professionals with ICT skills. The emergence of new communication technologies has also brought with it new legal challenges and the need for legal advice (Shariff & Hoff, 2007). For instance, to what extent are Internet service providers liable to act on reports of abuse? Is there a need to protect students' rights to freedom of expression? What are the privacy issues related to searching students' computers for evidence of cyber-harassment? Cyberbullying is associated with the potential for harmful text, videos, or images that can go "viral" and inflict distress, humiliation, and defamation on a much broader scale. The perpetrator of the bullying may be anonymous and there may be difficulties trying to remove harmful content from the Internet or trying to stop the rapid spread of videos or pictures via mobile phones. Thus, there are questions raised as to who is liable for the immense harm caused by the incident. To help schools navigate the legal implications of cyberbullying, partnerships with local and state police are beneficial, although a reliance on legal sanctions or threats to deal with cyberbullying may be largely ineffective, given cyberbullying is primarily a relational issue.

Building capacity for action

Several factors have been identified as relevant for the successful implementation of school health and education programs, including the availability of sufficient resources (staff, time, funding, materials), the commitment of school leaders, and the support of external partners, as well as compatibility of the program with the school's goals (Bosworth, Gingiss, Potthoff, & Roberts-Gray, 1999; Roberts-Gray, Gingiss, & Boerm, 2007). Schools may not be able to implement effective interventions if they do not have sufficient capacity, such as resources and systemic support (Cunningham & Henggeler, 2001). That the same or similar intervention methods have produced radically different results may be related to the thoroughness of program implementation in schools.

The readiness of schools and school staff to accept and satisfactorily implement a program is likely to be an important factor in the effectiveness of the program (Rigby & Slee, 2008). Principles of capacity building underlie all of the strategies discussed previously. The potential for any of these strategies to achieve success is dependent on their level of implementation and the commitment of the whole-school community, including parents. Intervention programs need to be intensive and long-lasting to have an impact on bullying (Farrington & Ttofi, 2009b).

Capacity building factors appear equally relevant to both bullying and cyberbullying prevention and intervention efforts. However, while a key factor to the success of whole-school health promotion programs is the active participation of students, teachers, and the wider school community in processes of planning, implementation, and evaluation (Cross et al., 2004), the involvement of parents and young people may be predominantly important to reduce cyberbullying. In particular, young people's proficiency with social communications technology enables them to be involved in all stages of the development and implementation of school policies, procedures, classroom curricula, professional development, and parent education. Students have the capacity and primary responsibility to develop and implement responses to cyberbullying. Moreover, fostering student ownership of school procedures and policies will increase the likelihood of students complying with the procedures.

Future Research Directions

It appears that some of what we know about traditional bullying and how to prevent and manage it is also relevant in the cyber context. However, the unique challenges raised by this new manifestation of bullying behavior requires empirical evidence of the effectiveness of specific cyberbullying related policies and procedures incorporating cyber safety elements and modeling the positive uses of technology into bullying prevention approaches. Schools also require more evidence to help them develop appropriate case management procedures when responding to cyberbullying incidents because of the potential anonymity of the perpetrator and the technical challenges posed by cyberbullying.

The role of the cyberbullying bystander in discouraging this behavior also requires further research. Because cyberbullying occurs where there is no authority and often involves a larger audience, there are greater and more imperative opportunities for bystander intervention. Strategies to encourage bystander action will be important, given they may feel less inclined to intervene because they usually can't see the impact cyberbullying has on the person targeted.

More research is also needed to understand how to encourage young people to seek help from adults about cyberbullying and importantly what kind of help young people need from adults (and peers) in cyberbullying situations. For instance, because adults may be less proficient with social communications technology, would young people talk to an adult about cyberbullying more for emotional support than practical help? Similarly, would young people be more likely to report cyberbullying to an adult who is technologically savvy?

Given the multi-causal nature of all forms of bullying and the apparent overlap between cyber and other bullying behaviors it appears clear that cyberbullying needs

Table 14.1 Strategies That May Be Effective in Reducing Cyberbullying.

1. Building key understandings and competencies of staff, students, and families about bullying and cyberbullying addressing:

- technical issues and cyber-safety to better understand the rapidly changing context of technology
- ways for adults to effectively respond to cyberbullying to increase the likelihood of young people seeking help earlier from adults
- positive uses of technology, given that young people's beliefs and attitudes about cyberspace are an important predictor of their online and offline behaviors
- general bullying awareness, bystander education, digital morality, and social skills training
- effective responses by young people to cyberbullying (both relationally and technically)

2. Developing proactive school policies, plans, and practices to encompass:

- clear and consistent policy and practices sending a strong message about the school's commitment to sustain a safe and supportive school environment
- positive behavioral expectations and moral conduct when online (and offline)
- the rights and responsibilities of staff, students, and families in response to cyberbullying
- effective online reporting and response mechanisms
- case management procedures for cyberbullying, especially given the potential for cyberbullying incidents to escalate in a short space of time
- consultation with IT professionals at the school

3. Creating and maintaining a supportive social environment, including the:

- provision of strategies such as extracurricular activities to enhance school connectedness, safety at school, and peer and emotional support
- encouragement of a supportive peer culture that promotes positive bystander intervention in bullying incidents

4. A protective physical environment including:

- promoting positive uses of technology
- making new technology available for students to use for both educational and social purposes
- providing satisfactory supervision in cyberspace

5. Collaborative school–family–community links including:

- promoting a coordinated and consistent school–home response to preventing and managing cyberbullying
- encouraging parents' responsibility and skills to monitor and positively support their child's online behavior
- engaging with service providers such as mental health professionals
- creating links with IT and legal services

to be nested within a whole-school effort to encourage positive social behavior online and offline (Vreeman & Carroll, 2007; Rigby & Slee, 2008). Hence while cyberbullying intervention elements may be limited if implemented in isolation, strategies such as the active engagement and cyber education of families, and the use of online self-help tools, may be particularly effective in reducing cyberbullying.

Summary

This chapter has reviewed a number of issues arising from the research presented in this book. It then moved on to consider a range of intervention strategies to reduce bullying and show their effectiveness. Based on the data presented in this book and other research, the extent to which these strategies may reduce cyberbullying was discussed. While it is likely that numerous whole-school intervention strategies to address traditional bullying would also be effective to reduce cyberbullying, some special characteristics of cyberbullying pose some new challenges. These challenges include the anonymous nature of cyberbullying, the potential scope of the cyberbullying audience, lack of authority in cyberspace, the 24-hour access to technology, and the rapid technological changes providing new means by which cyberbullying can be inflicted (Chapter 1).

The strategies that appear to be most effective are summarized in Table 14.1. The effectiveness of these specific intervention strategies to address cyberbullying would be limited, however, if the whole-school community of school staff, students, and parents does not have sufficient capacity for action. This capacity includes the commitment of school leadership and mobilization of resources. Further, the whole-school community needs to be involved as active participants in the planning, development, and implementation of policies, procedures, and program strategies. Given students' proficiency with social communications technology, ensuring student involvement and ownership of school actions to reduce cyberbullying is likely to be especially important.

References

Agatston, P. W., & Limber, S. (2007). Students' perspectives on cyberbullying. *Journal of Adolescent Health, 41*, S59–S60.

Arseneault, L., Bowes, L., & Shakoor, S. (2009). Bullying victimization in youths and mental health problems: "Much ado about nothing"? *Psychological Medicine, 29*, 1–13.

Baldry, A. C., & Farrington, D. P. (2007). Effectiveness of programs to prevent school bullying. *Victims and Offenders, 2*, 183–204.

Beran, T., & Li, Q. (2005). Cyber-harassment: A study of a new method for an old behavior. *Journal of Educational Computing Research, 32*, 265–277.

Beran, T. T., & Li, Q. (2007). The relationship between cyberbullying and school bullying. *Journal of Student Wellbeing, 1*, 15–33.

Bhat, C. S. (2008). Cyberbullying: Overview and strategies for school counsellors, guidance officers, and all school personnel. *Australian Journal of Guidance and Counselling, 18*, 53–66.

Bosworth, K., Gingiss, P. M., Potthoff, S., & Roberts-Gray, C. (1999). A Bayesian model to predict the success of the implementation of health and education innovations in school-centred programs. *Evaluation and Program Planning, 22*, 1–11.

Bronfenbrenner, U. (1977). Towards an experimental ecology of human development. *American Psychologist, 32*, 513–530.

Costabile, A., & Spears, B. (Eds.). (2011). *The impact of technology on relationships in educational settings*. London: Routledge.

Cross, D., Pintabona, Y., Hall, M., Hamilton, G., & Erceg, E. (2004). Validated guidelines for school-based bullying prevention and management. *International Journal of Mental Health Promotion, 6*, 34–42.

Cross, D., Shaw, T., Hearn, L., Epstein, M., Monks, H., Lester, L., & Thomas, L. (2009). *Australian Covert Bullying Prevalence Study (ACBPS)*. Retrieved June 4, 2009 from www.deewr.gov.au/Schooling/NationalSafeSchools/Pages/research.aspx

Cunningham, P., & Henggeler, S. (2001). Implementation of an empirically based drug and violence prevention and intervention program in public school settings. *Journal of Clinical Child Psychology, 30*, 221–232.

Espelage, D. L., & Swearer, S. (2003). Research on school bullying and victimization: What have we learned and where do we go from here? *School Psychology Review, 32*, 365–383.

Farrington, D. P., & Ttofi, M. M. (2009a). Reducing school bullying: Evidence-based implications for policy. *Crime and Justice, 38*, 281–345.

Farrington, D. P., & Ttofi, M. M. (2009b). School-based programs to reduce bullying and victimization. *Campbell Systematic Reviews*. Oslo: The Campbell Collaboration.

Gradinger, P., Strohmeier, D., & Spiel, C. (2009). Traditional bullying and cyberbullying. *Zeitschrift für Psychologie/Journal of Psychology, 217*(4), 205–213.

Hamilton, G., Cross, D., Hall, M., & Townsend, E. (2003). The role of extra-curricular activities in reducing smoking among adolescents: Final report. Western Australian Centre for Health Promotion Research, School of Public Health, Curtin University of Technology: Perth, Western Australia.

Hanewald, R. (2008). Confronting the pedagogical challenge of cyber-safety. *Australian Journal of Teacher Education, 33*, 1–16.

Hawker, D. S. J., & Boulton, M. J. (2000). Twenty years' research on peer victimization and psychosocial maladjustment: A meta-analytic review of cross-sectional studies. *Journal of Child Psychology and Psychiatry, 41*, 441–455.

Hinduja, S., & Patchin, J. W. (2007). Offline consequences of online victimization: School violence and delinquency. *Journal of School Violence, 6*, 89–112.

Hinduja, S., & Patchin, J. W. (2008). Cyberbullying: An exploratory analysis of factors related to offending and victimization. *Deviant Behavior, 29*, 129–156.

Hinduja, S., & Patchin, J. W. (2010). Bullying, cyberbullying, and suicide. *Archives of Suicide Research, 14*, 206–221.

International Union for Health Promotion and Education. (2009). *Achieving health promoting schools: Guidelines for promoting health in schools*. Retrieved August 20, 2010 from www.iuhpe.org/uploaded/Publications/Books_Reports/HPS_GuidelinesII_2009_English.pdf

Juvonen, J., & Gross, E. F. (2008). Extending the school grounds? Bullying experiences in cyberspace. *Journal of School Health, 78*(9), 496–505.

Kanetsuna, T., Smith, P. K., & Morita, Y. (2006). Coping with bullying at school: Children's recommended strategies and attitudes to school-based interventions in England and Japan. *Aggressive Behavior, 32*, 570–580.

Law, D. M., Shapka, J. D., & Olsen, B. F. (2010). To control or not to control? Parenting behaviors and adolescent online aggression. *Computers in Human Behavior, 26*, 1651–1656.

Li, Q. (2008). Cyberbullying in schools: An examination of preservice teachers' perception. *Canadian Journal of Learning and Technology, 34*(2), 75–90.

McBride, N., Midford, R., & James, R. (1995). Structural and management changes that encourage schools to adopt comprehensive health promotion programs. *Health Promotion Journal of Australia, 5*, 17–23.

McNeely, C. A., Nonnemaker, J. M., & Blum, R. W. (2002). Promoting school connectedness: Evidence from the National Longitudinal Study of Adolescent Health. *Journal of School Health, 72*, 138–146.

Ortega, R., Elipe, P., Mora-Merchán, J. A., Calmaestra, J., & Vega, E. (2009). The emotional impact on victims of traditional bullying and cyberbullying. A study of Spanish adolescents. *Zeitschrift für Psychologie/Journal of Psychology, 217*, 197–204.

Palfrey, J., & Gasser, U. (2008). *Born digital: Understanding the first generation of digital natives*. New York: Basic Books.

Patchin, J. W., & Hinduja, S. (2006). Bullies move beyond the schoolyard: A preliminary look at cyberbullying. *Youth Violence and Juvenile Justice, 4*, 148–169.

Pearce, N., Cross, D., Monks, H., Waters, S., Erceg, E., & Falconer, S. (2011). Current evidence of best practice in whole-school bullying intervention and its potential to inform cyber-bullying interventions. *Australian Journal of Guidance and Counselling, 21*(1), 1–21.

Raskauskas, J., & Stoltz, A. D. (2007). Involvement in traditional and electronic bullying among adolescents. *Developmental Psychology, 43*, 564–575.

Rigby, K. (2002). *A meta-evaluation of methods and approaches to reducing bullying on pre-schools and early primary school in Australia*. Canberra: Commonwealth Attorney-General's Department.

Rigby, K., & Slee, P. (2008). Interventions to reduce bullying. *International Journal of Adolescent Medicine and Health, 20*, 165–183.

Roberts-Gray, C., Gingiss, P. M., & Boerm, M. (2007). Evaluating school capacity to implement new programs. *Evaluation and Program Planning, 30*, 247–257.

Shariff, S. S., & Hoff, D. (2007). Cyberbullying: Clarifying legal boundaries for school supervision in cyberspace. *International Journal of Cyber Criminology, 1*, 76–118.

Slonje, R., & Smith, P. K. (2008). Cyberbullying: Another main type of bullying? *Scandinavian Journal of Psychology, 49*, 147–154.

Smith, J., Schneider, B., Smith, P. K., & Ananiadou, K. (2004). The effectiveness of whole-school antibullying programs: A synthesis of evaluation research. *School Psychology Review, 33*, 547–560.

Smith, P. K. (2011). Cyberbullying and cyber aggression. In S. R. Jimerson, A. B. Nickerson, M. J. Mayer, & M. J. Furlong (Eds.), *Handbook of school violence and school safety: International research and practice*. New York: Routledge.

Smith, P. K., Cowie, H., Olafsson, R., & Liefooghe, A. P. D. (2002). Definitions of bullying: A comparison of terms used, and age and sex differences, in a 14-country international comparison. *Child Development, 73*, 1119–1133.

Smith, P. K., Mahdavi, J., Carvalho, M., Fisher, S., Russell, S., & Tippett, N. (2008). Cyberbullying: Its nature and impact in secondary school pupils. *Journal of Child Psychology and Psychiatry, 49*, 376–385.

Smith, P. K., & Sharp, S. (1994). *School Bullying: Insights and Perspectives*. London: Routledge.

Sourander, A., Klomek, A. B., Ikonen, M., Lindroos, J., Luntamo, T., Koskelainen, M., Ristkari, T., & Helenius, H. (2010). Psychosocial risk factors associated with cyberbullying among adolescents. *Archives of General Psychiatry, 67*, 720–728.

Tapscott, D. (1998). *Growing up digital: The rise of the net generation*. New York: McGraw-Hill.

Tokunaga, R. S. (2010). Following you home from school: A critical review and synthesis of research on cyberbullying victimization. *Computers in Human Behavior, 26*, 277–287.

Ttofi, M. M., & Farrington, D. P. (2011). Effectiveness of school-based programs to reduce bullying: a systematic and meta-analytic review. *Journal of Experimental Criminology*.

Vandebosch, H., & van Cleemput, K. (2009). Cyberbullying among youngsters: Profiles of bullies and victims. *New Media and Society, 11*, 1349–1371.

Vernberg, E. M., & Gamm, B. K. (2003). Resistance to violence prevention interventions in schools: Barriers and solutions. *Journal of Applied Psychoanalytic Studies, 5*, 125–138.

Vreeman, R., & Carroll, A. (2007). A systematic review of school-based interventions to prevent bullying. *Archives of Pediatric Adolescent Medicine, 161*, 78–88.

Wang, J., Iannotti, R. J., & Nansel, T. R. (2009). School bullying among adolescents in the United States: Physical, verbal, relational, and cyber. *Journal of Adolescent Health, 45*, 368–375.

Williams, K. R., & Guerra, N. G. (2007). Prevalence and predictors of Internet bullying. *Journal of Adolescent Health, 41*, S14–S21.

Ybarra, M. (2004). Linkages between depressive symptomology and Internet harassment among young regular Internet users. *CyberPsychology and Behavior, 7*, 247–257.

Ybarra, M. L., & Mitchell, K. J. (2004). Youth engaging in online harassment: Associations with caregiver–child relationships, Internet use, and personal characteristics. *Journal of Adolescence, 27*, 319–336.

Ybarra, M. L., & Mitchell, K. J. (2007). Prevalence and frequency of Internet harassment instigation: Implications for adolescent health. *Journal of Adolescent Health, 41*, 189–195.

Index

Cyberbullying in the Global Playground: Research from International Perspectives, First Edition.
Edited by Qing Li, Donna Cross, and Peter K. Smith.